MATURITY

Not Everyone Who Grows Old
Chooses to Grow Up

IS A

CHOICE

MATURITY

Not Everyone Who Grows Old Chooses to Grow Up

IS A

CHOICE

KAROL HESS & DOUG McCULLEY

*Persevere so that you may be mature
and complete, not lacking anything.*
— James 1:4

Cover illustration by Mary Mouton Chambers.

For reproducible charts and seminar information please contact the
authors directly at Beacon Light Counseling Center, 10 Shawnee
Drive, Suite B-6, Watchung, New Jersey, 07060. (908) 668-0660

Printed and Bound in the United States of America.
All rights reserved.

Library of Congress Card Catalog Number: 94-70203
International Standard Book Number: 0-89900-679-5

TABLE OF CONTENTS

ACKNOWLEDGEMENTS. 7

FOREWORD 9

PREFACE 13

INTRODUCTION. 15

CHAPTER 1
The Road to Maturity. 19

CHAPTER 2
Straightening Crooked Thinking. 45

CHAPTER 3
Building Strong People 77

CHAPTER 4
Improving Family Dynamics 99

CHAPTER 5
Building Good Communication 121

CHAPTER 6
Bridging the Gender Gap 157

CHAPTER 7
Weathering the Storms and Disappointments in Life 177

CHAPTER 8
Overcoming Dysfunction and Healing its Wounds. 211

APPENDIX
Tools for Understanding. 261

BIBLIOGRAPHY 281

ACKNOWLEDGEMENTS

This book did not just happen. It was not waiting with baited, anointed breath to flow off the tip of the writer's pen. It was painstakingly eked out paragraph by paragraph. This has been a sporadic three year project of trying to put on paper what we have learned and taught over the last twenty years. It was difficult to try to coordinate our schedules and still be home in time to pick up kids from school.

There is one person in particular who deserves credit for being the greatest walking thesaurus and literary critic of all time. Thank you, Robyn Allen for not only being our faithful secretary and friend, but also being a skilled diplomat and referee — you probably deserve combat pay. Thanks EB!

Thank you Craig Lawson for confirming that the manuscript should be in print. Your editing skills and encouragement were invaluable.

A special thanks goes to the Beacon Light Staff, Deb Luedecker, Matie O'Brien, and Diane Giordano, for their support and input. Our greatest source of motivation came from Deb who week after week kept saying: "Isn't that book done **yet**?"

We love to teach and to counsel. We appreciate those who have been in Beacon Light's classes who have probably taught us more than we have taught them.

Thanks to Bruce for helping us move from being computer-hostile to being computer friendly.

My deepest love and gratitude to my husband, Bruce and my two daughters, Sandie and Katie for being the best family that anyone could ever have. I love you with all my heart.

Thank you Mary Beth Hauch for being my faithful friend and daily prayer partner all these years. We've seen a lot of answers to prayer.

Beacon Light and its outreach is a result of years of consistent prayer. I sincerely want to thank my board members, those who have been generous in their financial support and my Thursday Leadership Group for their faithfulness.

Last, but not least, thank you Mom and Dad for all you've taught me through the years. Your diligence to the Lord and your example of faith in action has equipped me to do the work that God has set before me. I love you both very much.

— Karol

With love I want to thank those who make up my wonderful home — my wife, Brenda, and our two teenagers Drew and Cassie. Thank you for making life a joy. You are loved and appreciated more than I could ever say.

I would like to thank my congregation for their support and for giving me the opportunity to serve the Lord here in New Jersey.

I want to thank all my family for what you have taught me. Thank you for your love and for just being there in some tough times.

— Doug

FOREWORD

A strange and sometimes heated debate is taking place in the church today. One side of the argument can be heard from some pulpits or radio programs. These make inflammatory statements like, "Psychology has infiltrated the church! What we need is a return to the Bible!" But this side of the argument also is seen in more private ways. Recently, a lady leading a recovery group in her church was approached by the chairman of the Women's Steering Committee. The chairman reported, "We've decided that you can't lead your group anymore. It's not good for the church. Some undesirable people have been coming since you've been leading that group of yours." The group leader assumed she was referring to those who had come to the group to get help for the pain and consequences of divorce, addictions, and compulsive problems in their lives. "I thought that was why we have the group," she lamented.

On the other side of the argument are those who react to stories like this. Many have gone to church for years without hearing how Christ could speak to their deepest fears and hurts. They have turned to "psychology" because they finally feel understood by those in the "recovery movement." The experiences of some of these people tell them that church is the last place where they will find safety, insight, and encouragement.

In the middle, of course, are millions of people who are confused and discouraged by the fire from both sides. (Most of us want to get relief from conflict like this, not get embroiled in it!) Each side seems right. Each side seems to care passionately about what it values. And we are forced to either take sides or hide from the fight. Why is the church relatively weak in pastoral ministries at this point in history? Some scholars say the energies of church leaders in the past century have been channeled to fight against liberalism and the attacks on the validity of Scripture. Very little creative energy is left for research and application in other areas such as pastoral ministries.

Why must we dichotomize and condemn? Why must we prove our points by building "straw men" of the opposing side and systematically tearing them down? The answer is that we don't have to do these things. We can value the intentions of both sides, find common ground, and provide light instead of just heat. As always, the Lord provides the best example of this blend. He consistently reached out to the hurting, the diseased, the disenfranchised, and the spiritually bankrupt to meet their needs. And he didn't do it from a distance. Over and over, the Scriptures say, "He *touched* them." But Jesus never lost focus on his purpose. He never turned away from the truth. He used that truth appropriately to comfort, to exhort, and to strengthen.

Doug McCulley and Karol Hess have written a book which exemplifies the best of this blend of grace and truth. In these pages, the dichotomy is resolved. We are encouraged with clear insights about the fallen, human condition, and we are given strong, clear, biblical principles to guide our progress.

Many "recovery" books give insights about the problems of addictions, compulsions, and painful emotions, but few books give so many "handles" so readers can identify and grasp clear choices in behaviors, thoughts, and relationships.

Actually, this is a book about responsibility. Its strength is in helping people overcome the passivity which bogs them down in a "victim mentality." For all of us, the Christian life involves taking responsibility for our emotions and actions. Those whose lives have been crushed by abuse or distorted by addictions are just like everybody else in that respect. They just need a little more help in seeing the choices, and they need a little more encouragement to take those steps — and keep taking them.

Maturity is a Choice is not "just another recovery book." It is an outstanding resource for any believer who needs insights and encouragement to deal with long-term personal struggles, and too, the outstanding charts provide quick references for counselors who want to show clients a visual demonstration of problems and opportunities.

I trust Doug and Karol's work will encourage you to apply the Lord's comfort and strength in your life and ministry.

— Robert S. McGee
February 16, 1994

PREFACE

The purpose of this book is to encourage our readers to develop skills in practical matters of everyday living. We cover the subject of maturity as a part of what it means to be truly spiritual.

Maturity is not a substitute for spirituality, however, for the Christian they are definitely related. One can be mature and not be spiritual; but one cannot be truly spiritual and *remain* immature. Eventually, our walk with God will bring us into the realm of truth and responsibility in all areas of our lives. To be honest, there are many non-Christians who are very mature and on the other hand, there are many long-time Christians who are still immature in everyday living.

We believe that God desires that we become whole and mature in all areas of living. We believe in the healing and redeeming power of God. It is our desire that our readers grow in depth in the knowledge of the Lord Jesus Christ and be intimate with Him with the goal of being able to live out in fullness the very purpose for which we were created.

INTRODUCTION

"Not everyone who grows old, grows up. There is a vast difference between age and maturity. Ideally, the older we are, the more mature we should be; but too often the ideal does not become the real.

"The result is problems — problems in personal lives, in homes, and in churches."[1] In our full-time Christian work, we see that immaturity — in one form or another — is usually the cause of these problems. We feel that this is an area that the church needs to address for the sake of its people and for the good of society.

We believe that one of the most important goals of the church in the next decade should be the restoration of the American Christian home. " . . . For the strength of a nation, especially of a republican nation, is in the intelligent and well-ordered homes of the people. And in proportion as the discipline of families is relaxed, will the happy organization of communities be affected, and national character become vagrant, turbulent, or ripe for revolution."[2]

"As Americans head into the 21st century, the family itself has become one of the biggest stories of our generation. At once venerated and vulnerable, this the most basic of society's institutions, is facing unprecedented change . . . the very nature of the family is in transition with the explosive increase in step-family households and the growth of other nontraditional families . . . ."[3]

It is frightening to realize how something so quickly broken apart can take so long to repair. For a little while (one generation), we have relaxed our moral code in order to indulge our selfish desires. Major compromises have redefined morality. What was once accepted as right is now considered to be wrong; and what used to be wrong is now considered acceptable and even preferable. The so-called freedom that we have attained has caused harm that will not be remedied in one generation.

Mature character is becoming an antiquated notion. Today's instant generation has little respect for diligence or tolerance for patience. Instant gratification is preferable to diligence. Cleverness has replaced character and integrity. We used to focus on building character and developing traits such as honesty, integrity, justice, fairness, courage, patience, initiative, personal responsibility, modesty and self-discipline. As a society, we have devalued the importance of maturity.

The goal of the church today is to get back to the basics, not only in biblical teaching, but in practice. Dr. James C. Dobson has been a prominent spokesman who has encouraged Americans to once again "Focus on the Family." The role of the family is to protect each family member from harm; to provide for each member's well-being; and to prepare each individual to become whole, responsible, productive, self-reliant, and mature, so that each person will be equipped to parent the next generation. This is how we pass the baton of moral character and spiritual maturity on to the next generation. All it takes for disaster to occur is to have one generation fumble the baton.

The church needs to grow up so that it can disciple its people, not only in Biblical truths, but in practical matters of life. Discipleship is much like parenting. Discipling was easier to do when people were already parented by their parents. Today, more people than ever before have been abandoned, neglected, abused and wounded by their parents. In decades past, we could begin the process of discipleship with individuals whose foundations were fairly strong, having had most of their basic needs met by their parents. Now, to a great extent, discipleship cannot begin until these needs are met. Discipling now requires knowledge of how to walk alongside those who are severely wounded, lost, afraid, insecure, and confused. We need to know how to help an individual regain a sense of personal wholeness before directing him on a course called discipleship.

The church must become a mature body that is able to heal the wounds of those who have suffered the consequences of a generation gone wild; to teach the truth of the power of God; to develop character and maturity in individuals; and to birth a vision that will turn the hearts of the parents towards home and family.

This book represents forty years of combined professional experience in working with families in the church, in schools and in professional counseling. It is an accumulation of material from all of our workshops, retreats, conventions, and counseling. We trust that this information will be as practical and helpful to the reader as it has been for the thousands of people we have served.

Introduction Endnotes

[1]Warren W. Wiersbe, *Be Mature* (Wheaton, Illinois: Victor Books, 1978), p. 5.

[2]Lydia H. Sigourney, 1851, (quoted in the *Pilgrim Institute Newsletter,* Granger, Indiana, January, 1993).
[3]Richard M. Smith, Editor-in-Chief (*Newsweek,* Winter, 1990), p. 8.

CHAPTER 1

THE ROAD TO MATURITY

Maturity

Workout sermon - 7/30/95 WCC

Maturity isn't something that just happens to us; it is something we must work at and actively pursue. Acquiring a measure of maturity is much like acquiring a specific skill, like driving a car, typing, learning to play the piano or a sport like tennis, for example. You must learn about it, practice it, endure the pain involved and press on through the setbacks and difficulties that are always involved when learning something new. If we really want something, the hardship involved in getting it seems minor in comparison to how we feel when we achieve our goal.

Maturity is a developmental process. It includes bringing something into completion or perfection. Personal maturity has to do with the development of *character* — positive traits or *characteristics* that a person possesses and according to which he acts.

Most of us know some people who are mature. They are a pleasure to be around, to work with and learn from. Mature people are dependable, responsible, and consistent. They have learned to take things in stride and seldom overreact. They have lived through the good and bad times in life and have learned, grown and even benefited from the hard times. That is to say — they have *digested* life.

We also know a few (probably quite a few) people who are immature. They have a tendency to make our lives difficult and exasperating. They tend to be irresponsible, undependable, overreactive and defensive. They have not matured from events in life, but rather have become *defined* by them. To them life is good when events are good, and life is terrible when circumstances are tough. Instead of learning from the hard times in life, they seem to have allergic reactions to them. They reject the idea that life will be difficult at times and throw a fit when things don't go their way.

We all have strengths and weaknesses; areas in which we are mature and immature. Maturity is not something you arrive at, but something you aim toward. Every situation can be addressed in either an immature or a mature fashion. Either we can be adult in our decision-making and plan ahead or we can drift along and just let things happen. We can react explosively when people criticize or disappoint us or we can respond with understanding and self-control. When problems arise, we can either avoid or address the real issues at hand. Our lives can be run by others and their opinions and antics or we can stand on what we know is right.

Alan is a 38-year-old manager of a growing company. A few years ago, his company began a new venture in another state that involved his department. There was a very strong possibility of an eventual relocation just as his daughter was starting her senior year in high school.

After praying about it and discussing the situation with his family, he and his wife agreed on a course of action. Alan decided to go back to school to get additional training that would give him a broader opportunity of staying with the company, but in a different capacity. *Planning* ahead paid off.

In the past, Alan would have been overwhelmed by this dilemma. He wouldn't have discussed it with anyone, even his wife. He would have just become quiet, gotten depressed and simply hoped that things would have worked out. In the past, any time he thought that something was beyond his control, he would become passive, irritable and verbally abusive toward his family.

Alan had learned to face the problem, talk about it and take action. In the process, he discovered that he was not alone in his problem, but had the help and support of his entire family.

Joanne is a woman who was tired of being afraid of people. All her life, she tried to please those around her. She was an excellent employee who did everything she was supposed to do. However, there was one thing she could not handle, and that was confrontation of any kind. She was promoted from secretary to office manager, and, with that promotion, came a variety of situations that involved confrontation.

One of these situations recently came up when the firm had moved to a new facility. Joanne was in charge of all the moving arrangements. During the move, the computer was damaged due to poor handling. Joanne called the movers and explained how the computer was damaged by one of their workers. Despite her explanation, the person on the other end of the phone refused to accept responsibility.

Before she learned how to confront, Joanne would have just left the problem here. She would never have taken it a step further like she did. Joanne, nervous as she was, took a deep breath and called the movers back and told them that she insisted that they take responsibility for the damage. What she got in return was a lot of excuses, accusations, and verbal abuse. However, she persisted and *calmly* asked for the supervisor and again clearly stated the facts and asked for his help in the matter. Her extra effort was rewarded in that the moving company finally cooperated.

Joanne felt like she lost ten pounds out of sheer nervous energy during this process, but it was worth it because she became more confident. She is enjoying her new managerial position more and more because she decided to conquer her fear instead of being stymied by it. Before, she almost dreaded going to work; now, she is enthusiastic about it. And it shows.

Bill and Sue came to a class on parenting a year ago. Both Bill and Sue are college graduates and are very bright. They have three children, two of whom are on the college track in school. Brian, their third child, has a learning disability and was struggling in school. Bill had difficulty accepting Brian's disability and refused to allow his son to be evaluated. He expected the same grades from Brian as his two other children, and when it didn't happen, he would become openly critical of Brian. Their relationship was horribly strained. Bill was ashamed of Brian, and Brian knew it.

The atmosphere at home became so toxic that Bill and Sue came in for counseling. It was only after Bill began to address his own fear and shame issues that his relationship with Brian began to change. Now, instead of attacking his son, Bill helps and encourages him. Their strained relationship eased. Brian feels better about himself and, with a specialized tutor, he is now doing much better in school. Bill has learned the best lesson of all—that Brian is a fantastic kid in spite of his learning disability.

Carl and Debbie were also very bright and successful, but seemed to genuinely be intimidated by their own children. It was as if they believed keeping the kids happy meant they had a happy home: It was truly a situation in which neither of them really knew how to stick with any type of discipline. As the children got older, they became more and more demanding, and finally the couple sought help regarding parenting skills.

With the counselor's help they began to understand how their own fear of rejection had influenced how they handled their kids. With this insight and a better understanding of the necessity of boundaries and rules, the parents began to establish some structure in the household. Their 12-year-old son, Evan, was the first guinea pig. Carl and Debbie sat down and explained that part of "first things, first" meant that there was going to be a limit on how much time he could play with his new Super Nintendo.

The rules were simple. Homework and chores must be done first before using the Nintendo, and he was limited to no more than one hour per day. Dad and Mom also explained what specific consequences would occur if the rules were broken. They ended the discussion by asking Evan to repeat back the rules and regulations in order to make sure there was no misunderstanding. Things went well . . . for a few days.

A week later, Evan came home from school and immediately started to pop a cartridge into the new Nintendo. His mom came in and reminded him, "Evan, your bed is not made and I'm sure you have homework to do. First things first. No more Nintendo." At first, Evan tried to beg, then began to argue, but Mom kept her cool and just replied, "First things, first." Next, he began to throw his usual little temper tantrum complete with tears and "you don't love me" (which usually worked in the past). Mom, determined to break this pattern, stood her ground even as the tantrum escalated. The temptation to give in to stop the antics was hard for her to resist, but she held fast with the long-range goal in mind — a home where the adults are in charge, not the kids.

Too often when we turn 21 — or graduate from college, or get married — we think that we have arrived at maturity. Unfortunately, this is when the process of maturity really begins. We all have room for improvement. None of us reaches adulthood fully mature. As time passes and we enter a new world of responsibilities, we usually find that we are not as mature as we thought we were or would like to be.

What type of person would you like to be? It is helpful to have a specific goal in mind to aim for. Sometimes we know an older, wiser, more mature person whom we would like to emulate. This is helpful. The following is an ideal description of a mature person. No one person has all of these qualities, yet each of us has some of these characteristics and certainly, we all have room to grow. We have to begin where we are and look at where we are going. This is the first step of maturity — recognizing where we need to grow.

A person on the road of maturity in general is a person who is growing in effectiveness as an individual, as part of a family and as a part of society. He is learning to make full and intelligent use of his natural abilities and is developing intellectually, socially, emotionally, morally and spiritually. He is becoming autonomous; learning what he believes and making decisions from that place of confidence. He does not live and move from a place of unhealthy dependency or out of a drivenness to overly protect himself. He is not motivated by some deficiency (fear, shame, failure, guilt, etc.), but from a platform of wholeness. For example, he does not please someone in order to make himself feel better, but rather he will choose to help someone because he thinks it's important. He is becoming more self-directed and less and less other-directed. He is becoming increasingly aware of what he thinks and values and is seeking to live in accordance with his beliefs.

A maturing person is learning to view the world around him objectively, seeing the world as it actually is, not as he might want it to be. Because of this, he is developing the ability to accurately judge what is true and what is false. He is not only gaining insight into *understanding* problems, but also is developing the skill to *solve* problems. He is a disciplined, responsible, reliable, and trustworthy type of person. He is genuinely affected by his surroundings and is compassionate, yet he does not allow emotions to cloud his judgment in his attempt to solve problems.

A maturing person is willing to be open-minded and flexible. He is not intimidated by the fact that others may be more knowledgeable than he is in certain areas and is therefore not overly defensive. He is quite ready to listen to and to learn from others. He has learned to accept himself with his strengths and weaknesses. He not only accepts himself, but can also accept others on the basis of their intrinsic worth as human beings — not on the basis of performance or achievement. He is tolerant of mistakes and failures and sees these as means by which future growth can occur. He is forgiving of himself and others.

A matured person is a freed person who is no longer bound by nor driven by guilt, fear, or shame. He has been freed to live to his potential and no longer feels that he has to live up to unrealistic, false expectations in order to be worthwhile.

Someone who is maturing is discovering his talents and is more able to enjoy his unique interests. He can be creative and innovative. He does more and more of his own thinking and dreaming and therefore is not bound by other's views. He is more able to be adventurous, spontaneous, fun-loving and willing to take reasonable risks.

A person who is growing lives and *digests* life and is more able to know what he thinks, believes, and stands for. He is gaining the personal strength along the way to be active in his pursuit of what is right, moral, and just. He is more able to commit to something beyond himself, even though it may cost a great deal.

A maturing person is growing in his compassion and empathy for others. He is aware of others' needs and potential. He genuinely likes people and is effective in working with them because he has learned to accept himself. He is more able to be patient with himself and others because he understands the concept of process — that growth and change is gradual. He knows the secret: maturity takes time.

Progress not Perfection

Maturity comes through learning lessons as life unfolds. For example, we have not experienced a full variety of roles in life by the time we reach our twenties and so we need to experience more of life and continue to learn. How else do we learn patience, except through aggravating circumstances? How else do we learn tolerance, except through having to accept what was once unacceptable? How else do we learn courage, except through fearful times? Continual learning through life completes us; it rounds out the rough edges of our character.

It's a relief to know that we all have areas of immaturity as we enter adulthood; but it would be irresponsible of us to stay immature. Life requires that we learn to meet the added responsibilities that come usually with age such as marriage, parenting, career, friendship and leadership. We are only young once, but we can be immature forever.

In our seminars, we use the illustration of a person who has been injured and now has difficulty using one arm and one leg. This person can get around. He can use crutches or lean on furniture or people for support. In fact, over time, the healthy limbs can become quite adept at compensating for the weaker limbs. But, none the less, there are still a lot of activities that he cannot do that require two hands or two feet. With physical therapy and much exercise, perhaps he could regain a significant amount of use. The problem is that exercising weak muscles is painful. Doubt can seep in as to whether continued exercise is really worthwhile. The truth is that it is worth it. The pain will eventually either pass or subside and the benefits will bring tremendous fullness into the quality of life that he now experiences. A key ingredient in the healing process is sticking with the exercise until the benefit is realized.

The point is that we all are incomplete in our maturity, therefore in our abilities and opportunities. We are like the injured person mentioned above. Overcoming our weaknesses takes effort and requires endurance, but the benefits will become evident and eventually enrich our lives.

Try to imagine what your life would be like if the weak areas of your character became strong. Imagine not being as fearful, or as irresponsible, or as impulsive, or as critical, or as defensive, or as intimidated. It would feel great and would open up such possibilities in living and in relationships. You would feel better about yourself: more confident, more capable, more courageous, more adventurous and creative. Instead of just existing, you would begin to *live* more and enjoy life more. It is a matter of gradually becoming stronger and freer so that we can live more fully. The phrase "three steps forward, two steps back" accurately describes how we learn and mature. Sometimes we make great progress and other times we seem to regress. But if we see this as normal, we are free to keep on trying in spite of setbacks. It is easier to try to make progress than to try to attain perfection.

Choice: Being Proactive

The word *proactive* is commonly used now in the corporate environment. It is a new term for an old familiar concept. Proactive is being active for something. The idea of being proactive involves more than just taking initiative; it encompasses ideas such as anticipation, vision, commitment, planning, responsibility, and diligence. Proactive people are those that have made conscious commitments to principles that they have come to believe in by actively upholding these principles, even in the midst of adversity.

To be proactive in the business environment involves seeing ahead; trying to anticipate new problems and opportunities so that you can prepare to meet the needs of tomorrow. The same is applicable in our personal lives. In the earlier example, Alan was proactive in anticipating a problem concerning his job which in turn would affect his family. He took steps to get himself trained in an area that would enhance his chances of not having to relocate.

Proactive is a way of thinking — thinking in terms of goals and responsibilities. A person who is proactive will take appropriate action to promote progress towards an objective. He will be tenacious and direct and, at times, may appear to be driven, pushy and outspoken. (This, of course, is not to condone inappropriate, stubborn or aggressive behavior.) It's a fine line between being tenacious and stubborn; and between being able to take initiative and being aggressive. In any case, a proactive person moves forward deliberately.

A proactive mindset is a prerequisite to maturity. In fact, it is the core requirement. The first step on the road to maturity is, simply, *choosing* maturity. It is not only making a decision to commit to the goal of maturing, but to the series of decisions and actions one faces every day in striving toward that goal.

For example, you may be on a diet and have a goal of

losing ten pounds. To reach that goal, you will be faced daily with many decisions that will test your willpower and perseverance. Giving in and eating that large slice of moist chocolate cake feels good for the moment, but later it becomes a bigger problem — literally. It may be very difficult to choose between an immediate gratification and continuing to press towards a distant goal, but if the goal is worthwhile, this must be done. And there are ways to do it. In order to succeed, you must "chunk it down" or set up a series of objectives which will gradually take you to your goal. You must learn to walk in the moment, doing what you *can* do *now* (rather than focusing on, and worrying about, what you *can't* do.) Little by little, step by step, it all adds up to success. Anyone who has lost a significant amount of weight knows how they have changed in the process, and how they have *had* to change. And the same principles can be applied in other areas. Diligence over time produces character — and results.

Keeping the Goal in Mind

Keeping your ultimate goal in mind is essential as you make daily decisions; otherwise you can all too easily lose sight of *why* you are doing *what* you are doing. Having a goal clarifies and lends perspective, purpose, and direction that makes it easier to endure the sacrifice and pain that accompanies responsibility and discipline.

Christopher Wren was the seventeenth century English architect who was chosen to design and build St. Paul's Cathedral in London. At one point during construction he needed a new supervisor. As the story was told, he was walking among the workers asking what they were doing. The first man replied, "I'm carrying bricks." The second replied, "I'm earning money to provide for my family." The third man answered, "I'm helping Sir Christopher Wren build the most beautiful building in England." What made this man different was that he had grasped the vision of why he was doing what he was doing. This is the man Wren hired as his foreman.

Having a goal also influences your attitude and approach towards responsibilities on the home front. For example, what is your goal in raising children? Survival? Sanity? All kidding aside, if you decide from the beginning that raising a child to be healthy, well-balanced and independent is a long-term but worthwhile goal, you probably will not be as easily discouraged by the amount of energy required to do the hard work of parenting. If you haven't kept the end result in mind, you may have come to view child-rearing as a duty, a chore, an extraordinary burden. Parenting can be frustrating enough without losing sight of the final goal.

Beginning The Process

In our work with children, we have found that having them take some kind of lessons (e.g., music, art, sports) is a great means of introducing them to the process that one must follow in order to attain maturity. You start from scratch and slowly, decisively, repeatedly practice what you're learning. The goal is the end result: a well-acquired skill which gives pleasure and expands one's capacity for enjoyment. Diligence, with the end in mind, develops areas of character such as patience, perseverance, tenacity and tolerance.

Is the sacrifice worth the result? Yes, it is, but this is impossible to know until you try it yourself. This is where a parent's encouragement and guidance is a critical part of the child's commitment to such lengthy endeavors. With a parent's help and encouragement, children will begin to experience the satisfaction of reaching a certain level of competence. If children are not encouraged to work towards a product that they have developed, they will not have the assurance that they "can do" things. If, on the other hand, a child is encouraged he can say to himself, "If I could do or learn something new once, then I can do it again."

Two Roads

What it boils down to is that the first step towards maturity is choosing to be responsible for the consequences of one's own actions. One way to visualize this is with an illustration of two roads: the mature road and the immature road. (See Figure 1 below).

FIGURE 1 – TWO ROADS

PROBLEM / PAIN

mature road	immature road
willingness to face pain	avoids pain
addresses issue	avoids real issue
open to feedback	closed to feedback
faces truth	rationalizes
responsible for own actions	does not want to be held responsible
thinks ahead	does not plan
solves the problem	wants others to solve problems
assertive	aggressive / compliant
endures pain for long-range relief	seeks immediate relief
responds	reacts
character matures	character is weakened

©Karol Hess 1988   **Pain**   **Pain**

Many times each day, whether we realize it or not, we choose one of these two roads. We have a natural tendency to *avoid* or *react* (responding to outside influence without thought) to those situations in which we are uncomfortable. For every situation that arises and for every goal that we set, we choose to follow one of two general courses of action. We will either choose to deal intelligently and proactively with the issues and situations at hand or we will choose to avoid or ignore them.

In general, the *immature road* skirts responsibility. A person usually chooses this road to avoid doing something difficult or painful. What must be done may indeed be very uncomfortable, but the overriding consideration is that it is important and necessary.

A common example is the person who consistently avoids settling down to the task of balancing his checkbook. Why? He may very well be afraid of having to face the unpleasant fact that he has unwisely spent more than he's earned, that he has very little money left, and that serious bills remain to be paid. He will not want to face the fact that he will have to change his spending habits if he is ever to remain comfortably solvent. He doesn't want to think about it. So he procrastinates.

This procrastination postpones the pain of reality, but only temporarily. This delay will only cause greater problems and pain later, not to mention underlying and growing stress in the meantime.

A more extreme example is not confronting someone who is being verbally abusive to you at work. Each time this happens you are faced with whether to deal with the problem or not. Of course, it's scary to think of doing so. Confronting someone else is rarely easy. However, if you avoid the immediate pain of necessary confrontation, you do nothing to solve the problem at hand. So the verbal abuse will continue, and will probably get worse, since the abuser now knows he or she has a victim who will not fight back. No one likes to be in that kind of situation. Yet, too often we find ourselves trapped by our own fear.

The *mature road*, on the other hand, leads us into actively facing our responsibility concerning life and the problems at hand. In the example of balancing the checkbook, getting to the facts (even if they are painful) is the only way to evaluate the budget. Decisions have to be based on reality, not wishful thinking. A secondary issue may involve changing spending habits and priorities. In the example of confronting verbal abuse, a mature stance would be to plan what to say to the person with the purpose of setting healthy boundaries and prepare for the attack that will most likely follow. (It may be helpful to practice in front of the mirror or with someone else to ease the amount of fear and anxiety that is involved.) The point is, the person on the mature road chooses to endure the short-term pain for the benefit of the long-term good. This does not always ensure that the *situation* will turn out successfully, but *he* will gain in strength and character and feel better about himself.

In order to make any progress along this road, perseverance and dedication will be required. Many times a day we face the decision to be, or not to be, a responsible human being. The failure to address problems almost always creates more problems, problems that are often more painful, more complex and more difficult to solve. We may acknowledge this to be true, yet we continue to procrastinate. We must learn how to handle the discomfort of facing our fears and our shortcomings, of learning new skills, and of being assertive, even if it means standing alone. The choice is *pay now or pay more later*.

Four Ways People Handle Responsibility

There are four distinct ways that we all handle or mishandle things for which we should be responsible. Ranging from the least responsible to the most responsible, they are: *passive, reactive, responsive, and proactive.*

Passive

The Bloomington PTA council has a problem. Jane Smith has served as PTA president for three years. Although she has positively contributed to the PTA, she has rejected all suggestions from others in the organization. Her executive council is very intimidated by her aggressive behavior and it has become increasingly more difficult to recruit PTA volunteers, since she monopolizes every project and dominates the agenda. It has gotten to the point that hardly anyone shows up for the general meetings anymore. Because the executive council has *passively* allowed Jane to intimidate and dominate everything, the organization is in a severe crisis. Their discussion to date has been passive, "Maybe she will see the problem on her own or we can hope that she will not run for office next year." Unless the council speaks to her about how she is affecting others, the PTA will inevitably continue to suffer.

Being passive is the opposite of being active. In regard to responsibility, a passive stance rejects any responsibility or concern for the problem or situation. It says " I don't think it is important enough to be involved" or " I shouldn't have to be bothered" or " I do not want the work involved" or "I don't want to be the one who is responsible or the one who targets a problem."

There are at least three reasons why people become passive. Sometimes they are simply afraid to assert themselves; sometimes they are lazy; or sometimes they are only practicing a learned pattern of behavior.

Being assertive is difficult. It is easier to be quiet and passive than to speak up and possibly cause a commotion. It is easier to do nothing and let others be responsible; that way I won't be held accountable for the results and perhaps the blame. Sometimes we are not responsible because we were not *taught* to be.

A general picture of a passive person is someone who stands by and watches someone else do the work. John, for instance, lets his wife, Ellen, do all the disciplining of the children, even when he is present in the room. One reason for this could be that this is how he was trained. Maybe *his* father sat by and let *his* mother be the disciplinarian. Another reason may be that he is afraid that his children won't like him if he sets boundaries. Or, maybe he feels that he has worked hard all day and shouldn't have to deal with any more problems at home.

On the other hand, Ellen does not want to know anything about the family finances. She leaves the responsibility of managing the budget to her husband while she continues to spend like there's no tomorrow.

In group settings, there are those who never participate in the discussion or those who just go along with the crowd. These are two more examples of how passive behavior really is avoiding responsibility.

Passive behavior merely postpones immediate consequences. In John's situation, his passiveness over time hurt his marriage. Ellen began to resent always being the "bad guy" in the disciplining of the children. Even the children began to lose respect for their father. When it came to Ellen's passiveness concerning finances, eventually the whole family suffered. The budget became a source of ongoing conflict, mostly because of Ellen's reluctance to learn how to budget.

Reactive

Whenever John and Ellen discuss either money or discipline, a shouting match ensues that too often ends in John slamming doors, leaving Ellen crying. Nothing gets resolved. They have been having different versions of this same argument for ten years. The problems are only exacerbated by their reacting to each other, instead of addressing the real problem at hand.

A reaction is a reflex, an automatic counteraction, a defense. A reactive person is a person who in a given situation simply reacts without thinking. A reactive person does not direct his course of action, but instead bounces off someone else's, much like a pinball ricocheting around inside the machine. He simply *reacts* to what happens to him. He does not *act* to take control of an unpleasant situation, but instead becomes its pawn.

Reactive behavior is defensive behavior. Steve is an employee who is being told to consider an alternate method of handling a problem. Instead of listening and cooperating, he argues back in a loud voice that is heard down the hall. Because of this habitual reactive behavior, his management has formed a low opinion of his abilities and he is now in jeopardy of losing his job.

The Jackson household is turbulent. Dan is moody, domineering, and sometimes volatile. His family is scared of him because *how* he reacts and *what* he reacts to is so unpredictable. No matter what his wife does, Dan is not satisfied. Communication is impossible because Dan always blames someone else for any problem that arises. Most of the dialogue in the family consists of defending oneself from Dad's attacks. The children avoid any discussion with their father and instead go to Mom for everything. As they have gotten older, the children are spending more and more time at their friends' houses. Dan is destroying his family with his reactive behavior.

People react for many reasons. For one thing, reactive behavior often gets the desired results (even though it may have a harmful effect on the relationship.) For example, yelling and screaming may make family members jump to do what you want, but they will do so with a lot of resentment. Intimidation works, temporarily, but the cost to the relationship is high.

Secondly, reactive people may not have enough confidence in themselves to withstand criticism or even normal feedback. At work, if someone is fearful of criticism they may take suggestions or criticisms too personally. Instead of *listening* to what is being said, they *react* to it. They either blow up (aggressive behavior) or become very withdrawn and uncooperative (passive behavior). Steve was in danger of losing his job because he would become openly hostile at the mere mention of any criticism or suggestion.

Thirdly, people who have not learned to endure the discomfort of *waiting* while unresolved issues exist often impulsively try to fix the person or problem quickly in an effort to maintain control or "make things right." Mary is the mother of a typical ten-year-old fifth grader who would rather play ball than do his homework. Andy consistently leaves his homework unfinished up until the last minute. When a book report was due on Monday, he appeared on Sunday night (with a tear in his eye), to ask Mom for help because he had not even started to write it. Of course, Mary wants her son to do well in school. So, rather than letting Andy bear the consequences for his procrastination, she panicked (reacted) and not only helped, but virtually wrote the report for him. Who's got the problem in this case? Mom does. She is not able to allow her son to face the consequences of his irresponsibility. Instead of letting him experience detention or poor grades, she rescued him to make herself feel better.

Responsive

First and foremost, responsive behavior involves intelligent thought about the situation at hand. A responsive person is able to absorb the impact of the situation and pause for reflection, before speaking or acting. The responsive person is not the victim of his emotional reactions, but rather is in control of his emotions, his thinking and his behavior. He has learned patience and self-control; they have become valuable tools which enable him to deal more effectively with the situations he may encounter in daily life.

Another way to look at it, is that a responsive person is able to "catch" the situation and look at it, instead of being "hit" by it. He is able to hold it, examine it, think it through, and choose how to direct it. For the most part, a responsive person has a pattern of responding as opposed to reacting. We will all react at times; but it is immature to be chronically reactive.

An effective way of responding is learning how to "option think." Option thinking is an open-ended way of viewing the situation at hand. It is seeing the situation from the point of view of a problem to be solved, rather than an event that has just happened to you over which you have no control. Problem-solving is a more familiar term; however, in our seminars, we prefer to use the term "option thinking" because it implies that there is more than one way of solving or approaching the problem.

Learning how to option think is part of learning how to respond. It is learning how to translate the incoming "darts" (personal attacks) into "issues" that need to be thought through and solved. This pause before responding may require only a few moments or it may involve taking a day or week. In the case where you need a considerable amount of time to think before you respond, it is better to respond immediately by saying, "I will need some time to think this over," and then giving an idea when you will be able to reply. This way you can think clearly, with less pressure, as you consider what is right or wrong, what are the options, what are the possible consequences of each option, as well as the timing involved.

Proactive

Proactive behavior is the same as responsive behavior, except that it sees ahead, plans ahead, and therefore is able to take steps to prevent problems as opposed to just responding to them. Proactive behavior, as we have already mentioned, involves actively thinking about situations, anticipating needs, and taking intelligent, responsible courses of action. The proactive person is aware of his own emotions, needs, and shortcomings, is aware of others' feelings and needs, has a realistic view of the situation, has collected the information needed to solve the problem, and is prepared and ready to proceed with a plan of action.

It is impossible, however, to be proactive about everything. We should not even try to be. You simply cannot anticipate everything. However, on the major issues of life (marriage relationship, family, finances, health, spiritual life, career, retirement) a mature person is proactive.

It is very helpful for parents to be as proactive as possible in the raising of their children. There are plenty of unexpected situations that will catch us off guard. Therefore, anticipate the common situations that will be coming up. Some issues that are helpful to discuss in advance are rules and guidelines concerning: homework, chores, piano practicing, TV viewing, language, manners, privileges, dating guidelines, telephone usage, and expected behavior of their friends while in your home.

Parents will have an easier time if they talk about the rules and guidelines beforehand rather than waiting until there is a problem. Being proactive allows for discussion, explanation, instruction, and guidance in a calm atmosphere rather than during a tense situation.

As their children entered school, Linda and Jim sat down with each one and discussed what school would be like; the importance of homework; a plan for when, where and how the homework was to be done, and the consequences of failing to do homework. The children complained a little about the new routine, but very quickly lived up to what was expected of them.

Sara and Matt, on the other hand, did not plan ahead. Every school day afternoon saw a tug-of-war between Sara and the children, who would rather watch cartoons than do homework. The kids saw Mom as an awful nag, and Sara felt drained by the daily hassle.

The discussion that occurs *after* a problem has arisen is not as effective as talking things out ahead of time because it is taken as punishment or correction. Done proactively, it feels more like "preventive medicine" — help to keep a problem from ever happening. Done after the fact, it can feel more like an attack. Linda's and Jim's children "grew into" the expectation of their parents. Sara's and Matt's children rebelled against what they perceived as constant nagging.

In the business world, policies and procedures are created to give detailed guidelines to prevent misunderstanding, miscommunication, or error. These are proactive, anticipatory measures that will hopefully save time, create efficiency and enhance the morale of the employees. Without them, there would be chaos, hurt feelings and wasted time.

Kingdom Principles

God calls us to maturity in character, in responsibility and in relationships. He calls us to address our weaknesses, to confess our sins, to make restitution for harm we have caused and to behave in a manner that glorifies Him. Though He knows that we are imperfect and immature in many ways, He still requires that we walk in truth and press on towards maturity.

There are several verses in the New Testament that refer to being perfect, complete, or mature:

. . . you know that the testing of your faith develops perseverance. Perseverance must finish its work so that you may be mature and complete, not lacking anything (James 1:3,4).

Wrestling in prayer for you, that you may stand firm in the will of God, mature and fully assured (Colossians 4:12).

He gave some to be prophets, some to be evangelists, and some to be pastors and teachers, to prepare God's people for works of service, so that the body of Christ may be built up until we all reach unity in the faith and in the knowledge of the Son of God and become mature, attaining to the whole measure of the fullness of Christ (Ephesians 4:11–13).

Be perfect, therefore as your heavenly Father is perfect (Matthew 5:48).

Therefore let us leave the elementary teachings about Christ and go on to maturity . . . (Hebrews 6:1).

All three words, perfect, complete, and mature are from the same Greek word, *teleios,* which means mature. *Teleios* in its various forms does not imply complete knowledge or complete perfection; but rather it implies being fully grown, being functional, being able to understand one's purpose in life.

William Barclay, a great New Testament expositor as well as longtime Professor of Divinity and Biblical Criticism at the University of Glasgow, comments that the word translated "maturity" in Hebrews 6:1 means two things. One is that as a person gets older he should have more and more things thought out for himself. A mature person should not only have a good grasp of facts but also understand the significance of those facts. Secondly, he should be reflecting the character of Christ, ridding himself of old faults and applying new virtues. As time passes, he should be growing stronger, finer, and more complete.

How does maturity develop? James 1:3,4 says it comes through testing. The purpose of testing is not to make us fall, but to soar. Just as a bird tests its wings to see if it is able to fly, so disappointments and sorrows test our faith. The Christian must expect to be jostled by trials. They are not meant to defeat us; we are meant to overcome them. Trials point out our weaknesses and give us an opportunity to develop the very area in which we are weak. They will make us stronger. This strength is developed in us for the purpose of maturing us so that we can do the work that He has planned for us.

Food For Thought

Use these questions to evaluate how proactive you are.

Personal

Do you consciously admit your faults and work to correct them? What do you do when you make a mistake — admit it quickly? Blame someone else? Think of an excuse? Or pretend it did not happen?

THE ROAD TO MATURITY

FIGURE 2 — HOW PROACTIVE ARE YOU?

PROACTIVE		REACTIVE
Do you . . .		Do you . . .
Anticipate problems and take steps to prevent them?	OR	Wait until problems happen and then fix them?
Think: What is the best in the long run?	OR	What can I do to fix this quickly?
Know specifically what your priorities, principles are?	OR	Let circumstances or other people decide what is important?
Acknowledge the positive emotions involved (mercy, compassion, sympathy) as well as the negative ones (anger, frustration, fear, jealousy)?	OR	Disregard emotions?
Base your decisions on principles?	OR	Make decisions based on emotions?
Know what is your respon- sibility and what is not your concern?	OR	Often get too involved in others and avoid your own responsibility?

Are you aware of your strengths? When can those strengths become weaknesses?

Are you actively pursuing good health (diet, exercise, medical checkups)?

Children

Do you plan time and activities to be with your children? Do you anticipate the stages they are going through and discuss this with your spouse?

Are you challenging and encouraging them in school work? Do you dream with them? Do you point out their strengths and show them how to deal with their shortcomings?

Do you discuss character issues and teach values and principles? Are you helping them learn how to handle problems or disappointments in a healthy, mature way?

Spouse

Do you take initiative regarding time for your spouse? Do you take time to listen and validate one another? Do you anticipate each other's needs?

Finances

Is there a realistic budget? Are you anticipating buying a home, saving for college, planning for retirement? Is the budget a joint decision?

Household/Auto Maintenance

Do you anticipate needs for maintenance, or are such expenses always a damaging surprise to the bank account?

Church/group

Do you see your importance to the group to which you belong? Do you volunteer for a fair share of responsibility or do you wait to be asked? Do you offer your talents and abilities?

Society

Are you informed? Do you know what the real issues are for your community as well as the country? Do you vote?

Friends

Do you have close friends? Do you initiate contact and activities or do you wait for others to reach out to you?

CHAPTER 2

STRAIGHTENING CROOKED THINKING

Why We Do What We Do

Ben, a well-respected high school history teacher, was an experienced vocalist and an accomplished musician. He shared this story:

> I had a solo in the Easter Cantata at church. Of course, we had practiced for weeks, and I was confident that Sharon, the accompanist, was as well prepared as I was. But the solo began badly. I couldn't believe that Sharon played the wrong chord so that the first note out of my mouth was off key. We both quickly recovered, though, and the program was well received. Nonetheless, I was really disappointed and embarrassed that Sharon had messed us up, although I didn't feel free to tell her.
>
> Later that week, when the choir was getting together to listen to the tape of the performance, I had mixed feelings. Sharon was a longtime family friend and an excellent musician, and I felt badly that she would hear her glaring mistake. On the other hand, I looked forward to being somewhat vindi-

cated, when everyone would know it wasn't my fault.

When we listened to the recording, I was in absolute shock. I'm a trained musician and I would have sworn before God that Sharon had played the wrong chord. I even thought, "Who doctored the tape?" But the recording didn't lie. I had just hit the wrong note— plain and simple— but I had instantly blamed someone else. I was able to distort the truth and convince myself that Sharon had made a mistake to excuse my own error. Since then, I often ask myself, "How often does this happen when there is no recording to point out my self-deception?"

Beliefs

A *belief* is a conviction that evolves over time as we see the world from our unique perspective. A belief is an assumption that certain things are true or real. It is a "given" premise upon which we base our choices and courses of action. It is the set of lenses through which we view and interpret life.

Your belief becomes the filter through which you view life. Your beliefs greatly affect how you live. For instance, if you believe that God will take care of you, you will probably not be so anxious about life. Also, if you believe that you are a likable person, you will probably have an easy time making friends. If you believe that you are capable of accomplishing most things that you put your mind to, then you will explore new ideas and be adventurous.

False Beliefs

If all the beliefs we lived by were true, we'd have a much easier time conducting the business of living. Unfortunately, all of us grew up in imperfect families, and we thus acquired some false beliefs along the way. A *false belief* is an inaccurate belief that interferes with how we perceive or interpret ourselves, others or the circumstances around us. Many times, these faulty beliefs hinder our growth and effectiveness. We may repeatedly suffer harmful consequences, while still failing painfully to understand the circumstance or situation in which we find ourselves.

Jill's situation is a very common example of how we can continue to be hurt and yet not understand why. She believes that her husband should know intuitively what she wants or needs for Christmas without telling him directly. Of course, this is impossible. So every year, Christmas is a major disappointment which develops into weeks of anger and depression. Unless Jill realizes that her belief is unrealistic to a great extent, she will continue to have hurt feelings year after year.

Phil

Phil is a bright, middle-aged man who has repeatedly chosen jobs that are beneath his ability. He is discontented and bored. He faces a struggle between wanting to change jobs, but being afraid to. Those close to him have tried to encourage him to seek a job with more potential, but he becomes very nervous at the mere suggestion. When asked why he is so afraid to take on a more challenging position, he replies, "I can't do it." In looking behind the scene, we find that Phil grew up with a lot of criticism, especially from his father. He was often told he was stupid and would never amount to anything, just like his older brother. Hence, Phil grew up to believe just that. Every time he came close to succeeding, he would sabotage the opportunity, and not allow himself to excel. It is amazing how powerful a false belief can be. In this case, his false belief that he was stupid became a "glass ceiling" on his life. Even though it wasn't true, because he believed it, his potential was limited.

The first step to solving the problem is to identify it specifically. This chapter discusses how to examine false beliefs and their effects on our lives and relationships; why we hold onto these false beliefs; and how to rectify them.

False Beliefs That Cause Problems

At the root of many of our problems lie common false beliefs (misconceptions, faulty concepts) that predispose us to trouble. For clarity, we have categorized and listed some of the most common false beliefs, or lies that we believe.

False Beliefs about Life

How we view life will affect our attitude and how we approach everyday circumstances. Some common misconceptions are:

- Life should not inconvenience me; it should flow smoothly without irritation.
- Life should be predictable and orderly.
- There should be a limit to the amount of discomfort or pain I should have to experience.
- Life should be easier for me especially since I'm a Christian.
- I cannot handle _____(fill in the blank). If that happens, I will be overwhelmed and I won't be able to survive.
- I should not have to live with unjust things that happen to me.
- Solutions to problems should be clean and easy.
- If something is wrong, someone must be blamed. We cannot just solve the problem. We must first place the blame on someone and *then* solve the problem.

False Beliefs about Self

What we think about ourselves greatly determines the level of our self-esteem. This in turn affects our relationships, our performance and our hopes.

In counseling, it is a joy to witness the changes that take place in a person's life as their self-esteem becomes healthier. A person's countenance, carriage, confidence and even communication display the positive transformation taking place. It is very important that we all examine how we view ourselves because it may very well be affecting a lot of other things in life. Here are some common lies we believe about ourselves:

- I must not fail or else I am not worthy.
- I must always be in control or else I'm not responsible.
- I am a bother to others if I need help.
- I am a mistake. I shouldn't have been born.
- Crying or showing any emotion is a display of weakness.
- I am what I am; I shouldn't have to change.
- I cannot change.
- I must be perfect and competent or else I'm a failure.
- I am what I do.
- I deserve _____(fill in the blank). I don't deserve_____(fill in the blank).
- I am no good; I'll never amount to anything.
- My opinion is not worth stating.
- I am always right.
- I shouldn't need anything or anyone.
- It's not okay to be (male or female).
- I can't embarrass my parents by surpassing them.

False Beliefs about God and Scriptural Principles

What we believe to be true about God and His care of us affects: how we approach Him in prayer; how anxious we are about life; and how we view our relationship to Him.

Some false beliefs about God and what He expects from us include:

- God's love must be earned.

- If He really loves me, He wouldn't let me suffer.
- "Loving one another" means "make everybody happy."
- A Christian should not be angry, anxious, depressed . . .
- The problems in my life are a punishment from God for my sins.
- I should always be modeling the victorious Christian life.
- God does not understand my problem.
- God is a cosmic killjoy.

False Beliefs about Relationships and Marriage

All of us enter adulthood with a partial understanding and with unrealistic expectations of what it means to be a friend, a spouse, a parent. We all have certain expectations of others and of our relationships. Some of these expectations are unrealistic, such as:

- I need others' approval in order to be happy.
- If I don't make others happy, I have failed in making the relationship work.
- If it takes hard work, it was not meant to be.
- Unity requires that everyone be in agreement (unanimity). Disagreement is synonymous with criticism and rejection.
- If someone disappoints me or hurts me, they are "off my list."
- I can't live without someone to depend on.
- I can't live without someone depending on me.
- If someone cares about me, they should anticipate all my needs, desires.
- Compromise is defeat.
- Good relationships don't have problems, e.g., conflicts, anger, misunderstandings.
- In a close relationship the two people involved do

everything together.
- Nobody will ever like me if they find out what I'm really like.
- I can only get attention when I am sick, whine, misbehave, etc.
- I shouldn't have to change; he/she knew what I was like when he/she married me.
- Romance equals love.
- If I express my feelings well, my mate should always be able to understand and empathize.
- If spouses really love each other, sexual needs will take care of themselves.
- Honesty is always the best policy. (We can be so brutally honest that we annihilate one another).
- There are set roles for husbands and wives.
- Anger is an attack.
- I can change the other person.
- Time will solve the problem.
- Once we are married (or when we have children, when the children are gone, when the job changes, etc.) our problems will resolve themselves.

False Beliefs about Family Roles and Expectations

Every family operates from a set of "rules" that govern roles and expectations. Often these rules are unspoken yet they nonetheless remain an extremely influential force in family life. Some of these are:

- Husbands (or wives) only have permission to spend large amounts of money without discussion.
- Men are allowed to be angry and aggressive (verbally or physically abusive).
- The family must always make allowances for Dad (Mom, problem child).
- The wife's duty is to always be there for whomever might need her.

- Only Dad (or Mom) is responsible for discipline.
- Never discuss disturbing, obviously destructive or bizarre behavior.
- Never talk about (_subject_) to (_person_).
- Steer clear of (_person_) if they have had a bad day.
- Boys are encouraged to prepare for a career; girls are encouraged to prepare for marriage.
- Anger, crying, or any other emotional display or weakness are not allowed.
- Do not show affection.

Subconscious Beliefs

Many of our beliefs develop *subconsciously*, i.e., without our awareness. For example, no one ever says that you have to be perfect to be accepted, yet many of us operate on this premise and subconsciously strive for a perfection that is actually impossible to attain. Other examples might be that being tall for a woman means that she is not desirable, or that you are not worth anything unless you are smart, or I have to make everyone happy, or spiritual Christians don't get angry.

Where do these come from? We weren't taught them directly, but rather indirectly through repeated impressions or behavior. Your parents may never have directly said "I love you more when you get 'A's." But if the only time you were given special attention and praise was when you made good grades, then you would probably, by default, not only begin to receive this indirect message, but also to operate from it.

It is important to realize that even though we are unaware of what we are thinking, we still react and make decisions from this (subconscious) place. We also react when things do not go according to our expectations, even though we may not consciously be aware of these expectations. Without this awareness, we are left puzzled as to why we feel the way we do and are genuinely bewildered by our actions.

Hidden beliefs that continue to remain unchallenged, buried in the subconscious, unexamined in the light of truth, are *very* powerful and will control our behavior as long as they are allowed to remain unchallenged. Truth sets us free. If we ask the Holy Spirit to reveal any hidden beliefs that are causing harm, we can then choose to correct them by renewing our minds with the truth. The Psalmist expressed this in Psalm 139:23-24.

> Search me, O God, and know my heart;
> test me and know my anxious thoughts.
> See if there is any offensive way in me,
> and lead me in the way everlasting.

Reality Check

If we take a closer look at the circumstances, our reactions to them, our feelings about them, and our thinking in them, we may discover the false belief, or outright lie, that causes us so much trouble.

This examination of our beliefs in a given set of circumstances is called a *reality check*. A reality check is a quick test to make sure that what we think we understand to be true is indeed true. We can ask ourselves such questions as these: Did I perceive the events, words, behavior correctly? Am I maintaining a healthy skepticism? Did I jump to a hasty and self-damaging conclusion? Is there someone I can ask for a more objective point of view? Because we all suffer from false beliefs and self-deception, we must continually maintain reality checks if we are going to be realistic, mature individuals.

A reality check is essential to our spiritual walk. "There is nothing worse than religion in which appearances are out of touch with reality . . . . The mind is a marvelous gift and has important and essential functions in the life of faith. There are times when it is the only means given to us for discriminating between truth and error, between sense and nonsense, between what is actual and what is illusion, between the popular insanity of the age and the enduring sanity of the gospel."[1] Spiritual maturity is the integration of faith and reality. Faith meets reality; it doesn't avoid it. Faith brings the supernatural dimension into the natural realm. Faith is based on truth — the truth of God and the truth of the circumstance.

Sanity— Healthy Thinking

One aspect of sanity involves healthy thinking, or seeing things as they really are, not just as they may appear to be or as we would like for them to be. Sanity also includes being able to stay in touch with reality; i.e., the facts and the feelings associated with real events. Sane thinking involves the ability to reason, to decide between alternative courses of action, and to uphold logic while maintaining Godly values, even while living or working in an environment that may be hostile to them.

We begin to lose touch with reality when we fail, or refuse, to recognize the truth of *what is really going on.* How does this happen? It happens when we experience a painful event (insult, rejection, criticism, shame, embarrassment, tragedy, victimization) which we find ourselves unable to deal with in a healthy and self-respecting way. So, we either block out the painful emotions associated with the event or we distort the facts of the event in order to make them more tolerable to us. In either case, *by backing away from the truth* of the situation, we try to insulate ourselves from the resulting pain. *Dissociation of feelings* from the reality of events is the breeding ground of mental illness.

The Safety Box

Everyone is a composite of strengths and weaknesses. We all have mixed feelings about ourselves. On the positive side, we can feel confident, significant, capable, lovable, and resourceful. But we can also feel ashamed, lonely, guilty, inadequate, worthless or fearful. We naturally try to project our best while trying to cover our shortcomings.

When we cover our weaknesses, our fears or our hurts, we are actually hiding. We retreat into a *safety box*, which serves to insulate us from the pain that is a part of life. These feelings of shame, guilt, loneliness, inadequacy, and failure are part and parcel of being human. No one wants to jeopardize himself by appearing vulnerable; so, we hide.

The devices we use to protect ourselves are called *defense mechanisms*. Defense mechanisms are mechanisms people use to protect themselves from harm and often from truth. It is easy to see how we can alter the facts to make the picture or situation safer and more palatable. We often have a hard time accepting ourselves as we really are, and so in our efforts to project a good image, we will blame, rationalize, argue, make excuses, avoid, deny, and complain. In the opening story, Ben was in denial about his own mistake and quickly blamed the accompanist for the mishap that marred an important musical performance. This anecdote is an example of a person subconsciously using the defense mechanism of blame in an effort to protect himself from embarrassment.

Validation

We also become very defensive when we are not validated. Validation is an act of acknowledging the validity of another person's feelings, problems, opinions, or concerns. When we are invalidated we feel like we must somehow "prove" ourselves or our feelings.

The idea of validation is used in everyday life. For example, we often get parking tickets validated by a movie theater or a store so that our parking fee is waived when we leave the parking garage. When we get the ticket punched or stamped we are validating the fact that we were there.

The idea of validation is used in a similar way in relationships. Just like getting our parking ticket stamped to show we have been there, validating another person acknowledges their presence, what is being said, and the feelings expressed. Validation occurs when one person confirms another, accepts what they are saying or feeling as legitimate, as valid, as important. Validation allows the other person to be free to think, to feel, to process, to change, to grow. Validation does not mean that we think the other person is always correct, right or that we approve of what they are doing. It just means that we receive their words and honor their worth as a human being. It is putting ourselves in the other person's shoes and trying to see and feel things as he does. It is first allowing the other person to simply *be*— be angry, sad, disappointed, frustrated, fearful, hurt as well as excited, happy or determined. Reality checks and further discussion is much more effective *after* validation has been given.

If your son was given detention for misbehaving and complains to you as soon as he walks in the door, you will have much more success in dealing with the situation if you first validate the fact that it is awful that he has to stay after school. Then, after you have validated his anger, you have a better chance of discussing the real issues involved. If you thwart him right from the start, you will more than likely start another feud. We all feel better and are more able to receive correction after we have first been heard.

Envision validation as playing catch. When you validate someone, you "catch" their words and feelings. Invalidating is missing the ball or shoving it back at them and walking away. Invalidation sends a message that "what you have to say is not important, therefore *you* are not important." Have you ever been angry and had someone tell you, "You have no reason to be upset." What was your response? Didn't it make you even angrier? On the other hand, if they had acknowledged (validated) that you were angry without putting you down, perhaps you would have been able to calm down sooner.

Validation is empathy in action. It is attempting to get a perception of what it is like to be the other person. It is putting yourself in his shoes. Validating says, "I believe in your right to be yourself, to feel what you feel and to be heard, and I will try to understand." We can validate another person's frustration, anger, or other strong emotions and yet not approve of any misbehavior. We have all heard the saying, "Love the sinner, but hate the sin." Easier said than done, but it works. Mature people can validate the person, even if they disapprove of his attitude or behavior.

If we are not validated at home, there are few other places where we are appreciated for just being ourselves. Growth only takes place in a nurturing, safe atmosphere. The importance of emotional safety cannot be stressed strongly enough. There is safety in a relationship when we are free to express how we really feel without being shamed, embarrassed, put down or ignored. (This does not condone bad or irresponsible behavior. More about this later.) True growth in esteem and identity can only develop in a safe place where we are allowed to *be*. If we are invalidated or ignored, we have a tendency to project a false front in order to be accepted. Real, solid esteem can only develop in a nurturing, safe environment.

Validators are *safe* people. In working with groups, we often begin the discussion on this subject by asking everyone to think of someone in their lives who has been a safe person— someone to whom you could tell almost anything. And we wait until everyone has this safe person in mind. (It is interesting to note that it always takes everyone much longer to come up with a safe person than an unsafe person.) What is this person like? What makes him/her a safe person? The responses were so consistent group after group that we have compiled these characteristics which we have listed in Figure 3.

FIGURE 3 —
CHARACTERISTICS OF SAFE AND UNSAFE PEOPLE

SAFE	UNSAFE
Listens to you	Doesn't listen
Hears you	Doesn't hear
Makes eye contact	No eye contact
Accepts the real you	Rejects the real you
Validates the real you	Invalidates the real you
Non-judgmental	Judgmental
Is genuine with you	Is false with you
Is clear	Is unclear
Boundaries appropriate and clear	Boundaries unclear; messages mixed
Direct	Indirect
No triangles	Triangles in others
Supportive	Competitive
Loyal	Treacherous
Relationship authentic	Relationship contrived
Has time for you	Doesn't have time for you

Codependency

If we grow up without validation we often become *codependent*. It is a very common way in which we attempt to protect ourselves from harm or conflict by appeasing another person so that they will not become angry, abandon us, reject us, ridicule us, condemn us, or merely think badly of us. Codependency is a relational dynamic that, to one degree or another, is present in all of us. At times, this dynamic is very evident, such as when a teenager gives in to peer pressure and does something he knows is wrong just to stay a part of the crowd. Another example is a wife who is afraid to confront her husband concerning his credit card debt because she receives the brunt of his rage every time the subject comes up.

At other times codependency is more subtle, but it still strongly influences what position we play in our relationships and what part we play in supporting or perpetuating a lie. Not being able to say "no" is a typical symptom of common underlying codependency. Many women fall into the trap of thinking that they need to please everyone around them. They believe that they must have done something wrong if someone acts hurt, disappointed, or throws a tantrum.

Joan is a mother who has difficulty disciplining her children. She gives in to even the most ridiculous of their demands. If she even attempts to say "no" the children misbehave to such an extent that she becomes embarrassed and quickly gives in to save face. Joan feels overwhelmed and inadequate at home. Outside the home, she has won the acceptance and favor from others when she volunteers to serve at church and school. As a result, she is driven to volunteer more and more just to feel good about herself.

No one is entirely free from being influenced by what other people think of us. We yearn for acceptance from others and may even allow this craving to override what we know to be right and true. *This is the essence of codependency.* To live for approval is to be at the mercy of everyone from whom we want that approval. It is letting someone else's thinking determine our course of action.

This state of affairs lends itself to being double-minded and unstable. Acute codependency is sure to affect every area of our lives, including our relationships, how we spend our time and money, how we raise our children, and how we implement leadership in the home, workplace, and church.

Mapping Our Thinking

The following figure is the tool that will be used in mapping our thinking.

FIGURE 4 – 1 ➡ 2 ➡ 3 ➡ 4 CHART

EVENT ➡ THOUGHT ➡ EMOTION ➡ BEHAVIOR			
1	2	3	4

The 1 ➡ 2 ➡ 3 ➡ 4 diagram is an illustration of how our thinking determines our behavior. 1 represents the *event* or situation. 2 is the *thought*– the way we interpret the event. 3 indicates the *emotion* caused by that thought. 4 is the subsequent *behavior* spawned by that emotion. This theory was developed by Albert Ellis and forms the basis for *Rational Emotive Theory*, which states that irrational (crooked) thinking and faulty belief systems are the root causes of emotional distress and its consequential damaging behaviors.

This diagram provides a practical means of *mapping our thinking processes* and seeing how they affect our feelings and behavioral patterns. It helps identify thought patterns and compare them to the truth, including the truth about God and the facts of any given situation.

Playing Detective

In order to fix what is wrong, we usually have to look back to see where it went wrong and why. If we want to know why we are feeling the way we are feeling or behaving the way we are behaving, we need to examine our thinking. Our feelings and behaviors are merely clues as to what we are really thinking.

Using the chart to play detective (using the clues to find the truth) is a tangible means for improving the level of awareness we have of our own feelings, motives, beliefs, and assumptions. It also allows us to see how they affect our everyday decisions, behaviors, and relationships.

In order to target crooked thinking, we must:

- Identify the event and the ensuing behavior or reaction to it.
- Ask ourselves, what must have been I feeling, for me to behave as I did?
- Did I perceive the event correctly? (Consult others as a *reality check*)
- What could have I been thinking, assuming or expecting to make me feel this way?
- Was that thought true or realistic, given the situation?

We have provided several examples of how to use the 1 ➡ 2 ➡ 3 ➡ 4 diagram at the end of this chapter.

Conformed or Transformed

The 1 ➡ 2 ➡ 3 ➡ 4 process helps to explain the difference between *con*forming (trying to change the behavior) compared to being *trans*formed (changing from the inside out by the renewing of our minds.)

We can use pressure or can enforce rules in order to cause others to conform to a certain standard of performance, excellence, or behavior. Sometimes this is appropriate. There are many times that a person in a position of authority must demand certain expectations. Even a government agency can demand a certain standard of criteria such as the Food and Drug Administration, which demands that medications be thoroughly and rigorously tested before being given approval.

However, when it comes to the subject of personal maturity, outward conformity does not necessarily produce inward change. Transformation, or inward change, happens when an understanding begins to take place that a change is not only necessary, but to be desired. Transformation begins, for example, when a child begins to think, "It's important to do my homework," rather than, "Mom will get mad if I goof off." True change takes place when you begin to "own" the problem and take the steps necessary to solve it. It is change that occurs in us because certain principles or values have become personal beliefs. Transformation takes place when we begin to *want* to change instead of feeling we *have to* (ought to, should, need to) change. One comes out of hope, the other comes out of fear.

How does transformation happen? It begins with giving the Holy Spirit free rein in our lives. We give ourselves to Him and look to Him for truth, power, direction, and motivation. He gives us just that. As He does, it then becomes our turn to walk in obedience to what He has taught us, shown us and empowered us to do. In the process, we change. Our minds are being retrained (renewed) and our perspective is being sharpened. We begin to see things differently and to experience Him more deeply. The reality of God is entering the reality of our lives.

God causes the growth; the working of the Spirit brings us into maturity. The process is called transformation. God is at work in every phase of transformation, but we can short-circuit this process by failing to cooperate. God has a plan for us— a plan for us to grow up. And we play an active role in this growing-up process.

Practically speaking, maturing is learning to become increasingly aware of reality, situations, and principles and choosing a proper response to them. Too often, we well-intentioned church members address only the behavior that is troublesome to us and think it is enough merely to demand conformity to our idea of what in fact may be moral, mature, correct behavior. But to alter behavior without working on the root problem is like trying to cork a steam kettle to prevent it from boiling over. Corking the kettle will stop the overflow for a moment, but the pressure will continue to build, until the cork explodes off the kettle. Willpower can correct bad behavior for a while, but unfortunately not for long. We must identify the source of our problems, and then take the steps necessary to effectively deal with them. Examining our thoughts and bringing them in line with the truth has the same effect as turning down the flame under the kettle.

This process is painful, but it has been our experience that God is utterly dependable and will bring to light those things that He wants to heal. When we determine to respond instead of react, lowering our defenses, the miracle of transformation begins its work in us. Transformation, not conformation, heals our deepest hurts and enables us to make choices that reflect growth.

Emotions

Many of us misunderstand the importance that emotions play in our lives. We may have been taught that emotions are silly, a sign of weakness or immaturity. Many people have wrongly relegated the subject of emotions to only the female gender. Women can talk about how they feel, but men are sissies if they do. This is unfortunate and certainly not scriptural.

Emotions are similar to the gauges on the dashboard of a car that indicate what is going on inside of the engine or how the car is functioning. The warning light may come on indicating that there is something wrong with the engine that needs to be checked. Likewise, emotions indicate what is going on in our conscious or subconscious thoughts.

Understanding the 1➡2➡3➡4 chart helps to explain the need to discuss and be aware of feelings.

If I am consistently aware of my car's temperature gauge or warning light, I should be able to take action to prevent the radiator from boiling over. Similarly, I usually can prevent overreacting to minor things if I am emotionally aware that I am in danger of overreacting due to tiredness or frustration. A maturing person is someone who is increasingly aware of his emotional response to what is going on around him.

It is important to know that emotions are:

- God-given and *of themselves* neither good nor bad;
- indicators of what is going on inside and directly related to our behavior;
- *very powerful* and important to understanding our thoughts and our heart-attitude;
- components of the maturing process.

Identification, awareness, and understanding of our emotions are all necessary components of the maturing process. Being aware of our emotions is the key to examining our thoughts. Often, we are mistaken about, or actually unaware of, what we are really thinking. Our behavior and attitude usually display what we really think or believe. Most of us can relate to the line our mothers said to us: "It's not *what* you said that bothers me; it's *how* you said it." We were confronted with the fact that *how* we said something conveyed our real attitude more than the actual words that we used. That's why we read that communication is more of an emotional process than a mechanical one. Body language and tone of voice are stronger communicators than words alone. (More about this in Chapter 5.)

Why Being Aware of Our Emotions and Examining Our Past Is So Important:

- To understand ourselves (why we do what we do).
- To determine what our expectations are of certain roles (parent, husband, wife)
- To uncover family false beliefs
- To understand family strengths and shortcomings
- To be aware of what we value — priorities
- To see how we do or don't resolve conflicts
- To realize what emotions were allowed and which ones were forbidden
- To discover how we handle pain, frustration, problems, crisis
- To understand how we nurture people in relationships.

The Ephesians 4:26 Principle

When Paul writes, "Be angry and yet do not sin," (Ephesians 4:26 NASB) his psychology is absolutely accurate. We can and must control our *behavior*; we can examine and change our *thoughts and beliefs*; we can even avoid certain *situations and events*; but while experiencing our emotions *we cannot change them simply by saying to ourselves that we should not feel the way we are feeling.* And yet many times this is exactly what we expect of ourselves and others. This is the difficulty we often have with emotions. Instead of trying to change how we feel, we need to use these feelings as gauges that signal how we are functioning and as a clue to what we are thinking. *It is possible to be aware of and discuss emotions without being overly emotional.* It is also possible to be aware of our emotions and use them to make rational decisions. It is important to be honest about how we feel without using this as an excuse for misbehaving.

FIGURE 5 —CONTRASTING EMOTIONS

ANGRY

annoyed, livid, frustrated, repulsed, hostile, undermined, hate, displeased, irritated, imposed upon, uptight, bitter, tense, impatient, out of control

AFFECTIONATE / PEACEFUL

caring, pleased, attracted, content, patient, loving, relaxed, helpful, at ease

DEPRESSED

despairing, gloomy, tired, angry, drained, weary, discouraged, resigned, suicidal, sad, stuck, useless, hopeless, shattered, broken

SATISFIED

cheerful, happy, full, encouraged, buoyant, grateful, glad, sunny, content, fulfilled, relieved, positive, joyous

HURT

rejected, blamed, mistreated, failure, deceived, unloved, put upon, misunderstood, disappointed, taken for granted, neglected, cheated, betrayed, used

WHOLE

accepted, belonging, comfortable, loved, eager, appreciated, refreshed, understood, invigorated, excited, rejuvenated, renewed, enthusiastic

ALONE

isolated, abandoned, left out, excluded, alienated, neglected, needy, cold, outcast, rejected, lonely

BELONGING

useful, included, warm, integral, desirable, precious, wanted, at home

CONFUSED

shocked	numb	hesitant
mixed-up	uncertain	surprised
torn	forgetful	double-minded
distracted		

CLEAR / AWARE

together	certain	determined
sure	confident	settled
directed	focused	sensitive
resolute		

AFRAID

anxious	worried	alarmed
paralyzed	dreadful	terrified
intimidated	scared	defensive
jealous	panicky	frozen
apprehensive		

HOPEFUL / SECURE

expectant	redeemable	worthy
trusting	courageous	right
confident	safe	free
vigorous	liberated	

SHAMED / GUILTY

unwanted	unnecessary	hated
worthless	embarrassed	unloved
redundant	burdensome	awkward
ugly	unimportant	despised
abused	insignificant	reviled
clumsy	beyond redemption	

WORTHY

acceptable	redeemable	worthy
desirable	unique	important
significant	affirmed	respected
valuable	honored	lovable
validated	cherished	

INADEQUATE

useless	incapable	helpless
insecure	inferior	clumsy
stupid	incompetent	disqualified

ADEQUATE

capable	well-equipped	resourceful
sufficient	qualified	smart
productive	well-prepared	successful
competent	useful	clever

Mixed Emotions

Another important key to understanding our emotions is that we very often have *mixed* emotions on a given subject. In fact, having several different emotions at the same time is quite normal, particularly if we are thinking of something of major importance to ourselves. For example, on the subject of our work: we may feel *grateful* that we have the job; we may feel *apprehensive* and *overwhelmed* about the project we are working on; and yet at the same time *enjoy* the challenge of it all. Another example is how we feel towards another person. We may *appreciate* our spouse and yet at times feel *annoyed* with him/her. We can feel *hurt* by someone and yet feel that we still *belong* to him/her. It is possible to feel *nervous* and yet *confident* in a given situation.

Using the Emotions List

We have found that a useful first step toward emotional awareness is to become familiar with a list of words that describe emotions. The following chart is a list of contrasting emotions:

Exercise

Using the preceding list of Contrasting Emotions, consider how you feel about . . .

- the Lord
- yourself – as a person, spouse, parent, worker
- your physical appearance
- parents, grandparents, uncles, aunts
- brothers, sisters
- friends
- marriage
- your spouse
- children

- your church fellowship
- your home (atmosphere)
- the neighborhood you live in
- work
- co-workers
- retirement
- the present
- the future
- finances
- status
- failure
- hobby – leisure time

Kingdom Principles

It is no coincidence that the Holy Spirit, given to us, is called the Spirit of Truth (John 14:17) and the Comforter (John 14:16) and the Teacher (John 14:26). He will continually nudge us towards the truth, showing us how to walk in it, supplying the power needed, and comforting us in the pain of the maturation process. "Walking in the light," even with the Comforter, can be a painfully uncomfortable experience sometimes, but we must remember that it is God's will to heal, strengthen, and equip us so that we might truly prove His love, grace and power. With prayer and *time*, God will replace your anger with peace, and your fears with strength.

The road of life at times is filled with heartache. God's intention is to restore us and bring us into deeper levels of maturity that will benefit us. As much as we hate to face it, these lessons often come through hard times and suffering. However, it is important to remember that God is *for* us, not against us. It is His *pleasure* to build us up, not tear us down or see how much we can bear. It is His *intention* to take all things and work them out for our good (Romans 8:28).

Principle # 1

We must believe that God is, and that He is a rewarder of those that diligently seek Him (Hebrews 11:6b).

Sometimes we struggle harder than we have to because we fail to understand two foundational principles of God. One is that we must believe that God is, and that He is a rewarder of those that diligently seek Him. *Believing that God* is does not mean some vague belief that there is a God; but that He is *living, present,* and actively *for us.* We must decide what we believe. Is God *for* us or do we have to win or earn His favor?

Our beliefs about God's character and His intention towards us are critical in the process of maturity. For example, suppose I imagine that God is some kind of critical dictator who is hoping that I'll make mistakes, and is ready to pounce if I do. Then, when I do make a mistake, I will feel afraid and most likely be hesitant to seek His help. If, on the other hand, I see God as a caring Father who genuinely loves me and is concerned for me, I will freely go to Him for help.

Principle # 2

The victory over our struggles is already ours.

"We are more than conquerors through him that loved us" (Romans 8:37). The victory has been given to us. It is a fact. We do not have to fight to attain it. We only need to hold onto it, against all challengers. God has already seated us with Christ in the heavenly realm (Ephesians 2).

Watchman Nee wrote,

> Has defeat been your experience? Have you found yourself hoping that one day you will be strong enough to win? Then my prayer for you can go no further than that of the apostle Paul for his Ephesian readers. It is that God may open your eyes anew to see yourself seated with Him who has Himself been made to sit "far above all rule, and authority, and power,

and dominion, and every name that is named" (Ephesians 1:20f). The difficulties around you may not alter; the lion may roar as loudly as ever; but you need no longer hope to overcome. In Christ Jesus you *are* victor in the field.[2]

Ephesians 4:11-19 relates knowledge and truth to maturity and stability. God requires that we grow up into Him (v.15), abandon the futility of our own thinking (v.17), and speak the truth in love (v.15). The result will be that we will no longer be infants tossed back and forth . . . (v.14). We cannot be anchored to the truth, if we do not know what the truth is. And in the absence of knowledge of the truth, we will be susceptible to every force that seeks to control us.

Principle # 3

He has rescued us from the kingdom of darkness (Colossians 1:13).

Christ came to redeem us from Satan's influence and to thwart his power. He came to bring light into the darkness, truth into deception, life into death, freedom into bondage. "If you hold to my teaching, (truth) you are my disciples. Then you will know the truth, and the truth will set you free" (John 8:31,32).

Again, what we believe about God and life greatly affects our general outlook. If we believe that God will lead us into truth and will give us everything we need pertaining to life and godliness, then we can be confident that the capacity to meet life's challenges, deal with failures, and survive heartaches will be available to us.

Principle # 4

Transformation comes by the renewing of your mind (Romans 12:2).

The *battle*, therefore, *lies in the mind where God's truth is chal-*

lenged by Satan and us. From the beginning, deception (distortion of truth) has been Satan's weapon to undermine man's relationship with God. The great deceiver's primary objective is to subvert the truth, followed by planting seeds of doubt. Jeremiah 17:9 describes this resulting phenomenon as "deceitfulness of heart."

Living in truth involves a redemptive process. It means letting go of the lies as they are revealed to you and replacing them with the truth. 2 Corinthians 10:5 gives insight to this. "Our battle is to break down every deceptive argument and every imposing defense that men erect against the true knowledge of God" (J.B. Phillips). "And . . . we take captive every thought to make it obedient to Christ." Personalizing this: *My* battle is to break down every deceptive defense that *I* erect against the true knowledge of God and replace it with the truth, becoming obedient to Christ.

How can we take our thoughts captive and bring them into obedience to Christ? We must play detective. We must be aware of our emotions, our thoughts, beliefs and expectations, bringing them under the light of truth and asking God for the grace and power to live the way He wants us to live.

Living in truth sets us free to develop a spiritual, moral, and responsible life. It involves stepping out of our safety boxes and becoming living sacrifices (Romans 12:1,2) — laying ourselves (in our vulnerable state) on the altar before God, where He rescues us because of His love, stands us upright in grace, and equips us to do the works prepared for us by filling us with His power.

Principle # 5

The Duality of the Christian Experience

Although the victory is ours we are still plagued by our old nature and live in a fallen world. It is a paradox in that we experience confidence in God and yet at the same time feel the despair of life's circumstances. Watchman Nee describes this.

> Scripture presents to us two kinds of Christian experience, both equally valid and necessary. On the one hand there are such strong, almost boastful affirmations as: (But thanks be to God, who always leads us in triumphal procession in Christ . . . 2 Cor. 2:14), (For to me, to live is Christ . . . Phil. 1:21), and (I can do everything through Him . . . Phil. 4:13). Yet on the other hand the very same people, with equal truth, have to confess: "We despaired even of life," "Christ Jesus came into the world to save sinners; of whom I am chief," and "We also are weak in him." This latter seems to be another kind of Christian, faulty, frail and fearful, and alarmingly lacking in confidence. But in fact the real life of a child of God consists in the co-existence of these two experiences. We would prefer of course to concentrate on the first only, to the exclusion of the other. But to know them both is to know Him who is the God of Israel—and the God of Jacob too![3]

Food for Thought

The following situations are examples of using the 1➡2➡3➡4 diagram. Read each example. How will changing the thinking eventually change the emotional response and the behavior in each situation?

Example 1

- EVENT and BEHAVIOR: I'm caught in traffic and will be late for my appointment. I react by yelling at myself, "Should have left earlier, you idiot!" and by honking my horn at the other cars in front of me.
- EMOTION: I feel extreme anger and frustration.
- POSSIBLE THOUGHTS: I am thinking that I cannot afford to be late or that I should never have to be inconvenienced.

SOLUTION

- REALITY CHECK: Did I not allow myself enough

time? Will the damage really be irreparable if I am late?

- CORRECTIVE THOUGHT: Given the situation (arriving late), I will have to make adjustments and salvage the appointment the best I can and hope people will understand. Next time I will make certain to allow for more travel time.

Example 2

- EVENT and BEHAVIOR: Parent discovers 14-year-old son failed an algebra test and overreacts with extreme punishment, rather than getting the child the help he needs.
- EMOTION: The parent is feeling fear, shame, guilt, anger.
- POSSIBLE THOUGHTS: "I can't let this happen. If he fails, it will look like I'm a bad parent."

SOLUTION

- REALITY CHECK: Is he capable of this level of math? Is he doing his assignments? Does he need more help?
- CORRECTIVE THOUGHT: I'm not a bad parent nor is my son a failure just because he is having difficulty in math. I will schedule an appointment with his algebra teacher, and ask if my son needs special tutoring.

Example 3

- EVENT and BEHAVIOR: 24-year-old secretary was not invited to join some of her co-workers for lunch. She reacted by isolating herself in self-pity.
- EMOTION: She was obviously hurt, felt rejected and left out.
- POSSIBLE THOUGHTS: "Everyone should like

me. If I'm not liked, I'll have to find another job."

SOLUTION

- REALITY CHECK: Was there a reasonable explanation for her not to be included?
- CORRECTIVE THOUGHT: "From time to time
  I'll make my own plans, I can initiate steps to
  making friends; some will pan out, others won't."

Chapter Two Endnotes

[1]Gerald Corey, *Theory and Practices of Counseling and Psychotherapy* (Monterey, California: Brooks/Cole Publishing, 1982), p. 170f.

[2]Watchman Nee, *A Table in the Wilderness – Daily Meditations* (Wheaton, Illinois: Tyndale House Publishers, 1978), November 7.

[3]Ibid., November 17.

CHAPTER 3

BUILDING STRONG PEOPLE

A mature person is a strong person. How do we become strong? In this chapter we will take a look at who we are, what we need, and how we develop.

Body, Soul, Spirit

God has created each one of us as unique multi-dimensional human beings.

Too often, however, we view each other as human *doings* rather than human *beings*. For example, when people are asked who they are, they often respond with answers like, "I'm a mother, I'm a dentist, I'm the Sunday school teacher." We tend to see ourselves and others as what we *do* more than as who we *are*. It is hard for us separate who we are from what we do.

Who we are is ultimately more important than what we do, although what we do reflects who we are. God is more concerned with our character than with our deeds. It is important to begin with understanding who we are.

People are relational beings made up of three parts: *body*, *soul*, and *spirit*. As we all know, the *body* is the flesh part of us that needs food and protection in order to grow in health and strength. It has appetites which develop from each of the five senses (sight, smell, touch, hearing, and taste). Our bodies crave to have these appetites satisfied and we can either satisfy them in healthy ways or attempt to satisfy them in harmful ways. The body is also subject to disease; and we have a responsibility to keep it in health.

The *soul* is made up of the *mind* (thinking), the *will* (decision), and the *emotions* (feelings). How we *think* (as we have discussed in the previous chapter) affects our perspective, attitude, priorities, and even our emotional state. Our *will* (where we make our decisions) greatly affects how we live and relate to others. *Emotions* are the barometer or gauge of how we are dealing with our circumstances.

The *spiritual* aspect of our being is that part of us that relates to God. Since the Fall in the Garden of Eden, we have a God-shaped void that can only be filled with God Himself. When we come into a relationship with God through His Son Jesus, His Holy Spirit comes to dwell within us; completing us. Thus the communion between the Creator and the creature is restored.

God created us not only for the purpose of being in relationship with Him, but with others as well. He created us as *social* beings. He never intended that we live alone or in isolation. He saw that Adam was lonely and needed another being like himself and so He created Eve. We are created to be in relationship, with God and with our fellow man. He placed us in a social setting and said that we are to love one another and walk in truth.

The following figure, depicting the whole person, is one way to illustrate I Thessalonians 5:23 which says: "May God himself, the God of peace, sanctify you through and through. May your whole *spirit, soul,* and *body* be kept blameless at the coming of our Lord Jesus Christ."

FIGURE 6 — BODY-SOUL-SPIRIT

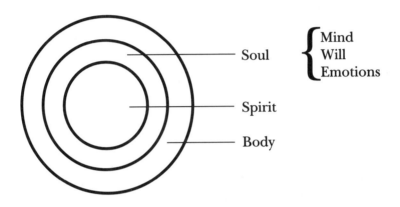

Even though the diagram depicts the three component parts of the person as being distinct from one another, in actuality they are closely interrelated. Each part influences the other parts. For instance, sickness can affect not only our bodies but also our outlook, our emotional state, and to some extent can even affect our spiritual perspective. Likewise, if we are worried about something, it is not unusual to become tense or tired physically and if prolonged it can even affect us spiritually. We may begin to have questions or doubts about God. If we allow outside circumstances and pressures to change us then we have conformed to the outside forces that are exerting these pressures. On the other hand, transformation is change that occurs from the inside out, when God's indwelling power begins to change our souls which in turn affects our behavior.

Basic Needs

A basic law of nature is that plants and animals don't grow or mature unless they are nourished. Just like a delicate rose, an individual can only grow or develop as basic needs are met. The remainder of this chapter will deal with the development of the physical, mental-emotional, spiritual, and social aspects of life. Listed below are the basic human needs that exist in each of the categories.

- *physical security* — including: shelter, food, medical care, physical contact and affection (holding, hugs, touch).

- *mental and emotional security* — providing a safe place to learn to reason and be creative; to find out who you are; for recreation, stimulation and challenge; to know validation, encouragement, love, and affection; to allow for individuation (becoming a unique and separate individual); to understand that pain and disappointment and healing are all a part of life.

- *social relationships* — sense of uniqueness; sense of integral belonging to the family unit and to a peer group; fostered by a sense of structure, consistency and boundaries; willingness to accept feedback; and development of a sense of responsibility to self and others.

- *spiritual relationship* — encouragement to find God (redemption) and your gifts, talents, and purpose in Him; to understand the process of transformation and its function on the road of maturity (grace, forgiveness, reconciliation and power).

Childhood Development

The basic needs listed above are fundamental to everyone, beginning at birth. The ways in which these fundamental needs are met greatly affect the way a child develops. For an infant, physical care and love are the most important needs that the parents and other caregivers can provide. In early childhood, a child becomes more independent as he begins to do more and more things for himself. The feeling of being separate, yet at the same time a part of the family, begins to develop. Encouraging a child to do and think for himself, while also being mindful of others, is an important need at this age. If a child is not permitted an adequate amount of activity to explore and play, then that child may lose a sense of curiosity and initiative and may even feel guilty for wanting to be "himself." If independence and creativity are encouraged within appropriate limits then the child develops curiosity, initiative and a sense of self-reliance.

As a child enters school, he needs to develop good self-esteem, a sense of adequacy and structure or routine. This is the time when he will learn new tasks as well as learn to take on some responsibility. If he does well, he will be confident and secure. If he does poorly, he will feel insecure, frustrated and badly about himself. At this stage of his life, he needs to be challenged and encouraged, given freedom within boundaries appropriate to his age, and consistency in discipline.

In the adolescent stage, a child will begin to further develop his uniqueness, a separate identity from that of his parents. The parents will spend more time in discussion, guidance and validation. If he is prevented from discovering his uniqueness and his own independence, he will become codependent, borrowing his identity from his parents or peers. If, on the other hand, he is encouraged to find his talents and abilities and to be aware of his weaknesses, he will develop a realistic, healthy self-concept.

The first column of Figure 7 lists five phases of development from infancy to adolescence. The second column gives the particular needs that are most important for each level. Column three describes the resulting qualities if the basic needs for each phase are consistently met. The last column indicates what happens when these needs are *not* consistently met.

As a child, our parents and teachers provided the boundaries and discipline under which we operated. As adults, we must become responsible for maintaining our own boundaries for being attentive to our duties and for our own growth. It is important to realize that as we mature, meeting these needs becomes more and more our responsibility instead of someone else's.

Finishing Unfinished Business

As we look at the basic needs list, we can identify needs that have been met in our lives and some that still have not been met. Very few of us have had all our needs met as we were growing up. These unmet needs are the issues that we take with us into adulthood. We all have *unfinished business.* We weren't born into perfect families or to perfect parents. Neither were our parents. We must learn to work with what we have and to begin to grow from where we are at the moment.

A matured person is one who has grown in *all four* aspects of living (physical, mental and emotional, social, and spiritual), who had the majority of his needs met in a *balanced* way. A gardener knows that his roses will reflect the quality of his care. He will take much time and deliberate effort in order to produce a bloom that is not only beautiful, but healthy. How much more so with people. *How well* a person's needs have been met will be reflected in his self-esteem, confidence,

FIGURE 7 – CHILDHOOD DEVELOPMENT

AGE	BASIC NEEDS	NEEDS IF MET PRODUCE	NEEDS IF NOT MET PRODUCE
INFANCY	• Physical security • Emotional security	• Trust • Contentment	• Mistrust • Fear
EARLY CHILDHOOD	• Creativity • Uniqueness • Separateness	• Self-reliance	• Shame and self-doubt • Insecurity • Dependency • Repression
PRESCHOOL	• Early stages of individuation ("I can do myself")	• Initiative • Industry	• Guilt for desiring to "be self," to discover.
GRAMMAR SCHOOL AGE	• Sense of Adequacy • To be challenged to complete a task • Need for structure, consistency, clear boundaries	• Assumption of responsibility • Industry – early development of completing a task • Sense of accomplishment	• Low self-esteem • Insecurity • Frustration
ADOLESCENCE	• Discovery – who "I am" (uniqueness) • Valued for oneself • Separate yet cared for • Guidance and validation • Encouragement	• Identity • Healthy self-concept • Stability	• Codependence • Identity is not formed

competence, resiliency, initiative, ability to give and receive, ability to relate to others, and breadth and depth of character.

A balanced, mature person can be likened to a person sitting on a four-legged stool (four aspects of living). Each leg (aspect) is necessary for stability, but that's not all. Each leg must also be the same length. Similarly, each aspect of living must be developed to the same extent. What would we be like if three of the legs were well developed and the fourth (social, for example) was immature? The fact is that if any of the legs are unequal, the stool is unsteady. You can *try* to balance yourself on only three legs so that you appear steady, but as soon as a substantial burden comes along, you will wobble. Human nature tends to be content with the status quo. It does not seek change. Instead of addressing the leg that needs attention, we compensate for our weakness by focusing our efforts on trying to balance ourselves on the other three legs.

A common example of this is the executive who can successively manage a large number of people, make difficult decisions, and lead his company in the workplace, and yet at home is unable to relate to his family. Unless he targets this area and makes a determined effort to learn how to nurture relationships, everyone in the family will continue to suffer to some extent. Sometimes to avoid the responsibility of developing relationships at home (his weak point), he may pour himself even more into his work.

Another example may be the woman who has not addressed or processed the tragedy and devastation of childhood sexual abuse. Without working through the trauma and necessary healing, she will probably be fearful and mistrusting and may have difficulty fully relating as a wife or mother on an intimate level.

Other examples might be people who neglect their physical health and appearance and don't understand why others shun them; people who continue to rely solely on themselves instead of the Lord and become tired and eventually disillusioned; parents that stress academic performance to the neglect of social and spiritual development. Any time we emphasize one aspect of living to the neglect of the others we run the risk of becoming unbalanced.

Maturity in the Church

Paul, in writing to Timothy and Titus, described the qualifications of elders and leaders within the church (1 Timothy 3:1-13; Titus 1:5-9). Leaders in the church had to know truth, to be able to teach truth, and to be able to refute those who oppose truth. They had to be discerning, able to judge, self-disciplined and honest. They were to be sociable— hospitable, gentle, not quick-tempered, quarrelsome or overbearing. They were not only to have earned the respect of outsiders, but also of their own children. They were not to be ruled by wine or the love of money. All these characteristics represent a well-balanced, mature human being.

God calls us to maturity in Christ. What does that mean? First of all, it means that maturity is possible. Before we were saved, we were slaves to sin, bound by it and to it. However, after we were saved, the rule changed. The bondage is broken and sin no longer has power over us. We are no longer slaves to sin. We struggle with sin because we have become so accustomed to its power and our weakness. We fail to grasp the new truth that says we are free and that we *can* change.

God has birthed in us a new nature which is more powerful than our old nature. 2 Peter 1:3-8 says:

> His divine power has given us everything we need for life and godliness through our knowledge of him who called us by his own glory and goodness. Through these he has given us his very great and precious promises, so that through them you may participate in the divine nature and escape the corruption

in the world caused by evil desires. For this very reason, make every effort to add to your faith goodness; and to goodness, knowledge; and to knowledge, self-control; and to self-control, perseverance; and to perseverance, godliness; and to godliness, brotherly kindness; and to brotherly kindness, love. For if you possess these qualities in increasing measure, they will keep you from being ineffective and unproductive in your knowledge of our Lord Jesus Christ.

This is proven Godly character.

Home Is Where the Start Is

It all starts at home. The process of growth and maturity begins early on, before we are old enough even to be conscious of the need to be mature. Growth begins from day one and it begins (traditionally) in the context of a family.

The family unit is the place where an individual's basic needs should be met. Specifically, the role of the parents in the family is to *protect* each member from harm; *provide* for each member's well-being; and *prepare* each individual to become whole, responsible, productive, self-reliant, and mature so that each person will be equipped to care for themselves, to serve others and to parent the next generation. This is a full-time job that demands top priority.

The level of maturity (physical, mental-emotional, social, and spiritual) of each member within a family is directly related to how satisfactorily and consistently his basic needs have been met. Everyone needs love and acceptance. If these needs are not met at home, we will look for them elsewhere. This is why it is so important for parents to provide a nurturing environment. It provides the very foundation upon which a child can begin to grow and develop into a mature and self-reliant adult.

Self-Esteem

Our level of self-esteem is directly proportional to the degree to which we have been nurtured. *Self-esteem* is the belief and respect one has in and for oneself. Healthy self-esteem is not conceit. It is a realistic assessment of one's strengths and weaknesses, a feeling of being on equal footing with others, not superior or inferior. The healthier our self-esteem, the greater the willingness to risk change, to stand, to hold to one's ideals, to be open to grow. Our self-esteem also greatly affects our abilities and performance. If we are not accepted at home, we will view ourselves as unlovable or undesirable and we will seek to find a group that will accept us. The need to be loved and accepted is basic to human nature and is so strong that we will find it, if it is not provided at home. Unfortunately, too many times it is found in unhealthy relationships.

Self-esteem is what we think and feel about ourselves, not what others think about us. It is the measure of our ability to think, learn, and perform as well as the measure of our eligibility for things that life has to offer such as friendship, respect, love, and fulfillment. Self-esteem is key to normal healthy development and growth and it affects every area of living. People with high self-esteem have been loved and well-nurtured in childhood. They are confident, resilient, creative, adventurous, able to express themselves, and able to set clear, healthy boundaries as to what they will (or won't) do or allow. Because they are more secure in who they are, their energy can be spent in being creative. They have the emotional energy that is needed to grow, to risk, to endure, to combat, and to adapt to life's challenges. These people tend to be more resilient and successful.

Those who have not been nurtured as well will have lower self-esteem. They will not have been raised to be as confident or self-assured and so will have a tendency to seek approval from others to "prove" their worth. They operate from an emotional deficit and so may not have as much emotional strength to endure or take on life's challenges. Because of this, they may have more of a tendency to avoid reaching out and risking the unknown. They may be more fearful, less sure of who they are, what they can do or what they are entitled to in life. They also may have difficulty setting healthy boundaries and can therefore easily become victims (and sometimes perpetrators) of abuse and disrespect.

Low self-esteem is curable at any age. If we are adults we can't expect someone to come along and nurture us and fix us. What we can do is seek truth, risk change and find healthy relationships. This takes courage and time, but it works. (More about this in Chapter 8.)

The saying, "garbage in, garbage out," is so true when it comes to nurturing children. What we, as parents, instill into our children will have lasting effect. It is so important for parents to love, nurture and train our children so that they know who they are, know what is right and be able to stand on their own.

The Goal: Moral and Character Development

Moral and character development is the process in which one's character becomes based on moral principles. These principles include concepts of moral strength, self-discipline, fortitude, courage, commitment, assertiveness, kindness, and love. Maturing is the gradual integration of these principles into the very heart and mind of an individual so that the person reflects the fullness of character that withstands the testing of time. The Bible calls this *proven* character.

Character does not just develop. It is the training or apprenticing of a person by someone who is more mature. It takes time to learn the truth and facts of life. And it takes even more time to practice (with guidance) applying these principles to everyday living.

Apprenticing or training takes place in almost every aspect of living: from work, to play, to household skills, to communicating. Apprenticing entails four steps: first is "I do, you watch;" second is "we do together;" third is "you do, I watch;" and fourth is "you do alone." Each step may take awhile, and often must be repeated.

The process of learning generally involves initial failure, followed by success. Daring to think and challenge and fail and rethink is what develops judgment and discernment—and hence, character. It is in the questions and failures and confusion that our time with our instructor is most vital. An effective instructor is one who does not panic over failure because he is able to see the student "in process"—just like God sees us in process.

Apprenticing can take place at any age, and hopefully it does. Learning should go on till the day we die, not only because of the practical value of learning new things, but also for the sheer enjoyment of it. Some of us have had excellent training in childhood; while others have not. Finding mature people to model in the body of Christ should be a common happening in the church. This is called discipleship.

Maturation, in short, is the process or transformation of an individual from being a dependent, self-centered child into a giving, responsible person. The more this process is understood, the better, so we have devoted the next two sections in this chapter to a more in-depth look into the maturation process. This closer look will help us to better understand where we and others are in the process of growing so that we are more able to help and to encourage one another on the road of life.

Progressive Stages of Moral and Intellectual Development

Egocentric Stage (self-centered)

We all begin as selfish little creatures, concerned only with ourselves and getting our needs met. Infants cry for a bottle or a diaper change or just to be picked up and held. Toddlers learn all kinds of ways to get their way; they pout, they whine, they cry, they hold their breath for remarkable lengths of time and, if all else fails, throw shrieking temper tantrums perfectly designed to drive long-suffering parents to abject surrender. The child's sweet smile of triumph after he's gotten what he wants is something with which every parent is grimly familiar.

In this preschool stage, young children govern their behavior according to external happenings or conditions. They focus on receiving rewards and avoiding punishment. In other words, it's okay to take a cookie without permission right before dinner, as long as they don't get caught with their hands in the cookie jar. The consequence (reward or punishment) governs the behavior. Children at this stage, left to their own devices, will eventually harm themselves. Parental guidance is absolutely necessary, and this is why it is so important for parents to take their roles seriously.

This stage is very fundamental to our maturity because it is the beginning of training. One thing to remember is that training is always going on whether you are aware of it or not. Children learn by what they see and what goes on around them. Preschoolers are not old enough to really understand the principles of right and wrong. They may connect a certain behavior with a parent's frown or smile, but they do not necessarily understand why Mom or Dad is angry or pleased. Their behavior is being conditioned or guided by the parent's response. Healthy development takes place when parents encourage patterns of behavior that are reasonable, practical, and age-appropriate. A child may not be old enough to understand the principles behind the discipline, but the patterns still need to be established. Understanding will follow later.

Extrinsic Stage (other-centered)

The extrinsic stage begins during the elementary school years when we begin to become aware of relationships and of the dynamic of "give and take." At this age there is strong motivation to conform to what is expected in order to gain approval. Children will naturally begin to seek the approval of their parents, another significant person (like a teacher), or someone of their own age.

This is a necessary stage in childhood. In the younger years, children will seek the approval of their parents and will conform to their parents' values in order to please them. This is good. This is part of the apprenticing process. It is also a way of getting needs met. For example, teaching a child to not repeat the swear words he heard at school is part of apprenticing values, and when he obeys (pleasing his parents), he receives approval and a sense of belonging to the family.

As children grow up into their teenage years, it is impor-tant for parents to remember to begin to allow their children to think and choose for themselves, while still acting in a supervisory role. We are supposed to be training our children well enough so that they are ready when it's time to leave home.

The motivation to conform to what pleases others can be a positive trait. For example, teachers who expect homework to be done neatly, thoroughly and on time will help their pupils to develop diligence, perseverance, and pride in their work. On the other hand, this need to conform can also work against the process of becoming a mature person. Peer pressure is a good example. Peer pressure exists at any age, but is particularly significant in the developmental years of childhood and adolescence because this is the time that values are formed. As children progress from the elementary years into the high school years they naturally become more independent. They identify more and more with others their own age than their parents. Peer pressure is a very strong influence, and in the right group of kids it is wonderful; but in the wrong group, it can have devastating results.

Kids whose basic needs have been met will seek out companions who are also healthy. On the contrary, kids whose basic needs have not been met in the home, such as acceptance, love, belonging, will try to find friends who will meet these needs. Kids who are healthy will tend to do activities that are constructive and creative. Kids who are unhealthy and needy tend to express their anger, resentment, disillusionment about family life. Unless this pattern is interrupted by a caring, healthy friend or adult, their lives become destructive rather than constructive. This is where youth groups, Sunday school, and church programs can be so vital to a young person's life. They are means of providing the opportunity to help meet the needs of today's youngsters.

To become mature, we must progress through this people-pleasing, codependent stage. We must move from a place of dependence, where others do the thinking and guiding for us, to independence, where we do our own thinking and choosing. It is moving from a place where others are responsible for us into a place of being responsible for our own decisions and actions.

Intrinsic Stage (principle-centered)

The most mature stage is the intrinsic, or principle-centered stage. Instead of making decisions to gain approval of others, we have learned to make decisions based on principles or values that we have adopted for ourselves. We have learned many lessons up to this point in life and have begun to integrate them. We understand concepts and principles such as justice, responsibility to others, equality and commitment, and to consider the long-term consequences that may result from our choices. We have moved from knowledge to understanding and wisdom.

We are able to stand for what we believe, in spite of resistance, considering the larger good of the family, society, or nation. For example, there is a battle in the education system over the subject of family living. Some parents are standing against having their children taught about "alternate lifestyles" as being moral and acceptable. They are in many cases taking much criticism and are being labeled in the community as being narrow-minded and discriminatory. Thankfully, many have stood firm and have successfully turned the tables and have been able to change the curriculum.

A good solid set of Christian values in childhood is a great foundation on which to build our lives. Our training begins in truth. It gives us a head start as we begin to mature through the growth stages we've discussed.

Progressive Stages of Social Development

The social realm is made up of relationships. Learning how to relate and communicate with others is a skill which like any other skill, has to be learned and apprenticed. Social development encompasses skills such as relating on a personal level; relating on a business level; learning how to express your opinions; learning how to confront constructively; learning how to lead; learning how to comfort and validate; and learning how to *respond* intelligently to situations instead of automatically *reacting* to them.

Another facet of maturity is learning how to "give and take" in relationships. It is not healthy to always be the "giver" or the "taker" in a relationship. Maturity is learning to operate not from a place of "need" (extreme dependence), nor from a place of isolated self-sufficiency (extreme independence), but from a place of where we can share (interdependence).

Interdependence is being able to both give and receive in such a way that it lends stability and balance to our relationships. People who are interdependent have learned to be dependent on others (able to receive), and who also have learned to be independent (self-sufficient), and now are able to integrate these two principles of interaction appropriately into everyday living.

An interdependent person can operate on his own, but desires and chooses to interrelate with others. This person allows for and elicits input from others for most significant decisions; cooperates appropriately; cares for himself and others; is able to give and receive (care, love, time, attention); is comfortable with being alone or being with others; is able to share feelings and opinions appropriately; is proactive; assertive; and is able to listen to feedback and consider change.

It is important that we check ourselves to make sure that we are not being inappropriately or dominantly dependent or too independent. A person who is predominantly dependent has a tendency to want others to make his decisions for him; to be passive, taking little initiative; to sacrifice his own values to please or appease others; to hide how he really feels or thinks; to accept blame even when it is undeserved; to avoid conflict; and to be ruled by other people's moods or opinions.

An independent person who has become an "island unto himself" is a very lonely person. He is operating from a place of extreme self-sufficiency (not needing or wanting interaction with another person). This person has a tendency to make decisions without feedback; to be self-centered, opinionated; and to be uncaring.

God intends for us to be in interdependent relationships, not isolated individuals. The Body of Christ is described as being made up of individual members who are joined and who contribute their talents, gifts, and roles. Isolated, they are not as effectual, but together they make up a mature, effective, functioning body. Each member must not only share his gifts but work in union, blending with the other members of the body. We must know ourselves in order to share ourselves.

Kingdom Principles

Peacemaker or Pacifier?

Matthew 5:9 says, "Blessed are the peacemakers for they shall be called sons of God." What exactly does that mean? We often misunderstand the term *peacemaker*. Jesus was a peacemaker. He was not a *pacifier*. It's important that we understand the difference between these two terms.

The goal of a *peacemaker* is to help bring about reconciliation, peace that results from bringing truth and compassion into a conflict or misunderstanding. Of course, this process does not always ensure peace. Sometimes the pursuit of peace results in war. Just because we are capable of discerning truth does not mean that others will accept it. A peacemaker addresses the *real* issues that are involved in a problem or conflict for the purpose of bringing about *real* peace. He does this with an attitude of grace, forgiveness and help. He confronts the people involved in love, while remaining steadfast to the principles of godly truth and justice. In Micah 6:8, we are reminded that God expects us to seek justice, love mercy and to walk humbly with Him. Loving mercy without seeking justice is not real peace. Real peace is that which comes from standing for and doing what is right before the Lord.

A *pacifier* has little or no concern with principled peace-making. To the contrary, he wants peace at any cost. His goal is just peace and quiet. A person who has a tendency to be a pacifier in a tense situation is usually afraid of conflict or displays of anger. Justifiably so, since past patterns of anger have probably been very painful. He is afraid of confrontation and the possibility of being attacked, rejected or abandoned again by the others involved. Hence, the real source of the problem is never addressed. He begins to compromise what he thinks, what he values, and what he stands for.

Pacifying a situation or person only temporarily relieves the tension, anxiety, fear, and discomfort. Pacifying only appeases the other person; the real issues involved remain unsolved. If a person continues to give in to untruth and harmful behavior just to avoid confrontation, he will inevitably continue to walk in fear, depression, frustration, and confusion. Injustice wins and everyone suffers. All it takes for evil to succeed is for good men to say nothing.

A peacemaker is someone who is strong in character, principled, and yet able to relate to people in a giving, forgiving, and loving way — but never at the expense of truth. He will never support sin in order to support the person; but rather will be gracious and supportive of the person while appropriately dealing with behavior that is harmful.

Jesus acted as peacemaker in the situation with the woman caught in adultery in John 8:3-11. Here, a group of Pharisees dragged this woman into Jesus' presence with the intention of stoning her (the legal penalty for adultery) for her sin. They purposely asked Jesus what he would do in this situation. Jesus replied by asking them, "If any one of you is without sin, let him be the first to throw a stone at her." He was not afraid to address the Pharisees who were actually using the woman to target him. He addressed the Pharisees by confronting their motives. Then, He turned to the woman and told her that he did not condemn her and to go and not sin again. Jesus graciously defended *her*, not her sin.

Food for Thought

The following chart can be used to examine how we handle conflict. In what subjects or situations do we tend to be a pacifier? With whom do we tend to be a pacifier? In what ways can we become more of a true peacemaker?

FIGURE 8 — PACIFIER / PEACEMAKER

PACIFIER (irresponsible)	PEACEMAKER (responsible)
Appeases	Confronts in love
Temporary relief	Long-term gain
Avoids conflict	Faces conflict
Avoids truth	Faces truth
Avoids real issue	Addresses real issue
Avoids others' wrath / anger / reactions	Faces others' wrath / anger / reactions
People pleaser	God-pleaser
Fear of possible outcome alters decisions — actions	Is not influenced by others' reactions
Problem is not solved	Working toward solving problem
Compromises values	Holds on to values
Not true to self	True to self
Loss of integrity, self-respect, self-esteem	Builds integrity, strength, character
Walking in fear, depression, frustration, confusion	Walking in hope, faith, truth, clarity, strength, contentment
Hurt continues, festers	Hurt diminishes
Result: little or no progress *anger, situation intensifies*	Result: peace of mind in truth possible progress becomes a *stronger person*

©Hess / McCulley, 1991

CHAPTER 4

IMPROVING FAMILY DYNAMICS

The Purpose of the Family

In the last chapter, we stated that the purpose of the family is to meet the basic needs of the individual by:
- *protecting* each member from harm;
- *providing* for each member's well-being; and
- *preparing* each individual to become whole, responsible, productive, self-reliant, and mature so that each person will be equipped to live a responsible life, serve the Lord and society, and parent the next generation.

Too often home and school focus on how to *make* a living. What we really need to learn is *how* to live. Life is full of many contrasting experiences: pain and pleasure, contentment and frustration, clarity and confusion, satisfaction and disappointment, joy and sadness, achievement and failure, rejection and acceptance, shame and approval. How do we learn how to handle life?

We learn through trial and error on our own. But we primarily learn by watching how our family handles life. This is what the family is for. The family is where we should learn *how* to live.

Structure and Atmosphere

Two main dynamics that determine how well a family protects, provides, and prepares its members are the *structure* within which the family operates and interacts; and the emotional *atmosphere* of how they relate to one another.

Structure

The structure of the family is made up of the *rules* (spoken or unspoken) that govern everyday living and the *roles* that each member is expected to fulfill. The rules and roles of the home affect the style of communicating, parenting and problem solving.

The structure of a family can be tight and rigid on one extreme or can be loose and chaotic on the other. A home encumbered with too many rules tends to be rigid, authoritative, and controlling. Perhaps you grew up in a family that had an overabundance of rules — rules for everything from how you brushed your teeth to how you tied your shoes, where any differences in style or method was taken as an infraction of the rules. Even unimportant things were either right or wrong. There was very little flexibility. Discipline was probably strict, and expectations were probably high. Communication was often in the form of commands and "problem-solving" often consisted merely of pinning the blame on someone.

On the other extreme, perhaps some of us grew up in sheer chaos. There were few rules, and whatever rules there were could change at a moment's notice. Misbehavior could be met one time with laughter and the next time with severe punishment. There were no set rules, role definitions or expectations. No one was in charge — the children had as much authority as the parents. Problems and personal conflicts tended to be avoided. When problems came up, they were never really solved, although there might have been a lot of fruitless discussion. In short, lack of clear direction and structure produces chaos.

Healthy structure in a home is a structure that is balanced. It is neither rigid nor chaotic, but flexible. This home has clear parental leadership that anticipates needs and communicates clear guidelines. When problems arise, options are discussed and decisions are made. Expectations are realistic. Rules are helpful, not burdensome. Rules and boundaries are for protection and training and are consistent and purposeful. When conflict arises between family members, the parents address the conflict as a problem to be worked out, rather than as a crime to be solved. Roles in this type of structure are defined but not rigid. Both parents see work at home as *our* work as opposed to *yours* and *mine*. For instance, Dad often helps Mom in the kitchen and Mom helps in the yard from time to time. Overall, healthy structure is sufficiently defined so as to provide direction and protection without being so rigid that it stifles flexibility, creativity and resourcefulness.

The purpose of healthy structure in any environment is to provide clear boundaries (of right and wrong, and what is and is not acceptable behavior); stability (realistic thinking); consistency; direction; and protection (both physical and emotional). These elements must be in place for effective communication and functioning. It is only in this type of environment that security and trust can be developed. Order breeds security; chaos breeds insecurity.

FIGURE 9 — FAMILY STRUCTURE

UNHEALTHY under-defined	HEALTHY	UNHEALTHY over-defined
• Too general • Little enforcement • Done in reaction to problem • Whimsical • No expectation of others	**RULES** (boundaries)	• Cumbersome – too many rules • Enforced harshly • Too rigid • Too many unspoken rules
• A lot of talk— no solution • Consistency is perceived as boring • So open-minded, unable to decide	**PROBLEM SOLVING** (addresses the issue open minded)	• Closed to options • Afraid of differences or change • Extreme deliberation — overkill • Not thought through • Little discussion — solution is imposed
• Passive • No clear leadership	**CONTROL** (assertive) appropriate clear leadership	• Aggressive • Authoritarian • Usually one person dominates / rules
• Haphazard • Ignores the problem • What problem? • Passive — lets others solve the problem • Comfort oriented	**CONFLICT** **RESOLUTION** (issue / solution oriented)	• My way only • Blames others • Win / lose approach • Attacks person instead of issue • Aggressive
• The child defines the parent's role • Parent's doesn't adjust to child's stages	**PARENT - CHILD RELATIONSHIP** (Anticipates and prepares for stages and changes)	• More concerned about being right than the well being of the child • Overreacts to change
• Unaware of any defined roles • No one is in charge or responsible	**HUSBAND-WIFE ROLE** (clear but not rigid)	• Stereotyped • Little give and take in sharing of responsibilities (e.g., house, kids)

The atmosphere in some homes feels warm and inviting, while the atmosphere in other homes feels cold and forbidding. What makes the difference? It is the amount of emotional warmth and safety within the home. It is the attitude of family members toward each other that determines the emotional climate of the home. This is part of what is meant by *family atmosphere*. The atmosphere in a home can be hot, warm or cold; suffocating, caring, or uncaring; anxious or calm; critical or accepting; comfortable or uncomfortable; tense or safe.

FIGURE 10 — FAMILY ATMOSPHERE

UNHEALTHY disengaged	HEALTHY	UNHEALTHY enmeshed
Non-caring	Care	Smothering
Anti-dependent	Interdependence	Codependent
Little need for loyalty	Loyalty	Loyalty demanded
Decisions made without discussion	Shared Decisions Family Time	All decisions need approval
Little interaction with family members	Indentifies (with family unit)	Little interaction with outsiders
Rejects identity with family	Discipline	Family defines who I am
No discipline, guidance, or correction	(with encouragement)	Discipline with criticism, shame, or threats

Some families are too close or *enmeshed*, while others are too distant or *disengaged*. An enmeshed family is one whose members lack a sense of separate identity or individuality, thus borrowing each other's identity. Family members can become entwined and dependent on each other to the extent that one person's problem can devastate the entire family. When relationships become this enmeshed, perspective and judgment are lost. For example, if Johnny does not graduate with honors like his father did, Dad may feel that Johnny has let *him* down. Instead of being just a little disappointed he thinks Johnny has let the family down. Another example of enmeshment would be a son/daughter who feels that he *must* take over the family business because of parental pressure.

Mary is an example of a person who is enmeshed with her mother. She is 28 and married with a small child. Her mother, Leah, lives in a nearby town and they talk almost daily on the phone. Mary had planned to go out shopping with some friends and had not thought to mention it to her mom. When her mom stopped by unannounced, Mary really felt she couldn't be honest and tell her that she had other plans. If she had, Leah would have been extremely hurt. Mary excused herself, went to her bedroom and called her friends to say she couldn't go shopping.

On the other hand, a *disengaged* family is too disconnected. Members of a disengaged family lack meaningful involvement in each others' lives. If Johnny does poorly in school, it's his problem. He is left on his own. Nobody cares very much. Often times one parent may be disengaged. A father may work long hours or be otherwise emotionally and physically unavailable to his family. Moms can also be so busy with church, clubs, work, and PTA that the family gets her leftover attention and time. (And that time is usually a distracted time.) Each person is too busy working out his or her own agenda or problems to even notice what is happening with the other family members. There is a feeling of indifference. There is little criticism, but also very little support.

Strong, healthy families, by contrast, have a degree of cooperation and involvement which is supportive but not meddlesome. Each person is seen as an individual, yet a part of the family. Each has their own set of activities and interests yet participates in family activities. Each individual has his own unique, separate identity as well as identifying himself with the family unit — a sense of independence *and* belonging.

A healthy family atmosphere consists of loving relationships that provide care, guidance, and encouragement. It is an atmosphere of safety in which a person can be themselves without fear of rejection or condemnation. Each person is confirmed and validated and not ignored or put down. This type of family talks *with* each other instead of *at* each other. All of the members are bonded to each other without smothering each other.

To summarize, healthy structure and atmosphere provide an environment that is supportive and nurturing.

Qualities of a nurturing environment:
- physical safety
- children are not shamed or put down because of their feelings or uniqueness
- children feel safe to talk about any subject
- children are validated, understood
- children are not used for adult role replacements
- rules are discussed and clearly defined
- rules are made for protection and for the well-being of the children
- rules are fair and consistent, rather than excessive or reactionary
- discipline consists of training rather than pressure or threats
- children are accepted where they are
- children are apprenticed
- parents show no favoritism
- children are encouraged in their interests, work, growth experiences
- parents express love in words and action
- parents model conflict resolution which is aimed at problem solving instead of blaming
- parents anticipate the needs of their children instead of playing "catch-up" (falling short and then over-compensating; disappointing and then overindulging)
- parents display consistency in words and actions.

The Dynamics of Disciplining Children

Discipline is not a bad word. However, most of us have a negative reaction to the idea of discipline. Many people associate discipline with punishment, anger, and pain. Perhaps our parents did more punishing than disciplining. Perhaps they inflicted rules and restrictions with an attitude of wrath. Maybe we felt put down instead of lifted up and left discouraged instead of encouraged.

Another word for discipline is training. Training implies a purpose, a method, a direction and a completion. Training or apprenticing is the process of imparting knowledge, skill, and wisdom from one person to another, from one generation to another.

In boot camp, the drill sergeant trains his recruits in the skills of war and survival. If he does a poor job, the recruits endanger their lives as well as those around them. A parent's job is to parent or to train his children in the skills of life — everything from problem-solving skills to relationship building. Parents should come up with a game plan of discipline that anticipates the normal problems inherent in the various stages of raising children. The purpose of the game plan is to prepare our children to be independent, and to train them to be responsible, loving, and caring people who are capable of contributing to instead of merely taking from society.

Four Steps in Disciplining

1. Self-check

Most parents would like their children to become whole, mature, productive individuals. Yet, most of us don't give much thought regarding how to discipline our children — we just automatically do what our parents did. If we were to be honest, most of us would have to admit that much of our "discipline" tends to be more of a frustrated reaction than a well thought out course of action. Often we may tell our kids a few times to stop making noise, ignore it until we can't stand it any longer and then take some sort of drastic action. We blow off steam, the kids feel the anger, and they reluctantly obey out of fear or resentment. There are hurt feelings, misunderstandings and strained relationships. Our screaming may have produced some changed behavior, but it certainly was not a result of training.

Training comes from a *proactive* perspective. We must remind ourselves of why we are disciplining. We have to continually check ourselves by asking: What do I want my children to be like? Is what I expect age-appropriate behavior? Is what I am doing effective? Do I know what I am doing? Do I need to learn *how* to discipline my children? Have I anticipated the situations that are common at this point in time? Have I thought ahead as to what will be in the next stage of development? (For example, discuss the rules of dating *before* the child begins to date.)

Am I trying to punish or train? Am I doing the disciplining in anger? Is what I am doing beneficial in the long run? Am I just reacting because I'm tired or frustrated or is this a genuine issue that needs to be discussed? Am I just trying to get rid of an annoyance or am I also concerned about my child?

Let's face it. Discipline isn't needed when the kids are behaving; it's needed when they are misbehaving. We are called upon to have a decent attitude just when we're worn out, frustrated, embarrassed or angry. We feel like throttling our kids, not calming down, composing ourselves, thinking and doing the right thing. It's in these situations that we find out just how mature or immature *we* really are. It's interesting that in raising our own children *we* are forced to grow up.

2. Invest in the Relationship

If we are really training our children, then we have to invest ourselves in our children. We need to be with them, love them, talk to them, play with them, encourage and teach them, and correct them when necessary. Correcting goes a lot more smoothly when there is a genuine caring relationship. A child will respond more readily to direction or correction better if he knows in his heart that you really care and want what is best for him.

It sounds obvious to say this, but get to know your kids. Learn to enjoy your kids. Find out who their friends are, what they like, what subjects they like and dislike, what dreams they have. Talk about their day over dinner. Who did they sit with at the lunch table? What games did they play at recess? How are their friendships going? How are they doing in school or in sports?

Treat your child with some special times. Take him for ice cream or to the movies. Take his best friend along and just have fun. You will see and hear your child in action in a setting that is away from home. It will give you insight into his world.

Tell your child that you *like* him. You're supposed to love him, but it's better if you like him, too. Point out specific traits that you can genuinely admire. *Precious talk* is important. Tell him that you think he's cute, adorable, wonderful. See his potential and paint a variety of pictures that enlarge his dreams. Help him to see himself as successful, able, competent, and unique. Explain why you are proud of him. Tell him that you are so glad that he was born to you and is a part of your family.

Realistically, we all get angry with our children and have a tendency to jump down their throats when something goes wrong. However, in a negative situation you can still encourage your child by offering positive statements and images. For instance, instead of criticizing your youngster for a bad test grade, help him to discover where his difficulty may be. Work with him to come up with ideas for solving the problem. Option think with him. *Help him to see that almost all things that go wrong are "fixable."*

Help and encouragement give the child the energy to keep going and to try again. A five-year-old may know how to pick up his toys and may do it for a while, but normally, he will slack off within a few days. Typically we say to him, "You know how to pick up; now just go do it like a good boy." This is unrealistic for that particular age. Parents need to clean up with them once in a while just to help them, to demonstrate support, to ease their burden, to show them what caring is.

Want to make points with your teenager? From time to time, pitch in and help them with their chores. Just jump in and give them an extra hand. Actually, this is appropriate at any age, with anyone. This is investing yourself and your time into your relationship. It shows that you like them and that you care. It is so nice to hear someone say, "How can I help? Need a hand? Let me help you."

Investment has its return. If you invest money, it should bring a good return on that investment. It's the same in relationships. The more you invest, the stronger the relationship.

3. Rules, Boundaries and Correction

Why do kids fail to do what we want them to do? There are four basic reasons. First, we may not have *discussed* with them what it is that we would like them to do — we may have just presumed or assumed a certain response. Secondly, we may have discussed some guidelines, but perhaps have failed to be *specific* or *clear* in our directions or expectations. Thirdly, maybe we need to *apprentice* them and show them how to do something (apprenticing involves a lot of repetition) or we may have jumped the gun in expecting too much too soon. Finally, kids often *rebel* and do not want to cooperate with us. It is human nature to be self-centered, lazy and irresponsible. We want to get away with as much as we can get away with. That is why God created parents. Hopefully, we are more mature than they are and can help them to learn to be responsible and caring.

Before jumping to the conclusion that our children are being rebellious, we need to double-check ourselves to make sure that we have indeed *discussed* the matter with them, that we were *clear* enough, and that they were *able* to do what was expected. If we think that our child is being rebellious, we need to check out our relationship. Sometimes, children do not cooperate with us simply because they have been ignored. If we shoot orders at them as they come in the door from school before even asking them how their day was, they will naturally resent our demands. Paying attention to them for ten minutes establishes the rapport for the day and goes a long way towards harmony and cooperation.

A good tip in setting rules and boundaries is to build in some measure of freedom in the process. It softens the orders and teaches children to make decisions. It allows for participation in the setting up of the rules and boundaries (within reason, of course) and teaches them how to think and to assume a measure of responsibility. Discipline done right produces a spirit of cooperation rather than one that is adversarial. The rules of the home become more reasonable and less smothering. Some examples:

"Sandie, you are old enough now to be able to clean your room yourself. So, I want you to clean your room once a week. (She has been taught how to clean her room). I definitely want it done by noon on Saturday. You may do it all at once or half on one day and the rest later. You decide that part, but I really would like it done by Saturday. Which way do you want to do it?"

"Cassie, your chore for the week is to empty out the dishwasher. I need it done before I start cooking dinner. I don't care when you do it, you may choose; just so I can use those dishes at supper time. You may empty it before you leave for school, when you get home, or before five o'clock. You decide."

"Drew, you can go out this weekend, but only one night. Which evening do you need the car? Let us know a few days ahead so that your mother and I can make plans."

"Katie, you know how much homework you have. I want it done by eight o'clock just to make sure that you have had sufficient time and haven't forgotten anything. So, you can do it right after school or after you play. Just make sure we can go over your work at eight."

Freedom mixed in with the everyday demands allows choice. When someone is given some freedom of choice there is less resistance and more cooperation. Defiance and resistance are normal reflexes to a dictatorial style of parenting. The more rigid and demanding a parent is, the more a child (or anyone) will naturally want to rebel. People like freedom, not bondage. It is very important for us to examine the style of discipline that we use. We must come alongside our children, not come at them. One is supportive and breeds love, care, trust, respect and confidence, whereas the other breeds hostility, self-protection, shame, guilt, fear and rebellion.

Human nature being what it is, there will be times of rebellion — when our little angels become demons who want their own way . . . Period! There will be times in which we will have to establish and carry out consequences for inappropriate, irresponsible or bad behavior. Probably, most of our heavy discipline will be in the category of addressing irresponsibility, forgetfulness, laziness, and sibling fighting. But, before laying down the law, there should be thorough discussion of why there needs to be particular consequences. It is important to remember to enforce these consequences without wrath. Try to be as matter-of-fact as possible. This focuses on the issue rather than the person; it focuses on correction instead of sheer punishment. Usually, our consequences feel like punishment anyway. So let us, as parents, try to develop an atmosphere of training as opposed to punishment. Training incorporates hope, whereas punishment for punishment's sake produces despair.

4. Maintain the Relationship Bond

After the heavy consequences have been handed down it is very important that we maintain the relationship with our child. Our natural reaction after an explosion or lively discussion is to isolate ourselves from our child. This is not good. As difficult as it may be to do, we should just *say* what the consequences are and then resume normal activity. Let the words you say (along with your follow-through) be the *power* in your discipline rather than using intimidation, hysteria, name-calling, etc.

For example, with your eight-year-old, you may have just finished another discussion of why we do homework before watching TV, only to find him the next day lying on the couch glued to the screen again. You may turn the TV off and say "We talked about this yesterday, Brian, and you have disobeyed again. As we discussed, you won't be going to the movies this weekend. I'm sorry that you will miss out on the fun." There probably will be a dialogue back and forth between you, but try to resume normal life again soon. Bridge the gap that normally occurs. Touch base with him. Make sure you bond again by eventually touching him. Say something like: "How much homework do you have?" Or,

"Do you want to do it down here with me while I make dinner?" Or, "After you finish half of your homework, come down for a cookie break." Or you may stop in his room in a few minutes after he's gotten started and just joke with him for a minute. There are many ways to break the ice after there has been an altercation.

It is vitally important to show that your relationship is not broken — that you love him — that you're not going to withdraw your love. There may be instances in which you have to let your child sit and think things over and come back with an attitude adjustment, but do not allow the "alone time" to become a brooding time. We need to remember that we are the adult in the situation. We need to initiate the love and reconciliation. We need to be the foundation of the parent-child relationship.

Most Common Mistakes Parents Make

- Lack of discussion or agreement between spouses concerning discipline.
- Parents disagree over what is important.
- Parents don't know what consequences to use.
- Parents do not follow through on their stated consequences.
- Lack of anticipation of problems that may lie ahead.
- Fighting about the children in front of the children.
- Parents are afraid to discipline their children.
- Implementing discipline *after* there is a problem instead of discussing it first.
- Allowing too much freedom of choice at too young of an age.
- Using fear, intimidation, shame or guilt to get results.
- Inconsistency in mood and discipline.

Kingdom Principles — Grace and Truth

Grace

God deals with us within the structure of truth in an atmosphere of grace.

God wants us to be in relationship with Him. Because of this, He has provided for us a safe relationship in which we can fellowship with Him, enjoy Him, and grow in knowledge and truth. He has provided a way so that we can approach the throne of grace with confidence (Hebrews 4:16). Grace creates a place of safety that supplies the love and power that is ever present to enable us to walk in responsibility. Grace encompasses our failure, disobedience, pride, immaturity, and weakness. Grace is actually *favor* towards us. Grace surpasses acceptance and declares that God not only loves us, He likes us; He delights in us. He enjoys us and wants to bless us.

When we believe that God is *for* us (Hebrews 11:6, Romans 8:31), seeking truth becomes a natural result — truth which actually works to our advantage. In contrast, if we don't really believe that God is for us, then we will not seek His truth.

Grace is always, endlessly, abundantly present, it is not just available, but actively present to heal our wounds and empower us to walk in His truth. Grace causes us to feel His affection for us as His own. David knew this when he asked God to "Keep me as the apple of your eye; hide me in the shadow of your wings" (Psalm 17:8).

In a sense, God validated us in the Incarnation. Hebrews 2:17 says that He had to be made like us so that He could be a merciful High Priest, one who makes intercession for us. He was not ashamed to be like us and be called our brother (Hebrews 2:11). He identified with us. He was tempted as we are; and He suffered like we suffer. Isaiah 53 says that he took up our infirmities, carried our sorrows, and bore our grief. He even bore our punishment that we might have peace.

Hindrances to Experiencing Grace

Why do we have so much trouble experiencing grace in our daily walk? For one thing, it is because we cannot earn it. Accepting grace goes against our sense of "work ethic." From the minute we are toddlers, we begin to realize that if I do this, then I get that. As I go to school and earn A's on my report card, I receive more favor from my teachers and parents. In sports, if I do well, I get the cheers of the crowd, I'm popular with my teammates, and I get a pat on the back from the coach. If I work hard enough, I will get rewarded. Because reward is conditionally based on performance, people usually carry that idea over to relationships. We come to believe that if our behavior is good, then love and acceptance will be ours.

God, on the other hand, loves and accepts us regardless of our sin. "While we were yet sinners, Christ died for us" (Romans 5:8). He does not love us more on our "good behavior" days and less on our "bad behavior" days. He does not approve of our sin, but our penalty has already been paid by Jesus (Isaiah 53:5). When we sin we will have to bear the consequences, to be sure; but the fact remains that God is *for* us, not against us. He wants to teach us a better way and to make the life we know on earth an abundant one. God takes no pleasure in watching us learn lessons the hard way; indeed, He never abandons us to manage on our own, but instead He endures with us and bears us up in it all.

Grace Realization

When we are confronted with and understand God's gift of grace, we are never the same again. Grace radically changes our relationship to God and to others and revolutionizes our self-assessment. We cannot be instruments of grace to others if we have not experienced grace ourselves. We cannot give away what we do not have.

The realization of the fact that we, as sinners, can be safe in the presence of a holy God is crucial to communion and intimacy with Him. This communion establishes sanctuary — a place of safety in which we can be healed and nurtured and freed to learn and to grow, to try and to fail — as we mature.

King David, who wrote most of the Psalms in the Bible, enjoyed this sense of sanctuary. Much of his writing shows us that he was unafraid to speak openly to God. The intimacy of the relationship that he shared with God created the atmosphere that enabled him to feel free to speak his whole heart and mind. He was unabashed and genuine about his humanity even in the presence of the God that he knew to be holy. He didn't soft-pedal his anger, hide his frustration, deny his fear or explain away his sin, but instead poured out everything to his trusted Friend. He felt no compulsion "to clean up his act" before approaching Him. David understood that his relationship with God was able to survive his shortcomings. It was in this place of sanctuary that he found the strength and courage to carry on and the freedom and power to grow.

Eugene Peterson writes, "*Freedom* is not an abstraction, and it is not a thing. It is a gift and a skill . . . . It is a skill that must be exercised by each person within the learned limits of reality. If we would understand freedom, we must be taught; if we would acquire freedom, we must be trained."[1] This is the nature of the growth process: the application of truth to the life already rooted in grace.

Truth

Grace and truth may seem to be contrasting ideas. They are not mutually exclusive, but rather work together. Grace is the essence of God's attitude towards us, and truth includes the reality of God's holiness and justice. Truth reveals my sin and points out my need for grace. Knowing and experiencing grace enables me to face the truth about my sin and God's holiness, which reminds me that I desperately need God's grace. *Both give life.*

Maturity results when revealed truth is applied to the individual life that is already growing in grace. Jesus referred to Himself as the Truth. When we are born again, His Spirit of Truth takes up residence in us to reveal the reality of all things — both visible and invisible.

Truth encompasses both God's principles and the earthly reality in which we must live. In order to be able to see and to think clearly and to be spiritually discerning, we need a balanced understanding of this duality.

God does not leave us to our own crooked thinking, but encourages us toward truth-based thinking *and* action. Satan's aim is to deceive and confuse; God's purpose is to enlighten, to cause us to know the truth — of His existence, His power, His redemption, and His perfect will.

Transformation occurs from the inside out as we begin aligning our lives with His revealed truth. It is the active work of remaking us into the image of Christ, as the Holy Spirit lovingly corrects, rebukes, encourages and instructs us in right thinking and right living. This is how we grow up into that "fullness of Christ" that is maturity.

Grace says it's okay to be human; that is, God accepts us as we are because of Christ's sacrifice. It does not mean our sin is okay or that our evil desires are condoned; but it does

FIGURE 11 — THE NEED FOR GRACE AND TRUTH

Grace with Truth **is** **Maturation Process**	• feel loved • encouraged • seeks my well-being • feel accepted, understood • plan for me • challenged • creative • sense of adventure and purpose • secure with values and boundaries • practical
Grace without Truth **is** **Sloppy *Agape***	• sincerity is all that's necessary • no clear right and wrong • avoids conflict • chaos; no boundaries • freedom bordering on license • issues are not addressed • lack of discernment • creativity is unbridled • free to "be" anything • few demands / expectations • no clear direction • no standards
Truth without Grace **is** **Legalistic Bondage**	• Dread, fear • black-and-white mentality • atmosphere of punishment, judgment • promotes approval seeking • creativity is squelched • motivated by fear and guilt • stressful • joy killed • life is hard

mean that God still loves us, sees potential in each of us, yes — even died for us — even though we are sinners. He restores us so that our wills are able to respond to God's love.[2] We are drawn by Christ's act of grace (John 12:32), rather than driven by fear of judgment.

God is grace — He *wants* the best for us.
God is truth — He *knows* the best for us.

Genuine maturity is a product of choosing to walk by faith in God's grace and to be subject to His truth.

Chapter Four Endnotes

[1]Eugene H. Peterson, *Traveling Light* (Colorado Springs: Helmers and Howard, 1988), p. 12.
[2]Ibid., p. 73.

CHAPTER 5

BUILDING GOOD COMMUNICATION

COMMUNICATION BASICS

It's not *what* you said, it's *how* you said it.
— Every mother who ever lived.

Larry and Alice are two lovers who probably say more with their eyes than anything else. Even at the restaurant, the way they sit at the table shows that they are infatuated with each other. Their attentiveness is shown by their gestures and facial expressions and the way they listen closely to each other.

A few tables away, Tim and Debbie are sitting in silence. He's pulled out the newspaper and she's staring into her coffee. Debbie is sighing deeply in frustration and he appears to be oblivious to her sighs.

On the other side of the restaurant, Mark appears to be

rambling on and on about something while Barbara is looking out the window with her arms crossed.

These three couples' relationships are obviously all very different, but in all three instances some kind of communication is going on.

There are two basic facts about communication within a relationship. First, it is impossible *not* to communicate. Communication is always going on whether or not you are saying anything. And second, communication is *not* just an *informational* process, but also an *emotional* process.

Studies show that 93% of communication takes place via *non-verbal* communication such as body language (physical posture, gestures, facial expressions), tone of voice, attitude, and timing. Only 7% of communication results from the actual *verbal* content — the words spoken.[1]

Communication is not so much a mechanical exchange of words, thoughts and opinions as an exchange of *intent*, *attitude* and *feeling* associated with a particular subject or person. In a conversation, the actual content is often overshadowed by the impact of the *emotional envelope* in which the message was delivered. Advertisers understand this. They spend billions of dollars on commercials trying to find the right emotional envelope in which to deliver their message. They use the right scenery, music, and people to capture a certain audience and evoke a specific response. The content of the commercial is not as important as the feeling they are attempting to generate inside their potential customers.

Mom was right. Many times it isn't *what* we say, but *how* we say it that communicates our truest feelings or thoughts. And without saying a word, we can communicate quite clearly. We often knew that we were really in trouble just by the *look* that Mom or Dad gave us.

Our lifestyles — what we do or don't do — are consistently communicating what is important to us. This is why some people believe there really isn't such a thing as a failure to communicate. We communicate what we *want* to communicate. By our non-verbal communication we can show approval or disapproval, frustration or appreciation, disinterest or affection. Paradoxically, even silence communicates the fact that we don't want to communicate. There may be *mis*communication (getting our information confused), or *failure* to convey information, but *in relationships* we are always communicating something.

Elements of Good Communication

Since communication is more an *emotional* process, (an interaction between people) than a verbal exchange, good communication is more about *who* we are and where we're coming from than *what* we say. Our *attitude* towards others is more important than the mechanics of what we say. Consequently, good communication is dependent on the following elements:

- *Openness* is an attitude of being approachable and receptive, even to points of view that differ from our own. Openness provides a safe environment in which a person can appropriately express himself without fear of judgment, rejection, or shame. To be open, we must be willing (within reason) to receive feedback — others' opinions, suggestions, and criticisms.

- *Self-disclosure* is the ability to share or disclose our real selves without pretense or false modesty. In order to do this effectively, we need a willingness to say how we feel; the boldness to ask for what we really want; the confidence to state our opinions, goals, and dreams; and the liberty to reveal dislikes and disappointments. It is being able to be free enough to genuinely express who we are and what we think and feel.

- *Credibility* is trustworthiness. Our credibility is based on earned trust, conduct that is authentic and reliable. It is exhibited in consistency of word and deed, dependable behavior, being someone whose word is binding; facing up to reality; practicality (as opposed to grandiose, puffed-up thinking); keeping priorities in good order; and in appropriately looking out for the interests of others, as well as for our own. We lose our credibility if our behavior does not match our words, if we break our promises, and if we fail to be realistic in our thinking and behavior.

- *Time* must be set aside for intimacy. Because sharing is at the heart of any relationship, we must make time for one another in everyday existence, as well as for serendipities and special occasions. If we want communication to flow easily, we must be available to discuss, to plan, to work and to play. The amount and quality of time that we give to each other is an indication of our priorities and values. For example, a parent may say, "I love you," to a child but if Dad or Mom are never around, the words are empty.

- *Validation* of one another. Communication is often thwarted because validation has not taken place first. If you want someone to listen to you, you must earn the right to be heard by validating their presence, feelings, and concerns. Identifying with someone goes a long way to remove any obstacle that could hinder communication.

- *An attitude of grace and encouragement* embodies the understanding that everyone fails sometimes. Encouragement focuses on learning and growth and works realistically with an individual's strengths towards attainable goals, rather than dwelling only on shortcomings.

- *Effective conflict resolution* involves skills that address the *problem* rather than the *personalities* involved. It is solution oriented, not attack oriented. Conflict resolution is working toward "win-win" solutions (where both parties gain something). It entails seeing conflict and differing opinions as an ordinary part of life. Conflict is normal and sometimes healthy.

How People Interact

As we have mentioned earlier, communication in relationships is an *interaction* between people. Too often, communication is seen as a mechanical process instead of a process of interaction. For instance, during marital counseling the subject of stopping by the cleaners came up. John confides, "I don't understand why she's upset . . . I just asked her to pick up my shirts after work." Mary replies, "I don't mind picking up John's shirts, but it's the way he shoots these orders at me that bothers me. I'm tired of being addressed as if I'm his employee."

In this case, it was not the verbal content that was necessarily the problem, it was *how* he related his request that Mary resented. It was the *emotional interaction* that took place that caused Mary's resentment. Mary doesn't feel that John is treating her like an equal when he shoots orders at her and makes demands.

Transaction Analysis Theory gives a useful model which is helpful in understanding how individuals interact. It delineates three *operating modes* or *states*: *Parent – Adult – Child (PAC)*.[2]

Parent — Adult — Child (PAC)

The *PAC* description of behavior pinpoints how people relate and is a helpful tool to use in addressing unhealthy communication. PAC categorizes behavior and feelings to reveal the styles and attitudes of interaction. It enables us to see what we are doing, how others react to us, and how we react to others.

According to this theory, everyone functions in three distinct patterns of behavior — *Parent, Adult,* and *Child.* Each category describes a position (attitude) from which we operate, communicate and relate to others. It is perfectly normal and healthy for an individual to function in all three of these states. There's a time to be nurturing (parent), a time to be business-like or responsible (adult) and a time to be carefree and fun (child). A mature person is well-rounded and operates in all three modes appropriately.

Understanding the PAC modes has proven to be one of the most helpful tools in improving communication in relationships at home as well as in the office. All of us have *blindspots* where we have no idea how we are coming across to others. As we describe the PAC roles in more detail, try to identify yourself in various situations at home and work. See if you can pinpoint the dynamics involved in your various relationships. It is so much easier to improve a relationship when we are able to see *how* we are relating to and affecting the other person involved.

The *Parent* state is the mode or function of *being in charge or responsible for others.* There are appropriate circumstances for this role such as actually being a parent, leader, teacher, manager, or any other occupation or position that involves having authority over others. Giving instruction, setting deadlines, giving orders, and making decisions for others are all functions of the *parent* role. Our relationships get into trouble when we forget that the role we play in one situation is not necessarily appropriate in another situation. In other words, operating in a parent mode is appropriate for a mother when dealing with her child or for a foreman on the job with his road crew, but inappropriate for the same woman relating to her husband or for the foreman relating to his wife.

The Parent mode has its good side. Parents are suppose to be responsible for and in control of their children, for instance. The negative side is if a parent (boss, coach, teacher, etc.) tries to force control through using harmful manipulation such as intimidation, blame, guilt, shame or name-calling. So, you can use the Parent mode constructively by setting boundaries or destructively by using harsh techniques.

The *Child* mode is marked by being carefree, trusting, fun-loving and spontaneous. The winsome, childlike traits of the *child* role are the magical elements that lend wonder and enthusiasm to life. We need curiosity, spontaneity, trust and a zest for living to enrich the routine of our everyday existence. On the other hand, *childish* traits, such as irresponsibility, compliance, passiveness or impulsiveness are extremely damaging in adult relationships.

The *Adult* mode is the state that we should be functioning in most of the time. A healthy, mature adult makes sound decisions, negotiates differences, plans ahead and listens objectively. He is not reactive but responsive. This is good. However, a person who functions merely in a business-like mode (without the nurturing or fun-loving sides) will have a tendency to take life too seriously. He may approach life in a robot-like fashion to the extent that he risks becoming a *"human doing"* instead of a *"human being."* In the school of life, he may earn an "A" on his report card for diligence, but will miss out on the joy of living.

It is normal and necessary for everyone to function appropriately in all three modes. There is a proper place and time to be operating in each state, and there are times and places where each state is inappropriate. Maturity includes the ability to "switch hats" or roles throughout the day. For the foreman, coming home from work will mean taking off the "boss" (parent) hat and putting on the "husband" (adult) hat as he relates to his wife; and when playing with the kids, switching to the "playmates" (child) hat. Playing the same role all the time, no matter what, prevents fullness in relationships.

In summary, each state or mode has positive and negative traits.

The Parent can be either

- nurturing or critical;
- advising or controlling;
- encouraging or intimidating.

The Child can be either

- childlike or childish;
- spontaneous or impulsive;
- trusting or gullible.

The Adult can be either

- an effective problem-solver, or a "human doing;"
- responsive or indifferent;
- diligent or rigid.

Problems occur in relationships when we function in the negative traits of any mode or assume an inappropriate role for the situation.

Following are some of the more common *unhealthy* family interactions described in PAC terms:

- When Mom or Dad tries to be one the "kids" instead of being the parent;
- When a parent still "talks down" to his *adult* child as if he were still a child — for instance, volunteering unsolicited advice;

- When one of the marriage partners is overly responsible (parent), enabling the other to be irresponsible (child);
- When one of the marriage partners is untrustworthy, forcing the other to be the "policeman;"
- When one of the marriage partners is primarily the "giver" (nurturing parent) and the other is the "taker" (irresponsible child);
- When one of the marriage partners is "helpless," thus forcing the other to be the "caretaker;"
- When one of the marriage partners is emotionally distant, thus forcing the spouse to supply all the nurturing needs in the marriage (thoughtfulness, affection, courtesy, caring);
- When one person in the family is the tyrant (e.g., harsh, patronizing, belittling) and others are the victims;
- When one person takes on the role of protector while the other takes on the role of helpless bystander;
- When one acts as dictator, not allowing for any discussion on major decisions;
- When one person always has to be right, forcing others to be wrong.

Food for Thought

If we want to improve our relationships, we must take a look into how we interact with and respond to others. Do we tend to become critical and controlling? Are we being bossy and manipulative? Do we try to intimidate? Perhaps we are *too* compliant, and play the martyr role. Are we irresponsible? Do we whine and complain and make excuses? Are we too serious or are we apathetic?

How do we feel when someone whines or displays inappropriate, childish behavior? When someone lectures or uses other controlling behavior? When someone gives advice without first taking the time to really understand?

FIGURE 12 — PARENT-ADULT-CHILD

	POSITIVE TRAITS	NEGATIVE TRAITS
P **PARENT**	**Nurturing Parent** · Love · Nurture · Care · Protect · Provide · Prepare · Apprentice · Discipline · Empathetic	**Critical / Harsh Parent** · Manipulate · Inflexible · Drivenness · Smother · Dictate · Lecture · Aggressive · Use power · Punish · Unsolicited advice · Talks but won't listen · I'm right (unteachable) · Too responsible · Unapproachable · Authoritarian · Abusive language or behavior · Use of guilt, shame, fear
A	**Proactive** · Planner · Thinker · Problem-Solver · Aware · Non-reactionary · Assertive · Give and take	**Robot-like** · Too serious · Disengaged · Preoccupied · "Human Doing" · Robotic · Apathetic · Overburdened · Stoic · Legalistic · Mechanical

	Positive	Negative
ADULT	· Not intimidated by differences · Comfortable with diversity · Rsponsible for self	· Unavailable · Unimaginative · Distant · Unable to empathize
C **CHILD**	**Child-like** · Fun · Trusting · Forgiving · Creative · Inquisitive · Teachable · Loving · Pleasing · Honest · Eager / Energetic · Spontaneous · Sympathetic	**Childish** · Compliant · Self-centered · Whiny · Pouts · Gullible · Impulsive · Undisciplined · Short-sighted · Fearful · Anxious · Underresponsible · Inconsistent · Thoughtless · People-pleaser · Martyr · Victim · Passive · Easily intimidated · Moods–high–low · "I can't"

Under what circumstances do we take on roles that are inappropriate? When criticized, do we tend to become childish or full of rage? Do certain types of people trigger certain roles? Does an assertive person intimidate us? When someone is irresponsible or seems helpless, do we rescue that person? What are the issues (finances, confronting, discipline) that frighten us, causing us to behave like an intimidated child? a controlling parent? a super-serious, rigid adult?

It's impossible to improve or fix anything without first identifying what is wrong. The PAC chart is a useful tool in examining our roles and interaction with others. It can help to pinpoint how we mishandle situations, to implement more appropriate behaviors, and to improve our effectiveness at work and at home.

Human Nature and Resistance

Every day we interact with other people. This involves being vulnerable. But, people do not like to be hurt. In fact, we do all sorts of things in an attempt to make sure that we are not hurt. We hide, pretend, rationalize, blame, comply, avoid, attack or employ other defense mechanisms.

Defense mechanisms greatly affect communication. We can use defense mechanisms to *resist* communicating. If we are too afraid of being hurt, we resist being vulnerable thus being honest. We retreat into our safety boxes.

Communication involves sharing who we are, what we think and how we feel. Communication is something we must *learn* to do. Good communication requires that we lower some of our defense mechanisms and come out of our safety boxes and share. This goes against our natural tendencies. Self-preservation is a natural protective instinct. We naturally want to defend ourselves. Our human nature would rather avoid interaction that might potentially put us at risk. However, we must overcome our vulnerabilities in order to mature.

For those of us who hate criticism, it can be a real effort for us to lower our defense mechanisms long enough to thoroughly hear what the criticism is all about. We must make a conscious decision to listen and not react. After all, they might be partially (or totally) right.

We must grow beyond our fears and face up to reality and truth, even if it is painful. However, it is this resolve in the face of difficulty that renders us stronger, more confident, and more able to relate and perform.

UNHEALTHY COMMUNICATION

Common Pitfalls in Communication

There are four main things we all do that hinder healthy, effective interaction. Addressing these unhealthy behaviors will smooth out our rough edges. Keep in mind that communication in relationships is not just an exchange of words, but also an emotional process.

- *Harmful attitudes* are reflected in the tone of voice used, the body language employed, and the selection of words used to convey messages. They come through in messages that say "I'm right, so you must be wrong," or "I'm smart, so if we disagree, then you're the dummy." Hurtful attitudes include those that cause others to feel intimidated, inferior, patronized, disqualified, devalued, embarrassed, or unworthy. We undermine communication when we display attitudes of helplessness, suspicion, condemnation, impatience, anxiety, or defiance.
- *Hidden agenda* is an ulterior motive or expectation. Very often we are not consciously aware of it our-selves. It is formed by our belief systems, conscious and subconscious. Even though we may be unaware of

our presumptions and expectations, our hidden agenda will still be played out in our attitude and behavior.

Some of our subconscious motives may include expecting someone to fix my problems for me; trying to control someone's behavior; getting my own way (period); wanting to ensure my safety beyond what is reasonable; punishing, blaming, or getting even; getting the credit for something good or avoiding blame for something bad.

- *Inaccurate information.* Many times communication falls short because the message relayed is unclear, incomplete, or incorrect. This is often the result of unstated boundaries (rules) or expectations (assumptions). This can be prevented by double-checking to make sure that you have the precise facts, and that you spend time in dialogue to verify that the other person understands what you are saying.

- *Double binds and mixed messages.* Double binds occur when we send two messages that contradict each other. Double binds include those that say "Sure, I love you — but don't get close;" "I need you — but you can't do anything right;" "I promise I'll do it next time — but don't count on it;" "You have to share your real feelings with me!" (but she panics whenever he hints at the slightest vulnerability.) These are called double binds because you are caught in a no-win situation. Sometimes we receive mixed messages due to the fact that a person's actions belie his words, as in "Of course I want intimacy," but he never stays home long enough to talk or get close, much less to share on an emotional level.

Games People Play

A relationship can only be as healthy as its communication. When we resist healthy communication by displaying our defense mechanisms, our interaction with others often becomes a *game*. There exists an entire spectrum of games that people will play to avoid direct, honest communication. Some of them are simple defense mechanisms; others are more intricate and extremely distressing. All of them thwart effectual communication and frustrate intimacy in relationships.

Many of the more common defense mechanisms need little explanation: avoidance, blaming, intimidation, "silent treatment," compliance, pigeon-holing, patronizing, sarcasm, minimizing, rationalization, justifying, and demoralizing, to name a few. However, there are three particularly destructive devices that warrant greater explanation: *passive-aggressive behavior, triangulation* and *crazy-making*.

Passive-Aggressive Behavior

We all recognize aggressive behavior when we see it. Yelling, threatening, blaming, and name-calling are good examples of aggressive behavior and they intimidate us, which is what they are intended to do. The intent of aggressive behavior is to gain and maintain control through intimidation.

Passive-aggressive behavior has the same intent, but is not as obvious and is usually unconscious. A passive-aggressive person retaliates (attempts to regain control), but not right away. He "gets even" later in a subtle, often unrelated way.

Both the aggressive and passive-aggressive individual wants the upper hand; both are motivated by fear and anger, though expressed differently. One uses the direct frontal assault: the other, unconsciously resorts to resistance as a means of manipulation.

Passive-aggressive behavior is a pattern of behavior that can include procrastination, pouting, tardiness, chronic forgetfulness, leaving, and doing a poor job. At first it masquerades as compliance, but later results in conflict or sabotage. A teenager may agree to do the dishes (false compliance), and off to the kitchen she'll go. But later, Mom will find the dishes in the cupboard rinsed, but not washed (sabotage).

Another example is a husband who has been abrasive with his wife. At the time, she says nothing. But later that week, when it's time to go to his annual business dinner, it seems that she just can't get ready in time, causing an embarrassing late entrance. In a similar situation, a husband was abrasive with his wife and in the next breath asked her to pick up his suit at the cleaners so he could pack for his business trip the next day. She agreed, but "somehow" forgot.

Sometimes the games in a relationship perpetuate each other. Usually, the more someone tries to control a situation (inappropriately), the more they will be met with resistance. For instance, if Mom resorts to name-calling and screaming in order to get the child to pick up his clothes, the child will usually comply at the moment but later be very uncooperative. Extreme force only breeds resistance and rebellion. Outwardly someone may comply but inwardly they are digging their heels in resistance. We all do this at times. We can be subconsciously angry with someone and not be aware how passively we express our aggression.

Triangulation

Triangulation is a common ploy used by people to avoid direct communication. When two people (or parties) are at odds, one of them often seeks out a third person. He may try to use the third person as the go-between or as the referee. For example, instead of Mom asking her son why he made a certain disagreeable comment at Sunday dinner, she will complain about it to her daughter the following day.

Another example is when two people do not want to speak to each other and use a third person as the messenger. If Mom and Dad have a big fight, and the dispute continues to simmer over several days, they might continue to express their unresolved anger with each other by using their children as go-betweens. Dad might tell his son to "Tell your mother I'm working late all this week" or Mom might tell her daughter to "Tell your father I need the checkbook for grocery shopping tomorrow." In severe cases of triangulation, parents try to force their kids to choose sides. Another example would be the wife who is discouraged by the lack of intimacy in her marriage and so turns to her daughter for comfort.

Triangulation doesn't happen only between parents or within families, but also happens in churches, in friendships and even in the office. Triangulating can split any group into sides and if not addressed properly can lead to warring parties. That's why Jesus said "If your brother sins against you, go and show him his fault, *just between the two of you*. If he listens to you, you have won your brother over. But if he will not listen, take one or two others along, so that 'every matter may be established by the testimony of two or three witnesses'" (Matthew 18:15-16, italics mine). Jesus taught that we are to be direct in our communication.

Another form of triangulation is *scapegoating*. While triangulation pulls someone into the conflict to take sides or act as a buffer, scapegoating pretends that the real issue is not the problem at all, but instead shifts the tension existing between two people to a third party or issue. It focuses on someone or something else in an effort to avoid dealing with the real problem.

For example, two parents cannot handle the fact that they failed to discipline their son (real issue). Their diversionary tactic is to then blame him for being a rebellious child who is bringing shame on the family. They effectively avoid dealing with the issue of proper exercise of parental authority and discipline, and target their son's "rebellion" instead. Since that is not the real issue, continuing to "address" it will do nothing to solve the problem.

Then there might be a husband who is under a lot of pressure at work. The company is scaling down and the amount of work remains the same. The deadlines have become ridiculously unrealistic. Problems at work often spill over to problems with relationships. However, he deceives himself into thinking that the stress is not affecting his marriage. Instead, he finds a way to blame his wife for tensions at home that can be directly traced to problems at work.

Spiritualizing is also a form of scapegoating. A person who refuses to learn how to manage a budget, for example, may blame his financial problems on demonic attack and oppression, whereas the real problem is the person's immature inability to live within his income.

A more subtle form of scapegoating is seen when individuals avoid resolving a conflict by focusing on a third person and *his* problems. For example, a couple that wants to pretend that they are not having serious marital difficulties may begin to concentrate instead on their son's performance at school. This effectively diverts attention from their own issues and allows the marriage relationship to continue at some level. But this is still nothing more than an avoidance technique. True, there may be less marital tension in following this procedure, but any such advantage will be at the expense of the child.

Triangulation can also be used as a ploy within families to play out the roles of persecutor, victim, and rescuer. The three players may include (respectively) father/child/mother; parent/son/older daughter; parents/child/grandparent; or any combination of these roles.

In a previously mentioned example, a mother has been offended by her adult son's comments made to her at Sunday dinner. By Monday morning, the offense (left unaddressed) has festered into resentment. Rather than bother him, she instead calls her daughter at work, who was also at the dinner, and voices her exasperation with her ill-behaved son, making sure that her hurt feelings are apparent.

The daughter, now thrust into the position of mediator (rescuer), contacts her brother, delivers the bad news and instigates a confrontation between her brother and her mother, which should have been the initial (and only) conflict to need resolution. Instead, we now have Mom upset with son; Mom (perhaps) upset with daughter for tattling to her brother; brother angry at sister for meddling; sister annoyed with brother's insensitivity to Mom; sister perturbed at Mom for unloading her problem with son onto her; son disgusted with Mom's hypersensitivity and cowardice at not speaking to him in the first place. It's a game no one can win.

This dynamic can also occur among executives — secretarial aides — middle management personnel; ministers — congregations — board members; three friends or acquaintances. Instead of working out issues directly with those involved, a third party is brought in to either gain support or to manipulate and control the outcome.

As you can see, *gossip* is often a part of the triangulation process. Not only does gossip prevent problem-solving, but it usually just makes matters worse. Hearsay, misunderstandings, and rumors are all a result of the indirect communication we call gossip.

Crazy-making

Perhaps you have seen the bumper sticker that says: INSANITY IS HEREDITARY — YOU GET IT FROM YOUR

KIDS. All of us who have dealt with adolescents know exactly what this means. They sometimes make demands as if they were absolute, all-knowing rulers, and then (when they don't get their way) resort to tantrums you'd expect from a two-year-old, not from someone who's just finished trying to tell you how grown up they are. They can have selective memory and hearing; they may specifically recall a promise you made a year ago, but entirely forget (within seconds) their promise to come home on time. They can project an air of complete self-sufficiency one moment, and the next come running, wide-eyed and frantic, desperate for immediate rescue. Trying to confront them about irresponsible behavior is at times a classic exercise in futility. They are capable of concocting excuses at lightning speed, and if *that* doesn't work can explode like a volcano if you continue to question their actions.

"Professional adolescents" (kids disguised in adult bodies) have these tactics down to a science. They are the slick, dishonest con men in relationships. They can be extremely charming, pleasant and fun to be around, but when it comes to specific details, matters of responsibility and any kind of accountability, these characters can convince us that *we* are the crazy ones if we aren't aware of this manipulation (and we usually aren't). Not only are they maddening to deal with but they make it virtually impossible to nail down the facts, which causes us to question our own judgment, sanity or perception of reality. Hence the term *crazy-makers*.

Crazy-making is a term coined by George Bach and Yetta Bernhard in their book, *Aggression Lab*.[3] Their definition states that it is a "subtle yet persistent strategy of one person or a group to upset the composure or psychological equilibrium ('having your head together') of another individual or group of individuals."

Simply put, crazy-makers want their own way and will do anything and everything (using every defense mechanism available) to get it. This person's safety box is a fortified bunker bristling with machine guns and cannons. They know all the games and can play any role — the dictator, the helpless child, and the super-logical adult — all at the same moment or in dizzyingly rapid succession. They will violate, contradict, double-bind, intimidate, ambush, blame, assassinate character, plead, cry, change subjects, triangulate and threaten. They often succeed because they are clever and quick. Holding them accountable would most likely be a thankless, full-time job, and probably only temporarily successful, if you get that far.

We all have done our share of crazy-making, but there are some people who exhibit this kind of behavior on a regular basis. They are extremely afraid of having to be accountable. These people just simply cannot and will not be nailed down on anything. They hate boundaries, rules, details and deadlines. They want to be free from any expectations that can be measured. To compensate for their shortcomings, they often are the most charming, generous people you could possibly meet. However, as soon as you begin to count on them for something, they begin to back off and do a lot of double-talk.

Crazy-making behavior destroys families and must be addressed with *tough-love*. As firm as we may have to be at times with a crazy-maker, we need to have compassion as well. We must remember that we learn many of our defense mechanisms from our parents. Members of a dysfunctional home have often learned how to use the crazy-making technique to keep others off balance and avoid facing their fear, inner pain, and irresponsibility. We must remember two things: one, that a crazy-maker is a very frightened person who desperately wants to avoid direct confrontation. He has probably been a victim of this himself growing up. Second, this is a learned behavior: this is how he was taught to handle problems and so he acquires the same technique. Unless this cycle is interrupted crazy-making will continue into the next generation.

141

We will describe addiction and dysfunction in chapter eight but it is important to understand that crazy-making is one of the chief defense mechanisms in an addictive family system. An alcoholic, for example, has to convince others that his drinking is not a problem, or that it is at least not his fault. If his drinking is mentioned by someone outside of the family, he may at first be very logical and sound extremely reasonable and may say it wouldn't hurt to cut back a little (reasonable adult), but reassures him that everything is under control. Continued pressing on the subject may lead to an angry response (controlling parent) that would drive most people away. If someone wades through the rage, eventually the last ploy used is that of the helpless child; "poor me; don't give up on me."

The only way to address this onslaught is to confront each tactic as soon as it is used. If you must deal with a crazy-maker, remain calm, detach emotionally, and concentrate on the single issue at hand. Do not allow yourself to become diverted from the specific item under discussion or fall for the "poor me" sob story. Just continually calmly restate (numerous times) what the problem is and what you want the crazy-maker to do (or not do).

HOW TO DO IT RIGHT

Appropriateness — Five Levels of Intimacy

The purpose of communication is to interact with others in an *appropriate* way that will enable us to communicate ourselves effectively, without causing undo harm. In his book, *Why I Am Afraid to Tell You Who I Am*, John Powell describes communication ranging from shallow small talk to intimate sharing. These five levels of intimacy are: *cliché, facts, opinions, feelings,* and *complete openness.*[4]

Most of us have had the unpleasant experience of inappropriate self-disclosure. We might be standing in line or perhaps have just met someone and the next thing we know this stranger is sharing their personal troubles with us. This situation is uncomfortable because this person has disclosed on a level of intimacy that is usually reserved for close friendships.

The least threatening form of communicating is the *cliché*-level. It is polite chit-chat. Phrases like "Hi, How are you?," "Have a nice day," "Don't work too hard" are all a part of the cliché-level communication. This kind of "small talk" is helpful in getting to know people and to break the ice in group settings. It has its place in everyday life, but it is important to know that relationships do not exist at this level.

Sharing non-revealing general *facts* about sports, the weather, the news, is similar to the cliché-level, but can lead to sharing more personal information, e.g., about our family, how many children we have, what type of work we do, hobbies and interests we have, and so on. Sharing facts is a little more personal; you are engaging another person in some level of interaction. They share some information; we share some information. It helps to carry on conversation on an acquaintance level.

When we begin to share our *opinions* about things, we are beginning to be vulnerable. Sharing an opinion is revealing what we think. That means that now we have a personal investment in this level of communication. We start to care about where our conversation will lead, and what the person we're talking to will think. Maybe he will agree with our opinion and make us feel good. But what if he doesn't agree with us? What if (worse yet!) he thinks our opinion is stupid? This level of conversation is more personal than the first two because it has a measure of personal risk (rejection, embarrassment, mockery). If we are involved in life at all we will *share* our opinions with others— at home, at work, in meetings, with friends. The more vulnerable we feel, the more reluctant we will be in sharing our opinions.

Sharing *feelings* is even more revealing. Feelings indicate where we are and how we are doing. It is deeper than just sharing what we think. Sharing positive feelings, like being pleased, happy or thrilled is fairly easy to do because these are non-threatening to others. However, to say I feel sad, afraid, angry, hurt, rejected, let down, disappointed or hopeless says we are wounded or fearful, which may be threatening to others. It takes a lot of courage to say how we feel, especially in close relationships. We usually share our feelings with those with whom we feel safe. That is why this level of communication exists mostly in friendships because this is where we feel secure and understood.

The deepest level of intimacy, *complete openness*, is where we feel safe enough to share anything — our opinions, dreams, hurts, joys. In short, it is found only in relationships in which there is *mutual* nurturing and caring for one another. Each person has the well-being of the other in mind. There is understanding, acceptance, appreciation and proactive communication of love and support. This is the level of communication that marks a deep friendship and ideally the relationship between a husband and wife.

Hopefully, we all have at least a couple of intimate friends with whom we can be completely open, other friends with whom we can share our feelings and opinions, and associates, co-workers, neighbors and others with whom we can relate on an acquaintance level. We need to learn how to relate on all of these levels — they are all important and useful in developing socially.

Directness

Another important feature of healthy communication is learning to be direct. One way to identify directness is to understand the difference between *I statements* and *you statements*. *You* statements presume blame. *I* statements allow for discussion. Most of us commonly use *you* statements. It isn't until we are educated about the impact of such statements that we begin to think more in terms of *I* statements.

For example: "you make me angry; why don't you pick up your clothes; you're trying to run my life; you're impulsive, selfish and irresponsible." When we use you statements, we put other person on the defensive. What happens then? The other person immediately feels that he personally is being attacked, and he reacts by deploying his defense mechanisms. After that, virtually nothing constructive can take place. Instead of rationally discussing the issue at hand, we find ourselves having to deal with their defense mechanisms. The conversation tends to become personal and emotional rather than focused on the issue or problem. A "cooling off" time becomes necessary before the problem ever gets addressed. This wastes a lot of time and, worse, causes strains in relationships that are difficult to put right.

On the other hand, I statements are more direct and clear. "I am angry; I want you to pick up your clothes; I think that what you're doing is selfish; I want to make my own decisions." I statements tend to pinpoint the issue, whereas you statements tend to be general complaints or attacks.

You will not get very far with your teenager, if you scream, "You are an absolute slob. Can't you keep your room clean at all?" All you are going to get in return is a very angry child. You will probably get much further if you let your anger subside a bit and calmly say, "I feel annoyed when I walk into your room. I really would like you to keep your room neater. I want you to pick up your clothes off the floor and make your bed now before you leave."

Another common situation is a husband who continuously fails to call when he is delayed at work. Ranting and raving doesn't help. The wife may be more successful by saying, "I feel aggravated when you don't call me if you are going to be late. I would like you to call me right away if you need me to postpone dinner. Would you please call me from now on?" In the event that she gets a lot of double-talk with no cooperation, she may then suggest a number of alternatives concerning dinner time. (Eat later, start without him at a designated time, or other options.)

A college roommate might be in a situation in which she has to say, "I am really ticked off that you borrowed my clothes without asking. And I am furious that on top of this you don't take care of my stuff when you use it. Next time, ask me first before you help yourself."

People who use you statements almost exclusively seem to have a need to punish. They are usually very angry people who look for someone to blame. They do not think in terms of something that is fixable or redeemable, but instead think in terms of blame and ridicule. These people are angry *at* people in general; that is why they must attack. The recipient of this kind of abuse feels ashamed, nervous, and stupid. People who use I statements may be angry at the person, but primarily the problem or situation. They are able to see beyond the problem and the person involved and see them both as redeemable.

Say-Ask Model

A helpful model for learning how to be direct and clear appears below and is made up of two parts: say how you feel and ask the other person for what it is that you want.

The say-ask model is effective because it helps us to communicate directly and clearly. We should keep this model in mind whether we communicate at home or at work. So

"SAY"	I feel . . . _____(emotion)_____ when . . . _(events, circumstances, facts)_ .

"ASK"	I would like you to _(preferred behavior)_ .
	Next time will you . . . (be specific!)?
	Wait for the response.
	     (He will now have to respond with
	     a yes or no answer — which is touchy.
	     We may hear what we don't want to
	     hear.)

many times feelings are hurt, projects are mishandled, and expectations are not met because of lack of clarity.

Taking a Stand — Drawing Boundaries

It's one thing to be direct in communicating what we want to say, but we all know that does not necessarily ensure that the other person will cooperate. There are times when we will have to enforce consequences in order to bring about correct behavior.

The say-ask model is helpful in that it pinpoints the problem and forces us to be direct and clear and forces the other person to respond one way or another. It nails the game being played. Sometimes the game being played is "I expect you to read my mind" or "I don't want to give you what you want but I'm afraid to tell you to your face."

It is important to remain focused on the issue at hand, the truth of the matter, our "I statements," and perhaps our consequences. For example, the parent dealing with a sloppy teenager may have to communicate clear rules (boundaries) regarding when and how the room is to be cleaned. And if it is not cleaned, then the consequences go into effect (e.g., no video, no weekend movie, no allowance).

Taking a stand is more effective if we can say what we need to say without being overly emotional while saying it. If we are overly emotional (acting hysterically), the other person will automatically react, defending himself from our hysteria. If we chronically lack self-control, others will dismiss the validity of the issue because of the hysteria involved.

Drawing boundaries involves stating clearly and directly what behavior we will and won't accept. Of course, this requires that we slow down long enough to understand what is going on, so that we can think about what is right or wrong, acceptable or unacceptable. The more principle-driven and proactive we are, the more confident we will become. It will become easier to draw boundaries, take control of our own lives and cease being victims of someone else's misbehavior or irresponsibility. This is becoming mature.

Think Win — Win

Mature people think win-win (we both win) as opposed to I win, you lose. Win-win is a state of mind that looks out for our own well-being, along with the well-being of every other person concerned in the situation. Paul wrote, "Each of you should look not only to your own interests, but also to the interests of others" (Philippians 2:4). When we stand for a principle we are more apt to deal with the people involved in a neutral, non-threatening way. We are better able to deal with issues and solve the problem instead of blaming people and are able to productively think about what is best in the long run.

Listen to Yourself

We humans have a difficult time being objective with

FIGURE 13 — COMMUNICATION DO'S AND DON'TS

DO'S	DON'TS
Validate	Use defense mechanisms
Respond	React
Stay on issue	Attack person
Address behavior	Focus on personal weaknesses
Be direct	Be indirect or triangle
Say "I feel . . ., think . . . want"	Say "You are . . ., You never. . ."
Be clear and concise	Be vague and talk on and on
Be solution oriented	Think win — lose

ourselves. We often do not see how we come across to others. Many times, we do not realize that we are angry, critical, controlling, invalidating. We must train ourselves to be aware of what we think, how we behave, how we feel, and what attitude we portray. An excellent way to begin is to listen to how we talk to ourselves.

We all do this. We're busy running around and next thing we know is that we are talking to ourselves. We say, "Okay, I've got that done, now I can sit down and take a break." We even call ourselves names! We come back from the supermarket, empty the grocery bags, and notice something's missing. Then we mutter, "You dummy, you forgot the toothpaste." We can learn a lot about ourselves, and hence how we treat others, if we pay attention to our self-talk.

Self-Talk

Self-talk develops whether you are aware of it or not. It is the running conversation we have with ourselves. We have included self-talk in this section because much of our self-talk is really parent talk and is usually reflective of how we were raised.

Healthy development is reflected in positive self-talk. When basic needs are being met, an individual will naturally be confident and thus positive in how he views himself. However, if you grew up in a critical home environment, you will probably have critical self-talk. If you grew up in a fearful home, your self-talk will tend to be filled with doubts and constant second-guessing. If you were spoiled, your self-talk will be more childish. The healthier the home, the more likely that your self-talk will be more objective and reasonable, and less anxious.

Positive Self-Talk

Positive self-talk is healthy. It is hopeful. It says *I can* as opposed to *I can't* or *I shouldn't*. A person who is positive in their outlook thinks in terms of choices and possibilities. He acknowledges problems and failures as a painful but normal part of life. He has become comfortable with the process of digesting life. He *responds* to life instead of *reacting* to it. Because his sense of self-worth is not dependent upon performance, he is free to try and perhaps to fail; to try again, to explore, to create, to live. Some self-talk statements:
- I can.
- I can become.
- I can think and make good decisions.
- I can forgive without whining or punishing.
- I like myself.
- I can forgive myself.
- I can allow myself to be human and make mistakes.
- I have a healthy sense of self-respect.
- I see myself as unique and worthwhile.
- I can ask for help.
- I can change.
- I can learn.

- I can adjust.
- I can feel pain.
- I can dream and wonder.
- I can set goals.
- I can fail.
- I can try again or do it differently.
- I understand I am "in process."
- I can love and accept myself and others.
- I am not overly critical of myself or others.

Positive self-talk can help us to change our negative thinking into realistic, positive thinking. Our perspective on relationships, work, responsibility, and life may actually change. Positive self-talk is beneficial in that it helps to create a healthy atmosphere conducive to growth.

Critical Self-Talk

Critical self-talk tears down instead of builds up. It prophesies doom and gloom. It makes the normal situations of life into an overwhelming burden.

Some of our critical self-talk involves yelling at ourselves and even calling ourselves names (unkind names). Key phrases include:
- I should.
- I have to.
- I ought to.
- I must.
- I'm such a jerk.
- I can't make a mistake.

Living under the weight of such critical self-talk is like living with a ongoing report card in which we are constantly grading ourselves. Our worth becomes tied to how well we deal with every item on the list. Translated, we are getting A's or F's. We are either good or bad.

Life becomes hard as each little task becomes a chore. Rules and results become the only things that matter. Self-worth becomes something that has to be earned everyday. People living this way for any length of time may describe themselves as feeling tired, frazzled, overwhelmed, guilty, trapped, depressed, angry, tense, pressured, coerced, ashamed, hopeless, inadequate, unfulfilled, panicky, dreadful, helpless. How we think greatly affects how we feel, emotionally, physically and perhaps even spiritually.

Negative Self-Talk

Negative self-talk is helpless talk, characterized by phrases such as "I can't," "who me?," "I couldn't possibly," "why me?," and "do I have to?" One aspect of this mode of behavior is that it always transfers the weight of responsibility onto others. Since other people are unlikely to appreciate the added responsibility, this puts a strain on relationships. These people are afraid to try, take initiative, and make decisions. Some examples of negative self-talk are:

- I can't change.
- I'm too afraid to try.
- I'm not smart enough.
- I must deserve the bad things that happen.
- That's not fair.
- I shouldn't have to do so much work.
- You must help me.
- You owe me.

Living in negative self-talk is very despairing. A person that lives with an "I can't" philosophy is living with a constant sense of inadequacy. Because he is afraid to be assertive, he will always be the victim of circumstances. Prevailing emotions are fear, anxiety, confusion, feeling trapped, hopelessness, and helplessness. This person may think that good things only happen to other people.

Kingdom Principles

The Bible addresses the subject of communication.

Since communication is more *who* you are than *what* you say, the main Biblical principal we would like to stress is:

WORDS + ACTION = MESSAGE

Our message or what we want to communicate consists of our words (what we say) *and* our actions. Words alone are not enough. In fact, if someone's words contradict his actions, which do you believe, what he says, or what he does? The answer is that we should believe the actions, despite whatever he might be saying, or pleading. Consistency in word and deed is imperative in all areas of living. 1 John 3:18 says, "Let us not love with words or tongue, but with actions and in truth." When what we say is different from what we do we begin to split; that is, we project a false front that is different from what we really think. The Bible calls this hypocrisy.

Learning better communication skills is beneficial; however the most important thing is to be honest with ourselves and others.

We also need to remember that words have the power of life and death (Proverbs 18:21). Words can heal, encourage, teach, edify, build, guide, empathize, nurture, comfort, lead into truth and clarify. Most of us can remember when someone spoke a word of encouragement to us that seemed to breathe life into us. On the other hand, words can kill, tear down, destroy, deceive, cause doubt, despair, cause dissension, assassinate character, or ruin a reputation. All of us know the sting and power of words that were meant to cut us to the quick. Unfortunately, all of us also know how we have hurt others by our words. It's very difficult to take back what has already been said. Even a fool when he keeps silent is considered wise (Proverbs 17:28).

"Name-calling" is a form of verbal abuse and should never be allowed in the home or anywhere for that matter. Mean-spirited kids do this, especially in elementary school, but it can happen at any age, and it is always devastating. Never, never, never call anyone (especially children) names, and endeavor to enforce this rule with your own kids. Never say, "you'll never amount to anything," or compare them unfavorably with someone else by saying, "why can't you be more like your sister?" or identifying them with a troublemaker, "you're just like so and so." Labeling someone literally creates a definition for them, that will control them in the present and in the future. It can and often does put a "glass ceiling" over someone, limiting their growth and potential. This is why Jesus had such a strong warning about calling people names (Matt. 5:22).

Conclusion

As we have mentioned, communication is more of an emotional process than a mechanical exchange of information — having more to do with who you are than with what you say.

Learning proper communication skills is a very important part in relating to people. However, people read people, not just what they say. In relationships, who you are speaks more loudly than the words or techniques you may use to convey verbal messages.

You can tell how mature someone is by how he communicates. Is he able to speak and act in truth? Is he able to control his tongue? Is he gracious, yet principled? Does he have a win-win approach to solving problems? Can he be intimate in family relationships? Does he validate others? Does he have compassion?

This is a tall order, but it is a noble and worthy goal. This is what God is looking for in His people.

Chapter Five Endnotes

[1] Norman Wright, *Training Christians to Counsel* (Eugene, Oregon: Harvest House, 1977), p. 18.

[2] Gerald Corey, *Theory and Practices of Counseling and Psychotherapy* (Monterey, California: Brooks/Cole Publishing, 1982), pp. 120f.

[3] Andre' Bustanoby, *Just Talk to Me* (Grand Rapids, Michigan: Zondervan Publishing, 1981), p. 147.

[4] John Powell, *Why Am I Afraid to Tell You Who I Am?* (Los Angeles: Argus Communications, 1969).

CHAPTER 6

BRIDGING THE GENDER GAP

Looking through the Sunday paper at the cartoons about marriage can be amusing. It also can be enlightening and unnerving. Husband to wife as he's reading the paper: "It says here that women tend to take things personally." She angrily replies, "I do not!"

Another cartoon portrays the husband yelling, "I know when to admit I'm wrong— and if I'm ever wrong, I'll admit it!"

Men and women are as different as apples and hand grenades. You laugh? We're serious. We recently heard of a book entitled *Men are from Mars: Women are from Venus*. That about says it all.

Regardless of funny cartoons, men from Mars, or women from Venus, the bottom line is that we all are stuck on earth with each other. A lot has deteriorated since the Garden of Eden, as you might have figured.

Our initial interest in the opposite sex is accompanied by wonder and excitement. It isn't too long before hormones take over, and the world becomes a wonderland of love and romance. For this brief period of time, we lapse into irrational, head-over-heels, bizarre romantic behavior. People who have graduated from this phase gaze upon the young lovers with both fond remembrance and empathetic pity.

Courtship is that stage in a relationship when both male and female pursue each other, yearn to be intimate, cater to each other's needs or desires and actually spend time communicating and listening to each other. We graciously minimize each other's weaknesses and failures, and are generous with our love and care as we enthusiastically support each other.

Reality kicks in when the infatuation fantasy begins to fade. As the rose-colored glasses become clearer, and our best courtship behavior wanes, the prince looks more like a frog and she begins to look and sound just like her mother.

How does such a euphoric relationship degenerate into what most people come to know as a marriage? After every wedding celebration comes a marriage commitment with all of its joys, adjustments, conflicts, and (hopefully) growth. The road to maturity is really tested when we have to live with another human being day in and day out, year after year.

Preface

In this chapter, it is our purpose to emphasize general characteristics and tendencies that correspond with each gender. What we are about to describe is what we see on a regular basis in our profession. As always, there are exceptions.

Our society has done considerable damage in fracturing the family structure and we want to bring into focus the need for building relationships— especially at home. We will be emphasizing the importance of the man's role in relationships. In doing so, we will be pointing out what is wrong or lacking and covering issues that will help restore and build a relationship. There are some fundamental attitudes that must be changed for harmony to exist in a relationship in a home.

The Main Difference Between Men and Women

Simply put, as we see it, the main difference between men and women is that most men tend toward self-centeredness while most women are other-centered. Women generally seem to naturally care for and nurture others, while men generally have their own agendas. The curious thing is that during courtship, the man is traditionally the pursuer. He emotionally invests in the relationship. He demonstrates this by being considerate, protective, proactive, and willing to share his feelings, thoughts, dreams, and goals. He even rearranges his busy schedule to make time for her and he cherishes her company. She, on the other hand, may feel that she has discovered her soul-mate and life's companion. She believes that the relationship they have established during courtship is the definition of what the marriage will be like after the wedding vows.

Sadly enough, this too often fails to be the case. Part of this is normal and to be expected. Husbands necessarily begin to focus more on providing for the family, and wives gravitate toward matters at home, particularly as children begin to arrive. For the most part, it is in the first year of marriage that many men begin to take their wives pretty much for granted. His major emotional investment migrates from his wife to his job or recreational activities. She may feel bewildered as he becomes less interested in her needs and quickly labels her a nag if she dares to bring them up.

In fact, if the wife gives up pursuit of the "relationship," the marriage often begins to crumble. We find that wives, in general, will make a supreme effort to keep the intimacy within the marriage viable, sometimes for decades; but when she runs out of energy or ideas, she often gives up for good. He, all too often, is caught completely off-guard, even though she has been trying for years to communicate the fact that she misses him in the relationship. She has verbalized this message calmly and/or hysterically; logically and/or pleadingly; and has possibly even threatened him with divorce, only to temporarily ruffle his feathers and interrupt his concentration at work. Another discouraging fact is that even when a couple comes in for joint counseling, very often the husband is responsive only as long as the counseling lasts. In other words, he will work to get an "A" from the counselor, but abandons his efforts when counseling ends and he is left on his own.

This scenario is by no means true of all marriages, but it does represent too large a percentage of them. Very often, this is the predominant cause of depression amongst married women. In our counseling experience, we see this trend vividly demonstrated on a regular basis. Statistically, there is a much higher rate of depression among women than men (not counting physiological reasons for depression such as PMS or menopause.)

So, the main issue becomes "who is responsible for nurturing the marriage relationship?" Talk about loaded questions!!

How Men and Women See Relationships and Intimacy

Who is responsible for establishing and cultivating the marital relationship and the relationships with the rest of the family? Most would agree that both husband and wife are accountable, yet, in practice, this is not what we see. The wife usually ends up being the one responsible for not only the marriage relationship, but for all the other relationships inside and outside the home. Even in churches, the "prayer chain" is often exclusively made up of women.

Women are expected to assume the responsibilities that come with the couple's relationships with others. For instance, the wife is expected to stay in touch with *his* family, as well as hers, to remember everyone's birthdays and anniversaries, and to arrange the holiday gatherings and the social calendar. There seems to be an unwritten rule that men can't be "bothered" with such trivial details.

As a society and as a church body, we have enabled and even encouraged men to assign personal relationships to a low level of priority. When it comes to cultivating relationships, the thinking has often been, "That's the women's role. Men are busy taking care of the critical needs in life," or "Don't expect men to relate to their wives or children. They are just naturally awkward at dealing with emotional issues."

In his book, *Thoroughly Married*, Dennis Guernsey writes: ". . . many mothers, often good Christian mothers, tend to spoil their sons to the point that they never really learn to be responsible for or to a woman. Sons are often taught to take from women and rarely to give. That's the tragedy. Who nourishes the wife if the husband doesn't?"[1] Sadly, quite often, no one does.

When it comes to *troubled* relationships, evidence suggests the following *tendencies*:

- Men tend to take family relationships for granted and presume that others will see to the care involved.
- Men fancy themselves as "islands"— self-sufficient and autonomous.
- Men acknowledge responsibility to or a need for a relationship only after the relationship is in trouble or ended.
- Husbands think providing for the family financially is equivalent to being in relationship.
- Men, in general, miss out on the joy of real, deep relationships.
- Women often burn out emotionally, trying to keep "the home fires burning."
- Wives often expect their husbands to meet all of their emotional needs.
- Wives desire closeness and yet often attack their husbands when they do come close.
- Women want to be treated like equal partners, yet tend to shy away from the intricate details of the financial picture.
- Wives tend to think that if they just try harder to please their husbands, that they will in turn respond accordingly.
- Wives want their husbands to be open and honest, yet tend to reject men if they show any weaknesses.
- Wives hesitate to say what they really want, expecting their husbands to be mind readers.

In *Love is Never Enough*, Aaron Beck writes:

> When it comes to talking out conflicts, again there is a sex difference. Many women, for example, take the attitude "The marriage is working as long as we can talk about it." Many husbands, on the other hand, have the view "The relationship is not working as long as we keep talking about it."[2]

We won't solve this male/female dilemma overnight, but it is important to understand other differences between men and women as we attempt to bridge the gender gap. The rest of this chapter will discuss some of the most significant differences including expectations of traditional gender roles; types of needs; the ways in which we think, listen, communicate and resolve conflict; the ways we each try to control circumstances; how we view power; the ways we view sex, love and romance.

Expectations of Gender Roles

Social expectations are dissimilar for girls and boys (and in many cases rightly so). Many times, the distinctions are subtle. In one study, classes of school children were videotaped to see if teachers interacted differently with each gender. The teachers were surprised to see themselves liberally excusing boys for not knowing the answers to grammar questions or failing to complete reading assignments and letting the girls off more easily when the subject was math or science. It would seem that, at least in the field of education (and more than likely the work force as well), men are expected to be more analytical and scientific and women to be more verbal and literary.

In many homes, the expectations of boys and girls are quite different. Boys take out the trash; girls do the dishes. Boys do the yard work; girls learn to manage laundry. When a brother and sister have an after-school snack at the kitchen table, David can run outside and play when he is done, but Sandie is expected to clear off the mess left behind. Many times, parents may accept that their teenage son's room will be an uncivilized mess, but the same parents will not tolerate the same type of clutter in their daughter's room.

Girls traditionally land the ongoing chores—those that are never really finished— like looking after younger siblings, cleaning up after others (dishes, dusting, straightening up), and anticipating daily needs (grocery shopping, cooking, laundry). Many times the tasks assigned to boys are less tedious; they are jobs done in "broad strokes." Doing the lawn may be a bigger project but tends to be needed only once a week. Boys' projects usually make a "bigger splash" when completed. They have a start and a finish and make an impact when they are done. "The lawn really looks nice," an appreciative parent may say, or, "Thanks for straightening the garage."

Girls' chores are more continuous. The lawn looks nice for a week; the kitchen looks clean for a few hours. Girls' chores tend to be acknowledged only when neglected, or if there are problems. "You didn't dry the pots and pans." "Why did you let your little brother spill milk all over the counter?" "You didn't put away the laundry." Because of these expectations, girls are trained to pay attention to detail and not to expect much applause for their daily duties. They tend to be trained to be care-givers, giving constant attention to other people's needs.

This distinction spills over into relationships. At the evening meal, who notices that the four-year-old needs her meat cut up? Who makes sure that homework is done? Who calls the teacher if there is a problem with one of the kids? Who anticipates and prepares for family birthdays? Who keeps in touch with both sets of grandparents? Who makes the plans and gets the baby-sitter for a romantic night out? Traditionally, all of these detailed responsibilities fall to the wife/mother, even if she is also working full-time outside of the home. (We must note that we are seeing a positive change in this trend with the younger generation.)

Nurturing relationships should not be a burdensome chore. Involvement with the members of our immediate family should occur naturally as a gift from one heart to another. Again, we communicate our real feelings by our attitudes. The attention given out of obligation is not only unwelcome, it is also resented. But unfortunately, too often this is precisely the feeling communicated by many men when it comes to relationships.

Although men traditionally seem to marry in order to win a relationship, many will set it aside for a career and then expect that he can just pick it up where he left off forty years later at retirement. Many men revert to the idea that all that they have to contribute to the marriage is a paycheck. After all, his paycheck provides for the needs of the family. This is truly a *major* lifelong contribution that deserves a lot of appreciation. However, the problem is that many men feel that it is their job to provide for the physical needs of the family *only* and it is the job of the wife to meet the emotional, spiritual and social needs of the family. Families need much more from the husband-father than just food, shelter and clothing.

We would like to state that we have seen a change in the younger men. More of them seem to be genuinely concerned about their responsibility in relationships, in parenting and in being the spiritual leader of the family by example. On the other hand, we have seen a dramatic increase of women entering the workforce in the last decade. Many have become serious "career" women that have taken on large responsibilities, leaving them little time or desire for investing in relationships.

It is important to know that the key to healthy relationships, especially marital relationships, is mutual caring. Relationships are healthier when each partner is actively concerned and aware of the other's needs (physical, spiritual, mental/emotional, and social). Marriages are much more than just "business partnerships."

In summary, when it comes to relationships, traditionally our society has groomed women to be proactively aware of the needs of those around them, and granted men permission to be passive.

Male and Female Needs

Men and women have needs that are gender distinctive. There is much discussion as to whether these needs are biological, divinely ordained, sin-perverted, culturally induced, or a combination of all of the above. In any case, most men express a need for respect, independence, space, and sex; women list love, security, intimacy, and affection as their fundamental needs.

If a man is to meet these needs of his wife, he will have to relinquish some of his space and independence. If a woman is to meet the needs of her husband, she may have to give him more space and not expect him to meet all of her intimacy needs. This is a tough assignment for both of them. It's important to note here that women by nature tend to be responsive creatures. A woman will readily respond to a man who genuinely and consistently cares for her and loves her unconditionally, and she will resent and resist him if he does not. When a woman is "given to" a man in marriage, traditionally, she not only gives up her name, but to a great extent, her independent identity and future (although this may be changing). She now lives "under his umbrella," so to speak. She hopes that this umbrella is sturdy and protective.

It is extremely difficult for a woman to respect a husband that she believes has devalued her by remaining remote and emotionally uninvolved. Moreover, she naturally feels used when she is still expected to invest herself into caring for his needs. Conversely, it is equally difficult for a man to communicate with a wife who clearly has lost respect for him.

In Ephesians 5:25f, Paul instructs Christian men to love their wives as Christ loved the church and gave Himself up (sacrificed) for her. A man is to love his wife as he loves himself. Christ died, not so that we could go to heaven (although that is definitely a result) but so that we could be restored to intimacy with God in close communion, fellowship, and relationship. He went on ahead of us to prepare a place where we will be together forever. A man who proactively goes out of his way to *demonstrate* his love for his wife and to win and hold her respect will usually have a wife who not only admires and likes him, but desires him in every way.

How Men and Women Think and Communicate

How Men and Women Think

It should come as no surprise that men and women do think differently! Men more naturally think about one main thing at a time. Women, on the other hand, seem to be able to think about many things simultaneously. Men compartmentalize; women generalize. Men can focus on a task without becoming easily distracted. Women are more aware of surrounding circumstances (which may be distracting) and seem to see how details fit into the larger picture or overall scheme of things. What we are about to cover targets the issues that harm relationships. Some things work fine in the work place but are harmful in family relationships.

Let's compare and contrast some general *tendencies* that seem to be gender distinctive:

Men tend to think in:

- a business or task oriented manner. This is more appropriate in the work place, but can be harmful in family relationships.
- competitive terms
- "black and white" terms— seeing things in terms of opposite extremes; right or wrong, good or bad, win or lose
- singular subjects: one idea, problem, or task at a time

- tunnel vision— seeing things only from their own point of view, often disregarding others and without considering possible options
- isolated events— not being able to see how one event affects another concerning relationships; e.g., husband provokes an argument in the morning and can't understand why his wife isn't interested in sex that night. He's forgotten all about the argument, but she sure hasn't!
- broad, non-specific terms— Dad might think that a vacation is a great idea, but more than likely won't think about the logistics, details, or additional burdens placed on his wife in order to make it happen.
- task-oriented terms, rather than in terms of relationship.
- a "Mr. Fix-It" or problem — solving mentality. (If a child is upset, Dad is more concerned about solving the problem than comforting the child.)

Women tend to think in:
- terms of relationships — how the people involved will be impacted
- cooperative terms — the way people could work together in order to bring about the desired result
- comprehensive terms — if one thing goes wrong, everything is affected in one way or another
- personal terms — If I do a good job, things will go well. If something goes wrong, it's my fault.
- specifics — details are important.

How Men and Women Listen

Because men tend to think analytically towards solutions to problems, they generally listen to pick up information. Long before a lecturer has finished his last sentence, a man will have made assessments as to the "bottom line" issue and formulated a plan to implement his idea for "fixing" whatever is broken. This analytic approach is great at work, but not at home. This "fix-it" mindset tends to be focused on the solution and disregards not only those involved, but their feelings and opinions. In the pursuit of the solution, he may interrupt others, offer unsolicited advice and in *general* unknowingly run over people. In doing so, he may send a message that people just aren't as important as the task at hand.

Listening is an important part of communication and validation. Men sometimes jump into a problem-solving mode as soon as they hear a complaint, a problem, or a disagreement. Instead of relaxing and just listening and participating in an exchange of information, they tend to short-circuit the process by quickly trying to solve the problem and make everything okay. This may seem to be a time-saver and be efficient, but when it comes to relationships it is destructive. Relationships are damaged any time problem-solving takes precedence over the people involved. Listening for understanding shows concern for the other person.

Women, because but they are more relationship oriented, listen not only for what is being said, but also for what is not said. Women listen for *how* the problem is affecting the person involved as well as the information being conveyed. They are more aware of non-verbal feedback in the form of facial expressions, tone of voice and posture. Women are more inclined to validate and to be active listeners. Even her body language and expression conveys that she is usually more interested in the person rather than the facts involved. She listens on a different level and for different signals.

How Men and Women Talk

Since men are more task-oriented, they tend to inform, lecture, advise or instruct. This communication style may be appropriate for a manager or teacher, but in personal relationships, it is naturally perceived as talking down to or talking *at* someone as opposed to talking *with* someone. Women in general, are people-oriented and therefore tend to be more nurturing. However, sometimes they can be so sympathetic that they may have a harder time holding to discipline. Their soft heart can sometime let the other person off the hook too easily.

In a group setting, men tend to prefer to lecture rather than to allow dialogue. They may unconsciously discourage feedback. In fact, men are more intent on delivering the information than on paying attention to the response of their audience (verbal or non-verbal). Men seem to be less aware of non-verbal feedback than women.

In a social setting, men tend to be competitive with other men. They will talk about sports, politics, and work-related subjects in order to determine who is knowledgeable and who is not. An ordinary dinner party can become a competitive arena in which to determine who has the upper hand. So, the players with the most points (facts, expertise, mastery or cunning) win, or at least make the best showing. Hence, a man, if he thinks he isn't as sharp as the next guy, will feel uncomfortable and intimidated.

Women in the same social setting are not as competitive when conversing. Instead, they tend to talk freely about family, interests, and current trends in an attempt to quickly put others at ease. They tend to go out of their way to include any non-participants in order to create a comfortable environment. This is not to say that women cannot be exclusive, catty or even vicious with each other, but in general, in a social setting, they tend to promote peace, not war.

Bottom line, men and women talk and listen in a different language. Men take on more of a direct and authoritative role, whereas women tend to take on more of a supportive role. In relationships, this difference can lead to problems. Men need to listen for understanding rather than to just get the problem solved. Women need to learn to be more direct in their communication.

How Men and Women Address Conflict

Aside from the main issues that cause problems in marriage, many marital conflicts arise due to the fact that couples simply have difficulty talking about unpleasant things. While women may procrastinate in dealing with a problem, men would generally prefer to avoid it altogether. If men can't fix it quickly, they have a tendency to rather not deal with it at all. Again, men are inclined to think that everything is okay as long as we *don't have* to talk about it, and women feel satisfied as long as things *are* being talked about.

When a situation has become tense, men and women naturally react differently. Not all defense mechanisms are gender-distinctive, but many seem to be. Men are prone to use intimidation, sarcasm, patronization, and criticism to recoup their advantage. Women usually try to get what they want by more indirect means, such as manipulation, inducing guilt, using flattery, or feigning helplessness.

Many times, the problem isn't really the issue. Conflicts usually arise over the issue of power—who is in charge. There are no power struggles in mature relationships. So how do we address the subject of power and authority?

Kingdom Principles— The Issue of Power and Authority

Tony Campolo makes a good distinction between the terms "authority" and "power." Power is having enough strength to *force* others to do as you want. Authority is the ability to *persuade* others to do as you want.[3]

Authority is earned respect. Power is an attempt to enforce respectful behavior. You either have authority or you don't. If you try to take authority, or enforce others into a submissive position in order to usurp authority, you have just proven that you do not possess genuine authority. You are simply a bully using force to get his own way. This is intimidation, which is unbecoming to an adult, especially a Christian adult.

The idea of headship (authority, leadership) in a marriage is often misconstrued to imply power. Jesus condemned a dictatorial style of leadership when he taught his followers about genuine authority and headship. Jesus said, "You know that those who are regarded as ruler of the Gentiles lord it over them, and their high officials exercise authority over them. Not so with you. Instead, whoever wants to become great among you must be your servant, and whoever wants to be first must be slave of all. For even the Son of Man did not come to be served, but to serve, and to give his life as a ransom for many" (Mark 10:43-45).

A true leader is the one who moves out first so that others can watch and follow his lead. Effective leadership involves working with people; cooperating, and pitching in together, and compromising where necessary. This idea was clearly modeled in times past, when the king himself would actually lead his warriors onto the battlefield. Today, generals command their divisions from remote, fortified headquarters. Years ago, owners of small businesses not only would manage, but would also work alongside their employees, even doing the menial chores connected with closing up the shop at night. Today, most large corporations keep their executives sequestered far away from their rank and file employees by many layers of organizational structure. Hence, over time, leadership has become more a matter of issuing edicts and less a matter of setting an example. This dynamic has naturally spilled over into men's views of leadership on the home front. Problems arise in the home when headship is misunderstood to mean demanding or enforcing respect or obedience, having the right to control, being the boss, or having the right to unilaterally make all the significant decisions.

True headship entails thorough discussion and listening to feedback from other members of the family, especially wives. Some Christian men wrongly interpret their position of headship or authority as an absolute divine right of rule. They perceive any criticism, suggestion, or disagreement as a challenge of their authority and a direct violation of Scripture. They put their wives down, ignore their input, and invalidate their feelings. The truth of the matter is that such men are in direct violation of Scripture in that they do not mutually submit, respect, serve, or devote themselves to their wives. In short, they are not loving their wives as Paul instructed in Ephesians 5:21, 25. In fact, if a man does not treat his wife with genuine respect, he will undermine his own authority in the home.

Tony Campolo relates a typical question that comes up in his lectures on marriage.

"Some guy always raises his hand and says, 'You haven't answered the real question.' This intrigues me. What is the real question? The guy will then continue, 'Who is supposed to be in charge? Who's the boss?' I would like to say to these guys, 'Real Christians don't ask who is in charge. They ask, 'How can I serve?'"

Mature people, especially mature Christians, aren't concerned about power and control, but about what is right, what does the other person need, what is best. Mature people see the value of mutual accountability, responsibility, and submission— "As iron sharpens iron, so one man sharpens another" (Proverbs 27:17).

Authority is born out of integrity. It evolves from a life that is honest, principled, open, moral, and upright. Integrity is more than being honest; integrity involves being proactive in the pursuit of what is correct, just, and honorable—even noble—not just for oneself, but also on behalf of others. Leadership is recognized, not seized. The one who initiates consistent care, establishes purposeful direction, and anticipates (and meets) individual needs is essentially the acting leader.

Intimacy

"This is true intimacy: being confident that what we reveal about ourselves will be understood and that the person with whom we disclose ourselves will accept us, seek our good, and communicate support and love."[4]

Intimacy is openness with someone who is safe. It is impossible to be intimate with a person who constantly ignores, blames, criticizes or is abusive. The more intimate we can be in sharing ourselves, the closer we feel to that person. Unfortunately, too many marriages have very little intimacy. For whatever reason, acceptance, understanding, love, and support have waned. The marriage has grown cold and it now functions more like a business than an intimate relationship.

Sex, Love and Romance

If the marital relationship has problems involving power, control, intimacy, or communication, the sexual relationship will reflect these difficulties. It is pointless to address sexual difficulties without first addressing issues of trust, respect, caring, validation, security, and understanding. If the marriage is in severe conflict, with a fundamental breakdown in any one of these areas, it is unlikely that the sexual relationship consists of much more than the physical. Without mutual respect, sex can (and usually does) degenerate into mere usage. Once this happens, any remnant of trust is destroyed. Re-establishing trust will take a very long time and a considerable amount of loving care.

There are some couples who would describe their marriage as a failure except for the sex. However, for emotionally mature human beings, the sexual relationship is much more than a physical act. It occurs at the deepest level of intimacy (not that sex can't be just for fun at times). In the heart of the marriage relationship there is a big difference between making love and having sex. The act of making love is the culmination of two people who desire to express their love for each other in a way that words cannot express.

Sex does not necessarily involve love; it can be simply a physical act of pleasure. Men will accept sex without love much more readily than women. Most women feel that making love should be the result of intimacy in the relationship. They see romance as the catalyst for love and love as the prerequisite for sex. The point we're trying to make is— first things first. In a marriage, a nurturing relationship should come before sex. Simply put, a lot of women are "turned off" to sex because their husbands don't pay any attention to them. A healthy dose of care and romance goes a long way to developing a good sexual relationship.

Conclusion

If marriage is to be a dynamic relationship, it must incorporate intimacy. To be intimate, both parties must assume responsibility for the sustenance of a caring, safe atmosphere in which the relationship can thrive. Intimacy requires the ability to communicate on an emotional level without fear of being abandoned, rejected, put down or otherwise invalidated. Therefore, both parties must be willing to accept, validate and to love one another— love that makes allowances for shortcomings and that looks out for the well-being of the other. The level of marital intimacy will directly correspond to the degree that these qualities are operative.

Intimacy is not a place but a direction. Either you are moving toward each other in an effort to share honestly in a caring manner, or you are moving away from each other and away from intimacy. Making a decision to begin to draw close to one another is the first step in the healing process.

Chapter Six Endnotes

[1]Dennis Guernsey, *Thoroughly Married* (Waco, Texas: Word Books, 1977), p. 36.

[2]Aaron Beck, *Love Is Never Enough* (New York: Harper — Collins Publishers, Inc., 1989), p. 18.

[3]Tony Campolo, *Authority and Power* (Sermon, National Youth Leaders Convention, Joplin, MO: January, 1982).

[4]Cynthia Heald, *The Creator My Confidant* (Colorado Springs: Navpress, 1987), p. 8.

CHAPTER 7

WEATHERING THE STORMS AND DISAPPOINTMENTS IN LIFE

There are all kinds of storms: light showers, thunderstorms, hurricanes and tornadoes. Storms come and go. Some storms inconvenience us for a while; other storms can wreak havoc and leave wreckage in their wakes. Severe storms may do so much damage that months, or even years, of repair and restoration are required before things are back to normal again.

Life is very similar to this. Things can happen to us that we did not expect or even deserve, and there are things that do not happen that we may have been counting on or hoping for. We experience "little griefs" over the little everyday frustrations and disappointments and "giant griefs" in response to traumatic events or irreversible catastrophes.

There is no way around it; life can bring us tragedy. How we choose to respond will either make us or break us.

The storms of life can usually be grouped into one of two categories: *transitions* or *crises*. Transitions are normal phases or changes in life that require us to adjust as our position or role changes. Simply put, a transition is moving from one point to another point: leaving the old and adjusting to the new; from what is familiar to what is unfamiliar. It involves accepting the change, adapting ourselves to the new responsibilities involved, and learning new skills. This takes time, and the transition from the old way to the new way is a process of learning and trying and failing and trying again. This process is rarely smooth, and it can be very painful. However, it is in this process that we become different people, hopefully better people, with greater perspective, increased tolerance, new abilities, and deeper compassion. This is all a part of the maturation process.

Maturity is tested strength. It is during these storms that your very soul sometimes is tested. To be healthy and strong, we must learn to integrate into our lives the good and the bad, the joys and the sorrows, the successes and the failures, the pleasures and the pain, the gains and the losses. If we feel only the good times and reject or deny the bad times, we risk becoming unrealistic in our thinking. God meets us in reality with all of its beauty and ugliness, its joys and disappointments, its victories and failures. He understands that growth takes time. He understands process (after all, He created it). He knows us in our strengths and weaknesses, and even in our anger against Him. He is not so small that He is threatened by our hurt and disillusionment. He sees the finished product.

Stages of Life

The necessary adjustments involved in an expected

transition are usually easier and shorter in duration than the adjustments required by a crisis or an *unexpected* tragedy. Normal transitions in life occur as we move from one stage of life to another. The usual expected stages of life are:

1. single young adult
2. newly married
3. married with small children
4. married with adolescents
5. empty nest — mid-life
6. changes in generational roles: becoming grandparents, retirement, perhaps caring for one's own parents
7. anticipating one's own death.

Adjusting

We all will go through many adjustments as the years go by. Going from being single to being married will bring different responsibilities. We suddenly find ourselves related to a whole new family— the in-laws (or out-laws). Christmas used to be fairly simple. Now it might be a significant tug of war between both families. In fact, all holidays, birthdays and other annual events become more complicated.

In the single state, most of us were responsible only for ourselves. When we married, we became responsible to and for our spouse. All of a sudden, as we made decisions, it became necessary to take into consideration another adult— our mate and partner.

Life becomes more complex as children enter the picture. We find ourselves with a major shock— having to be responsible to care for and raise a little bundle that is totally dependent on us. From this point on in life, almost everything we do will involve our children. In fact, everything we do and say now literally becomes a part of the development of this little person, since we reproduce in our children who and what we are ourselves.

Never before have we been faced with so many adjustments all at once: living without sleep, financial impact (especially if previously dependent on wife's income), curtailed social activities, and dealing with grandparents. As the family increases in number, there are still more adjustments: school and schoolteachers; refereeing sibling battles; increase in household chores and increasing amount of shopping; greater financial need; after-school sports, Cub Scouts and Brownies, car-pooling and more car-pooling; less time for ourselves, and for our spouse; and relentless exhaustion. Whew!

As our children enter adolescence, we are still adjusting (if we are still standing). Now there are bigger issues. Our children are making more and more of their own decisions; beginning to date; learning to drive; getting jobs; preparing for college and career, and craving their own independence as never before. If we are doing our parenting job correctly, this is a time of intense apprenticing, as we groom our young adults to be successful on their own. It is also a time of strong mixed emotions— we feel so proud of their maturation, but our hearts ache as we watch them gradually get ready to leave us.

As our nest begins to empty, we begin once more to have to face ourselves. We are alone with our spouse again. With the exodus of the children, our roles as mother and father for the most part end, and we once again become *acutely* aware of our marital relationship. Issues in the relationship are no longer masked by the responsibility of raising children. We may grieve a number of difficult changes: the role of caring for our children is ending, the daily company of our children is gone, our children's need for us is declining, the geographical distance that separates family members may widen. And we may also have to deal with a troubled marriage.

The empty nest may also be accompanied by mid-life issues. At this time in our lives we may become disillusioned with our careers, contemplate a career change, or consider moving back into the workplace after having been a full-time homemaker. We may feel overwhelmed by financial responsibilities and feel trapped. Perhaps we are struggling with self-image as we become aware that our youthfulness and perhaps health are slipping away. Our identity is changing. We may grieve the death of our dreams and our unfulfilled expectations. Our jobs may not have taken us where we wanted to go, our marriages may have let us down, and our children may not have turned out as we expected they would. At mid-life we generally find ourselves re-evaluating every aspect of our lives.

Just as we should be beginning to experience some freedom from the day-to-day care of children, we may find ourselves involved with the care and support of our aging parents. We may even face the death of our parents, and with this we painfully realize that we are now the "oldest" generation. The death of our parents confronts us with the fact that we too are mortal and naturally next in line to go.

Mid-life is that time when we experience being caught in the middle between two generations. Mid-life is just that; it is the mid-point of life at which we re-evaluate our past, present, and future.

The last stage occurs as we slip into our parents' shoes. The focus is on retirement, grandchildren, and plans for our last years of life. These new roles bring mixed emotions as well. Even though there may be excitement about retirement, on the other hand there are many adjustments, such as where to live, what to do, planning financial affairs and health concerns. These may involve a loss of title and identity, a change in life-style, having to make do with a smaller income, a loss of friends and associates, a possible change of residence and/or climate, a change of purpose, the possibility of renewed relationship in the marriage, and a lot of time to think. This can be a time of great fear and adventure.

Even though each of these stages of life appears to be quite different, they all revolve around five basic themes.

- *Integration of new people into our lives.* With each stage there is an introduction of new people into our families and peer groups. There is always a time of adjustment in integrating these new personalities into a family system or social structure that already exists (in-laws, friends, neighbors, teachers, etc.)

- *Adjustment and negotiation* are necessary to each stage. There are new roles, rules, and ways of helping and supporting each other at each transition. We need to adapt to each additional role as it comes along. Each stage has different needs; some stages are more physically and emotionally draining. These are the times when we have to renegotiate the roles and expectations involved. For example, a husband's role changes when a baby is born into his family. He can't just come home from work and expect things to run just like before. The new mother is physically and emotionally exhausted from taking care of the baby and sees her husband's arrival from work as RELIEF! The new adjustment requires renegotiation of roles, responsibilities, and job assignments. Renegotiation needs to accompany any significant change.
  Conflicts are common when a change occurs.
  "Strong families are not those which never experience conflict, but rather those which successfully manage it when it does arise. Conflict is a normal part of intimate relationships. Simply put, a conflict is a difference in opinion."[1]
  Healthy, mature people handle these conflicts as adjustments to be made, issues to be dealt with, and problems to be solved rather than as situations which require placing blame, defending ourselves, or simply denying that a problem exists.

- *Realignment of priorities and loyalties.* For example,
  when we get married, our primary loyalty should shift
  from our parents to our new partner in life. Many
  marital problems are due to the fact that one or both
  partners have not left home emotionally. Our spouse
  should be our new priority. When children come, they
  become our second priority. The extended family,
  although important, cannot be a *primary* importance.
  It is important to become separate and distinct from
  our parents and to establish our lives and, if we marry,
  establish our own family unit, with its unique set of
  values, priorities, traditions, and goals.
- *Commitment to maturity.* With every stage of every
  adjustment there comes a choice. We can either
  choose to be responsible to ourselves and others or to
  be indifferent and irresponsible; to be aware of
  problems and to be helpful or to be obtuse and let the
  responsibilities fall on others; to be proactive or to be
  passive; and to grow or to stagnate. Commitment to
  maturity helps us to see beyond the difficulties that
  come in adjusting to each stage of living.
- *Grief adjustment to losses in life.* These losses may
  involve loved ones, friends, financial status, identity,
  health, job, and relocation. Grieving is something we
  must all learn to do. Grief is common to everyone and
  may be experienced at any age.

Grieving Losses

Grieving is good. It is necessary. It is a process of mourning
over a loss. Some losses, since they have more of an impact on
our lives, are more significant than others. Some losses can
radically change our entire future. For example, a car accident
may leave someone physically disabled. His life and the lives of
his family members will never be the same again. Other losses
are less severe and thus require a shorter period of grieving.
For example, the death of a family pet may be devastating for

a time, but normal routine usually resumes fairly quickly.

We grieve over changes such as a child who leaves for college; a geographical move; a severe illness; friends that move away; a loss of freedom; or any major adjustment that we are forced to make. We miss the familiarity of the way it used to be, and we resist adapting to something new.

All families will face various types of losses such as:
- geographical moves (loss of friends, community, familiarity)
- loss of health or capabilities
- death of a loved one
- birth defects
- broken friendship
- miscarriage
- socio-economic change
- disappointments
- death of a dream
- loss of freedom, opportunities, or options
- separation
- loss of self-esteem, damage to reputation
- loss of belongings due to theft, fire, or calamity
- loss of control in a situation

Life isn't fair. Sometimes we are stuck dealing with something that has happened to us that we did not want and do not have any control over. Other times, we suffer deep disappointments over the loss of something we desired or were expecting. We also grieve over injustices, injuries, and violations that have altered our lives and destroyed our sense of well-being.

The Serenity Prayer

The Serenity Prayer offers insight into the subject of loss.

God grant me
the serenity to

accept the things I cannot change,
courage to change the things I can,
and the wisdom to know the difference.

In any given circumstance, including loss, there are things that we can change and things that we can't. A widow cannot change the fact that she has lost her husband. She will grieve for him and miss him for a long time; yet she can begin to learn the skills now necessary to live alone.

A victim of a car accident who is now partially paralyzed will mourn over the loss of his abilities, opportunities, freedom, and former way of life. He can, however, learn new and different ways of living. (Not that this is easy or simple.) Learning to adapt to a new existence— doing whatever it is that you *can* — transforms an individual from a complete victim to a partial victor. A person who has been impacted by tragedy must grieve, but he also at some point in time must begin to adapt and move forward. If he refuses to accept the reality of his physical condition, as painful as it is and do what he is able to do, he will remain bitter.

Grieving over major losses may take years. There are some losses that we will grieve over for the rest of our lives. The death of a child or a spouse is devastating. It destroys our future, our hopes, and our very being. Part of us has died, and yet we still wake up every morning. We still go through the motions of life, but with no vigor or energy. Everything seems gray. Life has become unbearably hard. Grieving rips our souls to shreds, and we feel that we will never again feel good. Life seems to have ended, and we wonder how it can be that everybody is still going to work and enjoying anything. It doesn't seem right.

People describe grieving with words like: sorrow, sadness, regret, melancholy, misery, heartache, affliction, gloom, despair, anguish, despondency, pain, worry, anxiety, agony, torture, lament, yearning, languish, longing for, brokenheartedness, distress, suffering, rage, anger, and emptiness.

Grieving is "digesting" these losses. It is a process in which losses are absorbed, pain is felt, adjustments are made, and new life is begun. It is a type of death and resurrection experience for us. Part of us dies, but that part can later be gradually brought back to life.

Understanding the grief process is important because it validates a normal experience of living. Grieving knocks us off-balance. If we have never known this experience before, it can be extremely frightening. The pain and sorrow can be so overwhelming that we may question our sanity, and even our faith.

The Grief Cycle

Grieving seems to follow a pattern that is commonly called the *grief cycle* which is composed of seven stages. For the sake of clarity, let's apply the grieving cycle to a situation in which someone close to us has died of a heart attack. Grieving begins with the shock of the event, tragedy, disappointment, or loss.

Denial

The first phase that we experience is a time of *denial* in which we are in a state of bewilderment, panic, disbelief and confusion. At the same time, we may be forced to make many important decisions, and make them quickly. This phase may last days, weeks, or even months. It's almost as if you have gasped for breath and are still holding your breath in. You're emotionally paralyzed for a while. When you finally exhale, the reality of the circumstance and the pain associated with it begins to register.

Anger

Anger is the usual response to the tragedy and pain. We resent this event, this disruption of our lives. We miss the person and feel that it is not fair that they have been taken from us. We're angry at God for not preventing this. We know He could have done so if He had wanted to, and we angrily wonder why He did not. Sometimes we are furious at the person or situation that caused the tragedy. We may even be angry at the deceased for having left. We hate the pain and are angry for feeling so devastated. We feel that we do not deserve this misery, and someone has got to be blamed for it. We begin to resent others for being happy while we suffer. We may even be hostile to those who offer genuine support.

This time of anger is like an allergic reaction to this new event in our lives. We hate it, and we are fighting against it, resisting it, and trying to drive it away. We have a surge of energy that is welling up inside us and needs to burst out. In our helpless rage, we may even scream and throw things. Along with our outbursts of anger, we may cry uncontrollably, off and on for days on end. In fact, during this time of intense emotional release, we can even become physically sick.

Bargaining

In the lull between the rages, we have energy to think and to ponder in an attempt to figure things out. We begin to *bargain* (we think) with ourselves, with God and even with reality. Bargaining is a mental exercise in which we try to make some sense of or to gain some control over something that is out of our control. We may feel guilty and think things like, "If I had only fastened my daughter's seat belt," "If only I had been a better wife (husband, parent, child) maybe this wouldn't have happened." We may believe, "If I had been a better Christian, maybe God wouldn't have let this happen." We may also rationalize with clichés like, "God must have needed him more in heaven," or "Only the good die young."

This bargaining phase is a way of trying to resolve what is in fact, unresolvable. We seem to need to exhaust every possible train of thought. We seem to think, "If I can just determine why this happened, then I can go on with my life." This search for the answer to our "whys" will go on until we run out of ideas or until the search leaves us completely exhausted. Throughout this process we feel frustrated and confused, and when we run out of plausible explanations of why the event has happened, we are depressed.

Depression

Depression is often called anger turned inward or emotional exhaustion. In this phase of the grief cycle, we often feel isolated and alone, even in the presence of others. We feel that no one, even God, understands or even cares. We can identify with the words of Jesus, "Why have You forsaken me?" We have lost interest in our friendships, and usual activities have completely lost their meaning. Despair sets in. Everything is overwhelming, and it is a struggle to accomplish even the simplest of chores. We have difficulty concentrating because our minds are entirely preoccupied with our loneliness and pain. We tell ourselves, "No one has ever felt as bad as this, and no one could even begin to understand how I feel," and we believe it, even though we intellectually know that this cannot be true.

Depression is a black hole that swallows us up. In the dark, we feel that we have lost all meaning, direction, not to mention hope. We have lost all sense of balance. We feel that nothing is worth anything, and we want to be left alone to die in peace. We feel that the very air has been sucked out of our lungs and we have no energy to go on. Depression is silent agony, and we can see no end in sight.

But somehow, out of the blackness and cold of winter comes spring, and with spring the renewal of life. The black of night slowly fades; eventually the pain is not as severe, as we begin to accept the reality of the situation.

188

Acceptance

Acceptance of a situation does not mean that we like what happened or think it is right or fair; it is merely the acknowledgment of what *is*. It is the first step toward living again. As sorrow lessens its grip, we occasionally begin to think about the future and its possibilities. We begin to try new things. We start to be more comfortable with people and to accept genuine offers of help. It's almost like we think, "I'm *not* going to survive this, but I can try to make the best of it."

Readjustment

Readjustment is the phase where hope begins to return. We begin to feel strong again as we begin new routines and activities. We accept new responsibilities and initiate contact with others. We have survived a long, hard struggle in which we were fighting for our very lives. We had become so emotionally depleted that we had literally shut down. But now, we have healed enough to be able to re-enter the world. We start to feel and think, "I *might* actually survive this after all."

Gaining Confidence

As we learn new skills and try things we previously didn't think we could possibly do, we *gain confidence* as we think, "I *am* going to survive this and I can move forward with my life." Purpose and meaning return after a long dark winter of despair. We have found our bearings again and we begin to move forward with a renewed enthusiasm for life.

Tragedy and grief are a part of life, just as are celebrations and joy. They impact us without our permission but, over time, lend us perspective. Crises cause us to re-evaluate our beliefs and to bring them into alignment with reality. We see life as we never have before. We understand people as never before. A little more compassion, strength, tolerance, empathy, insight and understanding has been added to our character. We are broader and deeper than we were before.

Going through the grief cycle takes time. Knowing information about the grief cycle does help but does not necessarily shorten our time in it, unfortunately. Different losses require different amounts of grieving. Children (and adults) grieve over the loss of pets, and this too can take time, before the process is complete. The grieving over the end of a relationship also takes a considerable amount of time. The grieving associated with the death of a loved one will usually take a minimum of two years. The grieving over an unwanted divorce may take seven years. The death of a child is perhaps the most devastating loss anyone could ever experience. If this tragedy happens to you, you will grieve over it, in some ways, for the rest of your life.

QUESTIONS ABOUT GRIEVING

Is Grieving Necessary?

The answer is YES! It is a time of letting go and of adjusting to the new reality. There are four main tasks of mourning.

The first task is *to accept* the reality of the loss. "When someone dies, even if the death is expected, there is always a sense that it hasn't happened. The first task of grieving is to come full face with the reality that the person is dead, that the person is gone and will not return."[2]

The second task is *to experience the pain* of grief. If we care about someone, we will experience the pain of the loss. It hurts. This pain includes even physical pain. Many people refuse to grieve and feel the pain. They literally shut down all of their emotions so that they don't have to feel anything.

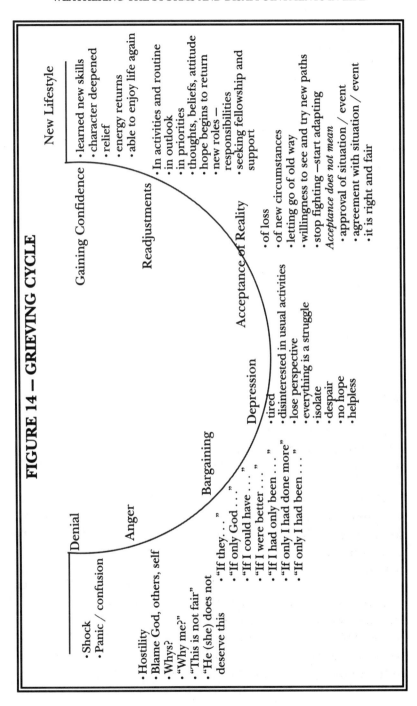

FIGURE 14 – GRIEVING CYCLE

Denial
• Shock
• Panic / confusion

Anger
• Hostility
• Blame God, others, self
• Whys?
• "Why me?"
• "This is not fair"
• "He (she) does not deserve this

Bargaining
• "If they . . . "
• "If only God . . . "
• "If I could have . . . "
• "If I were better . . . "
• "If I had only been . . . "
• "If only I had done more"
• "If only I had been . . . "

Depression
• tired
• disinterested in usual activities
• lose perspective
• everything is a struggle
• isolate
• despair
• no hope
• helpless

Acceptance of Reality
• of loss
• of new circumstances
• letting go of old way
• willingness to see and try new paths
• stop fighting —start adapting
Acceptance does not mean
• approval of situation / event
• agreement with situation / event
• it is right and fair

Readjustments
• In activities and routine
• in outlook
• in priorities
• thoughts, beliefs, attitude
• hope begins to return
• new roles – responsibilities
• seeking fellowship and support

Gaining Confidence

New Lifestyle
• learned new skills
• character deepened
• relief
• energy returns
• able to enjoy life again

The third task is ". . . *to adjust* to a new environment in which the deceased is missing. Adjusting to a new environment means different things to different people, depending on what the relationship was with the deceased and the various roles the deceased played. The survivor usually is not aware of all the roles played by the deceased until after the loss occurs.

Many survivors resent having to develop new skills and to take on roles themselves that were formerly performed by their partners. People work against themselves by promoting their own helplessness, by not developing the skills they need to cope, or by withdrawing from the world and not facing up to environmental requirements."[3]

The last task is "to withdraw emotional energy and reinvest it in another relationship. Many people misunderstand this fourth task and therefore need help with it, especially in the case of the death of a spouse. They think that if they withdraw their emotional attachment, they are somehow dishonoring the memory of the deceased."[4]

Are Faith and Grief Mutually Exclusive?

Sometimes people only quote the first part of I Thessalonians 4:13 telling others to "Grieve not," inferring that we should not grieve if we are Christians. The rest of the verse includes the words "we do not want you . . . to grieve like the rest of men, *who have no hope*" (Italics mine). We're told not to grieve as if this world was all there was.

Grieving is a process of readjustment to reality. Many of the Psalms seem to be a journal or diary in which David expresses his feelings as he processed losses and disappointments in his life. He felt feelings of anger (at times, anger at God), disappointment, isolation, shame and depression— all a part of the grieving process. Jesus grieved over Jerusalem. Jesus cried with those who mourned over Lazarus, even though He knew that He would raise him up.

When is Grieving Finished?

"One benchmark of a completed grief reaction is when the person is able to think of the deceased without pain. There is always a sense of sadness when you think of someone that you have loved and lost, but it is a different kind of sadness— it lacks the wrenching quality it previously had. One can think of the deceased without physical manifestations such as intense crying or feeling a tightness in the chest. Also, mourning is finished when a person can reinvest his or her emotions back into life and in the living."[5]

What are Normal Symptoms of Grieving?

Normal symptoms of grief can be anger, depression, sleeplessness, increased need for sleep, loss of appetite, some disorientation and confusion, some panic, a lot of crying, loneliness, some isolation, emotional pain, physical pain, and sickness. (Often illness is due to the fact that, while we are grieving, the immune systems works with less efficiency.)

Unhealthy symptoms of grief center around avoiding feeling the pain of the loss. These may include: no expression of emotion; prolonged period of isolation and depression; refusal or inability to make any decisions; hyperactivity (avoidance of pain); not talking about the deceased or the past; hastily selling or giving away items that belonged to the deceased; taking medication or drugs to avoid grieving; and seeking to communicate with the deceased.

What Can I do to Help Someone Who is Grieving?

Dr. Norman Wright suggests,

1. *Begin where the bereaved person is* and not where you think he should be at this point in his life. Do not place your expectations for behavior upon him. He may be more upset or more depressed than you feel he should be, but that is where he is nonetheless.

2. *Clarify his expressed feelings* with him. This can be done by restating his words in your own words. Help him surface his emotions. You might say, "You know, I haven't seen you cry for a week. If I were in your situation, I would probably feel like crying."

3. *Empathize—* feel with him.

4. *Be sensitive to his feelings and don't say too much.* Joe Bayley gave this suggestion: "Sensitivity in the presence of grief should usually make us more silent, more listening.

"'I'm sorry,' is honest; 'I know how you feel,' is usually not . . . . An arm about the shoulder, a firm grip of the hand, a kiss: these are the proofs grief needs, not logical reasoning."[6]

5. *Don't use faulty reassurances* with the person such as, "You'll feel better in a few days," or "It won't hurt so much after a while." How do we know that?

Remember not to give up helping the person too soon. The grief has been described in this way: "It seems when the initial paralyzing shock begins to wear off, the bereaved slowly returns to consciousness like a person coming out of a deep coma. Senses and feelings return gradually, but mingled in the good vibrations of being alive and alert again is the frightening pain of reality. It is precisely at this time when friends, assuming the bereaved is doing just fine, stop praying, stop calling, and stop doing all those little kind things that help so much."[7]

This is applicable in general, not just when someone is grieving over the loss of a loved one. Most of the time, people do not need advice, analyzing, platitudes, or their problems solved for them. They need to be heard, validated and understood.[8] Those who are grieving need to be encouraged to feel the pain and express any confusion they might be experiencing.

Often well-meaning Christians invalidate the pain of others by attacking them with "Bible bullets." Yes, God is in charge, and all things will eventually work out for good, but it is cruel to spout Bible verses at people who are in pain. We are to grieve with those who grieve! Again, Jesus wept with those who were grieving over Lazarus. He did not lecture them on their lack of faith nor did He try to get them to quit crying since He was going to "fix" everything. He apparently was moved to tears because He felt their grief. He also felt grief of his own.

Does Everyone Go Through the Grief Cycle?

We obviously grieve over the death of a loved one. But we also grieve over any loss over which we have no control. With major losses, we usually go through each stage several times. There is really no shortcut for experiencing the pains and disappointments of life. To deny the pain is to allow it to thrive underground; it won't go away, but will probably erupt later on.

Some people do not grieve when a relative (distant) dies. They sometimes feel guilty about this. However, this may be due to the fact that there was not a close bond in the relationship. Grieving is mourning over a loss. If there is no loss, there is no grieving. We may feel sad but not grieve. This explains why, for example, two of the grandkids are devastated by the loss of a grandparent and the other grandchildren are not. The first two may have been more closely bonded to their grandparent. For them it was a personal and emotional loss.

Can You Bounce Around the Cycle?

Yes! Often we feel we've accepted the reality of a new situation and have begun a new course in life, only to find a wave of anger washing over us all over again. Often an anniversary event or reminder comes along that jabs at the wound that is not yet healed.

Grieving isn't smooth. It is usual to go through each of the stages of the cycle a number of times in the grieving of one loss. Just as we think we are pulling out of depression, for example, we are faced with celebrating a certain holiday for the first time without a loved one, or remembering the birthday of a close friend that is now estranged from us. That often sends us right back into anger, bargaining, or depression. Sometimes, it doesn't even have to be a date that reminds us of our loss, but the smell of that person's cologne, a movie, a place, an object or phrase that sends us immediately back into some phase of the grieving cycle.

Acceptance happens in layers. Usually, when you've come into acceptance, the recovery time after a relapse is shorter than before. Each layer that we go through brings us closer to complete healing.

Will It Get Easier Next Time?

Yes. The first time a severe or challenging crisis comes your way, you probably feel that you will never live through it. The first time a severe loss impacts you, you fight it as if it were a life-threatening event. The next time, you are less frightened by it because you have been through it before and know that you will be able to survive. Given enough time and effective adjustment, you will begin to function again — probably to your own surprise. The pain may be as severe, but the fear of the grief experience is not as great (which is a measure of relief).

What If You Are Suffering from Several Losses?

It is exceptionally difficult to suffer a series of losses in a short time span with no recuperation period in between. Grieving and adjusting take time and energy. Help and support are essential during times like these such as can be provided by good friends and/or a trusted minister or counselor. Even though you may feel like withdrawing, it is important to stay in contact with others during this time.

How Long Is Each Stage?

As previously mentioned, the length of each stage (and the entire cycle) depends on the severity of the loss or crisis. However, there are points along the grieving cycle where we can get "stuck." One cause for becoming stuck is unforgiveness, which we will discuss at the end of the chapter.

Denial

A few people get "stuck" in the denial stage. They pretend that the tragedy or loss either did not happen or they minimize its effect on them. They may cover it with spiritual jargon, but the truth is that they are denying the actual impact of the loss and its pain.

Anger

Anger, left unaddressed, can turn into resentment. If it continues to remain unaddressed resentment will turn into bitterness; and bitterness can lead to hatred. This is what happened to Cain. God warned him about his anger, but Cain allowed his anger to develop into hatred and resulted in the murder of his brother, Abel.

We can destroy people in more ways than one. We can purpose to injure another emotionally or mentally to the point of destroying them or their reputations. If we do not resolve our anger, we risk becoming bitter, hateful, mean-spirited, negative, cynical, and judgmental. Our anger, instead of dissolving, has solidified like cement.

Isn't Anger Wrong?

No, anger is not wrong. Paul writes, "Be angry and yet do not sin" (Ephesians 4:26 NASB). Some people misunderstand meekness to mean never expressing anger. William Barclay translates "Blessed are the meek, for they shall inherit the earth" (Matthew 5:5), as:

> O the bliss of the man who is always angry at the *right time* and never angry at the wrong time, who has every instinct, and impulse and passion under control because he himself is God-controlled, who has the humility to realize his own ignorance and his own weakness, for such a man is king among men![9]

How *appropriately* we express anger is an important measure of maturity.

Two important facts about anger:

- Anger is a clue to what you value. You get angry over what is important to you.
- Anger is a secondary emotion. It is a reaction to a primary emotion such as:
    - hurt: disappointment, loss, rejection, abuse, insult, betrayal, embarrassment, unfair treatment, etc.
    - fear: of losing something important, of having something happen that you would like to avoid; of losing control.
    - frustration: low-level reaction to everyday

anxiety, pressure, strain, stress, and tension that interferes with your agenda.

Keys to Handling Anger

- Know what you are really angry about and why.
- Talk it out with yourself and perhaps someone else.
- Tell the offender that you are angry. Be civil. Use a normal tone of voice. Resist the temptation to avoid the person and or the issue. (This is tough to do!)
- Decide to be open to forgiveness. Your healing will take time.
- Leave vengeance to the Lord. (Romans 12:17-21)
- Make appropriate amends.
- If possible, or appropriate, think of a way to avoid repetition of the same scenario.
- Don't think WIN-LOSE, think SOLUTION.

Bargaining

We can also get stuck in the bargaining phase, rationalizing the "whys" of the tragedy and consequently landing in a place that is not in accord with reality. Sometimes, the smarter we are, the longer we can remain in this phase. Bargaining is an attempt to resolve or make sense out of a situation that is unresolvable. Sometimes we cannot rest until we figure out what went wrong and why. The truth is that many times there is no reason or cause for the tragedy that has occurred. And even if there is a cause, sometimes there is nothing you can (or should) do about it.

In searching for an explanation, we can subconsciously adopt a false belief or unrealistic explanation. For instance, a child who has lost a parent may conclude; "If I am real good from now on, nothing like this will ever happen to me again." Another common example is the child of parents who are going through a divorce who believes that he is the cause of the divorce. "If I had been better, this would never have happened.

If I am real good now, my parents will get back together." These false beliefs need to be addressed in order to proceed through the grieving cycle. The only way to get better is by facing the truth.

Depression

Depression is normal. It is a reaction to things being outside of our control. Depression is a phase that we go through in adjusting to disappointment or loss. "Dr. Archibald Hart says the probability is high that you or a close relative will experience a significant depression at least once in life."[10] Depression feels like death but, in time, it will lessen its grip. However, sometimes we can go beyond a normal reaction to a traumatic event and become self-destructive. We can begin to eat or drink too much, to abuse prescription medication or illegal drugs, to isolate ourselves for weeks on end, to make rash decisions, or even to make plans for suicide. When these things happen, we need to reach out to others for help. Part of the problem is that we are reluctant to admit that we are depressed. We are afraid of what others might think.

Unfortunately, many Christians attach a stigma to depression. Dr. Hart states that there are three main reasons for this.

First, in our culture we have strong expectations that people should be in control of themselves and their emotions. Depression is seen as a sign that we're out of control.

Second, this general fear is exaggerated by our notions of "perfection." Depression is seen as failure and is therefore stigmatized.

Third, we fear that depression in its severest form is a mental illness.[11] (We fear that we will have to be sentenced to a mental ward.)

Why Are More Women Depressed Than Men?

Dr. Hart gives four main reasons why women are more affected by depression: social factors, role changes, low self-esteem and biological factors. "For a long time, social conditions and attitudes in our culture have worked to the disadvantage of women. Depression, for many women, has had to become a survival strategy . . . . when living conditions are intolerable." Because of this many women slide into depression. Secondly, more women are entering leadership positions in the workplace and becoming the primary breadwinners in their families along with the women who are the sole support of their families (due to divorce).

"Next, the connection between diminished self-esteem and depression has long been known. Depression not only causes low self-esteem, but anyone whose esteem has been eroded is likely to be more prone to depression as well."[12] Finally, the reproductive function of women has also greatly contributed to their depression. They face problems such as infertility, singleness, PMS, and menopause, which are all related to her femaleness.

We have found that a large factor in women's depression is the fact that they are the ones in the relationship that carry the emotional weight of that relationship. They are the ones that do the worrying, caring, validating. The quality of relationships in the home depend on her. Everyone in the home depends on her. There is no break for her. Without the support and help of another adult, this responsibility becomes very heavy.

Could I Ever Need Medication for Depression?

Eighty-five percent of significant depressions are precipitated by life's stresses.[13] Pent-up anger is almost always at the root of clinical depression. Everyone suffers from some form of depression at some time; and although not all forms of depression include a chemical imbalance, some do and can be helped with medication.

After making an honest effort with the following guidelines, if you are still depressed, you may need medication. If you feel that medication is needed, you will need to see a psychiatrist, who is a medical doctor who is trained to evaluate and prescribe medication. Psychologists and mental health counselors cannot prescribe or monitor medication.

Keys to overcoming depression:

- Read the Bible and pray regularly. Ask God for clarification, direction, strength, options, courage, healing, attitude alignment, and accurate perspective.
- Maintain contact with friends and family. Do not isolate.
- Talk to someone (friend, minister, spouse, counselor) about why you are angry. Talk through possible solutions.
- Stick to your normal schedule or routine.
- Observe self-talk and keep it positive.
- Identify any false beliefs (see Chapter 2). Replace them with healthy ones.
- Develop new interests.
- Stay active – don't give in to your depression.
- Learn what you are "powerless over" and what you can control.
- Join a support group.
- Think before you act (respond instead of react).
- Plan some fun.

The above list feels impossible when you are depressed. Probably what you would like to do is stay in bed and hide. It is very important to know that you can be depressed and still carry on a routine. It is hard— but you can do it. A severe depression may require rest for a while, but in most cases, we can continue to live up to our responsibilities. You may be a little slower, be distracted and forgetful and require more sleep, but will eventually return to normal.

Again, depression is a part of life, even Christian life.

Kingdom Principles— Forgiveness

"Forgiveness is God's invention for coming to terms with a world in which, despite their best intentions, people are unfair to each other and hurt each other deeply."[14]

Forgiveness is a necessary part of coming to grips with the reality of injury and injustice that happens to all of us (without our permission). A lot of things happen in this life that are totally unfair, evil, harmful, crippling. Sin, with all of its consequence, invades and destroys what is good. Reality includes murder, incest, untimely death, theft, abuse, deceit, disease, accidents, wars and other tragedies.

The big question is, why does God let all these things happen? The Scriptures do not explain completely why God allows sin and evil to play such havoc with His children. We only know that He is coming back and will set all things aright.

This is easy to believe when we are not in the throes of pain. When we are hurting, it natural to question God. Hence, it is also natural to hold God responsible for the tragedy and even to be angry at Him. Accepting the unknowns as unanswerable questions is the first step towards resuming close communion with God. That is how we are healed.

Forgiveness is letting go of the desire for vengeance. According to Vine, the word forgive implies to "let go" or to dismiss or release the wrong.[15] Paul wrote, "Do not repay anyone evil for evil. Do not take revenge, my friends, but leave room for God's wrath, for it is written: 'It is mine to avenge; I will repay,' says the Lord" (Romans 12:17,19). "Forgiveness is not the alternative to revenge because *it is soft and gentle; it is a viable alternative because it is the only creative route to less unfairness.*"[16]

"Forgiving seems almost unnatural. Our sense of fairness tells us people should pay for the wrong they do. But forgiving is love's power to break nature's rule."[17] "For we create a new beginning out of past pain that never had a right to exist in the first place. We create healing for the future by changing a past that had no possibility in it for anything but sickness and death. And we heal the hurt we never deserved."[18]

Forgiveness is the key to healing. Being able to let go of the past or the hurt is the first step towards healing and finding the way out of suffering and depression.

Forgiveness is not easy. Most people often overlook small slights, aggravations, and disappointments but when we have been deeply hurt, genuine forgiveness is required.

Forgiveness follows a pattern which is much like the grieving cycle. It is a process of letting go of the injury and of distinguishing the hurt from the person who has harmed us. Although it sounds contradictory, many times some healing is necessary even before we are able to think about forgiveness. Sometimes we are so devastated that we are left broken and need help and comfort just to begin to recover enough to even think straight. Forgiveness happens later along in the healing process; but ultimately, forgiveness will be necessary for complete healing to occur.

The process of forgiveness is similar to the process of grieving in that we initially experience an injury or injustice and the accompanying sense of loss. Perhaps we have been rejected, mistreated, let down, or violated in some way. We begin a time of suffering in which we are angry, depressed, and perhaps vengeful. We do not want to forgive; we want to blame, and we want to hit back. We think that forgiving the guilty party somehow invalidates the victim's existence. We want to cling to the injustice until the guilty party is punished (thus validating the victim). The problem is that, very often, the injustices we suffer can never be set right, and so we get mired down in the quagmire of an irreconcilable situation—what we refer to as "being stuck."

The impetus that breaks through the inertia of pain or resentment is frequently the simple acknowledgment that we are at least open to the idea of forgiveness. Once we "make room" for God's grace in this way, the healing process can begin to take place.

Forgiveness is sometimes wrongly coupled with "forgetting." When we forgive, we let go of the idea of being judge, jury, and executioner. We can also begin to let go of the pain and sense of victimization that has developed.

But none of these ideas include failing to learn from the experience. We can forgive someone who betrayed our trust or confidence, but if we are wise, we will learn that it would be foolish to trust this person again before he has proven himself trustworthy.

Forgiveness does not necessarily include the idea of reconciliation, nor does it exclude the fact that an offender may rightfully suffer the consequences of his actions. In his book, *Love Must Be Tough*, Dr. Dobson describes what is now commonly called "tough love."[19] Our aim is to walk in forgiveness while standing for what is true and just. If a baby-sitter has been irresponsible, resulting in injury to your child, you may be able to forgive the baby-sitter; but that does not mean you hire the same teenager again, to "prove" that you have forgiven her. Likewise, if you have been sexually abused by your father or another family member, you may get to the place of being able to forgive him; but it would not be wise to leave him alone with your daughter. Forgiveness does not supersede common sense.

Forgiving a betrayal does not mean that you have to immediately trust the person who failed you. *Trust is earned, not given.* The person who caused the injury is responsible for taking the steps necessary to earn back the trust he has forfeited by his actions. A person who has stolen something from you may be forgiven, but he should also be made to make restitution. He should bear the responsibility for replacing what he has stolen, even if this means that he has to find a job to do it. Don't let anyone tell you that you are being unspiritual or unkind if you do not readily trust the forgiven offender again. Although forgiveness is a one-way process, reconciliation is a two-way street and requires a mutual effort to be accomplished.

Sometimes it is hard to make sense out of what may seem to be conflicting principles. It is hard to juggle grace and truth, forgiveness and accountability. When do we show mercy? When do we exact discipline? What do we make allowances for? And what do we demand? In his book, *Forgive and Forget*, Lewis B. Smedes says: "Forgiving is not forgetting. Excusing is not forgiving. Forgiving is not the same as smothering conflict. Accepting people is not forgiving them. Forgiving is not tolerance."[20]

Of course, we need to keep in mind that "we are seldom *merely* sinned against. We often contribute to our own vulnerability. We set ourselves up for hurt. Sometimes we invite pain, not because we love somebody too much, but because we are too stupid. Maybe we contribute to our being ripped-off because we are too lazy to look hard before we leap into a deal. Maybe we contribute to our spouse's infidelity by our unfeeling ignorance of their needs and desires. Maybe we contribute to our children's rebellion by our cold judgments and hot tempers. Surely, we know at least this much, that even if we are the hurt party, we are seldom a completely *innocent* party."[21]

We are all fallible and in need of forgiveness. Jesus tells a story about a king who was auditing his accounts. He came across one account of a person who owed him ten thousand talents. This man was brought to the king and was told to repay the debt. Since he had no money, the king ordered that he and his family be sold as slaves. The debtor fell on his knees and asked for patience and promised that he would pay back every cent. The king was moved with pity and canceled the debt and let him go. But this same man turned right around and choked another man who owed him only a small amount, demanding immediate payment. This poor man was thrown in jail because he also was unable to pay. He begged for mercy, but received none. When the king heard about what had happened, he was outraged and threw the first man who had received mercy into prison because he did not in turn, give mercy.

"The story is about God and us. If we act like the unforgiving servant, God will act like the king.

"Jesus grabs the hardest trick in the bag—forgiving—and says we have to perform it or we are out in the cold, way out, in the boondocks of the unforgiven. He makes us feel like the miller's daughter who was told that if she didn't spin gold out of straw before morning, she would lose her head. And no Rumplestiltskin is going to come and spin forgiving out of our straw hearts. But why is Jesus tough on us?

"He is tough because the incongruity of sinners refusing to forgive sinners boggles God's mind. He cannot cope with it; there is no honest way to put up with it.

"So he says: if you want forgiving from God and you cannot forgive someone who needs a little forgiving from you, forget about the forgiveness you want."[22]

In summary, forgiveness is an entryway into freedom. To refuse to forgive is to elect to remain in prison and to continue as the victim of others. Even when we cannot forgive, we can ask God to help us get to that place where we are open to it. Forgiving is a process. Many times it is two steps forward and three steps backward. There are days where we are able to forgive only to fall back into unforgiveness again. But as long as we call on the Lord to help us do what we cannot do we will continue to move forward in an attitude of forgiveness.

Chapter Seven Endnotes

[1]Jack O. and Judith K. Balswick, *The Family, A Christian Perspective on the Comtemporary Home* (Grand Rapids, Michigan: Baker Book House, 1989), p. 211.

[2]Worden, *Grief Counseling and Grief Therapy*, p. 10f.

[3]Ibid., pp. 14-15.

[4]Ibid., p. 15.

[5]Ibid., p. 16.

[6]Joseph Bayley, *The View From A Hearse: A Christian View of Death* (Elgin, Illinois: The David C. Cook Publishing Co., 1969), p. 40.

[7]Dr. Norman Wright, *Training Christians to Counsel* (Eugene, Oregon: Harvest House Publishers, 1977), p. 141.

[8]Karol Hess, *Communication and Resistance Workbook* (Watchung, NJ: Beacon Light Christian Ministries, 1989), pp. 9-10.

[9]William Barclay, *The Gospel of Matthew, Volume 1* (Philadelphia: The Westminster Press, 1975), p. 98.

[10]*Understanding Depression* (Focus on the Family Newsletter, March 93) p. 5.

[11]Ibid.

[12]Ibid., p. 6.

[13]Paul Meier, et al, *Introduction to Psychology and Counseling* (Grand Rapids, Michigan: Baker Book House, 1982), p. 266.

[14]Lewis B. Smedes, *Forgive and Forget* (San Francisco: Harper and Row, Publishers, 1984), pp. xi-xii.

[15]*Vine's Expository Dictionary of Old and New Testament Words* (Old Tappan, NJ: Revell, 1981), p. 123.

[16]Smedes, *Forgive and Forget*, p. 131.

[17]Ibid., p. xii.

[18]Ibid., p. 152.

[19]James Dobson, *Love Must Be Tough* (Waco, Texas: Word Books, 1983).

[20]Smedes, *Forgive and Forget*, pp. 38-46.

[21]Ibid., p. 147.

[22]Ibid., p. 150.

CHAPTER 8

OVERCOMING DYSFUNCTION AND HEALING ITS WOUNDS

PART 1: DYSFUNCTION

Dysfunction is a term that has become a part of common language. Much has been written recently about the subject of dysfunction and its effect on the family.

Dysfunction is defined as impaired or incomplete functioning. Dysfunction is the term used to describe families that do not meet the needs of its members sufficiently or appropriately. It is also used to describe the irrational, addictive or irresponsible behavior patterns of individuals impacted by their family of origin. The purpose of this chapter is to simply map out what dysfunction is, how it develops, how it impacts individuals and families and how we can break this destructive cycle.

It is possible to interrupt a destructive cycle. One individual who is willing to challenge old habits and patterns and to replace them with something that is better and healthier is the key. It is possible, with God's help, to align ourselves with the truth and to change things so as to drastically alter the course of the next generation within our family and hopefully within our society. This is every Christian's call to maturity: to walk in the light as He is in the light, being responsible for our own lives before the Lord. We are called to operate in truth in every aspect of living, while clothing ourselves with love, grace, mercy and compassion. We're not called to change others, but ourselves which will influence others and perhaps the next generation.

How Did Dysfunction Develop?

In the beginning, Adam and Eve walked and talked with God in the Garden of Eden. They lived in precious, intimate communion with their Creator. But then sin entered the picture. Sin severed the relationship between God and His human creatures, and Adam and Eve experienced shame, fear and guilt for the first time. They no longer felt safe in the presence of a Holy God. They became aware of their nakedness and made coverings for themselves (shame). When God called to them, Adam replied, "I was afraid and I hid" (fear). When God confronted their disobedience, Adam immediately began to blame everyone else (God and Eve) because he felt guilty. (This probably led to the first marital conflict in history.)

Ever since the Fall, shame, fear, and guilt have continued to keep us alienated from each other and from God. Once shame, fear, and guilt became a part of the human experience, man, out of his pride, began to distort, to cover up, to blame, to avoid responsibility— to operate contrary to his functional design; hence, the term *dysfunction*. Shame, fear, and guilt (unless addressed) will cause dysfunctional behavior, which will in turn cause others to experience the same thing. It becomes a vicious circle. This is a good description of how the sins of the father continue from generation to generation. Sin begets sin, and will continue to do so until it is stopped.

Awareness

The only way to break this harmful behavior is to see it, repent of it, and change. This, of course, begins with awareness. Awareness is being alert, cognizant, and attentive— to ourselves, to others, and to what is going on around us. Without awareness, we will continue to reinforce our safety boxes with the defense mechanisms that we have developed over the years, and we will perpetuate patterns that will be established in our children.

Awareness is not a secular idea or a practical gimmick to getting healthier; it is a spiritual imperative. It is the first step toward walking in truth. How can we align ourselves to truth unless we know what truth is and what part of my life it needs to affect? A major goal in discipleship involves applying truth to our everyday living so that we might truly reflect who God is. Discipleship is the process of integrating the reality of God into the reality of one's life. It is one person helping another to grow in truth, in direction, in responsibility, in power and in love. Its goal is spiritual maturity.

We, as Christians, can count on the Holy Spirit to guide us into truth and maturity. Coming into awareness implies that, at some point in time, we are unaware, blind to something, and have had our eyes opened to reality. We can ask God to reveal to us any beliefs, behavior, and wounds that are harmful to ourselves or to others. God will show us specifically how we operate out of shame, fear, and guilt and where we are living irresponsibly.

Types of Dysfunction

What is dysfunction anyway? How bad does it have to be in order to be called dysfunction and not just a "personality quirk"?

Each of us is different and unique. Everyone has distinct personality traits which make us interesting and which help to make life colorful and enjoyable. However, dysfunction is a *pattern* of living that has become harmful to ourselves and/or others. It is a pattern of behavior (which develops from our thinking) that has negative consequences for the well-being of others (or ourselves). It causes wounds of shame, fear, and guilt that in turn affect how we perceive reality, how we handle our responsibilities, and how we interact with others.

Although it is difficult to categorize dysfunction, it is necessary to be aware of certain areas of dysfunction if we are to make any progress. We have chosen to address dysfunction in terms of behavior, emotions, thinking, responsibility and family interaction. We have found that it is useful to understand dysfunction in these terms, although in actuality all five areas are interrelated and overlap.

Behavioral Dysfunction

Individuals with behavioral dysfunction tend to either try to control others or to allow themselves to be controlled by others. This is a rather simple statement, but how we go about doing either of these can be quite complex. And, it is also true that we do both, but we generally lean towards one or the other.

If we are the type of person that tends to be controlling, we may use intimidation, blame, anger, threats of rejection, belittling, lying or manipulation to accomplish our goal. On the other hand, if we tend to allow ourselves to be controlled by others we might play the victim, be passive, stop thinking for ourselves, rationalize, deny, minimize, act helpless, be silly or look only on the bright side of things. One seeks to run or control things; the other seeks to avoid things. In PAC terms, the first tends to be the *controlling parent* and the other, the *compliant child*.

A passive person (consciously or unconsciously) tries to gain control in covert ways such as passive manipulation, as opposed to overtly manipulating by use of intimidation. For example, a passive person may get his own way by feigning helplessness, whereas the aggressive controller may bark orders at others. Both are trying to coerce others to do what they want. The aggressive person tends to instill fear and shame in others; the passive person instills guilt and shame.

These patterns affect almost every area of our lives, from how we relate to people to how we approach a task. The more extreme our pattern of dysfunction the more severe the consequences will inevitably be.

Abuse is a popular topic today, especially on the afternoon talk shows. The general public is becoming aware of what abuse is and what it does to its victims. Abuse is the quickest and most devastating way to inflict shame, fear and guilt onto others. The more severe the abuse, the deeper the wounds. A person with an intense need to control will use extreme measures to get his way— to feel safe. Power and control are the two main themes of this person's life. Abuse takes many forms: emotional (verbal), economic, sexual, physical, usage, and confinement (isolation). Abusers are more often men, and the victims are their wives/girlfriends and children. Abusers are cowards disguised as bullies.

Emotional abuse takes the form of put-downs, name-calling, crazy-making, and other mind games. This type of abuse seeks to keep the other person off-balance, so that they cannot stand up for themselves. If you can successfully make someone feel that they are stupid, inferior, or inadequate, then they will not likely challenge any mandate you impose. They will feel they are incapable or unqualified to do so.

A sinister way in which husbands try to control their wives is to take control of the money in the family. He may accomplish this by preventing her from getting a job and earning money. He may purposefully keep her ignorant of his income, his spending habits and his bank accounts. In such cases, it is not unusual for a husband to forge his wife's signature on the income tax returns, insurance policies or other legal documents. In extreme cases, he controls the money to such an extent that he obligates his wife to have to ask for any money at all and to justify her spending, even for household necessities, doctor's bills, gas for the car and clothes for the children.

Lack of sufficient earning power is usually what keeps a woman trapped in an abusive situation. Even if she desires to leave, when she doesn't have the power or ability to support herself financially, she remains completely dependent upon her husband. This is not much different from a master/slave relationship.

Another insidious form of control is depriving a person of freedom of movement or self-direction. A husband may try to control whom his wife sees, whom she talks to, and where she goes. He attempts to isolate and sequester his victim, so that he is in total control of the home situation. He may screen phone calls, scrutinize phone bills, monitor the odometer on the car, make a scene in front of her friends so that she will be embarrassed and feel wary about seeing them again. He may also follow her to see what she does, forbid her to participate in any activities outside the home, and do anything further he can to try and dictate and control her every move.

Physical violence includes throwing objects, slapping, hitting, pushing, threatening or using weapons. Physical violence is the last-ditch effort a person uses in an attempt to control or punish another person. Violence follows a progression that will escalate unless the abuser is held accountable *publicly. Abusers never get better unless there is outside (usually legal) intervention.*

Often, before the onslaught of physical violence, an abuser

will harass, threaten, or use other ploys to intimidate, incite fear and cause alarm. He may use abusive language, damage personal property (car, clothes, dishes, pets) cherished by the victim, or threaten to harm either the victim or a family member. The abuser uses extreme forceful behavior to coerce the victim into doing what he wants.

Sexual abuse is by far the most crippling and devastating of all domestic abuse. Again, men are usually the sexual abusers, since men are generally bigger and stronger than women are. It is a violation of body, soul and spirit, rendering the victim wounded for life, causing extensive ramifications, even into the next generation. Sexual abuse (any type of force that is used to make a sexual encounter happen) between husband and wife is sheer usage and is dehumanizing. Incest is perhaps the greatest betrayal of all, because the father (or other relative) has invaded that which he was supposed to protect. He betrays trust and annihilates dignity to gratify his own perverted desires. Any person violated in this manner is shattered in a million pieces, becomes frozen emotionally and can come to exist merely as a shell of a person, isolated from much of what makes life worth living.

Almost all the abuse mentioned above is considered prosecutable as criminal behavior in most states. For example, the New Jersey Legislature passed the Prevention of Domestic Violence Act which declares that

> ... domestic violence is a serious crime against society; that there are thousands of persons in this State who are regularly beaten, tortured and in some cases even killed by their spouse or cohabitant; that a significant number of women who are assaulted are pregnant; that victims of domestic violence come from all social and economic backgrounds and ethnic groups; that there is a positive correlation between spouse abuse and child abuse; and that children, even when they are not themselves physically assaulted, suffer deep and lasting emotional effects from exposure to domestic violence. It is therefore, the intent of the Legislature to assure the victims of domestic violence the maximum protection from abuse that law can provide.[1]

C. Everett Koop, M.D., former U.S. Surgeon General, has identified violence against women as a global problem. He has said that "Battering is the single most significant cause of injury to women in the country." He further stated:

> Violence against females is everyone's responsibility. It is the responsibility of governments at the national, state and community levels. It is the responsibility of legislators and parliamentarians, city and village councils or panchayat leaders. It is the responsibility of the legal system, including the police, prosecutors, judges and probation officers. It is the responsibility of the health professions, including doctors, nurses and other health professionals as well as hospitals and clinics. It is the responsibility of educational institutions and educators; the communications media; the church and clergy.[2]

We would strongly urge women who find themselves in such situations to contact the police and/or the county services available to help them. We hesitate to suggest that women contact their church unless they are confident that the leaders understand abuse and the law. We have seen too many women devastated by well-meaning ministers who counsel them to stay in the abusive situation and try to win their husbands by their submissive behavior. When it comes to abuse, the situation will always get worse unless consequences for the abusive behavior are severe. Remember, it is grace *and* truth.

Emotional Dysfunction

Emotions are a God-given component of our total being. We all have emotions, whether we are aware of them or not. We all experience shame, fear, and guilt; but when they have been inflicted upon us by abuse, neglect, or trauma, they can result in emotional wounds which, if they are left unattended, can cripple us.

It is important to distinguish between healthy and unhealthy shame. Healthy shame is that painful feeling we have when we have behaved in an inappropriate manner thus embarrassing ourselves and losing respect from others.

Without healthy shame, we would be shameless— without a conscience, that is, having no regard for modesty or decency. Healthy shame helps to make us aware of how our actions affect others. It keeps us from acting out (misbehaving) and helps us to stay humble and teachable.

A State of Ineligibility— Shame, Fear and Guilt

Unhealthy shame is the emotion associated with feeling worthless, unwanted, undesirable, inherently bad, defective, deficient, unredeemable. People who are debilitated by this type of shame describe it as being not "good enough." They feel branded as a reject of society who should not expect to receive the same privileges, rights, or happiness as others. They have interpreted the bad things that have happened to them to mean that *they* are bad. Thus they feel like second-class human beings, who do not measure up to those whom they perceive to be normal.[3] They believe that they have already been judged and classified, "weighed and found wanting," and are therefore *ineligible* to qualify for anything good that life may have to offer. Many retreat into hopelessness and cease trying to fit into society while others feel that they have to constantly refute the judgment handed down and prove their worth, becoming people pleasers and/or very performance oriented.

Sally described herself as being insecure. Even though her performance reviews at work are excellent, she is fearful that they will find out that she is really inept. She often loses sleep worrying about being fired. At home she's afraid to stand up to her husband's verbal abuse. She rationalizes the abuse by believing that she somehow must have deserved it. She doesn't have any friends and is becoming more and more isolated and depressed.

In her excellent book, *Can Christians Love Too Much?*, Dr. Margaret J. Rinck states:

When children's basic needs are neglected, they begin to experience certain deficits and learn to view the world in a certain way. They learn to feel unloved, not valued, unimportant. As their needs continue to be consistently unmet, not only do they feel abandoned but these children learn to shame themselves for having the needs in the first place. The logic they unconsciously use goes like this:

It must be my fault that my needs are not being met. If I mattered or had any value, my parents would meet my needs. I must be hopeless and utterly without value. I'm no good. If I were good, then they'd care for me.

It never occurs to children that something might be wrong with Mom and Dad. After all, in their minds, parents are gods. Parents can do no wrong. Ultimately, the interpersonal link between the child and other humans breaks down, too. The child believes "I have no right to depend on or need anyone." Thus the child feels shame for being needy and for being alone (abandoned). Either way the child blames himself. Shame heaped on shame eventually causes the child to lose all awareness of basic needs. The child develops a phony self, which is usually compulsive in some fashion.[4]

Shame says I *am* bad; guilt says I *did* something bad. In this state of ineligibility, people feel ashamed for having basic needs and feel guilty about asking for them. Sally, for example, felt guilty for wanting to be treated with respect. This sense of *disqualification* makes it easy to feel afraid of everything, including having to ask for things, stating an opinion, being real, trying something new, failing and succeeding.

Sally expressed it this way: "It's like being a spy behind enemy lines. Constantly afraid that someone will find out this big secret. And the secret is that I'm ineligible. I'm a lower-class human being and don't deserve anything good. I'm constantly afraid that others will find out that I'm not normal. It's like even if I do something well, I can't take any pride in it, because I know that it was just a fluke and it's just a matter of time before I fail, and everyone will know that I am bad.

And when I do fail, it confirms the fact that I am worthless. I feel driven to achieve, so that one day I will become like everyone else." People branded by this feeling of ineligibility express this driven feeling as being like a car in which the engine is always racing, even when it should be just idling. They are constantly anxious.

In his book, *The Search for Significance*, Robert McGee describes this drivenness as a search to find worth. According to McGee we devise a destructive formula: What I do (performance) plus what others think of me (approval from others) adds up to my worth as a human being (significance). Worth based upon performance and acceptance is wrong. In God's eyes we are accepted as sinners. We don't have to measure up first. He knows that we can't do much of anything right for very long and that's why He's full of grace, love, and power. Satan desperately tries to keep Christians from realizing freedom from guilt and shame.

The Safety Box

We all instinctively protect ourselves from attack. This is the law of self-preservation. When we strive to perform or to gain approval in order to prove our significance, we have begun to operate from a false identity. We cover our true identity and construct a system of entrenched defenses around ourselves in order to avoid the pain of shame, the fear of standing up for what we know is right (especially if it means rocking the boat), the fear of failure, or the fear of being hurt again.

The more dysfunctional we are, the higher and thicker we build the walls around our safety boxes. All of us use defense mechanisms to some degree, but those who have been severely wounded may develop an inordinate reliance on these defense mechanisms to avoid being hurt again. Sometimes, in an effort to feel safe we become extremely controlling or demanding— trying to be in control of everyone and everything. Things have to go just right, or we become extremely threatened and anxious. We become unapproachable and unteachable and ultimately, very lonely and isolated. The result of this avoidance is that we become closed to any dialogue or any contact with the truth which would set us free.

Some of us can become so codependent that we only feel safe when we are making other people happy. We will forsake truth, violate justice, and disregard our own needs in order to keep the peace, to avoid rejection or abuse, or to pacify a tense situation.

Francine is a mother who is overwhelmed by her children's bad behavior. In counseling, she found out that the root of her dilemma was that she was afraid to discipline her children for fear of having them dislike her. She believed that she was only as good as how well she could make others happy. She not only got exhausted from doing everything her three children demanded, but became disillusioned when they misbehaved after all she had done for them.

Cognitive Dysfunction — Thinking

In the book, *The Lies We Believe*, Dr. Chris Thurman describes six distortions that we commonly use to misinterpret reality. The more heavily defended our safety boxes are, the more we use these distortions. Distortion is both the cause and result of dysfunction. It is important for us to examine ourselves to see which of these distortions we tend to use. We have rephrased some of his terms.

• *Magnification— The Mountain out of a Molehill Lie*

Thurman describes overreacting as taking a five-cent situation and magnifying it into a fifty-dollar issue. An example of overreacting can be illustrated in the following scenario. A son earns a poor grade on an important algebra test. Dad, who has to sign his test paper, seizes this opportunity to deliver a long lecture, during which he maintains that his son's prospects for future success have been seriously damaged, all because of a poor grade on one test. He distorts the situation completely out of proportion by saying, "You have to shape up, and shape up pronto. Otherwise, you'll just end up as a worthless bum, out on the streets somewhere." This father has magnified one event into a future of doom for his poor son. He used fear and shame in an attempt to motivate his son to improve his grades.

• *Personalization– The Taking Everything Personally Lie*

Jim is an example of someone who personalizes. He began his counseling session by complaining about the traffic. "This guy waited until *I* came by to pull out onto the highway. I had to slam on my brakes, while he went on as if nothing had happened. I can't believe he did that to *me*."

The counselor challenged Jim, "This guy sat at the side road waiting for *you*?"

"Well, I know he didn't, but it sure feels that way when someone does something like that to me." All of Jim's words reflected his distorted way of looking at events. It is normal to be upset that someone was driving carelessly. But it is unrealistic to believe that we are some kind of target. By talking it through, Jim had to admit that he had overreacted to this situation (and others) because he tended to personalize situations.

• *Polarization– The Black or White Lie*

People, in general, tend to think in terms of black and white. Things are perceived as either right or wrong, yes or no, just or unjust, good guy or bad guy. This type of thinking does not allow for any gray areas. All of life is put into one of two columns, the right column and the wrong one. Polarized thinkers tend to be legalistic, severe in their judgments, and unrealistic. Putting it bluntly, they do not see the world as it actually is. In the body of Christ, these people tend to label others as Saint or Sinner, i.e., a finished product, rather than seeing the whole person as a human being on the road to maturity. Within the church this type of thinking is deadly. It undermines grace, hinders growth, kills creativity and instills fear, insecurity, and despair. This kind of thinking encourages people to become "Christianoids" who conform to so-called Christian standards rather than being transformed by the work of the Holy Spirit.

This harsh "all or nothing" pattern of thinking is very draining and discouraging. If there are only two options in life— the good or the bad— then there is little room left for being imperfect. So much effort and energy is spent on trying to get into the right column, staying in the right column and convincing everyone else (including yourself) that you are indeed *in* the right column, that life degenerates into an exhausting, endless pursuit of trying to get everything right.

• *Selective Thinking— The Majoring on the Minors Lie*

Selective thinking focuses on some things to the exclusion of others. It puts emphasis on the small issues while ignoring the larger, important issues. It's a method of avoiding uncomfortable subjects or responsibilities. Focusing on the minors allows us to feel that we are working very hard, but in reality we are just staying busy to make it look like we are being responsible. This lie distorts our priorities and perpetuates dysfunction. We focus on the minor issues and fail to give our time and effort for the really important things.

George is a father who is trying so hard to provide for his family financially that he is never home to be with them. His children see him only a few hours on the weekend if they are lucky and even then he is unavailable because he is so tired.

Margaret is a neat freak. She is so concerned about keeping the house immaculate that it feels sterile and uninviting to the family and to others who may visit. Her obsession with cleaning leaves her little time for enjoying her family. Her kids prefer to play at other people's houses where they can enjoy themselves. When they are home all they want to do is watch TV because when they do anything else, Mom is constantly yelling at them to pick things up. By majoring on keeping everything neat she has in essence put her home before her children.

• *Generalization– The Always and Never Lie*

People who fall into the generalization trap use the words "never" and "always" in much of their language. "You always show up late." "You never put away your clothes." "I always mess things up." "I'm always (or never) right." "We always do it this way." "You can never count on her."

Using never and always about ourselves and our circumstances excuses us from changing because it categorizes a person with a summary conclusion. This "pigeon-holing" effect can be devastating. It is hard for most of us to forget words like, "You'll never amount to anything; You'll never change, You're always slow." People who generalize often use shame (humiliation) in an attempt to motivate or to punish. Using shame, guilt or fear to motivate usually does nothing to promote or encourage healthy motivation, and it damages the relationship involved by destroying trust and respect.

Using always and never also hurts our credibility. One husband said, "As soon as she says, 'You never hang up your coat,' I don't hear anything she says after that. I'm busy proving her wrong by thinking, 'There must be at least one time in the last 15 years that I have hung up my coat.'"

- *Being Run by our Emotions–*
  The "Don't Confuse Me with the Facts" Lie

Since we are prone to seeing only what we want to see, it isn't unusual to let our emotions overrule facts and truth. Once again, this is where shame, guilt, and fear become our enemies. When we let these emotions define who we are, we will tend to interpret all input through the impressions that these emotions have left on us. For example, a person with a lot of shame will have difficulty accepting compliments, trying new things, or being creative. Even when he does a fantastic job, his mind cannot hear the compliments. His shame overrides the facts.

Someone who is stubborn or obstinate is almost always operating from a place of intense fear. Fear filters reality. Usually, this person has difficulty hearing anything new that might be different from his perceptions. Accepting a change means that is was wrong to begin with. He is so fragile that he will greatly resist any feedback.

All these distortions lead to dysfunction. We will be dysfunctional to the degree that we distort reality. What we think will affect what we do.

Responsibility Dysfunction—
Being Over- or Under-Responsible

One of the common indicators of dysfunction is being over- or under-responsible. One of the earmarks of maturity is being able to discriminate between those things for which we are and are not responsible. Many of us continue to do for others what they should be doing for themselves. Janet is the mother of two grown sons, who *thinks* she has to do the laundry for her twenty-two-year-old son who still lives at home. Her older son lives on his own, but Janet still *thinks* that she must call him every day to make sure he is alright and it's not unusual for her to clean his apartment at least once a month.

An over-responsible person feels a real need to do something to help out or to prevent problems, regardless of whether or not it's his responsibility to do so. He is driven to make sure that everything and everybody are taken care of. This person feels that if he doesn't do it, it won't get done (or at least it won't get done "right"). Things will fall apart or someone will be left without. In other words, the onus falls on him to be the "responsible one." In short, he places himself in the position of being responsible for things for which he is not in fact responsible. It follows that this super-person becomes the hero of the family, the rescuer at work, the caretaker in a relationship, and the over-achiever in life. His motto is "If you want it done right, do it yourself."

The under-responsible person fails to acknowledge his responsibilities for things that clearly fall within his realm of obligation. Janet's sons have grown to expect Mom (women) to take care of them. When they get married, they will likely think; "I shouldn't have to; it'll get done; someone else will do it, things will take care of themselves, things have a way of working out." An under-responsible person relies (consciously or unconsciously) on others to do his thinking, his planning, his job. He is more passive than proactive, and, because of this, will most likely have problems at work. His main defense is to blame others for his problems, which is just another way of passing onto someone else the responsibility that rightfully belongs to him.

Under-responsibility in relationships is a major factor in marital conflict. When one spouse is under-responsible, the other spouse ends up bearing the total responsibility of caring for the other, nurturing the relationship, mending the rifts, and communicating information, plans, and dreams. When the responsible partner wants the marriage to work, he or she is forced to take the initiative and do all that is necessary to keep the relationship stable. As the years go by, however, the responsible person will become emotionally and physically depleted, and will eventually feel used. The resentment and bitterness that usually follows adds even more strain to the relationship, which in turn may lead to the demise of the marriage.

Addiction and Codependency

"Addictions have always been a part of the human predicament."[5] In today's instant society it is so easy to become ensnared in a variety of forms of addiction. It is not hard to find a substance or behavior that helps to calm our nerves, lift our spirits, or numb the anxieties and pain of life. "We can become addicted to any substance or behavior which alters our mood, or which anesthetizes us to our emotional pain."[6] Of course, habitual use of mood altering drugs or behaviors can only lead to addiction or slavery.

There are all kinds of addictions that enable a person to avoid being responsible for themselves and to others; things such as: drugs, alcohol, gambling, eating, people (codependency), sex, exercise, perfectionism, spending (or saving) money, religion, sports and work. The adjective which best describes the essence of addiction is compulsive. A behavior becomes a compulsion when a person is driven or controlled by the substance or addiction. He must have the drug. Instead of being in control, the addiction is now in control of him.

Addiction is a disease of feelings. An addict actually forms an emotional bond with the substance or behavior being used. The substance or behavior replaces people. An addict becomes bonded to the addiction because it gives him something in return — comfort or relief. When faced with a confrontation, he will defend his addiction just as someone would defend a best friend who has been falsely accused. Anyone attempting to infringe on this relationship can expect fierce opposition.

Addiction provides the ultimate escape from the reality of living a responsible life. Irrational thinking and unreasonable behavior escalate as sanity, reason and values diminish and ultimately vanish. Self-preservation is all that matters to the addict who sees himself as a victim whose only defense and comfort is his drug or habit. Rationalization, manipulation, crazy-making and every other kind of defense mechanism will be displayed to evade the truth and to perpetuate his addictive behavior.

Addiction and Dysfunction

Addiction and dysfunction feed on each other. Addiction develops as an individual seeks to satisfy (on his own) needs that should have been filled by someone else (usually a caring adult). Instead, the voids that have been created by dysfunction (neglect, abuse, abandonment) are now painful wounds that need careful attention. This is where addiction provides temporary relief. Compounding the problem is the fact that the addictive substance or behavior rewards the addict by temporarily alleviating his pain. It is difficult to conquer an addiction when the substance used makes you feel good (for a while). It provides a means of escape and a place of refuge. If we don't learn how to ease our pain by meeting our own needs in a healthy way, we will tend to seek out temporary relief in an unhealthy way.

In short, addiction and codependency short-circuit the normal maturation process. It cripples "normal" people at an alarming rate. We must learn to identify harmful patterns of behavior (regardless of how common they are) and to stop them and learn how to handle life and pain in a more mature fashion. It's "back to the basics" of character building.

Addictive Cycle

Addiction and dysfunction operate in vicious cycles. Both are usually born out of either unbearable shame or intolerable pain. A person suffering this intense pain may seek relief in a substance, such as alcohol or cocaine, or in a behavior such as bingeing, overspending, gambling or sex.

In a perverse way, addictive behavior does "work." The pain does indeed subside, but only for a while. However, as the effect wears off, the pain returns; only this time, along with the pain comes the resulting consequences of the irresponsible behavior. If a person has binged or overspent, he or she now feels guilty. And no wonder. After the binge, you feel awful. And after the spending spree, there's less money to take care of the bills, or even groceries for the rest of the week. The alcoholic may have missed work, had a black-out (no memory of the incident), or perhaps fallen down the stairs and injured himself so that he is in even more pain than ever. In any case, feelings of guilt and remorse are overwhelming, and the pain has become completely unbearable. Once again, he cannot endure the pain and is unable to solve his problems, and so he takes another drink or another drug or he gambles one more time, in order to find relief. And that just starts the cycle all over again.

It is absolutely necessary to break out of this cycle. Unfortunately, there's no easy way to do it. The *only* way out of this cycle is to feel the pain, address the truth and genuinely repent. The first step is to be able to feel the pain and not panic or anesthetize it. The person cannot, and should not, go through this alone. We feel that it is almost always necessary for someone to be in counseling (with someone who is trained in addiction) through this process. If a person suddenly stops his addiction without addressing the voids and unmet needs underneath, he will either relapse into the same addiction or choose a new one. It is not uncommon for an alcoholic to stop drinking, only to become compulsive in one of the other areas previously mentioned. People who give up smoking for example, often overeat.

FIGURE 15 – THE ADDICTIVE CYCLE

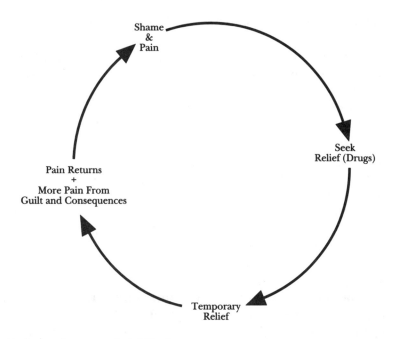

Codependency and Addiction

"Codependent behaviors are panic reactions to another person's addiction or compulsion."[7] We are all codependent to some extent. It's part of human nature. We react to other people's moods. We appease the intimidator, we compensate for the irresponsible by doing their work, fix problems, and rescue the wounded. Some of us almost make a livelihood out of codependency. We can become driven to do it all and do it perfectly.

Codependency allows addiction to continue. "The fear, anger and helplessness a person feels when someone they love is addicted can lead to desperate attempts to 'take care of' or control the loved one. Unfortunately, these behaviors are not helpful. Instead, both the addicted person's behavior and the frenzied codependent behavior combine in a destructive downward cycle."[8] Both the addict and the codependent need to be in recovery.

Tough Love and Intervention

As the addict becomes less and less willing to assume his rightful responsibilities, he forces those around him to be over-responsible in order to ensure that the work gets done. The others are forced into making a decision to either take up the slack for the irresponsible family member or to enforce accountability and responsibility (tough love). Knowing when to take a tough-love stance is not always easy. Two conditions that can indicate when "enough is enough" are easily spotted: 1) if someone's behavior is causing significant harm to himself or others, and/or 2) if a family's basic needs are chronically going unmet—then taking a hard stand becomes necessary to prevent any further damage, damage which might be irreparable.

It may be that taking an accountability stance becomes necessary in the workplace. Perhaps an employee is not fulfilling his job requirements because of addictive behavior or chronic irresponsibility. Whether the breakdown occurs in a family or in the workplace drastic measures may be appropriate. An *intervention* (secular term for tough love) may be necessary to enforce responsible behavior.

An intervention is an active strategy that decisively interrupts the cycle of dysfunction. An intervention involves specifically confronting the addict's irresponsible or destructive behavior, by forcing him to either cease the behavior and live responsibly . . . .Or else! The consequences must be painful enough to produce results and must be upheld faithfully.

To be effective, interventions should be overseen by experts who are trained in addiction counseling. An intervention team is usually made up of family members, friends or authority figures as well as the trained professional. The purpose of the intervention is to convey a message of genuine concern for the addict as well as a specific plan for recovery.

An intervention is just what it implies: an action from an outside source to restore discipline and sanity. If the addict could get back on track himself, it would be called self-discipline. In the absence of self-discipline, an intervention is a means of exerting discipline from an outside source that is used for the sole purpose, not of punishment, but of restoration. We do the addict no favor by allowing him to continue to live irresponsibly and to destroy his family and career. If an intervention is not done, all those in relationship with the addict will suffer. At the office, morale suffers and productivity drops. In the family, relationships fall apart and home life disintegrates.

Dysfunction, Society and the Family

Dysfunction is a term that has come into vogue in the '80s and '90s. There are several reasons for this.

One factor is the increase in the number of individuals and families who are severely impacted by divorce, addiction, abandonment, abuse and neglect. The children of divorced parents of the '60s are now parenting the children of the '90s. They bring with them the baggage of a broken home where their basic needs were to a great extent unmet and where they had little sense of security. Many have assumed the role of "parent" without the foundation and role modeling necessary before one can be a good parent.

Another issue in dysfunction is that our society in the '90s is seeing more single parent and two-income families where kids are left on their own to a greater extent. These children are left alone without supervision (and getting into trouble) and often have to assume responsibilities (laundry, dinner, baby-sitting) that are adult responsibilities.

Our society has become busier than ever before. Even when there is time available for children to spend with their parents, that time is often pre-empted by a myriad of scheduled outside activities. It's a sad commentary on our own culture when classes dealing with stress and time management are being taught in our middle schools. Much of our effort today is spent in just trying to cope and survive the demands of each day. Little energy is left over for anticipating and meeting the needs of those around us. Sadly, our society has become a very self-centered one. We have forgotten the importance of the family.

Our society has become amoral. There has been a major change in values that has contributed to the extent of dysfunction today. Major compromises have redefined morality. What was once accepted as right is now considered to be wrong; and what used to be wrong is now considered acceptable, and even preferable. The so-called freedom that we have attained has caused harm that will not be remedied in one generation.

In his insightful book *All Grown Up and No Place to Go* sociologist David Elkind describes one cause for dysfunction today.

> In today's rapidly changing society, teenagers have lost their once privileged position. Instead, they have had a premature adulthood thrust upon them.... Many adults are too busy retooling and retraining their own job skills to devote any time to preparing the next generation of workers.
>
> And some parents are so involved in reordering their own lives, managing a career, marriage, parenting and leisure, that they have no time to give their teenagers; other parents simply cannot train a teenager for an adulthood they themselves have yet to attain fully. It may be summed up that we have immature parents raising immature young adults.
>
> The media and merchandisers, too, no longer abide by the unwritten rule that teenagers are a privileged group who require special protection and nurturing. They now see

teenagers as fair game for all the arts of persuasion and sexual innuendo once directed only to adult audiences and consumers.... In today's society we seem unable to accept the fact of adolescence, that there are young people in transition from childhood to adulthood who need adult guidance and direction.[9]

He describes our society as one that is pushing children towards a *pseudo-maturity*. Children are more sophisticated, street-wise and independent than they were twenty years ago; but they only seem to be mature because they appear to mechanically function as small adults.

Another aspect of today's dysfunction is that we have created an *instant generation* that has little respect for diligence or tolerance for patience. Today we can see most any problem "solved" within a thirty-minute television format; we can deliver packages around the world overnight, and we can microwave a complete dinner in a few minutes. We are constantly bombarded with the message that we deserve to have every whim or desire immediately gratified. There seem to be some hidden statements: "I shouldn't have to invest too much;" "It shouldn't be so hard or complicated;" "I shouldn't be inconvenienced;" or "I shouldn't have to wait for what I want."

Although he does not use the term pseudo-maturity, Stephen R. Covey describes a similar phenomenon in his book, *The 7 Habits of Highly Effective People*. Covey documents a change in the description of success and leadership.

> . . . much of the success literature of the past 50 years was superficial. It was filled with social image consciousness, techniques and quick fixes... In stark contrast, almost all the literature in the first 150 years or so [of our nation] focused on what could be called the Character Ethic as the foundation of success— things like integrity, humility, fidelity, temperance, courage, justice, patience, industry, simplicity, modesty, and the Golden Rule.[10]

He then describes the *Personality Ethic* which is similar to Elkind's pseudo-maturity— where appearance and street-smarts have replaced character as the criterion for success. Hence, the ability to survive and look good while doing it has replaced genuine character as qualification for leadership.

Covey's assertion that *appearing* confident is considered more important than integrity is illustrated by a salesman's comment, "I may be wrong, but I am never in doubt." These immature attitudes have made an impact. *Looking* good is more important than *being* good. Appearance is more important than substance. Instant gratification is preferable to diligence. Cleverness at manipulation has replaced character and integrity.

Back to Basics

In Chapter 4, we wrote that the purpose of the family is to protect each family member from harm; to provide for each member's well-being; and to prepare each individual to become whole, responsible, productive, self-reliant, and mature. This has to be done within a structured, safe atmosphere and with a balance of truth and grace.

A strong or healthy family is one in which each family member's basic needs are being consistently met; where parents are parenting with love and care; where there is the sense of belonging to a family; where children are being trained to be responsible and sensitive; where the family operates under healthy rules and boundaries; and where there is a foundation of Christian values and principles that shape the entire life of the family.

All families are dysfunctional in some area of family dynamics. Some have only a few areas that are out of balance, whereas others may have much work to do. One way to determine areas of weakness is to identify the specifics that are causing problems, either in relationships or responsibilities. These areas should be targeted in order to identify the real problem (unmet needs, painful voids, results of irresponsibility). Then the goal becomes to learn whatever is necessary in order to live in a healthier way.

Maturing these areas may be as simple as acquiring insight or as difficult as learning a completely new life skill and changing the way we communicate, confront, listen, anticipate, plan, resolve conflict, care and love.

Unhealthy Characteristics of a Family System

To summarize, the more the following characteristics are built into the family system, the more unhealthy the system is. Pinpointing a particular unhealthy issue that has been troublesome is the first step to taking responsibility in moving towards maturity.

We have constructed a rather lengthy, comphrehensive list of unhealthy characteristics. We are not trying to overwhelm you, but it is necessary to be specific for the sake of understanding. Hence, the list is long. Reviewing this list may be a bit painful. All of us will identify with some of the following characteristics. It is better to identify the areas that we need to work on, painful though this is, than to ignore it and let it grow. We would like to encourage you to to face some issues that you may have been ignoring for a while. We humans have a tendency to do this — avoid pain.

Unhealthy Characteristics:
- Families seek help only when the pain or stress becomes overwhelming; when a particular crisis happens again; or when the children start to have problems.
- Marriage partners don't know what is expected of them concerning their roles as husband and wife.

(The marriage license does not come with a manual.)
- Parents use children to meet *their* needs.
- Parents have little understanding of the process involved in training their children.
- Parents rarely discuss values and principles involved in everyday situations.
- Children (and often spouse) live in dreaded fear of abuse (verbal, emotional, physical, or even sexual).
- Parents model indirect communication, disrespect, insecurity, poor problem-solving skills, inconsistent behavior.
- Parents use shame, guilt, intimidation, force or punishment in an attempt to control a child, instead of disciplining with love, keeping the long-term goals in mind.
- Instead of encouragement, parents often resort to name-calling and blaming in an effort to discipline the children.
- Parental rules are reactionary, inconsistent, inflexible, or non-existent.
- Rules are for the convenience of the parent, rather than the child's welfare.
- Parents expect too much or too little for the appropriate age of the child. (very common)
- Parents fail to show affection in words and action.
- Parents on one extreme are acting as dictators or are so passive that they allow the children to dictate the rules.
- Children are not taught to be respectful or obedient to proper authorities.
- Atmosphere is one of insecurity.

  - Children don't know what to expect from parents at any given time.
  - Children don't know what is expected of them.
  - Anxiety level is high.
  - Family operates around the mood of one individual.

- Children feel that they are a bother or are unwanted.
- Family members have low self-esteem.
- Children feel unduly pressured to conform to expected roles.
- Children feel anger due to extremely rigid rules.
- Children are not allowed to feel, speak, or think differently from the parents.
- Physical affection is either non-existent, conditional, manipulative, or intrusive.
- Children are not taught how to solve problems.
- Family lives from crisis to crisis.

- Life skills often are weak in the areas of:
  - Budgeting and financial planning.
  - Managing time.
  - Establishing and working toward long-term goals.
  - Problem-solving skills.
  - Making decisions.
  - Completing a task thoroughly.
  - Self-control (is impulsive or reactive).
  - Communication.

- The family members may view life unrealistically.
  - Often grandiose about self and abilities.
  - Sees family system as "just fine."
  - Has no reference as to what "normal" is.
  - Normal events and problems often perceived as crisis.
  - Does not know a "real" crisis when it does happen.
  - Surprised by the amount of diligence required to get a desired result. Hence, give up quickly.
  - Has difficulty in adjusting to the normal stages of life.

- Family members may take on distinct roles, such as:
    - Controller/abuser: use of intimidation, power, blame.
    - Pacifier/enabler: defuses the anxiety in the home. Nurtures and cares for the wounded.
    - Comedian/mascot: uses humor to defuse a volatile situation.
    - Wallflower/lost child: is the lost member in the family. Flows with whatever is happening. Avoids everyone, does not want to be recognized.
    - Scapegoat/rebel: known as the "black sheep" in the family. Thought to be the source of the family's problems.

Sometimes, a list like this sparks some people to over-analyze and dissect themselves unmercifully. This is not our intent. However, if some of these characteristics have become a *pattern* in your life and are causing undo confusion and harm, then it is time to get serious and do your homework.

Progress, not perfection is the motto. God does want us to mature, but perfection is unrealistic. Take it easy — yet be conscientious.

Characteristics That Build a Healthy Family

It is easier to remove unhealthy characteristics if we know what should replace them. Listed below are the traits of a healthy family system. It's unfortunate that this subject is not required in school. All of us can benefit from reviewing this list from time to time, if only to be reminded to apply these worthwhile principles:
- Parents have a commitment to family.
- Parents demonstrate and discuss values, goals, faith.
- Parents promote the child's sense of well-being.
- Parents affirm and support each other and their children.

- Parents model trust, respect, responsibility, open communication, consistency, proper handling of crises.
- Parents take the time to apprentice their children in tasks appropriate for their age.
- Parental rules are explicit, yet flexible.
- Parents treat children with respect and encouragement.
- Parents express love in words and action.
- Parents anticipate and are responsive to the needs of the children.
- Parents model admitting needs and faults.
- Parents model seeking help and problem solving.
- Family spends time together (meals, fun, church).
- Atmosphere is one of safety.
  - children trust they will be taken care of.
  - children feel safe in confiding in parents.
  - children feel guided, not dominated.
  - children know that they are wanted and liked.
  - children are allowed to be unique.
- Atmosphere is one of affection.
  - in personal conversation (including precious talk.)
  - in behavior (bonding, hugs, kisses, touching.)
- Atmosphere is relatively consistent.
- There is no perfect home:
  - yelling happens, but not typically.
  - will be anger and hurt, but not chronic.
  - may be times of unhappiness, but not constant.
  - may be arguing, but not regularly.

Results of a Healthy Family

A healthy family produces healthy individuals who are not afraid of truth and are able to perceive reality without distortion; to learn from failure; to make restitution when necessary; to face responsibility. In short, healthy functioning involves not letting fear stand in the way of being responsible. Dysfunction occurs when fear or other strong emotions overrule reality and what should be responsible behavior. Healthy people can endure the pain involved in dealing with hurt, frustration, conflict and disappointments. They don't run away from problems or issues that need to be addressed but are self-disciplined and principle-driven. They are willing to suffer short-term heartache for long-term gain. Therefore, they are better able to learn, risk, fix, change, forgive, fail, love, and care. They are sufficiently established in who they are and therefore are able to think and care beyond themselves and their own world.

PART 2: RECOVERY

Kingdom Principles — Recovery and Restoration

Life Recovery Guides from InterVarsity Press begins the booklet, *Recovery from Addictions* as follows:

> First, we are in need of recovery. The word *recovery* implies that something has gone wrong. Things are not as they should be. We have sinned. We have been sinned against. We are entangled, stuck, bogged down, bound and broken. We need to be healed.

> Second, recovery is a commitment to change. Because of this, recovery is a demanding process and often a lengthy one. There are no quick fixes in recovery. It means facing the truth about ourselves, even when that truth is painful. It means giving up our old destructive patterns and learning new life-giving patterns. Recovery means taking responsibility for our lives. It is not easy. It is sometimes painful. And it will take time.

> Third, recovery is possible. No matter how hopeless it may seem, no matter how deeply we have been wounded by life or how often we have failed, recovery is possible. Our primary basis for hope in the process of recovery is that God is able to do things which we cannot do ourselves. Recovery is possible because God has committed himself to us.[11]

There are two things that we have found to be extremely

helpful in the recovery and restoration process. The first is the Serenity Prayer, and the second is the Twelve Steps of Alcoholics Anonymous. Working through the Twelve Steps is truly a life-changing experience that can benefit everyone, not just those suffering with addiction. We have used this format for nearly a decade in a course called *The Nuts and Bolts of Christian Living.*

Many people have been able to overcome habits of addiction, overcome fear and depression, and codependency. Many marriages and parent-child relationships have greatly improved and even those dealing with difficult relationships that had not significantly improved have reported that they, themselves felt more sane and stable. The most rewarding results were the numbers of people who had received Christ as their Savior.

The Twelve Steps has become a way to "chunk down" problems into workable, solvable pieces. Those who have participated in *The Nuts and Bolts of Christian Living* class, have reported that the one outstanding result was that they found peace while learning how to live responsibly.

The Twelve Steps originated with Frank Buchman in a Bible Study-Prayer Group called the Oxford Group which was active in the 1920s and 1930s. Buchman believed in spiritual transformation and stressed absolute honesty, purity, love and unselfishness. Bill Wilson became involved in the group, devised the Twelve Steps, and began to apply them to the problem of addiction. Although the Twelve Steps originated in a very evangelical setting, over time the spiritual aspect has become watered down. It is, nonetheless, based on sound biblical principles.

The Serenity Prayer

We see the Serenity Prayer everywhere— on plaques, refrigerator magnets, desk ornaments and bumper stickers. It's so common that it has almost become a cliché. However, we have found the Serenity Prayer to be one of the most meaningful and powerful prayers we have come across. It literally verbalizes the first key necessary to unlock the door that leads to recovery and restoration.

> *God*,
> Grant me the
> *Serenity*
> to accept the things
> I cannot change
> *Courage*
> to change the things
> I can, and the
> *Wisdom*
> to know the difference.

These words are packed with effectual insight. When a situation calls for prayer, and we do not have the understanding or the appropriate words to pray, this is the prayer to use. It suits any circumstance or situation. It leads us to expect wisdom from God and causes us to think and take action. The Serenity Prayer gets to the core of truth, dysfunction, and responsibility.

One of the key issues in dysfunction is not knowing what we *are* and *are not* responsible for. And so we begin by asking God to give us His wisdom. Over time, God will teach us, through a variety of sources, what we are and are not responsible for. This formula sounds simple, but working it out in the daily activities of our lives is much more complicated. Sometimes we get into trouble because we violate the boundaries of responsibility and attempt to control and manipulate the lives of others. On the other hand, in the exact same situation, there may be times that we have to take a *tough-love* stance. Every stage in every situation needs to be submitted to God, and His wisdom must be sought.

This prayer is intended to focus in on our specific decisions and actions. This prayer makes us slow down, think, and seek God. The Serenity Prayer, if taken seriously, can become the start of an increasingly close walk with the Lord. It encourages us to develop a relationship with God where we learn to listen and apply our faith to every aspect of our lives. It brings His presence and power into our daily situations.

The Serenity Prayer brings us (our wounds, shame, fear, guilt, depression, bitterness), our problems, and our situations to the throne of grace. It is in this place of sanctuary that we find grace and peace — especially when we must accept things that we cannot change. It is here that we can talk over and cry over our hurts, fears, and confusion and find that He won't leave us or let us remain in darkness. He will begin to teach us where we need to be responsible and where we have been irresponsible. He will teach us how to "let go" of the things that are outside of our control while promising to sustain us with His peace (serenity) as we stay close to Him.

This place of sanctuary is appropriately called the throne of grace, for it is where we are understood, validated, cared for, healed, and helped. He doesn't scream at us and blame us; He talks to us, holds us, wipes our tears, and speaks ever so gently. He knows we are weak, wounded and frightened, and so He moves us gently and slowly, but always towards the truth.

The Serenity Prayer focuses on the main issues in recovery which are:
- learning to talk honestly with others and with God
- learning to express feelings to others and to God
- learning to trust others and God.

Three of the unstated rules that seem to be characteristic of a dysfunctional family system are: don't talk, don't feel, and don't trust. These are the same issues that keep us from speaking the truth, acknowledging and expressing our feelings, and relying on those who are trustworthy. The Serenity Prayer brings us back to the point of facing each of these issues. With God's help, we can overcome old obstacles and stand firm in the knowledge that He is able to make us new.

The Twelve Steps

The Twelve Steps are for believers and unbelievers alike. For the believer, they are steps toward restoration and spiritual maturity. For the unbeliever, they are also often the steps that lead to their salvation.

Step 1 We admit that we are powerless over certain areas of our lives, and that our lives have become unmanageable.

> I know that nothing good lives in me, that is in my sinful nature. For I have the desire to do what is good, but I cannot carry it out. Who will rescue me from this body of death? Thanks be to God— through Jesus Christ our Lord! (Romans 7:18, 24b-25a)

Step 1 is the admission of powerlessness or helplessness, the same kind of powerlessness that Paul experienced. Facing the reality of our powerlessness is the first step in the recovery process. The Serenity Prayer asks God to help us to identify what it is that we are powerless over. This is a significant step for those of us who have learned (and expect) to be in control of everything. Even admitting to ourselves that we have a problem is a drastic eye-opener. We have grown up relying on our own understanding and ability either to fix whatever is wrong, or successfully avoid the issue. But instead of admitting that we are powerless, we try to desperately hide this fact. Step 1 helps us out of denial and out of hiding and brings us into the open where we can hear ourselves admit that there are things in our lives that we can't handle, that we, in fact, can do nothing about.

Some of the addictive things that render us powerless may include: alcohol, drugs or other addictive substances; work or achievement; money— overspending, gambling or hoarding; approval-codependency; food; sex; exercise or sports; physical appearance; religiosity; perfectionism or obsessive-compulsive behaviors; or materialism. We can also experience a sense of powerlessness when it comes to the past, the future, an illness or disability, other people, and even God. It is acknowledging that we have come to the end of our willpower, we don't know what to do next and have found that the harder we have tried, the more unmanageable our lives have become.

Step 1 can also be used to address issues involving anger, shame, guilt, fear and hurts. It is the admission that we are unable to heal ourselves or to get better on our own. It is the first step in giving up the struggle and allowing God to begin to restore us to emotional health.

Simply put, Step 1 helps us to specifically identify and own the "it" that is causing us so much trouble. You can't begin to solve a problem if you don't know *what* the problem is. And you can't solve it if you don't *own* it, if you don't *admit* that the problem is yours.

Step 2 Came to believe that Jesus Christ has the power to restore us to sane, healthy thinking, emotions, and responsible behavior.

> And the God of all grace, who called you to his eternal glory in Christ, after you have suffered a little while, will himself restore you and make you strong, firm and steadfast (1 Peter 5:10).

> For God did not give us a spirit of timidity, but a spirit of power, of love and of self-discipline (2 Timothy 1:7).

Now that we have admitted what we are powerless over, we have to ask ourselves, do we believe that Jesus can and will help me? This requires an exercise of faith. It may also require realizing that some previous ideas we had about Jesus, about God, and about Christianity are entirely wrong, and must, before we go any further, be replaced by the truth. He is not out to punish or shame us; He is devoted to helping us get better. His power is extended to us to give us life, not death. He yearns to lift us up out of our weakness and to enable us to become strong.

Step 2 says "Came to believe that Jesus could restore me to sanity." It does not say I believe. It says "I came to believe." Coming to believe that Jesus has the desire and power to restore me is usually a process of small discoveries, rather than one large instantaneous revelation. So don't be upset if you find it difficult to trust Him right away. Perhaps the most difficult aspect of this process is that it entails time— time spent waiting for the results to appear. When our lives are unmanageable, waiting is usually just the thing that drives us even crazier. Hindsight gives birth to much faith; but hindsight only occurs after the passage of time. That's why believing sometimes takes time. God even helps us in our unbelief.

Step 3 Made a decision to turn our will and our lives over to the care of Jesus Christ, as Lord.

> Therefore I urge you, brothers, in view of God's mercy, to offer your bodies as living sacrifices, holy and pleasing to God — which is your spiritual worship (Romans 12:1).

> "For I know the plans I have for you," declares the Lord, "plans to prosper you and not to harm you, plans to give you hope and a future. Then you will call upon me and come and pray to me, and I will listen to you. You will seek me and find me when you seek me with all your heart" (Jeremiah 29:11-13).

As we come to believe that Jesus has the power to restore us to sane thinking, sane relationships and a sane lifestyle, we can then progress to a place where we are able to decide to submit our wills and turn our lives over to His care. Paradoxically enough, it's one thing to believe that God is all-powerful, but quite another to actually yield my will to Him and entrust my life to His care. We want to ask questions like, "What will He do with me? Where will He take me? What will He make me do?" These are all details that we would like to have settled before turning our lives over to Him. We want some guarantees, so that we can feel that we are in control again. It's hard to turn our lives over to Him, trusting that *He* will care for us. We're so afraid of being hurt, of being vulnerable, of being in despair, of being powerless.

Turning our will and our lives over to His care is a conscious, deliberate, and ongoing decision. We need to make one critical decision that begins this process, but that is not enough. We must consciously endeavor to follow a new way of life. We will have to affirm this decision many times over as we encounter and walk through difficult circumstances. But the more quickly we learn to relinquish control and rely on God's care for us, the sooner we will see our lives begin to become more manageable, stable and healthy.

"Cast all your anxiety on him because he cares for you" (1 Peter 5:7).

Step 4 Made a searching and fearless moral inventory of ourselves.

> Let us examine our ways and test them, and let us return to the Lord (Lamentations 3:40).

> Do not think of yourselves more highly than you ought, but rather think of yourself with sober judgment (Romans 12:3).

A self-inventory is simply a self-assessment. It is taking stock and making a list of our assets and liabilities. Some people misunderstand humility to mean never thinking about one's self. Humility is having a consciousness of one's defects or shortcomings as well as our strengths. It's important to know our strengths so that we can move in the gifts and talents that God has given us. It is also important to be aware of our shortcomings; areas where we need to grow and mature; areas where we are easily tempted; and areas of harmful behavior that need to be addressed.

Many problems remain impossible to solve simply because we have not bothered to take an honest look at ourselves. We should be cognizant of our feelings, motives, actions, and attitudes. To remain unaware is a form of irresponsibility. Our goal is to be teachable, open, moldable, always moving toward the truth, and doing what is right. The purpose of compiling an inventory is not to punish or blame ourselves, but to help us gain insight and understanding so that we can fully become the person that God intended us to be. The more we are able to do this, the freer we will become. We are less "weighed down" because we not only are not afraid of our shortcomings, but we are overcoming them. We thus become stronger, more proactive, more creative and more courageous. We are always more effective if we operate from a place of honesty, strength and confidence than from a place of ignorance, avoidance and fear. Truth does set us free and enables us to live fully.

It is significant that Step 4 uses the adjective "fearless" to describe this moral inventory that we must make. There can be no denying that it will take a good amount of courage to look at ourselves honestly, to invite feedback from others, and to take a hard, realistic look at what our weaknesses are. It is only as we objectively examine our heart attitudes and outward behavior, considering how we affect those around us, that we can begin to see the necessity for, and actively to embrace, change.

Change is invariably painful at first, but the results are extremely freeing and rewarding later. Doing fourth-step work is a tough beginning that introduces us to our own humanity; and if we can own our humanity (our uniqueness with its imperfections), then we have begun to live freely and without fear.

It is interesting to note that when we do twelve-step work with groups, many group members drop out at the pivotal fourth step. But those who make it past Steps 4 and 5 stand a good chance of learning to be at peace with themselves as they grow into a greater understanding of what it means to be a human being living in grace.

Step 5 Admitted to God, to ourselves, and to another human being the exact nature of our wrongs.

> Therefore confess your sins to each other and pray for each other so that you may be healed (James 5:16).

> God is spirit, and his worshipers must worship in spirit and in truth (John 4:24).

God never calls us only to an intellectual understanding of His principles; He calls us to action. James writes, "Do not merely listen to the word, and so deceive yourselves. Do what it says" (James 1:22). God wants our words and our deeds to be mutually consistent. Too often, we excuse our shortcomings by saying, "I know I am impatient, critical, unreliable, etc., and should do something about it." Acknowledging our shortcomings is easy; changing is work.

We begin with our words. We admit to God, to ourselves, and to someone else the specifics of our faults and failures. Admitting the worst about ourselves to an appropriate and trustworthy confidant eases the burden of guilt and secrecy and frees us up to move on to change. We actually hear ourselves admit out loud where we have gone wrong, how we have offended others, and how we are harming ourselves. If you have never done this before, it is a surprisingly therapeutic experience. To fail to do Step 5 is refusing to come out of our safety boxes. That strong denial, reinforced by pride, will prevent growth. Humility is the primary attitude that allows for the degree of honesty necessary to successfully accomplish Step 5.

Step 6 Were ready to have God remove these defects of character.

> If we confess our sins, he is faithful and just and will forgive us our sins and purify us from all unrighteousness (1 John 1:9).

Steps 6 and 7 are closely related. Step 6 is the "getting ready" stage. We are saying that we're ready to be different. It's one thing to agree that a change is necessary and desirable, but it is another thing to be ready for that change.

So often we prematurely jump into something before we are ready. A diet is a good example. We may know that we need to go on a diet. We may agree that we should lose weight. But we will not be successful at it until we are actually ready. We are ready when our *thoughts*, our *emotions* and our *wills* are aligned. Too often we know we should be different and may feel guilty that we aren't, but if we don't have the desire, lasting change will not happen.

We must therefore be honest. Do I just want to feel less guilty or do I want to be a different person? Why do I want to be different— just to please other people or because I really believe in what I am doing? Do I just think I should change or do I really want to change? Do I just want to avoid punishment or am I really ready to ask God to change me?

Step 7 Humbly asked Him to remove our shortcomings.

> Blessed are those who hunger and thirst for righteousness, for they will be filled (Matthew 5:6).

Step 7 is the "action" step where we humbly ask God to begin to remove our shortcomings. Sometimes (not often) this is neat and easy. God may actually remove a harmful desire. We have seen this occasionally with those who have been miraculously delivered from addictions to alcohol or other drugs. However, this is the exception and not the rule; and most of the time, self-discipline and humility are required to effect change. God will remove our shortcomings by allowing us to see how we affect others, by sending us feedback from others, and by having others confront us. Usually God does not force enlightenment; He allows us to decide to seek His ways.

Step 8 Made a list of all persons we had harmed, and became willing to make amends to them all.

Do to others as you would have them do to you (Luke 6:31).

Step 8 serves as the preparation for the action of Step 9. An *amend* is "righting the wrong." It means fixing what we have broken, replacing what we have stolen, mending what we have torn, rebuilding what we have destroyed. Sometimes this may mean that we have to make financial restitution, return what is not ours, ask for forgiveness, and begin to do the things that are right. Making restitution for things that we have or have not done is acting on our beliefs; it enables us to gain a clear conscience.

Step 9 Made direct amends to such people wherever possible, except when to do so would injure them or others.

Therefore, if you are offering your gift at the altar and there remember that your brother has something against you, leave your gift there in front of the altar. First go and be reconciled to your brother; then come and offer your gift (Matthew 5:23-24).

Step 9 takes a lot of wisdom and a tremendous amount of courage. Making amends in relationships is not simple. It takes time to rebuild trust and respect. It is unrealistic to expect someone to quickly forgive and to lovingly respond to us when we seek to make amends for injuries committed over a long period of time. Trust reappears only after we have earned it again, and we can't expect this to happen overnight. We must be prepared to go far beyond an apology. Often, people desire to change solely in order to win the other person back; and when that fails, they return to their old ways. We need to be convinced of our wrong and be determined to truly change because it is the right thing to do. We must be prepared to do what is right and responsible, regardless of whether others respond as we would like them to respond. We must also realize that rebuilding relationships is a delicate task, and that sometimes, our effort may simply be too little, too late. The extent of the damage we have done is simply too great to rectify apart from a miracle of God.

There are times when it might be inappropriate to go back into a situation because it may cause more harm than good. It is important to examine our motives, and to be sure that we don't use this as an excuse to avoid making amends. If we have serious questions about making amends with a particular person, it may be wise to seek advice from a trained counselor.

Step 10 Continued to take personal inventory and when we were wrong, promptly admitted it.

> Humble yourselves before the Lord, and he will lift you up (James 4:10).

> Search me, O God, and know my heart; test me and know my anxious thoughts. See if there is any offensive way in me, and lead me in the way everlasting (Psalm 139:23-24).

It is impossible to change everything all at once. Changing (transformation) is an ongoing process of living. It is easier to keep a house in order by cleaning it weekly than cleaning it once a year. And so it is with our personal housecleaning. In order to be mature, we must daily be mindful of our attitudes and actions, promptly admit our mistakes, and willingly do what we can to make things right when we have done wrong.

Step 11 Sought through prayer and meditation to improve our conscious contact with God, praying only for knowledge of His will for us and the power to carry that out.

If any of you lacks wisdom, he should ask God, who gives generously to all without finding fault, and it will be given to him (James 1:5).

This step has three parts to it: seeking to improve our awareness and relationship with God; praying for knowledge of His will; and asking for the power to do what He has shown us.

Maturity in our relationship with God comes from desiring to know Him and to follow Him every day in every aspect of our lives. Too often, we become negligent and only seek His help when we find ourselves embroiled in a crisis. We fail to pray regularly about work, relationships, family, our future, major purchases, and what He may want us to do. Step 11 encourages us to seek His will for *ourselves*, not for everyone else.

Once He has shown us what is right in a given situation, we may feel afraid or inadequate to follow through. Asking for His power to carry it out places us in a position to rely on His strength to enable us. This is how we come to know that God is faithful, reliable, and, best of all, He is for us, not against us.

Step 12 Having had a spiritual awakening as the result of these steps, we tried to carry this message to others and to practice these principles in all our affairs.

In the same way, let your light shine before men, that they may see your good deeds and praise your Father in heaven (Matthew 5:16).

Brothers, if someone is caught in a sin, you who are spiritual should restore him gently. But watch yourself, or you also may be tempted (Galatians 6:1).

A genuine spiritual experience occurs when we come into an awareness and acceptance of Jesus as Savior and a surrender to Him as Lord. Awakening to the fact that our God does in fact care about every aspect of our lives helps us to realize that He cares for us and loves us, no matter what we have done or are even doing now. We can believe that God really wants to establish an intimate relationship with us whereby we can become whole and experience life abundantly in order to fulfill the very purpose for which He created us.

When we discover such a truth— that God exists and that He loves us— we naturally desire to share this message with others around us. To help others come to know Him as we have come to know Him is the most satisfying experience we can have.

Processing the Twelve Steps is a beautiful way to come to *know* Jesus Christ. Throughout these steps, we experience His presence, His forgiveness, His healing, His guidance, His richness, and His truths.

CLOSING PRAYERS

Portions of Psalm 51

Have mercy on me, O God,
according to your unfailing love;
according to your great compassion
blot out my transgressions.
Wash away all my iniquity
and cleanse me from my sin.

Cleanse me with hyssop, and I will be clean;
wash me, and I will be whiter than snow.

Let me hear joy and gladness;
let the bones you have crushed rejoice.
Hide your face from my sins and blot out
all my iniquity.

Create in me a pure heart, O God,
and renew a steadfast spirit within me.

Restore to me the joy of your salvation
and grant me a willing spirit, to sustain me.

Then I will teach transgressors your ways,
and sinners will turn back to you.

Paul's Prayers
paraphrased from Philippians 1:9-10
and Colossians 1:9-14.

And this is my prayer:
that our love may abound more and more
in knowledge and depth of insight,
so that we may be able to discern what is best.

God, we ask that You fill us with the knowledge

of Your will
through all spiritual wisdom and understanding.
And we pray this in order that
we may live a life worthy of You
and may please You in every way;
bearing fruit in every good work,
growing in knowledge of You,
being strengthened with all power according to
Your glorious might
so that we may have great endurance and patience,
and joyfully giving thanks to You, Father,
for You have qualified us to share in the inheritance
of the saints
in the kingdom of light.

For You have rescued us from the dominion of darkness
and brought us into the kingdom of the Son whom
You love,
in whom we have redemption, the forgiveness of sins.

AMEN !

Chapter Eight Endnotes

[1]Deborah J. Pope-Lance and Joan Chamberlain Engelsman in the *Guide for Clergy on the Problems of Domestic Violence*, (New Jersey Department of Community Affairs, 1990), p. 5.

[2]From presentation to Pan-American Health Organization, May 22, 1989, (quoted in *Guide for Clergy on the Problems of Domestic Violence*, 1990), p. 4.

[3]Rich Buhler, *Pain and Pretending* (Nashville: Thomas Nelson Publishers, 1988), p. 64.

[4]Dr. Margaret Rinck, *Can Christians Love Too Much?* (Grand Rapids, Michigan: Pyranee Books, Zondervan Publishing House, 1989), p. 60.

[5]Dale and Juanita Ryan, *Recovery from Addictions* (Downers Grove, Illinois: Life Recovery Guides, InterVarsity Press, 1990), p. 11.

[6]Ibid.

[7]Ibid.

[8]Ibid.

[9]David Elkind, *All Grown Up and No Place to Go*, (Reading,

Massachusetts: Addison-Wesley Publishing Company, 1984), pp. 3-4.

[10]Stephen R. Covey, *The Seven Habits of Highly Effective People* (New York: Simon and Schuster, 1989), p. 18.

[11]Dale and Juanita Ryan, *Recovery from Addictions,* p. 3.

APPENDIX

Tools for Understanding

Healing and restoration come through self-awareness and understanding of your point of view and resulting responses to life's situations. We unconsciously learn patterns of relationships and behavior from watching our parents, who learned their patterns from their parents. If our parents were appropriately responsible, we learned responsible behavior. However, in those areas where our parents tended to behave inconsistently or immaturely, we learned to think and act immaturely.

There are two tools which have proven to be very useful and practical for self-awareness and understanding, the *life line* and the *genogram*. A life line is a tool used to document what we personally have been through and the genogram (genealogy diagram) is used to document what the family has been through. The life line puts down in visual form the major events that have occurred in our lives to date. The genogram is a systematic way of uncovering family patterns that influence how we function in our current roles and relationships.

It is impossible to fix a problem if you don't know what the problem is or why it keeps happening. Once we see our individual and family patterns, it is easier to move on to healthier ways of living.

The Life Line

A life line is a chronological list of important events that have impacted one's life. For example: Elizabeth.

FIGURE 16 — ELIZABETH'S LIFE LINE

AGE	EXPERIENCES
4	• Sister born with physical handicap
7	• 1st of six moves in 12 years
10	• Grandma's death
16	• High school
	Began with good grades
	Tennis
	Parents separated, filed for divorce,
	but moved back together (very tense)
	Forced to change schools
	• Became rebellious, poor grades
18	• Community College 2 years
20	• Married Mark
22	• 1st of several miscarriages
25	• 2nd miscarriage
	• Son, Steve, born
27	• 3rd miscarriage
	• Daughter, Donna, born
	• Bought first home
	• Bought larger home
32	• Mark (husband) quite ill — off work 6 months
36	• Layoffs, Mark without real work for 1 year
37	• Dad heart attack — retired disability
	• (Mom becoming more dependent on Elizabeth)
44	• Very depressed, sought counseling

Significant events would include things such as:

- circumstances of one's birth
- school experiences: academic performance/ activities/ friends
- strong emotions: stress, anger, rage, depression, fear, insecurity
- impact of the birth of siblings
- relationship to siblings
- state of health (allergies, illnesses, surgeries, accidents)
- losses (friends moving away, deaths, miscarriages, abortions)
- traumatic experiences (abuse, incest, rape, addictions, accidents)
- relocations
- dating experiences
- financial status of the family
- employment (type of work, number of jobs, terminations, satisfaction level)
- religious/spiritual life

When we sit down and look at our own life line, we view our experiences on a piece of paper. Seeing how many experiences we have had in a given period of time may help to explain the level of stress that we have been living with. It may also explain why we may feel tired, confused, depressed, hurt or overwhelmed.

The Genogram

A genogram is a diagram of a family tree that identifies the family members and their relationships to each other. It helps to shed light as to why family traits and styles (both healthy and dysfunctional) repeat themselves from one generation to another. The value in using the genogram is that you can quickly see the cast of characters with their patterns of behavior, relationship dynamics, problems, and issues. It helps you to see yourself in the context of the larger picture.

In order to gather some of the information to complete the genogram you may need to seek out parents, grandparents, or other family members. This may be difficult to do. Your relatives may be scattered all over the country. However, doing a genogram may be just the thing that would help to revive a lost sense of family.

A genogram should show life realistically, including good times and bad times; celebrations and tragedies; births and deaths; successes and failures. We should avoid dressing up the family tree in order to make it look good (as we do when we are having our pictures taken). It should record things like illnesses, moves, abuse, temperaments, addictions, divorces, deaths, accidents, bankruptcy, or other events or patterns that have had a significant impact on the family. The purpose of filling out a genogram is to paint a multi-generational picture that helps you see your position in a broader scheme of history thus lending understanding of yourself and what your family has been through.

For almost everyone, this process leads to discovering information previously unknown, such as facts like the following: My aunt's real name was Gertrude. I didn't know that my mother had a sister that was stillborn or that Mom had so many miscarriages. Aunt Suzy is a diabetic. Dad almost died from pneumonia. Grandpa lost everything in the Depression. Uncle Bob was an alcoholic. And we may discover things that are dreadfully painful, such as incidences of incest, rape, violence, suicide, alcoholism, jail sentence, homosexuality, or mental illness. Though uncomfortable, these facts are nonetheless important because they may explain some of the patterns that have occurred in the life of your family.

How to Complete a Genogram

To begin, get a large piece of paper and draw Figure 17. Record the data about each individual on the genogram. If you run out of room on the genogram use a separate piece of paper.

Siblings are listed in order starting with the oldest child being listed to the left of the marriage line. Record the following data that is applicable: complete names, dates (birth, marriages, death, divorces, relocations), jobs, major illnesses, religion, and other important life events (crises, tragedies).

FIGURE 17 – GENOGRAM SYMBOLS

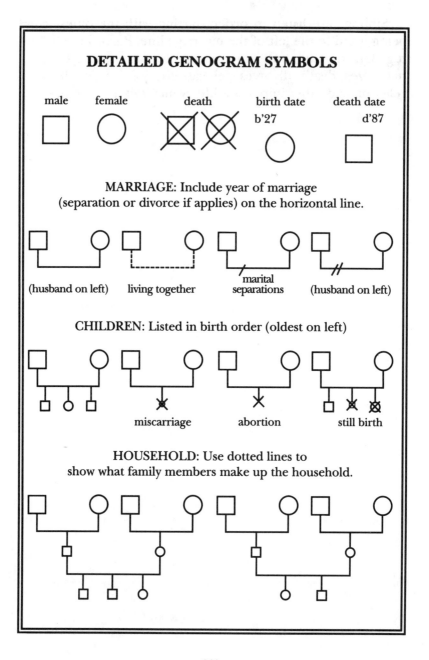

DETAILED GENOGRAM SYMBOLS

male   female   death   birth date   death date
b'27   d'87

MARRIAGE: Include year of marriage
(separation or divorce if applies) on the horizontal line.

(husband on left)   living together   marital separations   (husband on left)

CHILDREN: Listed in birth order (oldest on left)

miscarriage   abortion   still birth

HOUSEHOLD: Use dotted lines to
show what family members make up the household.

FIGURE 18 — GENOGRAM EXAMPLE

Example #1: Elizabeth's Genogram

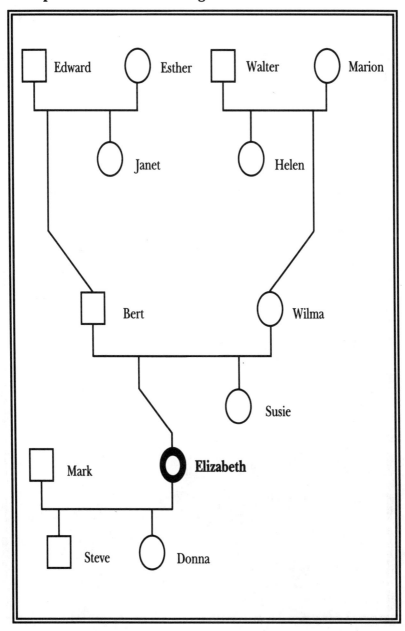

FIGURE 19 – ROGER'S GENOGRAM

Example #2: Roger Adams

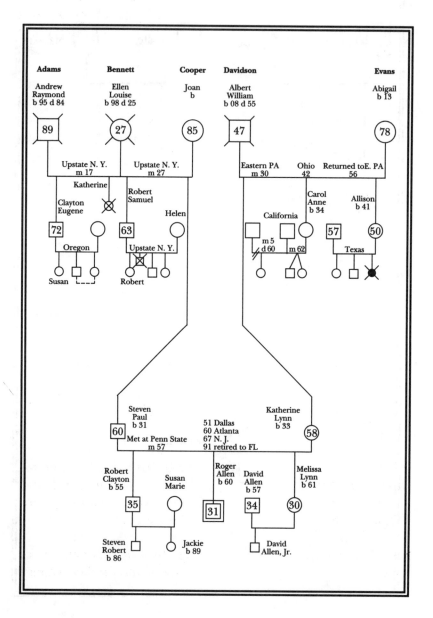

The following statements can be made by reading Roger's genogram:

Roger is the middle child. His father, Steven, is the youngest of three boys. The first wife (Ellen) of Steven's father (Andrew Raymond) died giving birth. Katherine was stillborn. Roger's paternal grandmother is living with uncle Robert and Aunt Helen in upstate N.Y.

Roger's mother is the oldest of three children. His Aunt Carol is divorced and remarried; her second husband adopted her son. They later had a pair of fraternal twins. His Aunt Allison has two children and her miscarriage was a baby girl.

Example # 3 Paula

Paula's case study illustrates how the genogram can help us to understand how a tragedy from the past can affect a person in the present.

Paula, a college sophomore, attended a local church and was active in the college fellowship group. During a share time, she broke down in tears that she had "lost a brother." After the group meeting was over, the minister suggested that Paula make an appointment to see him.

At their meeting, the minister began making a rough genogram. (See Figure 20.)

Upon noting that Paula's grandfather and brother had died within a few months of each other, the minister helped Paula construct a genogram that would represent the family's experience of that particular year. (See Figure 21.)

"I didn't realize how close together all this happened." Paula saw that her life had undergone several radical changes

FIGURE 20 – ROUGH GENOGRAM, PAULA'S FAMILY

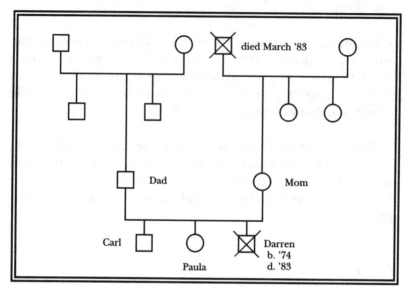

FIGURE 21 – PAULA'S FAMILY IN 1983

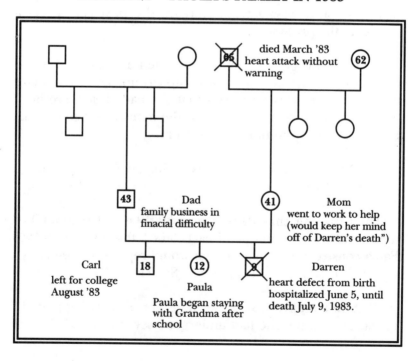

in a relatively short period of time and was nearly overwhelmed by this unexpected transformation.

In discussing the events of that year, it was apparent that the family had been in shock from the deaths and busy trying to keep the business afloat. Paula had been left on her own to grieve. She had no one to help her sort through the confusing messages she heard. ("Don't cry." "It's God's will." "You shouldn't be upset." "Be strong for your mother." "We shouldn't mourn, because they are with the Lord, and we will see them again.")

Even though these events had taken place eight years before, Paula realized that she had never really grieved over them. She had never been given permission to grieve over the loss of her brother and grandfather. It was such a relief to hear that the mixed emotions — anxiety, anger, confusion and depression — that she were experiencing was perfectly understandable.

Example #4 Bill and Janet

Both Bill and Janet were frustrated in their marriage. Janet insisted that they seek counseling with a counselor. Her presenting problem was that Bill was being irresponsible in many ways and she often complained, "I have to do everything!"

The counselor began the session by completing a genogram. In the process of getting the information, Bill started to feel more comfortable and even laughed about how he was almost named after Uncle Marion Milhouse Montrose III.

FIGURE 22 – BILL AND JANET'S GENOGRAM
(simplified version)

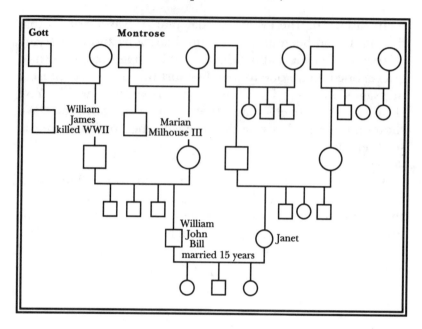

After filling in the basic data, the counselor began directing questions to Bill, eliciting information about his family, what was it like having three older brothers and sisters; being named after a "hero" (he was named after his dad's brother, who had been killed in World War II); how Dad's excessive traveling affected the family; and other details about growing up in the Gott household.

For Janet, questions included: What was it like being the oldest? Were you expected to take care of the other children? Were you given unfair responsibility? Which parent did the disciplining in your family?

In discussing how their parents handled conflict, they discovered (with the counselor's help) that they handled conflict in much the same way as their parents. Janet saw how she tended to be over-responsible and critical, jumping in quickly to take over any time Bill didn't carry out some task as quickly as she wanted him to. Bill was able to talk about his tendency to shy away from conflict, much as his father did. By seeing the issue as a pattern, it was not as threatening. The genogram was an effective tool for neutralizing an otherwise very touchy subject. It became easier to talk about the issue at hand, rather than the persons involved.

Bill had anticipated that he would be blamed for their problems, expecting that Janet wanted the counselor to take her side. As it turned out, Bill and Janet left the session feeling better understood and even hopeful because the counselor helped them to see the family *system* rather than just the presenting problem.

Over the next few months, Bill and Janet continued to work with their counselor on these issues and their effect on child-rearing. Janet was much more strict with the children than Bill liked, and he would often side with the kids against her. Again, by looking at his family of origin, Bill saw that since his dad traveled extensively, almost all of the responsibility for discipline had fallen to his mom. He remembered very few times that his father had corrected him. Without this awareness, Bill would have just continued the pattern. Now that his part is identified, he can consciously choose a better approach to the problem.

With a great deal of effort and hard work, and sound guidance from their counselor, Bill and Janet were able to talk more openly about their expectations of each other and were able to come to some agreement about their roles in parenting the children. Although there continued to be tension within the marriage, it was not as pronounced because of the awareness and understanding they both had gained. One good skill they learned was to address the *issue*, rather than to attack the *person*. This, by itself, relieved a great deal of the tension between them.

Putting information, including the presenting problem, down on paper can help to neutralize and depersonalize an extremely sensitive subject. It helps to get the problem off the persons involved and set it on a neutral piece of paper, where a more objective look is possible. Also, seeing the problem within its context lends perspective to the painful situation at hand.

Questions for More Insight

As we discuss our family history a clear picture begins to emerge as to how the family members each deal with crisis. Patterns (e.g., style of communication, defense mechanisms used, abuse, addictions) become apparent, revealing core issues such as commitment, trust, respect, control, problem-solving skills and responsibility. How the family reacts in crisis is the key indicator of the family member's maturity.

The following is an exhaustive list of categories and questions that we can use in gaining a fuller understanding of our background. You may find it helpful to write down your thoughts and impressions.

Family Members and Other Important People

- Describe each individual (positive and negative traits) in your immediate family (parents, siblings). Describe how you feel toward them.
- Describe your extended family (grandparents, aunts, uncles, cousins). What, if any particular feelings do you have about these relatives? To whom did you feel close? Was there anyone in particular that you strongly liked or disliked (felt uncomfortable with)?
- Has anyone else ever lived with your immediate family?
- Who were the important non-family individuals who were involved with you or your family?

Dynamic Events and Impact Issues

- Dynamic events include:
    - births, unwanted pregnancies
    - handicaps, disabilities, serious injuries
    - abortions, miscarriages, stillbirths
    - deaths
    - serious illnesses
    - family moves
    - job changes, changes of financial status
    - one or both parents in school
    - separations, divorces, extra-marital affairs

- Impact issues
    - addictions (alcohol, drugs, gambling, spending, eating)
    - abuse (physical, sexual, verbal, emotional)
    - lawsuits, criminal record
    - mental illness, clinical depression
    - absentee parent due to career
    - large financial debts or pressure
    - military service
    - layoffs, firings

- Delicate issues
    - Were you ever sexually fondled as a child by anyone inside or outside the family?
    - Are there any periods of life you cannot remember?
    - Did your parents consistently display disapproval to you regarding your appearance, abilities, or behaviors?
    - Were you subjected to ridicule or shame?
    - Did family members of the opposite sex maintain appropriate modesty or did they undress in front of each other?
    - Was bed-wetting a problem? If so, were you shamed for it?

- How did the family respond to a crisis?
  - How did each family member react to a crisis? (hysterical, calm, rational, blaming, focused on other things)
  - Did the family cooperate during times of crisis or did they attack each other? Focus on the real problem or become diverted by being busy with other things? If applicable, did each individual own up to his/her own responsibility or did the family designate a scapegoat on whom to blame everything?
  - Who became responsible and took care of a crisis?
  - Who felt the weight of the stress— was it shared or did one person carry all the responsibility?
  - Was everything a crisis? Did your family create crisis where there was none?
  - In times of crisis, did the family tend to make rational or emotional decisions?
  - Was the family open to seeking outside help for its problems?
  - What has been the family's experience with doctors, lawyers, or other professionals?

You and Your Family

- Describe yourself in relation to the family.
  - In your opinion, which family member are you most like? How?
  - What are your strengths and weaknesses?
  - Which family members do others compare you to?
  - Which family member differs the most from you? How?
  - To whom did you feel closest?
  - From whom do you feel the greatest distance?

- Your Parents
  - How did your parents meet? How long did they know each other before their marriage? What was their parents' reaction?
  - Looking back, how did you perceive your parents' relationship? Were they affectionate?
  - How did they handle decisions and disagreements?

- Family atmosphere
  - What kind of adjectives describe your family? (distant, close, strong-willed, together, warm, cold, indifferent)
  - Who had the power in the family? How was this power exerted and how did others deal with it?
  - Who was the "life" of the family, that is who "energized" the family?

- Nuclear Family Unit
  - How many times a week did your family eat together?
  - Did you hold family discussions? How often and for what purpose?
  - What kind of play time did the family have and what games or activities did the family enjoy together?
  - Family vacations— what were they like, how often, with whom?
  - Did the family worship together?
  - Did family members spend time sitting and talking with each other?
  - How much television did you watch?
  - What activities separated the family unit? How many times a week?

Communication

- Parents
  - Could you only discuss certain topics with only one parent?
  - If you had a personal problem, which parent would you go to and why?
  - Were you:

encouraged	or	criticized
endeared	or	just there
important	or	a bother
guided	or	punished?

  - When you talked, did you feel you were really listened to?
  - Were there certain subjects that were forbidden to be discussed?
  - Could parents admit their mistakes or were they always right?
  - Were you allowed to discuss your parents' decisions with them?
  - How did your parents express disappointment in your behavior?
  - Did your parents provide a "safe" atmosphere for discussion?
  - How did you and your siblings manipulate your parents to get what you wanted? (We all know how creative kids can be at this.)

- Emotions
  - How was anger expressed by each family member?
  - Were there certain feelings that could be expressed only if they were justified?
  - What emotions were allowed to be displayed? What emotions were unacceptable?
  - How did each parent attempt to motivate each one in the family? Did they use blame, guilt, shame, encouragement, intimidation, threat, modeling, discussion, apprenticing?

- How was affection expressed?
- What were the double-binds or mixed messages that existed in your family? (see Communication, page 134)

- Problem solving
  - Were problems discussed or were they ignored?
  - Did someone have to be blamed for a problem?
  - Who was excused from having to be responsible?
  - If a decision affected the whole family, did each family member have input in the decision?

Rules and Roles

- What were some of the spoken rules within the family? (first things first; let your parents know where you are; be on time; phone if you are going to be late; answer when called; homework before TV; you are going to college; you're on your own at 18; you will go to church; we have to meet your friends; no opposite sex friends in the house unless a parent is home)
- What were some of the unspoken rules in your family? (don't: play, ask questions, cry, enjoy, trust, fail, succeed, let us down, be close, fight, speak up, feel, tell anyone, grow up)
- Were there double standards— behaviors that were okay for some family members but not for others? (spending money, school, career, leisure activities, display of anger)
- Was one parent the disciplinarian and the other lenient?
- Were rules a reaction to an event (made after a problem surfaced) or were they preset (anticipating possible problems)?

- Were rules overly demanding or permissive; arbitrary or consistently enforced; clear or vague? Were consequences inappropriate or did the punishment fit the crime?
- Did you feel rules were designed for the best interest of the children or were they too often made for the sake of what was convenient?
- What were the roles that family members (especially the children) had?
    - Which family members tended to have which of the following roles: the smart one, the clown, the black sheep, the peacemaker, the caretaker, the hero?
    - Were some labeled: sick, talented, attractive, very responsible, carefree, or clumsy?
    - Were some designated to be professional or career-oriented and some expected to always be at home?
    - Did any of the children parent the parents?
    - How were these roles and expectations communicated? What happened when family members tried to change their roles?

Is there a Current Problem?

- Have you sought help at this time?
- How long has this been a problem?
- Who else knows about the problem?
- How do they view it?
- How have they responded to the situation or the fact that you are seeking help?
- Who else in the family has had similar problems?
- How have you tried to solve this problem so far? What (if anything) has helped?

BIBLIOGRAPHY

Augsberger, David. *Caring Enough to Confront*. Ventura, CA: Regal Books, 1983.

Balswick, Jack O. and Judith K. *The Family, A Christian Perspective on the Contemporary Home*. Grand Rapids: Baker, 1989.

Barclay, William. *The Gospel of Matthew, Volume 1*. Philadelphia: Westminster Press, 1975.

Barnard, Charles P. and Ramon Garrido Corrales. *The Theory and Technique of Family Therapy*. Springfield, IL: Charles C. Thomas, Publisher, 1979.

Beck, Aaron. *Love Is Never Enough*. New York: Harper-Collins Publishers, Inc., 1989.

Buhler, Rich. *Pain and Pretending*. Nashville: Thomas Nelson Publishers, 1988.

Bustanoby, Andre. *Just Talk to Me*. Grand Rapids: Zondervan Publishing House, 1981.

Corey, Gerald. *Theory and Practices of Counseling and Psychotherapy*. Monterey, CA: Brooks/Cole Publishing, 1982.

Covey, Stephen R. *The Seven Habits of Highly Effective People*. New York: Simon and Schuster, 1989.

Elkind, David. *All Grown Up and No Place to Go*. Reading, MA: Addison-Wesley Publishing Company, 1984.

Heald, Cynthia. *The Creator My Confidant*. Colorado Springs: Navpress, 1987.

Lerner, Harriet Goldhor. *Dance of Intimacy*. New York: Harper and Row, 1989.

McGee, Robert S. *The Search For Significance*. Houston: Rapha Publishing, 1987.

Nee, Watchman. *A Table In The Wilderness – Daily Meditations*. Wheaton, IL: Tyndale House, 1978.

Peterson, Eugene H., *Traveling Light*. Colorado Springs: Helmers and Howard, 1988.

Rinck, Margaret, *Can Christians Love Too Much?* Grand Rapids: Pyranee Books, Zondervan Publishing House, 1989.

_____. *Christian Men Who Hate Women*. Grand Rapids: Pyranee Books, Zondervan Publishing House, 1990.

Ryan, Dale and Juanita. *Recovery from Addictions*. Life Recovery Guides. Downers Grove, IL: InterVarsity Press, 1990.

Smedes, Lewis B. *Love Within Limits*. Grand Rapids: William B. Eerdmans Publishing Company, 1978.

_____. *Shame and Grace*. New York: Zondervan Publishing House, division of Harper-Collins, 1993.

Springle, Pat. *Codependency, Emerging from the Eclipse.* Houston: Rapha Publishing, 1989.

Swindoll, Charles R. *Strike the Original Match.* Portland, OR: Multnomah Press, 1982.

Thurman, Chris. *The Lies We Believe.* Nashville: Thomas Nelson Publishers, 1989.

Wright, Norman H. *Training Christians to Counsel.* Eugene, OR: Harvest House Publishers, 1977.

———. *Crisis Counseling.* San Bernardino, CA: Here's Life Publishers, 1985.

PRAISE FOR *THE RIDE*

"[A] riveting story of the r-- ͐
human spirit . .
—Sister Helen Prejean,

"A loud and memorable ͐
unbearable tragedy with ͐   ͺɑssion."
—John Walsh, host of A, ... Most Wanted

"In tracing one man's journey beyond violence, Brian MacQuarrie's
excellent book becomes a chronicle of hope for us all."
—David Kaczynski, brother of the Unabomber and executive director
of New Yorkers Against the Death Penalty

"An absolutely gripping story. . . . Brian MacQuarrie is masterful in
finding the humanity and light in such darkness."
—Michael Connelly, best-selling author of
The Scarecrow and *The Brass Verdict*

"This book—ultimately a book about hope—promises to
change all who read it."
—Michael Patrick MacDonald, author of *All Souls* and *Easter Rising*

"*The Ride* is a powerful affirmation of life. . . . It is not a pretty story,
but it is a beautiful story, and MacQuarrie tells it the right way."
—Dan Barry, author of *Pull Me Up* and *City Lights*

"An engrossing page-turner on the worst—and best—humanity
has to offer. Redemption instead of revenge as a grace note
in a world of hurt."
—Gerard O'Neill, coauthor of *Black Mass*

"A first-rate combination of true crime and social history."
—*Kirkus Reviews*

"This is a gripping, unusual true crime tale, likely to move readers
to tears and sure to inspire personal contemplation."
—*Publishers Weekly*

"If you have an interest in the question
of putting people to death, read it."
—*The Federal Lawyer*

THE
RIDE

*The Jeffrey Curley Murder
and Its Aftermath*

BRIAN MACQUARRIE

DA CAPO PRESS
A Member of the Perseus Books Group

Designed by Pauline Brown
Set in 11.5 point Fairfield Light by the Perseus Books Group

Library of Congress Cataloging-in-Publication Data

MacQuarrie, Brian.
  The ride : a shocking murder and a bereaved father's journey from rage to redemption / Brian MacQuarrie.
       p. cm.
  Includes index.
  ISBN 978-0-306-81626-0 (alk. paper)
  1. Curley, Bob. 2. Fathers of murder victims—Massachusetts—Boston—Biography. 3. Curley, Jeffrey, d. 1997. 4. Murder victims—Massachusetts—Boston—Case studies. I. Title.
  HV6533.M4M32 2009
  364.152'3092—dc22
  [B]
                                                    2008055397

PB ISBN: 978-0-306-81872-1

First Da Capo Press paperback edition 2010
First Da Capo Press edition 2009

Published by Da Capo Press
A Member of the Perseus Books Group
www.dacapopress.com

Da Capo Press books are available at special discounts for bulk purchases in the U.S. by corporations, institutions, and other organizations. For more information, please contact the Special Markets Department at the Perseus Books Group, 2300 Chestnut Street, Suite 200, Philadelphia, PA 19103, or call (800) 810-4145, ext. 5000, or e-mail special.markets@perseusbooks.com.

10 9 8 7 6 5 4 3 2 1

To the Curley family
and to all missing children.

CONTENTS

Prologue   1

1 Inman Square   3

2 A Ride to Hell   25

3 The Face of Evil   51

4 The Long Journey Home   79

5 Storm at the State House   103

6 Uncharted Ground   135

7 Collateral Damage   153

8 Questions and Beginnings   167

9 Resurrection   195

10 The Road Home   217

11 Into the Light   237

Epilogue   253

Notes   255
Acknowledgments   259
Index   263

Illustrations follow page 160

vii

Prologue

HUNDREDS OF PEOPLE huddled in the autumn air, waiting for the words of a grieving, shattered family. Parents held their children, mouthed a prayer, or simply hugged their numbed neighbors in a communal search for solace. Bob Curley, a Fire Department mechanic, approached a bank of microphones and looked into the stunned and disbelieving faces of East Cambridge, a community shaken to its core by his son's horrific death.

The unthinkable had happened here.

Bob had never spoken to a large group before. But today, with a compelling natural eloquence, he issued a chilling warning, coupled with a loud call for action.

"My Jeffrey's not going to feel no more pain," Bob said, his voice clear, angry, and commanding. "But my Jeffrey died with the heart of a lion. I know that. And that's why God put this on us. Because we're gonna take it, and we're gonna go forward, and all you people remember this!"

Bob's neighbors nodded, many of their faces lined with tears. Children who could not understand this agitated man, but were frightened by his rage, tugged their mothers a little closer.

"Remember Jeffrey!" Bob said. "Remember the pain you feel now! Remember how scared you are now! We'll all stand tall as a community, and we'll work to change the laws. We'll work to keep maggots like this away from our children."

The time had come to bring the death penalty back to Massachusetts, Bob ranted, in the opening salvo of a bitter, personal crusade that would radically transform his life.

"God love you all," Bob concluded, his voice cracking with emotion. "Thank you so much. It's been so hard."

————

$\underline{\qquad}$ 1 $\underline{\qquad}$

Inman Square

BOB CURLEY rolled out of bed, tossed a glance toward the Boston skyline three miles away, and dressed for another day's work at the Cambridge Fire Department. There would be no dawdling for Bob, a broad-shouldered, good-looking man with thick brown hair, glinting blue eyes, and the no-nonsense look of this edgy neighborhood, where grit was as embedded in its men as in its cracked and crumbling sidewalks.

Bob hustled out the door at 6:45 A.M., only a quarter hour after waking up and less than two miles from the firehouse, where he and another mechanic repaired and prepped the ladder, hose, and pumper trucks that raced through one of the most densely populated cities in the country.

The morning was October 1, 1997, a warm, Indian summer Wednesday when New England was awash in a season-bridging spectacle of color.

Bob, at forty-two, commuted to work on a battered bicycle, coasting down a steep hill from his new home in East Somerville, a curmudgeonly cousin to the Inman Square streets where he was raised and now worked. At the bottom of the descent, Bob blocked out the jarring sound of heavy trucks bouncing in and out of gaping potholes and banked hard into a right-hand turn.

There, Bob entered what he called "the ghetto," an unsightly stretch of ungroomed growth pocked by jagged, uneven pavement; honking, impatient traffic; and a hilly warren of narrow, one-way streets. Focusing on the pedals, not the panorama,

Bob passed a grimy repair shop, a Brazilian church, the tired facade of Buddy's Diner, and half-organized graveyards for used
auto parts, where old mufflers and piles of rusting radiators lay
stacked against the neglected sides of sagging buildings.

Just after a confusing slalom of twists and turns through
Union Square, Bob rose from his bicycle seat, legs pumping like
pistons, to scale a short, tough incline beside the commuter-rail
tracks. Atop the crest, breathing hard, Bob cruised through a
cheek-by-jowl neighborhood of modest, two-story, wooden homes,
a well-tended place of front-yard Madonnas and corner stores
that had yet to fall victim to the gentrification creeping through
Greater Boston's blue-collar core.

Finally, after catching his breath, Bob veered left on Springfield Street several blocks away, where he could see the Renais-
sance design, graceful bay doors, and soaring bell tower of the
century-old Inman Square firehouse. And near the square, where
scraps of early-morning litter blew across a junction of six chaotic
city streets, a small sidewalk sign marked the indistinguishable
boundary between Cambridge and Somerville.

Here, in Inman Square, Bob had matured from boy to man,
fathered three children, and found a steady job among the people,
sights, and sounds that had anchored him in good times and
bad. The neighborhood was his turf and always had been, a cocky,
changing crossroads of Irish pubs, upscale coffee shops, gay
bookstores, and Portuguese social clubs that had managed to re-
tain a spit-on-the-sidewalk chippiness from its immigrant past.

Whether it was the sports talk that attracted Bob to the
bare-bones Abbey Lounge or the politically incorrect banter from
third-generation firefighters, Bob loved this place as much as ever,
even as the hard-drinking men's bars and bottom-dollar barber
shops that had long ruled its unpretentious social life had all
but disappeared.

The place remained a comfort zone that kept Bob grounded,
even if trauma had distorted his childhood there. His father,
John, a transplant from St. Joseph, Missouri, had been a gambler and serial womanizer who left the family when Bob was
twelve. Money was scarce, clothing could be shoddy, and do-

mestic tranquility was seen only on television. To escape, the boy sometimes retreated to an attic room he called "the Tomb," where he could lock out, if not forget, the dysfunction that roiled his family.

For family outings, Bob's father would cart some or all of his six children across the city to Suffolk Downs, a scruffy, third-rate, thoroughbred racetrack in East Boston, where the desperate could bet on a miracle from an overused nag. And while John Curley tried his luck, something he did nearly every day of the racing season, the children amused themselves in the racetrack parking lot. If John won, the clouds lifted, and the family would stop for ice cream on the ride home or venture to Revere Beach for a roast beef sandwich at Kelly's. But if he lost, which was often, there were neither treats nor conversation. Bob, a quiet kid not quite seven years old, thought this was how most people spent their summers.

On October 1, 1997, those days had long been consigned to the past. And at 7:00 A.M., Bob wheeled his bicycle into the landmark brick firehouse, home to Engine 5, where a hose-carrying truck and bright red pumper screamed through Inman Square more than two thousand times a year. The men of Engine 5 called the company "The Nickel." And like firefighters everywhere, their camaraderie was a palpable, living thing that bound them with an intimate communal history, where shared worries and hopes, success and failures, were often felt more intensely than within their own families. "If you get in a pickle, call The Nickel," boasted the company's informal motto. And Curley, who had worked at Inman Square for three years, was an integral, upbeat, dependable part of that fraternity. Nearly everyone liked Bob, whose quick humor, passion for Boston sports, and stoic work ethic fit neatly into the fabric of Engine 5.

A man of routine, Bob walked to the rear of the firehouse to a cramped repair area he called his "office," a place where a box of corn flakes and a container of milk always lay stashed in a small refrigerator. After breakfast, Bob strolled past the dispatcher's desk and climbed the stairs to the second-floor kitchen for coffee, gossip, and head-shaking regrets that the Boston Red

Sox, a fourth-place team in the death throes of a dreadful season, would not be World Series champions for the seventy-ninth consecutive year.

From this men's club perched in the heart of the square, Bob and the firefighters could watch the ever-changing urban drama unfold on the star-shaped intersection below. They watched the fistfights, judged the women, and sneered at their left-leaning neighbors as they ambled across the street.

Bob didn't participate in, or even talk much about, politics. Like most of his coworkers, Bob thought "liberal" was pretty much a four-letter word, even though he rarely voted Republican and joked that the working class should be registered Democratic at birth. But for political radicals in a city only half-jokingly nicknamed the "People's Republic of Cambridge," the firefighters reserved a special, vitriolic scorn. To Bob, they were "phonies," which to him was just about the worst label he could pin on anybody. To the firefighters, the world of Engine 5 was different, a place where grown men referred to each other as brothers and where risking one's life was a given, not a choice. They cooked for each other, pulled pranks on each other, and went drinking together at the Abbey and the Druid. And to ensure that their mission never lost focus, the yellowing photographs of Inman Square firefighters from the past, some of them killed on the job and some dating back a century, hung on the wall as a constant, silent, inspiring reminder.

Life had taken an upward trajectory for Bob. He loved the firehouse and now had a spacious Somerville home bought four months before, thanks to the financial resources of a petite, attractive, and effervescent psychologist named Mimi, a native of Colombia with whom he had been living since late 1995.

Bob was separated from his wife, Barbara, who lived five blocks from the firehouse in a small condominium that Bob had helped buy before he left. His two oldest boys, Bobby Jr., nineteen, and Shaun, seventeen, were in good health. And his youngest son, Jeffrey, a precocious ten-year-old, was a constant, frenetic presence in the neighborhood, a boy who often whiled away his time at the firehouse, bantering with the men, riding to fires in the trucks, and peppering everyone within sight with a never-ending barrage of questions.

Bob had seen Jeffrey the previous day at Barbara's condo, where Shaun had badgered his father into helping him repair his Buick Regal, an abused, decade-old dinosaur that Shaun had bought for $400 a few weeks before. The car, Shaun's first, wouldn't start. So, Bob drove his mechanic's truck to the house, charged the battery, figured that a little gasoline would prime the carburetor, and sent Jeffrey scurrying into the house to find a small plastic cup to pour the fuel.

Jeffrey did as he was told, always eager to help his brothers and father negotiate this fascinating men's world of tools, lawn mowers, weed whackers, and snowblowers. Despite his age, Jeffrey—a four-foot, six-inch, seventy-seven-pound tornado—had a fearlessness and urban street smarts that made him seem much older.

Bob used the occasion to lecture his youngest boy about the dangers of gasoline.

"This is dangerous stuff. Be very careful how you use it," Bob said, cleaning his hands before hopping back in the truck to continue his rounds of the city's firehouses.

"Okay, I will," said Jeffrey, a broad smile exposing his crooked front teeth. "Nice going on the car, Dad."

Jeffrey, a blue-eyed boy with close-cropped brown hair, had left his fifth-grade class at the Charles G. Harrington School earlier that day. A school nurse had called Barbara, a slow-to-smile woman with auburn hair and a weary gaze, to tell her the boy felt nauseous. Barbara, who worked nearby, left early from her cashier's job at Bradlees, a discount department store, to retrieve her youngest son.

After walking the zigzagging half mile together from school to home, Barbara gave Jeffrey some medicine and looked ahead. Though not scheduled to work the next day, she could not afford to stay away for an extended illness.

"Jeffrey, why don't you stay home tomorrow," Barbara said. "If you get yourself run down, then Mommy's going to have to miss work Thursday."

Jeffrey nodded, turned, and trudged upstairs to bed.

The relationship between mother and son was a rare and close one, bound even tighter since Bob had left the spare, three-bedroom condo. While the older boys inhabited a world of girls, beer, sports, and mischief—living at home but not entirely of it—Jeffrey remained Barbara's link to a world of maternal nurture and family norms that had all but shattered for her.

When the separation began and the pressures of parenting increased, Barbara switched from part-time night work at Bradlees to a forty-hour week of day shifts. Any extra income, she knew, was needed to support the family and pay the mortgage.

Bob continued to contribute the bulk of the money for the household. Often, when no one was home, he would stop at the olive-green building, walk up a short flight of stairs, and leave most of his paycheck in a cabinet over the stove.

Times, admittedly, had been hard when Bob and Barbara lived together. "We were struggling with the kids, and there wasn't enough money," Bob said. "Her working nights all the time, me working days—it was tough."

In those days, Bob seemed focused on three priorities: food, clothing, and a roof for his family. In return, he asked Barbara simply to have dinner on the table at 5:00 P.M. before she went to work. The family never went out to eat, and Bob's after-work routine, usually conducted from the couch, revolved around Budweiser and the television remote control.

Despite the domestic tension, Bob's decision to break up nineteen years of marriage devastated Barbara. "She just became more miserable every day," recalled Bobby Jr., who suddenly found himself the man of a cramped house from which much of the joy had been sucked away.

As much as Bob claimed these streets, the neighborhood's familiar blocks were Barbara's, too. Her late father, a Cambridge firefighter for thirty years, worked two jobs and brought home just enough money to raise five children across from the Harrington School. There, in a small apartment, Barbara and her four siblings were taught to respect their country and the Roman Catholic Church—and to take no lip from anyone.

Like Jeffrey, Barbara had attended the Harrington School, and the adjoining ball field where he became a Little League all-star was the same green oasis where Barbara had scampered as a child. The games there of jump rope and hide-and-seek, which Barbara played until the 8:00 P.M. horn sounded at the Woven Hose Company, were replayed in 1997 by a new generation that was more Hispanic and African American than the Irish and Portuguese who had dominated the neighborhood in the 1960s. But as the twentieth century drew to a close, most of the ethnic wariness in and around Donnelly Field remained the province of the parents.

Barbara had met Bob in early 1977, at a time when guys and girls from the neighborhood would gravitate to the street corners to conduct the generations-old mating ritual of one-liners, easy laughter, and flirtatious one-upmanship. Barbara knew of Bob as a popular, funny, tough guy from the heart of the square. And after they met, she learned that "everything I had heard about him was basically true." Bob had a truck mechanic's job during the day; a night job tending bar at the Mad Hatter, one of Boston's most popular discos; and a joke for nearly every waking minute.

Less than a year after the pair met, they were married in a small civil ceremony at the Middlesex County Courthouse, just up the street from Inman Square. The no-frills reception was held at the house of Bob's sister Francine, a rambunctious affair for which Bob supplied the alcohol and Francine supplied the food.

After a brief stint in Somerville, the couple rented an East Cambridge apartment around the corner from Barbara's parents. And into this cocoonlike world of grandparents, aunts, uncles, and cousins, Bob and Barbara brought three boys, who renewed and embraced a clanlike attachment to family.

More so than his brothers, Jeffrey was an ever-visible, peripatetic presence in the neighborhood, one of the poorest and most crowded in a city better known for Harvard University, the Massachusetts Institute of Technology, and activist, brainy intellectuals. A confident imp who thought nothing of bicycling alone in city traffic, Jeffrey knew all the shortcuts in this working-class enclave, all the side streets, and nearly all the neighbors, both the upright and the shady.

To Bill McGovern, one of those neighbors and a longtime Engine 5 firefighter, Jeffrey embodied this insular universe. "I'd be working around the house, fixing the front stairs, and he'd yell, 'Hey, Magoo,'" said McGovern, whose thick glasses had spawned his cartoon-character nickname. "He was always with the questions. They were rebuilding the park across the street one summer, and the guys had laid new granite slabs. And the whole time the guys are working there, he's over there, talking to them, asking questions. He was pretty much a hands-on individual."

Jeffrey thrived on a whirlwind of activity. He'd hitch a ride on city garbage trucks and pocket a couple of dollars for his trash-collecting efforts. He'd help a Cambodian bicycle mechanic on the next street; shovel ice shavings from the local rink during hockey games; make flavored ice at Sarchioni's, the corner grocer, in exchange for a sandwich and a soda; and even rush to blazing fires, either on his bicycle or in the trucks that screamed from Inman Square. "Give him twenty-five cents or a pat on the back, and he was the happiest guy in the world," said Shaun, who marveled at his little brother's energy.

The day before he became ill, Jeffrey and his class of city kids had traveled to a country orchard. On their return, Jeffrey stopped at Sarchioni's store, holding his apple-picking haul proudly in hand. At first, he gave away a few to the corner regulars. But keen beyond his years, he soon realized there was money to be made and began selling apples for fifty cents apiece.

To Barbara, Jeffrey was a shining light in a world turned upside down since Bob had left to live with Mimi. Barbara initially thought Bob had decided to bunk at the firehouse. And in October 1997, although Barbara knew of Mimi, she still did not know exactly where they lived. "I kept hoping he'd come home," Barbara said of Bob. "It was like losing someone that you loved dearly, like them dying and passing away. I was crying; I was scared; I was all those things. I had been with Bob since I was twenty years old, and then, just like that, I'm thinking, How am I going to pay a mortgage and raise three boys? Who's going to watch the kids if I work nights? It was hard for me because I had always been home with my children."

Jeffrey saw many of her tears. And when she lashed out at his father, Jeffrey would try to console her. "Mommy, don't worry," he'd say. "I'll always take care of you. I love you, Mommy."

At age ten, Jeffrey continued to sleep in the same bed as his mother. He roller-bladed to Bradlees in the summer to join her for pizza. And he often greeted Barbara at the end of their thirty-yard driveway, astride his beloved bicycle, when she walked into view at 5:20 P.M. after yet another shift.

The boy's cockiness defined him, but Jeffrey had a soft side that returned and redoubled his mother's love. He would sit by her side on the living room couch, watch the television series *Home Improvement*, and match her critiques with knowing nods and giggling wisecracks. And in a summer outing to Canobie Lake Park in New Hampshire, he once persuaded his mother to join him on a thrill ride, where he held her hand to calm her fears.

In return, he always received the most fuss and the best Christmas gifts. "My mother would have new roller blades for him, new outfits, new schoolbags, new books," Shaun said. "Jeffrey got everything from her, and he couldn't be away from her." If the household's division of affection seemed skewed, the older boys rarely mentioned it, except as a joke. They recognized the strain on their mother, who saw in Jeffrey, her "little pooh," something innocent and vulnerable in a life of hard, unanticipated edges.

Jeffrey also enjoyed the company of Barbara's mother, Muriel Francis, who lived a block away and was a near-daily source of after-school soft drinks and companionship. For Barbara, her mother was another layer of supervision for the ten-year-old son of a working woman. The older boys helped fill that role, too, and Barbara would call them frequently to check on Jeffrey. But being teenagers, the boys were not natural babysitters. "It would be like, 'Ma, will you stop it? He's in the neighborhood. Don't worry about it,'" Barbara recalled. "And I would say, 'That's my job, to worry about it.'"

Bob was also a familiar presence in the neighborhood, driving past the condo on congested Hampshire Street nearly every day to check on the boys and catch up on their activities. In this close-knit world, Bob's biggest worry was that Jeffrey would be hit by a car.

When Bobby Jr. and Shaun were younger, the Curley sports world revolved around hockey practice at the nearby Gore Street rink, where Bob would change Jeffrey's diaper while sitting on unheated stands in near-freezing temperatures. Although Jeffrey began skating at age four, money had become tight in the Curley household, and the cost of organized hockey meant the boy was destined for less-expensive sports. For Jeffrey, that meant baseball, baseball, and still more baseball. In 1997, Bob umpired in the Cambridge Little League—it was more of a hobby than a job at $20 a game—and watched Jeffrey play for the Marlins. Bob loved baseball as much as Jeffrey did. And that September, as the days grew short, Bob would take Jeffrey to a ball field on the Boston side of the Charles River, where he tossed sky-high pop-ups to his wide-eyed son.

Jeffrey had been to his father's new home only once, but he became immediately fascinated by Bob and Mimi's top-to-bottom renovation of a bland, funereal place into a bright and vibrant home. There were walls to strip and floors to refinish, and Jeffrey congratulated his father and his girlfriend on doing the work themselves. Captivated by "this beautiful little boy," Mimi, who had no children of her own, hoped to know Jeffrey better in the months ahead.

By the morning of October 1, Barbara remained adamant that Jeffrey stay home and rest. This way, she could help him recuperate, as well as enjoy the uninterrupted pleasure of his company. While Barbara woke to see a pleasant autumn day on Hampshire Street, Jeffrey slept late into the morning.

Sixty miles to the north, in Manchester, New Hampshire, Charles Jaynes awoke at 9:00 A.M. in a tawdry, one-room apartment he rented for $105 a week under the name of Anthony Scaccia. Jaynes had used the alias, lifted from a Massachusetts man killed by a hit-and-run driver in 1987, to elude seventy-five arrest warrants for a notoriously impressive string of bad checks and ATM theft. In August, the newspaper in Jaynes's hometown of Brockton, Massachusetts, had published his photograph in a "Most Wanted" feature. By then, Jaynes had moved out of state, first to Maine and then to Manchester, where he wrote in his rental application that he wanted "a change of scenery."

The scenery in his three-story downtown building, which housed twenty-four apartments and an Army Navy surplus store, was unrelentingly drab. Many of the tenants had no family, no contacts, and no cars to ferry them from a bare-bones, pay-as-you-go pit stop where a fugitive could feel relatively safe.

Unlike many of the building's tenants, Jaynes could boast a semblance of a social life. By October 1, he had lived there only two months but already had an unsavory reputation for loud, obnoxious parties. One neighbor was struck by the party-goers, mostly teenagers, whose tastes tilted toward nose rings, tongue piercings, and messy, multicolored hair. Jaynes also enjoyed a few other amenities. His doting mother paid the rent and even hauled his laundry back and forth to Brockton. The phone was listed in the name of Laurie Pistorino, his out-of-town girlfriend.

Living off others was not unusual for Jaynes. By his mid-teens, he had learned that scamming and scheming were much more lucrative than minimum-wage work. In one brazen example, Jaynes obtained a driver's license after persuading his best friend to let him use his Social Security number. Once he had the license, Jaynes opened several checking accounts in the friend's name, diverted the bills to a third-party address, and ran up thousands of dollars in bad checks and bad charges. A year later, the unsuspecting friend, a high school senior, was blind-sided when he learned that seven arrest warrants had been filed against him.

When Jaynes did work for his money, he cleaned new cars for his father in the Boston suburb of Newton, Massachusetts. He also had experience pouring coffee behind a Dunkin' Donuts counter.

Wherever he went, Jaynes cut a distinctive figure. The caramel-colored son of a black father and white mother, Jaynes carried three hundred sagging pounds on a five-foot, nine-inch frame. The sight could be startling, at least according to one Manchester neighbor, who once stumbled on Jaynes standing in the hallway wearing only his underwear, talking on a cell phone in the middle of the night. He had a squeaky voice, and a pizza parlor cashier in Kittery, Maine, was struck by his "weird eyes." His seventh-grade reading teacher, Rebecca Moffitt, found his presence more unnerving—glowering, know-it-all, and menacing—than that of any other pupil she had taught in thirty years.

If Jaynes's appearance and manner repulsed people, he seemed oblivious or uninterested. Growing up in Brockton, he always held a high opinion of his worth. He even styled himself a savant and an artist, once winning a regional art award as a twelve-year-old. A decade later, the award from the *Boston Globe* still hung in a place of honor in his parents' home. However, the ten years that elapsed between award winner and car cleaner had shown that Jaynes would not pursue much of anything creative besides finding new ways to steal money.

To outsiders, Jaynes seemed just another rootless, overage adolescent in search of the next party. But inside his Manchester apartment, in places only his closest friends saw, the décor, possessions, and paraphernalia offered a raft of ominous clues that Jaynes had other, twisted predilections.

Born in 1975 under the Zodiac sign of Leo, Jaynes found meaning in the astrological symbol of the lion and became obsessed with the movie *The Lion King*. Posters of the film were tacked on the cheap walls of the apartment. *Lion King* figurines and knickknacks lay clustered on small tables. A *Lion King* towel even hung on the bathroom rack. One friend said she had seen the movie with him at least a dozen times.

The walls were also papered with posters of child actor Jonathan Taylor Thomas, a star of the series *Home Improvement*, who had supplied the voice of Simba, the cub son of the Lion King. The images showed Thomas in languid poses designed to stir the hearts of preadolescent girls. But to Jaynes, the pictures spoke to unnatural desires he had harbored for a decade.

Those thoughts took disturbing expression in his senior year at Brockton High School. After being lectured for disrupting a study hall, Jaynes left an unsigned note in the teacher's office. In the letter, described by Rebecca Moffitt as the vilest she had ever read, Jaynes wrote in shocking, deviant detail of an imagined sexual attack on the study-hall supervisor. The letter contained the teacher's home address, the names of her children, and where they boarded the school bus. The handwriting was eventually traced to Jaynes, who was expelled. The terrified teacher moved to a new home far from Brockton.

About this time, Jaynes began to tell friends he was sexually attracted to boys as young as six years old. He kept a pair of binoculars in his car and barked and whistled out the window when he passed a teenager or someone younger whom he found attractive. "I'd like to do that boy," he'd shout. On one trip to New York City, friends recalled, Jaynes repeatedly stopped the car outside arcades near Times Square. As his annoyed companions stewed in the automobile, Jaynes strolled inside to ogle his imagined prey. "He discussed it very freely," said William Pelligrini, a friend. Drawings of nude boys could be found strewn about his Cadillac.

Jaynes seemed constantly on the prowl for new targets, acquaintances said, and his appetite seemed insatiable. To pique those desires, Jaynes kept pornographic material in his apartment. He stored gay porn magazines in a duffel bag as well as below a shelf near the head of his king-size waterbed. He corresponded with the North American Man/Boy Love Association (NAMBLA), an organization that advocates legalized sex between men and boys. A NAMBLA membership card, made out to Anthony Scaccia, lay in his kitchen closet. A half dozen NAMBLA bulletins had been placed by his bed.

Writings about pedophilia also were scattered throughout the apartment. One book was titled *Loving Boys*. Another, his hard-cover diary, contained a meticulously written record of Jaynes's sexual experiences and fantasies, including memories of his first intimate encounter with another boy, when both were eleven years old. He also recorded that he once paid a boy $120 for sexual favors.

In the diary, Jaynes wrote that he did not begin to understand his desires until 1996, when he read a NAMBLA bulletin. The organization, Jaynes said, "helped me to become aware of my own sexuality and acceptance of it." Founded in Boston in 1978, NAMBLA two decades later had grown into a loosely knit group of a few hundred people across the country. Its Web-based manifesto proclaimed support for "the rights of youth as well as adults to choose the partners with whom they wish to share and enjoy their bodies." The group aimed, in its words, "to end the oppression of men and boys who have mutually consensual relationships."

For Jaynes, the vision of a mentoring, nurturing, sexual bond between an adult and a child struck a soul-altering chord. He rhapsodized about the possibilities. "Warm breezes, green grass, the air is fresh and crisp," he wrote in his diary. "Spring will soon roll into summer. Beautiful boys in shorts and T-shirts play basketball at the park.

"Boys in shorts with smooth, tender, muscular legs and arms, not yet ruined by adulthood.

"Ruff [*sic*] boys with their arousing arrogance.

"Impoverished boys, with their discerning attractiveness, that I wish to hold and caress in my arms."

NAMBLA, Jaynes wrote, helped him realize he was more than merely bisexual. Now, he also understood that he had the sexual desires of a pedophile and that others accepted that urge in themselves without shame.

Meanwhile, Jaynes continued to pursue relationships with adults of both sexes. Laurie Pistorino considered herself his fiancée. Pistorino had spent the night of September 30 in the Manchester apartment, where Jaynes cooked before they watched *The Tonight Show*. On the morning of October 1, stumbling over and through unsorted heaps of dirty clothes, some of them stacked knee-high beside the couch and waterbed, the two prepared to drive to Boston.

As they traveled south on I-93, Jaynes stopped briefly at the Massachusetts border for coffee. Less than an hour later, he dropped Laurie off at the Boston Public Library in tony Copley Square, where she stocked shelves until 9:00 P.M. Jaynes planned to report to work at 4:00 P.M. at his father's car-cleaning business eight miles away. But before then, he had time for a quick trip across the Charles River to East Cambridge to meet his new best friend, Salvatore Sicari.

Sicari, an unemployed twenty-one-year-old misfit, had met Jaynes in 1996 when they both lived in Brockton. The introduction came courtesy of Sicari's girlfriend, Charlene Letourneau, who had just left an abusive relationship with Jaynes's brother. At first, Letourneau believed she had found a soul mate in Sicari, an unloved outcast whose experience as an abused child, like her own, might foster a bond between them. She even found Sicari a job by persuading Jaynes's father to hire him. But that good deed was punished when Sicari, who had bragged of his mechanic skills, proved he could barely change the oil.

Edward Jaynes Sr., a bald, muscled man nicknamed Kojak, found he had no use for Sicari shortly after he hired him. "He was nothing but a thief and selling drugs when I met him. Ask him to put a water pump on. Ask him where to put the antifreeze," Jaynes said, scoffing at the notion. "He looked at my son and said, 'I got something here.' And my son said, 'Hey, I got a friend.'"

Edward Jaynes eventually fired Sicari, and Letourneau broke up with him, worn out and frustrated by his chronic dishonesty, philandering, and unwillingness to find a job. Sicari moved back to his mother's apartment in East Cambridge, but he maintained a close friendship with Jaynes. And the pair, cruising around in Jaynes's hulking gray Cadillac, quickly established themselves as neighborhood fixtures.

To Sicari, who rode a bicycle to get around, Jaynes was a winning lottery ticket with a big payoff. Suddenly, Sicari had access to transportation, and his new friend was generous with other people's credit cards. This was a good thing for Sicari, a high school dropout who had quit the twelfth grade at a Boston-area school for struggling adolescents when he could not find the energy or the muscle to pass gym class. He had never held a steady job, already had two children by two women, and was wandering through life with the snarling, defensive front of a hopeless sociopath. But now Sicari had Jaynes. And even after he was fired, Sicari would help his friend at Kojak's, for free, as the world passed him by in the early fall of 1997.

For Sicari, the high-energy atmosphere of a busy car dealership was a refreshing change from his second-floor apartment, where the blinds were nearly always drawn, the thwack of slaps was common, and the family was considered the strangest in the neighborhood. "He was a loose cannon," said Kris McGovern, who hung out with Sicari and a half dozen other friends nearly every night on the street corner below Sicari's apartment. "He didn't seem like he had any kind of stability at home or any kind of support, morally or physically. He just—I don't know—his life was just weird." Indeed, one of Sicari's elementary school teachers said he might have been the most neglected child she had ever taught, a sad little boy nicknamed "Pigpen" who seemed on the fast track to a sorry, stormy life.

If Sicari felt neglected at home, he never seemed self-pitying to his small circle of nightly acquaintances. It was always Sicari the tough guy, even if he stood only five feet, seven inches and weighed 160 pounds. He'd break into cars with them, smoke pot on the corner, and steal from friends and strangers alike. "He would act out a little bit more than the rest of us," McGovern said. "Exaggerate his hand gestures, maybe, or the look on his face. But you could see right through it."

According to McGovern, Sicari's ambitions fell far beneath the very low bar set by most teenagers and young adults on the corner, where most of the guys thought only about the next day. "Salvi never worked. He just ripped people off," McGovern said, using Sicari's nickname. "Riding around and smoking weed, that was pretty much his thing."

Sicari already had an extensive criminal record by October 1997. He had been arrested five times, convicted of seven offenses, and given a six-month suspended sentence for assaulting the mother of his twenty-one-month-old daughter at a Brockton doughnut shop. Letourneau witnessed that beating, in which Sicari stomped the woman after she and Letourneau confronted Sicari in a stinglike ruse. They both suspected him, correctly, of cheating on them with the other woman. "I had to pull him off of her," Letourneau said of the May 1997 assault. "He took off running."

Sicari's other child, a boy from a different mother, had been born within six days of his daughter.

Worse trouble arrived at the Sicari household in September, when Sal's sixteen-year-old brother, Robert, was indicted and later convicted on charges of raping a young Cambridge boy from the neighborhood. To ingratiate himself with the youngster, Robert Sicari had dangled the promise of a new bicycle.

Both Sal and Robert Sicari were well known to Jeffrey Curley, who often rode his bicycle past the Sicari apartment on Market Street that summer. He would stop at the curb to listen to the spicy conversation on the stoop, offer smart-ass comments, and often return any of the obligatory ribbing with an extended middle finger. Jeffrey knew the Sicaris were different and dangerous, particularly after Sal body-slammed him on the hood of a car in late July. The contact was hard enough to leave a dent, but Jeffrey shrugged off the incident, even laughed, as he rolled off the hood and rode off on his bike. Jeffrey could dish out the insults, but he made a point of showing the older crowd that he could take them, too.

Barbara did not know Sal Sicari well, but she had heard about Robert, and she repeatedly warned Jeffrey to stay away from him. Any infraction of that rule, Jeffrey knew, would mean automatic grounding.

As the summer of 1997 crept into August, Jeffrey began seeing a new visitor to the neighborhood. And that visitor, Charles Jaynes, soon made Jeffrey feel like he had a new buddy—one with a big car, surprise gifts, and hours of available attention. The attention was inviting because Jeffrey's best friend, an inseparable cousin, had moved forty miles away that year. And Jaynes's Cadillac, with its plush seats and preening self-importance, was a vast, exciting world of its own. Jeffrey and Jaynes, surveying the world from the front seat of the oversize car, cruised the familiar streets of East Cambridge several times that summer. Occasionally, they roamed farther afield.

One such trip, on September 11, took them to Assonet, a village thirty miles to the south, where Jaynes picked up Robyn Neil, a nineteen-year-old friend who had asked to spend the weekend with him in New Hampshire. When the Cadillac pulled into the driveway, Robyn did a double take at the sight of a young boy in the passenger seat. Robyn had never seen or heard of Jeffrey Curley, but she did know that Jaynes had prurient interests in boys. The previous year, she discovered a book in Jaynes's bedroom that showed photos of boys engaged in sex. Also, Robyn knew that Jaynes kept gay pornographic books and letters in that room, locked tight in a purple-and-aqua Rubbermaid container.

If she had any concerns, Robyn concealed them. She readily climbed into the backseat, and the trio headed north on busy Route 24 toward Cambridge. Once on the highway, cruising at sixty-five miles per hour, Jaynes asked Jeffrey if he would like to steer the car. The boy jumped at the invitation, shifted to the middle of the front seat, and placed his left hand on the wheel. For fifteen minutes, tucked against Jaynes's side, Jeffrey lived a boy's dream as he "drove" the mammoth Cadillac.

Once in Cambridge, Jaynes dropped Jeffrey near his home. The ride, and its unexpected thrill, would not be mentioned to mother or brothers. Other outings with Jaynes would not be mentioned either, such as the trip to a shopping mall where Jaynes posed in a photo booth with the boy on his lap.

The picture, framed with an Old West motif, read "Wanted" on the bottom.

The details of the night of September 16, when Jeffrey dined at Vinny Testa's, a popular Italian restaurant in the heart of Boston's fashionable Back Bay, would also remain a secret. Laurie Pistorino had expected to be dining alone with Jaynes that evening. But when the Cadillac pulled up outside the Boston Public Library at 9:00 P.M., a boy she had never seen was sitting in the car.

"Who's this?" Pistorino asked.

"J. C.," Jaynes said, using the nickname he had given Jeffrey.

Laurie remembered now that he had mentioned the boy before. During the short ride to the restaurant, Pistorino asked Jeffrey a few questions: How many brothers and sisters do you have? Why are you out so late?

Jeffrey ordered spaghetti and meatballs; Laurie, the chicken *picante*; and Jaynes, the baked chicken. As Jeffrey dug into his meal, Jaynes and Pistorino bantered about her day at work. Jaynes also asked if she could pick up two complimentary passes at the library so that Jeffrey and he could visit the Museum of Science.

The dinner ended at 10:30 P.M., when Jeffrey was finally driven the few miles to his neighborhood. "Have a good night. See you tomorrow," Jaynes called out as the boy scampered toward his house. Inside the condo, Barbara was angry. Jeffrey, in need of a quick explanation, cobbled together an alibi that he had gone to the movies with a friend and her mother.

During that summer, Jeffrey had also become a familiar face at Honda Village in Newton, where Kojak's Reconditioning occupied a cramped and gloomy space in the basement. Jaynes brought the ten-year-old to work at least a half dozen times, sometimes in the company of Sicari. There, in this little boy's heaven of gleaming new cars, Jeffrey would roam the shop at will, peeling white plastic coverings off the automobiles and chasing his older friend with the water hose.

To many employees, Jeffrey seemed to crave Jaynes's company. One worker recalled seeing Jeffrey leap into Jaynes's arms, screeching with delight. Another saw Jaynes give him piggyback rides. For some at Honda Village, their camaraderie raised a host of troubling questions. When one worker asked about the child, Jaynes answered simply that he was babysitting. "No," Jeffrey shot back with a grin, "I'm babysitting *him!*"

But for other workers, their childlike friendship seemed natural. Jeffrey might have been the son of an old family friend. The two might have known each other for years. How else to explain the boy's big smile or the way he would run to Charlie, yell his name, and give him a hug?

Henock Desir, a lot manager at Honda Village, spotted Jeffrey riding on Jaynes's shoulders one day. Jaynes was spinning Jeffrey around and around in the basement, teasing the boy, and playfully threatening to toss him in the air.

"I'm going to drop you. I'm going to throw you away," Jaynes said.

"No, no, don't do it! Don't do it!" Jeffrey protested with a laugh. "You can't do that!"

Another time, receptionist Sharon Snow looked up to see Jeffrey in the middle of a school day, standing in front of her desk with Jaynes and Sicari.

"What are you doing out of school?" Snow asked.

"I'm going to get a bike today," Jeffrey answered eagerly.

Later, Jeffrey was saddened to learn there would be no new bike that afternoon.

Jeffrey and bicycles had been a sore point in the Curley household that summer. Jeffrey had lost three, the latest one only recently, and his mother now refused to buy another until Christmas. This way, maybe, Jeffrey would learn responsibility. "Jeffrey, I've told you, and your brothers have told you," Barbara lectured him. "You need to bring the bike in the house. Now, you're going to have to wait until Christmas. I'm sorry, but I can't afford it. You've had three strikes, and now you're out."

Jeffrey had another option, however, which he shared obliquely with his mother. A friend of Sicari's, whom he did not name, had promised to give him a bicycle, Jeffrey said. Barbara immediately tried to douse that idea. "Nobody gives you anything and doesn't expect something in return," she said in their living room. Case closed, or so she thought.

Teenagers in the neighborhood knew that friend to be Jaynes. Tashika Ellis, who lived beside Sicari, had heard Jeffrey say several times that Jaynes was planning to buy him a bike. In exchange, Jeffrey said, he would have to do something for Jaynes. But what that was remained a mystery.

Barbara did not worry about Jeff's pronouncement, delivered almost as an aside. After all, for someone who had lived her entire life within shouting distance of family and friends, neighborhood security was almost a given. The dangers of the age, trumpeted endlessly in the media, hardly seemed real in the short walk from the Harrington School to Hampshire Street. Despite the petty crime, the fistfights, and the adolescent roughhousing that permeated this crosshatch of crowded blocks, the streets of East Cambridge seemed safe enough.

Even Jeffrey adopted that sensibility. When Sicari had slammed him on the hood of the car, Jeffrey reacted with laughter instead of tears. But ten-year-old bravado did not come so easily in mid-September, when Sicari locked Jeffrey in the trunk of Jaynes's car, revved the engine, and kept the boy captive for five terrifying minutes. Rochelle Cruz, who lived nearby, heard banging from inside the trunk as Jaynes casually watched the scene from beside the driver's door.

"What are you doing? Let him out of there!" several neighbors screamed.

Jaynes and Sicari downplayed the fuss. "It's just a little joke," Sicari said. "We're just playing around. Don't worry about it."

Jeffrey emerged red-faced and sweating. But almost immediately, like a child trying to be a man, he burst into laughter.

Despite Sicari's occasional bullying, Jeffrey prowled the neighborhood throughout the summer, as feisty, undeterred, and unbowed as ever. But his growing familiarity with Jaynes, the newcomer, prompted some of Sicari's friends to urge Jeffrey to be cautious. Tashika Ellis saw Jeffrey alone with Jaynes in the Cadillac many times.

"Why are you hanging with him?" she asked Jeffrey. "You don't need to be with him. He's too old to be around."

In his inimitable way, Jeffrey fired back, "Mind your own business."

But as he roamed his turf, forever in search of adventure, the boy remained blissfully ignorant of Charles Jaynes's predatory intentions.

William Pelligrini, Jaynes's friend, first heard of those intentions during a September drive to the Manchester apartment. His excitement palpable, Jaynes confided that he had found a darling boy in Cambridge with chubby cheeks, a batch of freckles, blue eyes, and crooked teeth. With help from the Sicaris, Jaynes said, he would steal the boy's bike, buy him a new one, and demand sex in return. And if the boy refused, Jaynes continued, one of the Sicaris would "take care" of him.

In his apartment, on a piece of lined notepaper, Jaynes rendered his evil more lyrically. "I was out visiting friends in the fair city of Cambridge. While on the excursion that should never have started, I glanced a glimmer of a beautiful boy about 11 or 12 years at most," he wrote. "Beauty, beauty. Lord, why have you forsaken me to carry this burden? He had a lovely tan and crystal-blue eyes."

A Ride
to Hell

JEFFREY WOKE at midmorning on October 1, a rare late start to the day for him. He walked slowly downstairs to the kitchen, where Barbara, already up and about, was looking ahead to a few hours of quiet time with her youngest son. Pale and without an appetite, he clearly had not recovered from the bug that sent him home from classes the day before. Still, pushing the envelope as much as ever, he began to badger Barbara about whether he could go to school, even if only for half a day.

"I'm fine, Ma," Jeffrey said, fidgeting on the couch as he watched the Nickelodeon channel.

"Jeff," she answered wearily, "stay home with me today."

The boy reluctantly surrendered, and at 11:00 A.M. he began to feel well enough to ask for a bowl of his favorite soup, Oodles of Noodles. After eating, Jeffrey left the table to peer out the window for any hints of adventure on Hampshire Street. The neighborhood was quiet, at least for a ten-year-old boy. "Mom, I'm gonna take a shower," he announced.

As Jeffrey clambered up the stairs, Barbara turned on the television to watch live coverage of a sensational murder trial, in which a fifteen-year-old Somerville boy had been charged in the brutal stabbing death of his best friend's mother. The family of the victim, Janet Downing, was friendly with Bob Curley's niece, so Barbara had a tangential connection to the case. Like most of Greater Boston, she had been both horrified and captivated by the crime. Today, a verdict was expected against the defendant, a pudgy former altar boy named Eddie O'Brien, who allegedly stabbed his neighbor ninety-eight times in what prosecutors called an uncontrollable frenzy of frustrated sexual obsession. The murder of Downing, a divorced forty-two-year-old mother of four, had been so alarming that Middlesex district attorney Thomas Reilly had decided to prosecute O'Brien himself.

As Barbara watched the proceedings at Middlesex Superior Court, less than a mile away, Jeffrey reappeared about noon and asked his mother if he could walk to Sarchioni's. He was feeling better and had a craving for another of his favorite foods, a large Italian submarine sandwich, loaded with all the fixings, including hot peppers, which made Jeffrey unique among the neighborhood kids.

Barbara shook her head in disbelief. "Momma just made you some soup," she protested. "I think you need time for that to digest." But Jeffrey was persistent, as always, and Barbara allowed him to head to the corner store, where soda, candy, and a few staples had been squeezed into every available inch of the cramped shelf space.

In fifteen minutes, Jeffrey was back, just in time to see Shaun return from a half day at trade school, where he had shown a knack for carpentry and hockey. Shaun had recently returned from a "boot camp" on Cape Cod for juvenile criminal offenders, and the mixture of tough love and no-compromise discipline he received there had tilted his choices toward the straight and narrow. A few days before, Shaun had tackled the popular Doc Linskey road race in Cambridge. He ran beside his father, finished the five-mile course, and felt good about the result. Suddenly, life was looking up for an often reckless kid who had earned the nickname "Crazy Curley."

Shaun's car now started at the turn of the key, thanks to his father's hands-on attention the previous day. With a short day of school behind him, Shaun planned to drive the Buick to an out-of-town junkyard to find a replacement for the rusted front fender. Jeffrey loved junkyards—particularly ones with old cars, where he could climb in the seats, pretend to drive, and fiddle with the knobs, dials, and moving parts—and pleaded to tag along.

"You can't go," Shaun shot back. "We have to go all the way to Billerica. We don't have a car seat, and this car's not safe, anyway."

Jeffrey, crushed and crying, ran into the house to complain to his unsympathetic mother. Shaun had gone, his friends were in school, and he suddenly felt much better. For a hyperactive ten-year-old, confinement to the condo was not a pleasant option.

Unfortunately for Barbara, her plans for a quiet day at home had been upended. Jeffrey was badgering her, and the patience of both mother and son began to wear thin. Finally, about 2:00 P.M., with the O'Brien verdict expected any minute, Barbara relented and gave Jeffrey permission to return to Sarchioni's.

Jeffrey seemed agitated on this visit, enough that the help took notice of his hyperactive behavior. His restlessness didn't end after the short walk home, where Jeffrey spotted his oldest brother, Bobby, standing at the end of the driveway with the family dog, a Rottweiler named Tyson.

Bobby also seemed agitated, but for complicated reasons of late-teen romance. A girlfriend had stopped outside the condo to confront him, angrily asking why he hadn't called her all day or the night before. And Jeffrey, unaware, walked straight into the middle of a roiling tempest.

"Can you take me to do something?" Jeffrey asked Bobby, a tough, husky kid who had graduated from high school the previous year.

Bobby had no inclination to do any such thing. His girlfriend was giving him a hard time, and Bobby was too busy navigating the fine line of laying down the law without damaging the relationship. As Bobby attempted that delicate maneuver, Jeffrey continued to nag him. The strategy backfired. With more than a little attitude, Bobby barked at his brother.

"Go wash the dog, okay? I'll take you later," he said. The message: Get lost and don't bother me. He sweetened the deal by throwing in $10.

A small victory in hand, Jeffrey ran inside the condo, where Barbara agreed to let him walk the dog to his grand-mother's house, two streets away. There, under her eye, he could shampoo Tyson just like he had done so many times before.

"Throw a warmer coat on you," Barbara said.

"Ma, I'm fine, I'm fine. Stop worrying. I don't need a jacket," answered Jeffrey, who wore only a Boston College foot-ball jersey and a pair of denim shorts.

"Okay, but try not to get yourself wet, because then you're going to get sick all over again," Barbara pleaded.

Jeffrey lifted his head, gave his mother a kiss, and dashed outside.

"I love you," Barbara said.

"I love you, too, Ma."

"Remember, Jeff, I don't want you taking off from Nana's," Barbara added, well aware of the boy's wanderlust. "After you wash the dog, bring him back, and we'll chain him in the kennel so he can dry."

The walk was second nature to Jeffrey, who regarded Muriel Francis as a second mother and her two-story wooden house as a second home. A seventy-year-old widow with a hard, chiseled face, Francis was accustomed to seeing Jeffrey at least twice a day.

On this afternoon, Jeffrey decided on a whim to bypass the house for a few minutes and walk Tyson down the block to Market Park. There, a small patch of street-corner greenery and playground equipment offered children and young adults a neighborhood alternative to the dusty sidewalks and sagging stoops where they usually congregated.

As he neared the park, Jeffrey spied Sicari and Tashika Ellis walking toward him from Sicari's apartment a block away. Ever the scamp, Jeffrey sensed a delicious opportunity to turn the tables on a tormentor who had teased and bullied him

throughout the summer. Jeffrey tightened the leash and prodded the Rottweiler to exact his revenge.

"Get him! Get him!" Jeffrey urged the dog. Tyson, strain-
ing at the leash, began to snarl. And Sicari, only yards away,
began to panic.

"You little punk!" Sicari screamed at Jeffrey. He grabbed
a brick, hopped a small metal fence, and yelled again. "Get that
dog out of here before I fuck up both you and the dog!"

Jeffrey, smirking, called Tyson off and continued toward
the park. Sicari, fuming, headed toward Izzy's, a small Spanish
shop where Ellis, a twenty-year-old single mother, planned to
buy a takeout lunch. Only a block away, after turning a corner,
they spotted Charles Jaynes, leaning against his Cadillac on
the side of a busy street.

"I'll wait here for you," Sicari told Ellis, who suddenly
sensed that he had expected to see Jaynes there. "I'm going to
talk to him."

Ellis shrugged and strolled to Izzy's, where, after a few
minutes, she retraced her steps and found Jaynes and Sicari,
side by side, immersed in deep conversation near the Cadillac.

Jaynes, as usual, was annoying.

"How's the food? I've never eaten there before," Jaynes
chortled in his high-pitched voice. He helped himself to some
of her order and then offered Ellis a ride home, an unusual bit
of chivalry considering that she lived only two blocks away.

Why not? Ellis thought. She slid into the back of the
Cadillac, while Sicari claimed his accustomed place of honor
in the front passenger seat. Two minutes later, after several
sharp turns on a few, short, narrow streets, Ellis stood outside
her door. And as she did, she saw Jeffrey walk his dog away
from the park and disappear from sight.

Only fifty familiar yards separated the park from Jeffrey's
grandmother's house. He opened a chain-link fence, climbed a
short flight of concrete stairs, and heard his grandmother and
his uncle Arthur talking in the kitchen. The sounds of their
voices, floating out the door, were yet another comforting
thread in the tapestry of this boy's circumscribed world.

Arthur Francis visited the home at least one afternoon a week so he could linger with his mother over a cup of tea after his shift as a maintenance foreman for the Boston subway system.

Jeffrey greeted his grandmother and uncle and promptly set about a well-worn routine: tethering Tyson to a post beneath the stairway and unraveling a green garden hose to wash the dog. Mother and son could hear water pulsing through the hose as they chatted, warm and reassuring, until they were interrupted by the crash of an opening door. Jeffrey burst into the kitchen, no time to spare, in a whirling rush of sound and movement.

"Nana, I have to go. I have to go somewhere. I'll be back in a little while," Jeffrey said.

"But the dog?" she asked.

"Don't worry, Nana. I'll be back in ten minutes!"

Jeffrey placed the shampoo on the floor and darted out the door. As he left, his maroon football jersey disappearing from the kitchen, Muriel Francis paused and smiled. Her irrepressible grandson, she mused, seemed happy today. At that time, 3:15 P.M., Muriel Francis didn't give another thought to this abrupt change in plans. After all, this was quintessential Jeffrey: a nonstop, upbeat, unpredictable tornado. And, despite all the motion, he almost always was dependable. She couldn't have known what lay beyond the door.

Outside, a lumbering gray Cadillac idled at the curb. Charles Jaynes sat nervously expectant behind the wheel. Salvatore Sicari slumped low in the passenger seat to avoid being seen. And Jeffrey, smiling and ecstatic, bounded into the backseat. A months-long promise was about to come true. Charles Jaynes, his bearlike friend, had declared he would buy Jeffrey a brand-new bicycle today.

Jeffrey leaned forward, as he often did, extending his arms sideways on the upholstery, his crew-cut head jutting forward between Jaynes and Sicari. Jaynes told Jeffrey they would pick up the long-anticipated gift in Newton. The eight-mile trip would be quick and easy, only one exit west on the

Massachusetts Turnpike and not far from the car dealership that Jeffrey knew so well.

On this trip, however, Jaynes did not stop at Honda Village. Instead, he cruised through other parts of the affluent, leafy suburb until he reached a Mobil gas station in the busy Four Corners neighborhood near Boston College. There, pulling his Cadillac close to a self-service bay, Jaynes pumped eighteen gallons into the car.

But as he did, Jaynes interrupted the job to place a rag over the flipped-down license plate and douse the cloth with fuel. Jaynes used an American Express card in his father's name to pay the $27.76 tab, then tossed the rag on the rear floor.

The Mobil station was close to International Bicycle Centers, where Jaynes and Sicari had shopped in September. During their first visit, on September 8, the pair ordered an adult-size, metallic-red Trek 850, a mountain bike for which Jaynes gave $60 as a down payment on the $330 bill. On September 26, Jaynes and Sicari visited again to say they had changed their minds and now wanted a bike for a ten-year-old.

Fabio Selvig, the assistant store manager, showed them the children's bicycles. The pair chose a red model already on the display floor, a Trek Mountain Cub 97. Because the bike was dented, Selvig suggested a blue version, a ready-to-roll model that they could take immediately rather than wait a week for another red one. Jaynes, who used the name of Anthony Scaccia for the purchase, liked the suggestion. "He won't care about the color," Jaynes said.

To Selvig, the comment seemed odd. From experience, he knew that a child who is set on a color wants only that color. Plus, Selvig thought, these men did not seem like the usual customers for children's bicycles.

If Jaynes planned to give Jeffrey the Trek 97, he didn't bring the bicycle on the trip to Newton. Instead, after he left the Mobil station, Jaynes drove the car toward the rear of a small shopping center across the intersection.

Jaynes, who needed to urinate, was joined by Sicari and Jeffrey as they relieved themselves near a brown Dumpster and a stack of empty milk crates. Here, Jeffrey was just one of the guys, reveling in a midday adventure, his mind far away from a Rottweiler that by now had begun to bark for lack of attention.

Jaynes and Jeffrey finished their business first, returning to the car in a misty rain as Sicari lingered in the alley. In Jeffrey's mind, a good day was about to get better. In addition to the bicycle, Jaynes had said Jeffrey now stood to make the astronomical sum of $50.

Finally, Jeffrey would hear what Jaynes expected in return. The price of his generosity, Jaynes explained, was a sexual favor. The boy, horrified, refused a demand he could barely understand.

Jaynes reacted with a burst of volcanic fury, grabbing Jeffrey with single-minded force and dragging him to the backseat of the car. Sicari turned just in time to see Jeffrey disappear into the Cadillac. Stunned, he bolted toward the car, racing around the vehicle and slamming all the doors. He threw himself into the driver's seat, looked around, punched the gas, and sped out of the parking lot.

Behind him, a violent battle had begun. Jeffrey was fighting for his life, flailing against a three-hundred-pound predator who had sat on him to pin him to the cushion. Still struggling to subdue the boy, Jaynes reached for the rag and held the fuel-drenched cloth to Jeffrey's face, pressing harder and harder, smothering the boy's nose and mouth and forcing him to inhale the toxic vapors.

"Don't fight it!" Jaynes yelled. "Don't fight it."

Instead, Jeffrey lashed out with his arms and legs, again and again, in a furious effort to fight off the killer he had thought was his friend. Unable to see, he strained to find and release the door handle, his short, groping fingers jabbing for the lever under Jaynes's crushing weight. Despite his size, Jeffrey refused to succumb. By now, the gasoline had reached his brain, his blood, and his lungs, searing Jeffrey's respiratory tract and raising raw, painful blisters on his face and neck. Amazingly, Jeffrey continued to battle as the Cadillac mingled with afternoon traffic. At one point, in a final, futile signal for help, the boy's arm shot straight up. Frightened and angered by Jeffrey's resistance, Jaynes grabbed the arm and slammed it down.

The struggle continued for twenty interminable minutes, as Sicari, his eyes darting between the rearview mirror and the rush-hour congestion, nervously steered the Cadillac on an aimless path to no set destination. At one point, a Newton police cruiser pulled up behind the Cadillac, its blue lights flashing, as Jeffrey continued to fight.

Sicari stiffened. He hit the gas again and lost sight of the officer, unaware that the police had been dispatched on an unrelated call. Now, seemingly safe for a moment, Sicari screamed at Jaynes, "What the fuck did you do?"

By now, Jeffrey's long, desperate struggle had ended, and he lay dead, the frantic fight for life too great for his seventy-seven pounds. His blue eyes stared blankly toward the roof as his small body lay prone on the backseat of a car that reeked of gasoline. Bruises marred his gums, arms, knees, and buttocks. And on Jeffrey's upper left shoulder and arm, the diamond-shaped weave of his football jersey lay imprinted on his skin like a cattle brand.

Jaynes panted while lines of sweat poured down his face. He gasped for breath but seemed oblivious to his deed. Instead of horror, he showed scorn. Instead of fear, he spewed derision. Instead of guilt, he blamed Jeffrey.

"The kid is not going to con a conner," Jaynes snapped. "He thought he was going to get a bike and the money for nothing."

Sicari pulled the Cadillac off the street and into a parking lot, out of sight of traffic and pedestrians. There, Jaynes gagged Jeffrey with the rag and duct tape.

"Ride in back with the kid," Jaynes said.

Sickened by the sight of the corpse, slack on the seat with wide, open eyes, Sicari refused. Jaynes, however, had no such qualms. He used his fingers to lower Jeffrey's eyelids, placed the body on the floor, and rolled the front seat back to hide as much of Jeffrey as possible.

The time was 4:15 P.M., only one hour since Jeffrey had bounded away, smiling and excited, from his grandmother's house. In Cambridge, the boy's restless Rottweiler remained tied to the pole outside Muriel Francis's home. Although Jeffrey had not returned, his grandmother credited the tardiness to a longer-than-usual case of Jeffrey being Jeffrey.

At 4:30 P.M., however, she had heard enough of Tyson's barking and called Barbara. Jeffrey had wandered off with friends, she told Barbara, and not come back. Could someone stop by the house and take the dog? Barbara agreed to retrieve Tyson. On the walk home, she speculated that Jeffrey must have stopped by Donnelly Field. Par for the course for that little rascal, she mused.

In any event, Barbara was preoccupied with other thoughts. Close to the time that Jeffrey hopped into Jaynes's car, the jury returned with a verdict in the Eddie O'Brien case. First-degree murder with extreme atrocity, the foreman proclaimed on live television. The sentence: a mandatory term of life without parole for the cherub-faced seventeen-year-old. A chill coursed through Barbara as she, and most of her neighbors, watched the verdict. How could such a horrific crime happen to such a woman, Barbara wondered. How could it happen in this community?

Those questions also tugged at Bob Curley, who watched the verdict with several firefighters who had clustered around the upstairs television at Engine 6, an old firehouse near the Charles River. Bob had not known the victim, but his sister Francine and her daughter had been traumatized by the murder of a friend found butchered on the kitchen floor. Like Barbara, Bob felt insulated from such savagery, even though petty crime was a frustrating fact of life in the working-class neighborhoods where they had spent their entire lives. Murder had never visited his family, and, like many of the firefighters around him who shook their heads, its impact was incomprehensible.

Unknown to them, another horror had just hit the community.

A few miles away, Jaynes and Sicari cobbled together a cover-up. The first step led them to a bustling shopping plaza in a crowded, commercial bend of the Charles River near Honda Village. Jaynes, who worked less than a mile away, knew the place well and directed Sicari to park the Cadillac in a side lot, close to an NHD Hardware store where Jaynes would shop for supplies.

As Sicari fidgeted in the driver's seat, fingering the thin growth of beard that lined the edge of his jaw, Jaynes entered the store. His nervousness made an instant impression on Roque Alfaro, a Newton high school student who worked one of the cash registers. Jaynes hurriedly asked Alfaro to point him toward the duct tape. In response, Alfaro summoned Dale Bisson, an assistant store manager, who started to back away when Jaynes began moving toward her, agitated and aggressive. Jaynes was perspiring heavily, and Bisson thought she detected a faint odor of gasoline as she led him to the duct tape. As they moved through the aisles, Bisson made sure she kept fifteen feet away from Jaynes and turned her head repeatedly to track his location.

Once they reached the tape, Jaynes asked Bisson where the tarps were stored. "Just show me where they are," he snapped. "I don't need you to come with me." Bisson, however, escorted Jaynes to the tarps, although she left as soon as she pointed them out. "He frightened me," Bisson said later. "I'll never forget his face." Jaynes chose a nine-by-twelve-foot tarp to go with four rolls of duct tape, all of which he billed to his father's American Express card.

Sicari started the car as soon as he saw Jaynes turn the corner from the store. But before they could leave, Sicari was forced to wait while a medical-office worker, on her way home, walked directly in front of the Cadillac. The worker, Jacquelyn Avant, took a good look at the two men. She noted Sicari's "scrubby beard" and the way he cut his hair: close on the sides, but thick and curly on the top, just like hers. Sicari, sweeping a hand over the top of the driving wheel, politely waved Avant past the car.

From the plaza, the pair drove less than a mile to Honda Village, where Sicari backed the rear of the Cadillac against a wall of the dealership. Jaynes was expected at work that afternoon, and he was determined to stick to his routine, even though his car still carried the warm body of Jeffrey Curley.

As Jaynes walked down a ramp to his job in the basement, Sicari rearranged the Cadillac. He laid out the tarp in the trunk, lifted Jeffrey's body from the rear passenger floor, and carefully placed the corpse in the plastic wrapping. Then, he removed the duct tape from the boy's face, which had been badly bruised. Ugly black-and-blue welts, almost like the remnants of a beating, disfigured his face and eyes. Sicari then moved the Cadillac to a narrow, lightly traveled street beside the dealership. A Honda salesman, Jason Drew, saw the car there about 5:00 P.M. and thought it odd because Jaynes regularly parked in the basement.

To other employees, the day seemed to be business as usual for Jaynes, who prepped new cars as always. Jaynes even joked with some of the workers, including mechanic James Gavell, who sat in the customer lounge about 5:45 P.M., reading a newspaper before the end of his shift. "You aren't really too busy, huh?" Jaynes said, chuckling. "Or busy doing nothing."

While Jaynes was typically wisecracking, upbeat, and obnoxious, his friend Sicari seemed the emotional opposite. While Jaynes placed calls on a dealership phone, Sicari took a seat near Gavell, hung his head, and stared at the floor.

Jaynes phoned Charlene Letourneau, Sicari's former girlfriend, to insist she tell his mother not to drive to his New Hampshire apartment that night. Letourneau and her two-year-old child, the son of Edward Jaynes Jr., had been living at the Jaynes home in Brockton since the beginning of the year. Jaynes also placed a call to Laurie Pistorino at the Boston Public Library. She, too, had plans to stay overnight in Manchester, but Jaynes said he suddenly felt ill.

Two loose ends had been tied, so Jaynes returned to work for two more hours on a slow night. About 8:30 P.M., he ambled back to the customer lounge, where Drew and his sales manager were watching a baseball game on television. Jaynes asked for permission to leave early, and the manager gave him the go-ahead.

Meanwhile, in East Cambridge, Barbara was becoming concerned. Her first reaction to Jeffrey's decision to leave the dog alone had been mild annoyance. After all, he had stayed home sick from school, pestered her to go outside, and then abandoned Tyson. The time had come for Jeffrey to be held accountable.

Barbara walked into the condo shortly before 5:00 P.M., looked at the clock, and frowned. Dinner would be on the table at 5:30 P.M., although no one else was home yet. At 6:00 P.M., she would attend a condominium meeting at one of four other units in the complex. Jeffrey was playing somewhere close, she was sure, and this meeting was important. So, after cooking three meals for her boys and placing them on the kitchen table under plastic, Barbara fumed and headed out the door of an empty house.

Shaun arrived home minutes later, following a successful scavenger hunt to replace his car's rusted bumper. Missing the 5:30 P.M. dinner was routine for him, so the sight of his supper under wraps was expected rather than extraordinary. Shaun also knew what lay on the table: one of four meals that Barbara rotated for the boys. His favorites in the culinary batting order were chicken cutlets and meatloaf, but Barbara cooked a New England boiled dinner on special occasions—corned beef, cabbage, potatoes, and carrots—that topped all the others in Shaun's mind.

True to form, Shaun didn't linger long. His cousin's parents were vacationing in Aruba, and dozens of neighborhood teenagers had been descending on the house since midafternoon. The prospects of beer, unattached girls, and friends from the hockey rink were plenty of motivation to get out of the condo as quickly as possible.

Bobby already was at the party when Shaun arrived. After dispatching Jeffrey to wash the dog, Bobby had walked the few blocks to the G&J Variety Store near Donnelly Field to

rendezvous with his friends on the corner. The group headed
to the party, where about twenty people had gathered by the
time Bobby arrived, cooking hamburgers outside, drinking
beer, and swapping jokes. When a light rain began, the crowd
migrated to the porch and then the attic, a single open room
that had been converted into a party-perfect apartment.

The beer came from one of two sources, neither of them
legal. Shaun and his crew had mastered the art of breaking
into trains in the Cambridge rail yards near Boston's North
Station, loading up shopping carts with cases of beer, and
stashing the booty in someone's basement. The stakes were
impressive: a single heist could yield the group enough free
beer for two to three weeks. Another option was the beer truck
that stocked the Windsor Tap, a tired gin mill only a short
stone's throw from Bobby and Shaun's condo. When the driver
wheeled a delivery inside, usually once a week, Shaun and his
buddies would climb into the rear of the truck and scamper
away with a few cases.

Not surprisingly, the party's agenda included drinking
games. In one favorite, a two-liter plastic Pepsi bottle was
turned upside down, the bottom cut off, and three or four
beers poured into the container. A hose attached to the bottle
delivered as much beer as the wide-eyed person on the receiving end could handle—and usually more. The games were in-
toxicatingly effective, and the party picked up momentum.
Raucous, rowdy laughter mixed with loud, thumping music.
Life was good, at least for the moment, in a neighborhood
where life's options were often limited.

A few blocks away on Hampshire Street, Barbara returned home at 7:30 P.M. to find no sign of Jeffrey.

"He's going to be in big trouble," she muttered, then did
an abrupt about-face, pulled her jacket tight, and left the
building for a brisk walk to Donnelly Field. All the sunlight
had left the evening sky by the time she scoured the edges of a
park she had known for forty years, searching all the places
she knew Jeffrey liked to sit, play ball, or perform stunts on
his bike.

"Okay, no Jeff here," she said aloud. Pivoting for home, Barbara made a mental list of all the parents she would call to track him down. "Does Jeffrey happen to be there with Brian?" she asked one mother on the phone. "Have you seen Jeffrey?" she asked another. Over and over, for forty-five minutes, Barbara dialed two-dozen homes where Jeffrey might have been that day, or where he might be playing still. And over and over, the drumbeat of disappointing answers perplexed and worried her.

At 8:30 P.M., she paged Bobby, who left his cousin's attic to phone his mother. "Your brother's not home," she said. "You boys need to start riding around looking for him. I don't know what's going on." The good times ended with a thunderclap. Bobby and Shaun Curley left immediately to prowl the neighborhood, and with them went much of the party. "Everyone split out of the house after my mother's call—on feet, in cars, whatever," Shaun recalled. Everyone there knew Jeffrey, so Bobby and Shaun's problem suddenly became their problem, too.

Bobby started his search on foot, first to a house a few steps from the party, then to a home two doors from the Curley condo. When those door-knocks turned up nothing, Bobby drove to playgrounds and parks in the immediate area. He scoured the neighborhood until 10:15 P.M., when he broke off the hunt and left for his first night of work at a printing company fifteen miles away. "He'll come home," Bobby said to himself, more miffed than mystified by Jeffrey's disappearance. "He's out there causing mischief."

Shaun also took to the streets, hopping into his beat-up car and crisscrossing East Cambridge in the dark—up by the rusting Lechmere stop on the subway line, down by the posh Galleria shopping mall, and over by the courthouse. "I know Jeffrey," Shaun said to the friend riding with him. "He's street-smart. He's a strong kid. Nothing's gonna happen to him."

As the Curley boys began their search, Jaynes and Sicari left Honda Village and headed to the Bradlees department store in nearby Watertown, purposely avoiding the branch in

Somerville where Barbara Curley worked. The pair arrived just before 9:00 P.M., and Jaynes found his quarry in short order: a green-and-gray Rubbermaid Rough Tote container just big enough to hold the body of a ten-year-old child. The price: $39.99. "I guess I'll spend forty dollars on the kid," Jaynes said.

Sicari lugged the container to the cash register, where he leaned the forty-two-inch bin against the counter and rubbed his eyes, while Jaynes used his father's credit card again to pay the bill. The transaction complete, Sicari awkwardly stretched two arms around the container and followed Jaynes dutifully out the door.

The shopping expedition then shifted a few miles to Somerville, where Jaynes bought a fifty-pound bag of cement and some granulated lime at The Home Depot. By the time of that purchase, at 10:21 P.M., Jaynes had solidified his plan: weigh down the container with cement, cover Jeffrey's face with lime to speed decomposition, and dispose of the body in a watery grave somewhere north of Boston. The scheme resembled a hypothetical scenario that Jaynes had posited to friends two years earlier in a casual, but macabre, conversation. "If I killed someone," he had said, "I would put them in something, put cement on them, and throw them into the ocean."

Jaynes now had what he needed, but he remained worried that his mother would drive to Manchester that night. To ensure that she stayed in Brockton, he phoned her home a dozen times. Letourneau answered most of the calls while Jaynes's mother made her long, obsessive rounds of the Brockton grocery stores, hunting for the absolute best bargains on every item she purchased.

As the night wore on, Jaynes became more anxious with every call. "Tell her she *cannot* come to my house tonight! She *cannot* come!" Jaynes ordered Letourneau, who promised she would relay the message. Jaynes, however, remained unconvinced and continued to phone the house. "Is Ma there yet? I really need to talk to her," he said in one call. "Look, I'm not going to be home, okay? I'm busy. My room is messy." Letourneau, who kept house for Virginia Jaynes in return for lodging, shook her head. Your room is messy? she thought. Your life is messy. I don't get this.

At one point, Jaynes accused Letourneau of lying to him because he knew she despised his interest in pedophilia. That animosity was well founded. Letourneau had found child pornography in his room in Brockton. She had witnessed his vulgar come-ons to young boys. And she had sorted the mail that came to the house from NAMBLA. Letourneau had also discovered four pairs of boys' underpants in his room, underwear that had been worn, folded up, and neatly packaged in ziplock plastic baggies. Jaynes, to her, was evil incarnate, and she never left him alone with her son.

By midevening, Jaynes was frantic and snarling.

"You're just not telling her," Jaynes snapped into the phone. "I'm sure she's called to check in by now, and you're just not telling her!"

"Charlie, I don't know what to tell you," Letourneau said, tired of this strange and maddening back-and-forth.

But Jaynes was only half the problem. Letourneau also had been fielding a fusillade of calls from Sicari. One after another, like a coordinated relay, Jaynes and Sicari had been alternating their calls to Brockton. Letourneau did not realize the two were together. If she had known, she would have been incensed. Letourneau had forbidden Sicari to fraternize with Jaynes if he wished to communicate with her.

If Jaynes sounded panicked, Sicari seemed his usual, emotionless, unrattled self. Although his complicity in Jeffrey's murder grew deeper by the minute, much of his talk with Letourneau revolved around run-of-the-mill arguments between fractious ex-lovers. Letourneau had considered getting back together with Sicari, but she was furious because he had lied about having a job. Back and forth the chatter went: Letourneau's anger at his deception and Sicari's meek attempts to defend himself.

Occasionally, Sicari would digress into a vague, baffling, unrelated riff concerning a search for cement. At one point, Sicari told Letourneau he might be in a fix.

"What are you doing with cement?" Letourneau asked.

Sicari replied that he and two friends were buying concrete to put up a basketball hoop that night. An hour later, he said they were hunting for even more cement.

"How much cement do you actually need, and why couldn't you buy it at one store?" Letourneau asked. "What the hell is going on?"

Sicari's answer jolted Letourneau from suspicion to alarm.

"I really can't talk about this on the phone, and I really have to get this finished up," he said. "If I don't get this finished up, I'm going to be in a lot of trouble."

Letourneau demanded an explanation.

"I've hurt somebody really bad," he said.

"Tell me what you're talking about!" Letourneau shot back, her anxiety rising and her patience exhausted.

"Remember what we talked about yesterday?" Sicari asked in his characteristic monotone, referencing a fatal car accident that they had discussed.

Letourneau, no longer merely confused, suddenly became hysterical. Had Sal hit someone with his car? Had somebody died? That seemed to be the implication, and Letourneau began screaming. "You're on the phone telling me you just killed somebody?" she asked incredulously. "And you have no remorse?"

Sicari answered with a callous disdain that was chilling for its nonchalance. "I could give two fucks," he said. "It's like a bowl of cereal to me. I could either eat it or walk away."

The phone call ended. This could not be true, Letourneau told herself. Sal had told her too many lies, too many tales of fights and beatings that had never happened, too many inventions of street-punk machismo to make himself bigger in her eyes.

Letourneau had put her closest friend on hold to take Sicari's latest call. Now, she clicked back and bombarded Michelle Ward, a taxi dispatcher, with a frenzied, rapid-fire summary of their talk.

"What do I do?" she pleaded. "Should I call the police? I don't know what to do!"

Ward, at work, paused for a second, then whispered, "Holy shit." To her, this development seemed darkly ominous. She had always disliked Sicari and had long worried that he might harm Letourneau. But these cryptic clues, in some indefinable yet undeniable way, seemed dangerously different.

Unsure of Sicari's meaning or Letourneau's legal liability, the pair decided not to notify police before consulting their relatives the next day. Meanwhile, Ward ordered a taxi to the Jaynes home. Letourneau woke up her son, retrieved a few belongings, and was whisked back to the cab company. There, she huddled with Ward until daylight before moving to her friend's apartment.

By this time, Jaynes and Sicari had begun their fifty-mile drive to Manchester. But before they merged onto I-93 for the quick trip to New Hampshire, the pair made their final purchases of the night. At an Osco Drug store in the Twin City Plaza in Somerville, Jaynes brandished his father's credit card once again, this time to buy a box of Garcia y Vega panatela cigars and three packages of NoDoz caplets. The time was 10:33 P.M. The NoDoz would be needed to keep them awake. The Dominican cigars were valuable for their leaf wrappers, which could be unrolled and reused to hold the marijuana that Jaynes had recently begun to enjoy. For Sicari, pot was almost a dietary staple.

Before leaving the plaza, Jaynes placed the car's trunk key in the ashtray. If a police officer wanted to inspect the trunk, Jaynes figured, he'd simply shrug his shoulders and say he couldn't find the key.

Their shopping complete, the two merged onto the highway at a nearby entrance ramp and hurtled north in light, comfortable traffic. As they did, Bobby Curley might have sped past as he hurried to his new job in suburban Lynnfield.

As usual, Jaynes drove. He prided himself on his sense of geography, and he had become well acquainted with southern New Hampshire and southern Maine since he moved from Brockton to escape arrest. Jaynes's mother had paid for months of accommodation in that swath of semirural New

England to shield her son from prosecution, Letourneau recalled. Nothing was too good for Virginia Jaynes's favorite son. But when resort-style lodging on the Maine coast became too costly, Letourneau said, Jaynes packed his clothes in trash bags and moved to less-expensive digs in Manchester.

Jaynes knew the interstates, the back roads, and the rest stops where couples would meet for furtive trysts under the cover of night. A favorite for Jaynes was on I-93 in New Hampshire just across the Massachusetts border. In his experience, the police rarely checked there. He also frequented venues closer to Boston, particularly garages at mass-transit stations and dimly lit, after-hours corners in fast-food parking lots.

By October 1, according to Jaynes, he and Sicari had been sexual partners for six months. He had been interested in Sicari, however, for twice that long, dating to the day in 1996 when Letourneau introduced them and Jaynes made a brazen offer. "I'll give you fifty dollars if you let me suck your man off," Jaynes told Letourneau, who recoiled at another disgusting, predictable remark from a man she loathed.

Later that day, Sicari became enraged when Letourneau told him of the request. If he later entered a physical relationship with Jaynes, he never spoke of it. Indeed, Sicari routinely bashed gay men in conversation, Letourneau said, and "acted like the most homophobic person you'd ever met in your life." But, like much of Sicari's life, that front might well have been a lie.

On this night, Jaynes and Sicari had work to do. They arrived in Manchester shortly after midnight and parked in the rear of Jaynes's apartment building, several dozen yards from busy Elm Street and the late-night commotion at the popular Black Brimmer bar. Near the back entrance that led to his second-floor unit, Jaynes unlocked the Cadillac's trunk, looked around, and carefully picked up the tarp that held Jeffrey's body. Sicari carried everything else: the Rubbermaid container, the duct tape, the lime, and the cement.

The wooden stairs creaked as they climbed, turned left, and paced halfway down the empty hall before opening a set of louvered doors at Apartment 206. The place, as always, was a shambles. Piles of dirty clothes lay jumbled just inside the entrance, spilling out of cardboard boxes or tossed haphazardly on the cheap blue carpet.

Jaynes crossed the boxlike space that served as living room and bedroom, passed under a Honda Village dealer plate, and lowered the tarp to the kitchen floor. Methodically, meticulously, he slowly took the clothing from Jeffrey's stiffening body: the Boston College football jersey, the denim shorts, the socks, the Reebok sneakers, and the underwear. Then, using a single-edge razor blade, Jaynes sliced a waist button and a label from the shorts that Jeffrey's mother had bought at Bradlees for an employee discount. These were Jaynes's souvenirs, he told Sicari, two small trophies from his first murder victim, which he would carefully preserve as life-long keepsakes.

Jaynes placed the items on the kitchen table. Then, with Jeffrey's naked body before him, he prepared to plumb the depths of his criminal fetishes. Across the kitchen, he spotted a long-neck bottle of Coors Light beer. As Sicari looked on, he later told police, Jaynes lubricated the top of the empty bottle with petroleum jelly, bent to the floor, and inserted it into Jeffrey's rectum.

Sicari, sickened, retreated to the bathroom.

"Stop being a baby," Jaynes barked. "Come out here and help me hold his legs. He's getting stiff."

When Sicari returned, he witnessed more of the unthinkable. Jaynes rolled Jeffrey over and placed his penis between the boy's buttocks. Later, with Jeffrey on his back, Jaynes used his mouth, hands, and feet to manipulate the boy's penis.

Jaynes encouraged Sicari to sodomize Jeffrey's body, but his friend refused. No matter. Jaynes had added the ultimate horror to his growing inventory of pedophile experiences. And he seemed satisfied, if somewhat surprised. "I didn't know I was a necrophiliac," he told Sicari. "I didn't know I would like having sex with a dead body."

Nearby, a poster of child actor Jonathan Taylor Thomas added color to the drab walls. A few feet from Thomas, a *Lion King* ad read, "Hakuna Matata," a Swahili phrase for "no worries," in bold, childlike lettering. And on an end table near the couch, carefully folded, lay a child's mesh maroon football jersey, smelling of gasoline and bearing the number worn by Heisman Trophy winner Doug Flutie, a Boston College hero. Jaynes wanted to keep the jersey, he told Sicari, because "it smelled like Jeffrey."

His perversions completed for the night, Jaynes prepared to dispose of the body. He and Sicari stirred the cement, used the pasty mix to line the bottom of the Rubbermaid container, and then inserted Jeffrey's corpse. Sicari heard something snap, probably a joint, as they sharply flexed Jeffrey's neck, arms, hips, and knees to fit inside. The boy's bruised and blistered face tilted up toward the opening. To speed decomposition, Jaynes and Sicari spread lime on Jeffrey's mouth and eyes. They snapped the green lid down and secured it with a crosshatch of duct tape.

Two hours after they arrived in Manchester, the pair had nearly completed their gruesome work. Jaynes and Sicari retraced their steps down the stairs, placed the container in the car's trunk, and parked the Cadillac two streets away. Now, all that remained was to choose a place to dump the body.

As they walked back to the apartment, the Black Brimmer's patrons began spilling onto Elm Street. Despite everything that had happened, only minutes after placing Jeffrey's body in the trunk, Sicari suggested they try their luck with the women. Never one to skip a party, Jaynes went along.

The pair approached two girls, struck up a conversation, and persuaded them to visit the apartment. Sicari made progress with one of them, a girl whose blood-alcohol level might have masked the apartment's mess and locker-room smell. Jaynes, however, was a different animal. Rudely arrogant and grossly overweight, he quickly offended the other

girl, who made for the door after only a few minutes. Sicari's
would-be companion jumped up. "Let me see if I can talk to
her," she said. The woman followed her friend into the hall,
but Jaynes had gone too far.

The liaison had been only a diversion, and Jaynes knew
he could not afford a distraction. After the girls left, he immediately redirected his attention to something more important:
disposing of the container. Jaynes opened an atlas and studied
the area near the border of southern Maine and New Hampshire. Tracing his finger along the map, he stopped suddenly
at the junction of a small river and rural highway. "That's
where we'll dump Jeffrey Curley's body," he said.

The tired streets of downtown Manchester were deserted as they returned to the Cadillac. The sidewalk outside
the Black Brimmer was empty, a chill laced the early October
night, and the only sounds on Elm Street were the rustle of
leaves and two pairs of footsteps. Jaynes steered the car back
onto I-93, this time heading north toward the state capital,
Concord, before meandering east on a secondary highway to
Portsmouth, a historic seaport on the southern bank of the
Piscataqua River.

The pair reached Portsmouth just over an hour later, at
4:30 A.M., and stopped at a Bickford's restaurant at the main
highway circle outside the city. There, Sicari and Jaynes found
a Dumpster, where they tossed the empty lime and concrete
bags and some of Jeffrey's clothing.

So far, the cover-up was problem free. But, like the bum-
bling amateurs they were, the pair returned to the car to discover they had locked themselves out. The trunk key, which
also opened the doors, lay stashed in the ashtray.

Jaynes, panicking, scurried into Bickford's for a wire coat
hanger. As a few customers watched, the waitress told him to
try the front desk of the adjacent Howard Johnson's Motor
Lodge. There, a sleepy receptionist found one, and Jaynes and
Sicari were on their way.

Less than a mile north on Route 1, Jaynes pulled into a
twenty-four-hour Exxon station just as a driver for Poland

Springs water stopped on the opposite side of the highway. The driver, William Merrill, had coffee on his mind when he heard someone yell at him from the Cadillac.

"Do you know any cheap motels in the area?" Jaynes asked.

Merrill leaned down to the passenger-side window and told Jaynes of a few motels just south of the gas station. As he did, he spoke across Sicari, who seemed nervous and kept his head turned from Merrill for the entire conversation.

The roads around Portsmouth had become busier, daylight and the morning commute were approaching, and Jaynes decided that the time had come to dump the container. After a short drive across the Piscataqua River into Maine, Jaynes left Route 1 and headed north on a winding, two-lane road that roughly paralleled the New Hampshire border. After twelve miles and twenty minutes, Jaynes found his spot: a short bridge in the small town of South Berwick that spanned the meandering Great Works River.

Even here, the predawn traffic had picked up, carrying workers to the navy yard in Kittery, Maine, and the Seabrook nuclear power plant in New Hampshire. Afraid of being seen, Jaynes made several trips back and forth across the bridge. He turned around on dirt roads lined with pumpkins and rusted cars and even used the driveways of the few, scattered homes. "No, no, don't put the coffee on," he joked at one house. "We're not staying."

Eventually, they stopped about fifty yards north of the river, popped open the trunk from inside the car, and carried the container to the bridge. From the guardrail, where they rested the box, Sicari could make out the slow-moving current. In the darkness, he noted lily pads, trees on the banks, and bending grasses. Jaynes dropped his end of the container over the side, and Sicari followed suit. When the bin hit the water with a loud, jarring splash, Sicari's throat tightened. A motion sensor suddenly brightened at a nearby ranch house.

While Jaynes and Sicari scurried back to the car, William Smith drove past the Cadillac on his way to the nuclear plant. The car and its location struck Smith as very odd. Here was a car with Massachusetts plates, heading away from Sea-brook and the navy yard, parked on a sand embankment with no visible occupants. Smith checked the side of the road as he drove past, looking for a driver who needed help. He saw no one and proceeded to his job.

Jaynes and Sicari, their deed unseen, reentered the car at 5:22 A.M., according to the dashboard clock. Ten minutes later, they stopped at the Dover Point Variety Store in New Hampshire, where Tracy Carr had just opened up. Sicari, her first customer of the day, walked in and ordered two coffees, a pack of cigarettes, and a Danish. Greg Garvin, a regular customer, was about to enter the store when he saw Sicari exit. Garvin stopped, waited for Sicari to pass, and greeted him with a cheery "Good morning!" Sicari, startled, never uttered a word.

The killers returned briefly to Manchester before driving back to Cambridge. When they reached Sicari's apartment at 9:00 A.M., Jaynes took a moment to consider the anguish that was building, minute by minute, at the Curley household a block away.

"You should go over and knock on Barbara Curley's door, and ask her where Jeffrey is," Jaynes said, savoring the cruelty. "We'll torture her. Next weekend, we'll kill Shaun Curley. The weekend after that, we'll kill Bobby Curley. And then we'll keep calling the mother, asking for her kids."

His goal, Jaynes told Sicari, was to be a famous killer. Just like Jeffrey Dahmer.

———

—— 3 ——

The Face
of Evil

IN CAMBRIDGE, the evening of October 1 crept toward midnight as Barbara Curley sat anchored to a window seat facing the driveway. Shaun continued to drive the streets and
back alleys of East Cambridge, and Bobby reported to work.
Finally, at 11:30 P.M., Barbara confronted the inevitable and
filed a missing-persons report with the Cambridge police. The
officer who reported to the condominium told Barbara that
police would be alerted immediately about Jeffrey but that the
child would not be considered missing until twenty-four hours
had passed.

Barbara was incredulous. "You've got to be kidding me,"
she said.

"If he's not home by morning, call us back," the officer
replied. "He could be sleeping at a friend's house. Call us in
the morning."

For Barbara, there would be no sleep. Instead, she began
to feel the pangs of panic, even as she clung to the hope that
Jeffrey would come bounding toward the house at any second.
"He's just at a friend's. He's going to come home," she told
herself over and over again. "I'm going to be so upset with him.
And then we're going to laugh afterward, and I'm going to hold
him and kiss him and never let him out of my arms again." But
as the hours marched past midnight, instead of Jeffrey's smile,

Barbara saw only the harsh glare of lonely streetlights on nearly empty Hampshire Street.

Across the city line in Somerville, Bob Curley and Mimi were asleep when Barbara contacted the police. Bob had worked in the garden after an uneventful day at work, watched a television special on Cuban baseball, and greeted Mimi when she walked in the door at 7:30 P.M. after another exhausting, ten-hour day of counseling.

Barbara, who deeply resented Mimi, did not have their telephone number. Instead, when the phone rang at 1:30 A.M., Bob woke to hear his sister Francine's voice.

"Bob, it's about Jeff," said Francine, who had heard the news only minutes earlier and was now at Hampshire Street. "He hasn't come home. The boys are trying to find him. Barbara's hysterical."

"Okay, okay, I'll be right over," Bob said, still groggy. "He's all right, Francine. Don't worry."

"I don't know, Bob," Francine said, her voice trembling slightly.

Bob hurriedly threw on some clothes, leaned over the bed, and murmured to Mimi, "I have to go. I have to go."

"What happened?" she asked.

"Jeff hasn't come to the house."

On the short ride to Hampshire Street, Bob tried to digest what he'd just been told. He was concerned but not fearful. Everyone knew Jeff could be a handful. That little son of a gun, he thought, pulling something like this. But at the condo, as he walked down the driveway to the door, Bob could see the play of shadows in the home. Suddenly, he felt a knot of worry. This can't be, Bob assured himself.

When Bob entered the living room, Barbara turned from her window seat. "The baby's missing," she said quietly.

Her brother Charlie and three friends had joined Francine at the house, phoning hospitals and dissecting the situation. Bobby Jr. called regularly for updates, but he couldn't concentrate and returned home at 3:30 A.M. to join the vigil. Shaun had parked his car near the courthouse on Cambridge Street, fallen asleep, and then woken with a start. Was this all a dream? he asked himself. By 4:00 A.M., when he arrived home, more relatives and friends had congregated there.

In the predawn darkness, the brothers resumed their search, by the subway tracks, by the Charlestown bridge, and by the idle freight trains where Shaun would steal his beer and Jeffrey would light railroad flares and shake them in the air. At the condo, Bob and Barbara believed daylight would bring a good conclusion. Hope, as yet, had not given way to despair. Someone made coffee, others cobbled together information for a flier, and another person checked the hospitals one more time.

When dawn broke, Francine encouraged Barbara to call the police again, but Barbara, reluctant to cause a fuss, wanted to wait until 10:00 A.M. Unable to hold out, Francine took matters into her own hands and called Officer Frank Pasquarello, who handled the department's public relations.

"What are you doing about my nephew?" asked Francine, who was Pasquarello's insurance agent.

Pasquarello assured Francine that a search had begun. Almost immediately, three officers arrived at the Curley home, including Detective Sergeant Lester Sullivan, a seventeen-year veteran of the department, who investigated domestic violence and sexual assault.

As the police began their work, using standard procedures for missing-persons cases, the Curleys were flummoxed and unprepared. As police are fond of saying, everyone is a suspect, and no one is a suspect. So, when one officer stopped Francine to ask if Bob might have taken Jeffrey to punish Barbara, Francine fired back with an indignant, emphatic, "No!"

The boys also began to wonder if they had become suspects. Shaun became irate when police said his account of the previous day didn't match the versions provided by other members of his family. "You know something, buddy," Shaun snapped. "My point of view might have been different from my mother's. It might have been different from my father's. It might have been different from my brother's. But you just asked me the last time I remember seeing my little brother, and this is what I'm telling you!"

The officer, sensing an altercation in the making, abruptly ended the interview. "All right, all right, we're going to get this stuff together."

Bobby became offended when he saw police sifting through his belongings. "What the hell's going on?" he barked. "This is my personal stuff!"

By late morning, word of Jeffrey's disappearance had begun to spread throughout the community, and clusters of neighbors walked to the condo to offer help. By early afternoon, their numbers had swelled to the hundreds.

Sullivan now had a full-bore community crisis to manage. To better coordinate the investigation, he asked for the department's mobile command vehicle, a van equipped with phones, tables, maps, and computers, which he stationed near the house. Police began a door-to-door canvass of the entire neighborhood, encompassing hundreds of homes and businesses stacked side by side in an urban jumble. Jeffrey's teachers also had been contacted and asked to compile a list of his friends and classmates. Police knocked at the homes of each of these children, and teams of volunteers scoured streets, alleys, backyards, playgrounds, sheds, garages, and everything in between.

Thousands of fliers, printed and copied that morning by Francine and others, carried a treasured family snapshot of Jeffrey, a bright-eyed ten-year-old with a Little League cap on his head, a bat on his shoulder, and an open, gap-toothed smile. The fliers were tacked on hundreds of telephone poles, showered on commuters at subway stops, and handed to motorists who slowed to a crawl as they passed by the throngs gathered outside the condo.

Bobby Curley continued his painstaking search, both on foot and by car, as the day progressed. The work helped distract him from the dark possibilities lurking behind Jeffrey's disappearance. Bobby knew more about the neighborhood's criminal underbelly than many of the police, but he chose not to dwell on that scenario. In any event, he ceded the early investigative work to the professionals.

That strategy began to change in late morning when a friend, Elvis Gonzalez, told Bobby that his nephew had just mentioned something interesting. A guy named Charles Jaynes supposedly had offered Jeffrey a bicycle the previous week. And Jaynes, the nephew said, was a friend of Salvatore Sicari's.

Bobby's antennae shot up, and he and Gonzalez began the short walk to Sicari's apartment. On the way, they spoke to a neighbor who knew Sicari and said she had seen Jaynes in the area. "Yeah, friggin' Jeff's been over here," the neighbor said. "They horse around with him. They even threw him in the trunk of a car."

Bobby and Gonzalez rang Sicari's ground-floor doorbell. The sound woke Sicari, who, rubbing his eyes, answered the door dressed only in boxer shorts.

"Where were you last night?" Gonzalez asked.

"I was out drinking with a couple of girls. I just got in," Sicari answered.

"Where's Jeffrey? You seen Jeff?" Gonzalez said.

Sicari paused for a few seconds, stunned by the question and wondering what Gonzalez knew and how anyone could have connected him to Jeffrey's disappearance. He answered that he had seen Jeffrey walking the Rottweiler the previous afternoon.

"Okay, who's this Charles Jaynes character?" Bobby asked. "What's he look like? How do we get a hold of him?"

Sicari mumbled that he had seen Jaynes around the neighborhood but did not know how to reach him.

"All right, put your shit on," Bobby snarled. "Let's go."

Sicari dressed quickly, pulling his Georgetown Hoyas sweatshirt over his head as he stumbled back downstairs, where Bobby and Gonzalez walked him to the front of the Curley condominium. As Bobby pondered his next move, Sicari immersed himself in the volunteer effort. He grabbed dozens of fliers, handed twenty to a Cambridge police detective, and stood in the middle of Hampshire Street to flag down passing cars.

Gonzalez, meanwhile, entered the house, where he told Francine that he and Bobby had spoken with someone who saw Jeffrey the day before.

"Ask him to come inside," Francine said.

Clutching a fistful of fliers, Sicari joined Francine at the Curleys' kitchen table, where he told her about the altercation with Jeffrey and the dog. Unprompted, he also told Francine that he had met a friend, Charles Jaynes, after the confrontation. He and Jaynes then drove to the Boston Public Library, Sicari said, before stopping at Honda Village in Newton and Jaynes's apartment in Manchester, New Hampshire. There, they met two girls and drank until the early morning.

Why is he telling me this? Francine wondered. Still, she was grateful for the information and asked Sicari if he would speak to the police. Sicari agreed. Across the room, Barbara sat dazed and drained, fighting a losing battle to maintain hope. Shaun Curley spotted Sicari and introduced him to his mother.

"Ma, this is Salvi," Shaun said. "You know Salvi. He's been passing out fliers for Jeff."

"Oh, thank you," Barbara said softly, just as she had thanked dozens of people that morning. As she turned back toward the window, Barbara noticed a fresh cut on Sicari's left palm.

In the meantime, Sergeant Sullivan entered the home, where he saw Sicari standing with a cluster of Curley family members.

"I have some information," Sicari told Sullivan.

The detective suggested they talk in the privacy of his police cruiser, where Sicari, speaking quickly and seeming eager to help the authorities, elaborated on the story he had told Francine.

"You know, I've seen this guy Jeffrey's befriended lately," Sicari said.

"How old is he?"

"About twenty-five, about three hundred pounds, drives around in a gray Cadillac," Sicari answered.

"And he befriended a ten-year-old?" Sullivan asked.

"Yeah, he's been with him. He gives him rides in his car. He offered him a bike," Sicari continued.

To Sullivan, a veteran investigator, something seemed wrong. "I'm taking it all in," the detective recalled later, "and I'm thinking, How does he know all this stuff?" Sullivan handed Sicari a cell phone and asked him to page Jaynes. After fifteen minutes and no reply, the two walked to Sicari's apartment, where they tried again on a home phone, whose number Jaynes would recognize. Again, no return call.

The sergeant thanked Sicari and said police might contact him later. When he returned to the command post, Sullivan called headquarters for background checks on Jaynes and Sicari. What he heard—seventy-five outstanding arrest warrants for Jaynes—amplified his steadily increasing alarm.

Sullivan next called Detective Sergeant Patrick Nagle, a Vietnam-era navy veteran who handled Cambridge homicide investigations.

"Pat, I think you want to come down here," Sullivan said. "We have a missing child, but it might end up being much more. There's media here. They're giving out fliers. It's kind of wild."

"I'll be right down," Nagle replied.

Sullivan added a kicker. "I was just approached by this guy," the detective said. "We got to talk to him a little more. There's something here."

Nagle needed only a few minutes to reach the command van. Sullivan briefed him on his talk with Sicari, whom they could see passing out fliers only a few feet away.

Nagle approached Sicari and introduced himself. Sicari once again related his story as they walked through the neighborhood—past Jeffrey's grandmother's house, past Market Park, past Sicari's apartment, and back to the command post. He had last seen Jeffrey near Market Park about 3:00 P.M. the previous day, Nagle was told, when Jeffrey whipped his "hundred-forty-pound, big-ass Rottweiler" into a frenzy. The dog tried to attack him, Sicari said, before Jeffrey left for his grandmother's house. After the confrontation, Sicari continued, he met his friend Charles Jaynes, and the two spent the night at Jaynes's apartment in Mansfield, New Hampshire.

"There is no Mansfield, New Hampshire," Nagle said.

"Well, something like that," Sicari replied with a shrug.

Before they separated at 12:45 P.M., Sicari gave Nagle a beeper number for Jaynes and agreed to speak to the detective later.

As Nagle returned to police headquarters, Sicari returned to the Curley driveway, where family members, volunteers, news media, police officers, and the merely curious mixed in a crush of concerned and angry people. Bob Curley stood with Francine on the single concrete step that served as the household "porch," watching the surreal scene swirl around them. Up to this point, Bob had been reluctant to concede the worst. But now, exhausted and disheartened, he confided his fears to his closest sibling.

"I know Jeff. He'd be home now," he said to her. "I know Jeff is dead."

Francine placed her hand on Bob's shoulder, rubbed the back of his suede leather jacket, and offered a few words of comforting encouragement. Unknown to him, she shared his conclusion but had not yet found the ability, or the willingness, to verbalize the unspeakable. Bob had designated himself the on-scene coordinator for the family's search efforts, but Francine remained the unflappable, emotional rock. She kept her distress to herself, smiled at her brother, and wandered over to the police van for another status report.

As she did, Sicari approached Bob.

"I'm sorry what happened. I hope Jeffrey comes home," Sicari said, leaning forward to hug Bob. "Whatever I can do, just let me know."

Bob nodded, accepting this unexpected empathy from a neighborhood oddball and petty thief. In Bob's world, even thieves had shown small decencies in trying times, and he was willing to concede this generosity of spirit to Sicari. "He was always doing something wrong," Curley said later of Sicari. "But that was nothing that I was unaccustomed to, growing up around here. I knew guys who would steal cars, guys who would do bad things. I didn't hang around with them, but I got along with them, you know? That was kind of the way I viewed him, too."

Then, in a reprise of his conversation with Francine, Sicari began blurting out a riff of unsought information. Not content with a few simple words of consolation, Sicari launched into a bizarre, run-on diatribe about Charles Jaynes, someone Bob had never seen or heard about.

"You know, a lot of people have talked about Jaynes and me being queers," Sicari began. "But there's no way that Jaynes could be fucking queer. Because when we're driving down the street and he sees a girl that he likes, he says, 'I'd like to fuck her,' you know?"

Bob was dumbfounded and unnerved. Sicari's statement about Jaynes, following his awkward embrace, had been so bizarre that Bob immediately became suspicious.

Sicari turned toward the street to hand out fliers, passing Shaun Curley on the way. Shaun was exhausted, and he approached his father for reassurance.

"Dad, Jeff's coming home, isn't he?" Shaun asked. "He's gonna be all right, isn't he?"

Bob hesitated. "No, Shaun, Jeff ain't coming home," he answered, his eyes narrowing. "Something's wrong here, and I don't know, but I think Salvi's got something to do with it."

Sicari stood one hundred feet away, half-hidden by the crowd. But Shaun could see him watching their conversation with what seemed to be a smirk.

"Dad, listen, I've known that kid my whole life," Shaun said, perplexed. "The kid sold drugs, he did whatever, but there's no way, Dad."

"I'm telling you, I think he had something to do with your brother's murder," Bob said. With that, he dropped his head on Shaun's shoulder, chest heaving, and began sobbing for the first time since he heard of Jeffrey's disappearance. "Listen, this fucking piece of shit right here had something to do with your brother," Bob whispered into Shaun's ear, his voice low, insistent, and desperate.

"Listen, Dad," Shaun pleaded. "I'm telling *you*, there's no way."

To Shaun, the idea that Sicari had murdered his brother was preposterous. Sicari was a nobody, a skittish recluse from the shadows of the neighborhood who had always lived in fear of the Curleys. But Shaun had never seen his father cry before. And he respected his father's gut instincts, honed by a lifetime on these gritty streets. Maybe, Shaun thought, his father knew something.

Now, their arms around each other, Shaun cried, too.

"We've got to pull ourselves together," Bob said, struggling to regain control. "Talk to your brother Bobby, okay? But don't say nothin' to anybody else about what I've told you."

"Okay, Dad," Shaun replied. "Okay, okay."

Bobby, however, had already relayed his suspicions about Sicari to police, who assured him they would take care of the police work. The message, as Bobby recalled, was to take a seat on the sideline. Bobby wasn't interested in that option. This was his brother, and no one was going to tell him what to do.

Bobby consulted with Gonzalez. "Okay, forget the police, forget everything," Bobby said. "We're gonna figure this out." The friends became their own street detectives, circulating through the neighborhood, asking questions, and digging deeper into this murky figure named Charles Jaynes.

Sicari took a break from passing out fliers and returned home. Wayne Garber, who lived above him, was heading out the door as Sicari approached the building.

"Garber, what's up?" Sicari said.

"What's going on?" Garber answered.

"Did you hear little Jeffrey's gone?"

"No, what are you talking about?" Garber asked.

"Little Jeffrey's missing," Sicari repeated. "I'll be going back down to the mother's house and help them put up fliers and stuff."

A few minutes later, Sicari felt his beeper vibrate with an urgent page from Detective Nagle.

"Sal, can I speak with you at the station?" Nagle asked when Sicari returned the call. Sicari agreed, and Nagle dispatched two detectives to pick him up. Like Sullivan, Nagle sensed Sicari might have valuable information he hadn't offered. And he was bothered by an evasive phone conversation he had just finished with Charles Jaynes.

The exchange began when Jaynes returned a page from an unfamiliar number. When Nagle answered and identified himself as a police officer, Jaynes apologized for dialing the wrong person.

"No, you didn't," Nagle answered. "Could you come to the Cambridge police station to answer a few questions?"

"Why do you want to speak to me?" Jaynes asked.

"It's regarding a ten-year-old boy named Jeff Curley."

"I don't know any Jeff Curley."

"Where are you?" Nagle pressed.

"I'm working in Dunkin' Donuts."

"Okay, which Dunkin' Donuts?"

"In Brockton," Jaynes replied. "I can't come to Cambridge. I'm working a double shift."

Back and forth the pair went. Jaynes tried to assure Nagle he would call the next day, but the detective relayed his concerns to his supervisor, Deputy Superintendent Thomas O'Connor.

"I don't know where this kid Jeffrey is, but we have to make it top priority," Nagle said. "Right now it has Lester Sullivan's interest, and it has mine, too."

Top city management agreed to ask for outside help. Within hours, the Massachusetts State Police, Federal Bureau of Investigation, and National Guard committed personnel and resources, including uniformed officers, detectives, helicopters, and dogs. The news media's interest also grew exponentially. Dozens of reporters had begun gathering outside the house, and by midafternoon, local television trucks had secured the few remaining parking spaces near the home. Microphones and notebooks seemed to be everywhere, and Jeffrey Curley's name, as well as his Little League picture, began appearing regularly on TV throughout Greater Boston. By now, the hunt for a missing ten-year-old, unseen for only twenty-four hours, had become the most intensive investigation in the city's history.

Bob Curley continued to circulate outside the condo, doling out encouragement despite his certainty that Jeffrey was gone. After another obligatory hug, he stopped himself, shaken by the encounter with Sicari and by his own bleak acknowledgment of the worst. This is not fucking happening, he told himself. I can't think here. I don't know who to listen to. The best thing right now is to try to do something normal. With that, Bob trudged to Inman Square, where he sat alone on a stool at a coffee shop, a broken, disbelieving father in a world where every street corner was familiar but every painful emotion was now devastatingly new.

Barbara felt overwhelmed by similar emotions as she sat by the window, surrounded by well-meaning family and friends but unreachable in the depth of her suffering. She had left the seat only briefly during the day, afraid she might miss Jeffrey's return. Her thoughts had not yet turned to murder, but she seriously considered the likelihood that her child had been kidnapped. And in her heart, Barbara also considered the terrifying possibility that Jeffrey had been raped. I wonder if he's calling for me, Barbara thought. He must be cold. He must be hungry. Oh my God, he only had shorts and a shirt on.

As she agonized, an unending stream of food and drink arrived at the house, as did a steady flow of guests—some known, many not—whom Barbara's sisters screened before admitting them. The phone rang constantly. Reporters from all of the Boston media outlets asked for interviews, and Francine's work supervisor even called to report that his psychic believed Jeffrey was alive. Next door, a fight broke out at the

Windsor Tap, where an innocent patron was assaulted because he seemed suspicious. The wife of the beaten man tried to broker a truce, only to be dispatched to a hospital emergency room with injuries of her own.

Inside the condo, the Curley family had reached a lull, their energies sapped by the long search, the lack of leads, and the relentless, circuslike frenzy. For a few moments, they savored a weary, needed, midafternoon silence.

Suddenly, the front door burst open, the quiet shattered by a shrill, shrieking cry. "Barbara! Barbara!" a woman screamed. The family bolted upright from the couch and the chairs, startled but hopeful that this could be a thunderclap of happy news. The woman's next words, however, served only to crush the family with their bland and unintentional cruelty. "Barbara, I just heard," the woman said. "I'm so sorry." Deflated and despondent, the family sank back in their seats.

As they did, Sicari climbed into the back of a Cambridge police cruiser for the short ride to headquarters, where Nagle asked him to settle into a chair in the Grainger Room, an interrogation and meeting area furnished with a long oval table, a television and videocassette player, and a blackboard. The third-floor corner room, named for a former police chief, was fitted with three large windows whose architectural grace had been compromised long ago by iron grates. The bars were installed in the late 1960s after Cambridge activists targeted the police station in a protest against the Vietnam War.

Nagle now felt in his gut that something criminal had happened to Jeffrey Curley. "I was willing to be wrong, I would love to be wrong, but I was suspicious," he said later. Nagle sat opposite Sicari, who seemed as eager as ever to cooperate. This time, for the record, Nagle told one of his detectives to take notes as he asked Sicari to recount his last encounter with Jeffrey.

Sicari revisited familiar ground: He had seen Jeffrey about 3:00 P.M. the day before; the boy had threatened him with a Rottweiler; he had seen Jeffrey enter his grandmother's house. Then, Sicari added even more about Jaynes, whom he said had been sitting with Jeffrey in his Cadillac two weeks before. Sicari confided that he had taken Jeffrey aside afterward. "I told him he should go home and shouldn't be hanging with older people," Sicari said. He also told Jaynes "it didn't look right" to be in the company of young boys.

Nagle nodded, invited Sicari to continue, and then listened as Sicari spoke at unsolicited length about Jaynes's supposed female interests. "He made sure that I knew that Jaynes has this girlfriend and that girlfriend," Nagle recalled. "I mean, he's pounding away at these girlfriends. And I'm starting to go, The guy's three hundred pounds, and he's telling me how many girlfriends he has? Are these two gay? Is there something else going on here?"

Despite his unease, Nagle could not hold Sicari. No evidence had surfaced to connect him with Jeffrey's disappearance. And besides, Sicari had provided police with what little information they had about Jeffrey's activities the previous afternoon. Nagle thanked Sicari for his cooperation.

"If you need any more help or questions," Sicari said, "you can reach me on my beeper. I'll call you back."

Sicari was back at the Curley condo in fifteen minutes. And as he picked up a stack of fliers, Sicari heard his name at the head of the driveway. Bobby Curley, Gonzalez, and another friend beckoned to him from Curley's car, a year-old Toyota Camry.

"Hey, Salvi," Bobby yelled. "We're going over to Somerville. We're gonna hang up some of these fliers. Come on!"

Eager to appear helpful, Sicari quickly worked his way through the crowd and took a seat in the rear. To Sicari's left sat Gonzalez. In the front passenger seat, staring straight ahead, loomed Manny, an older friend of Barbara's whom everyone called "the Portugee." No one spoke until the police and volunteers had vanished into the background. In the meantime, another car with Bobby's friends had pulled in behind them.

Bobby, cocking his head toward the rearview mirror, locked eyes on Sicari and asked, "Who's this Charles Jaynes? Where is he? Do you have his phone number?"

"I only got a pager number," Sicari answered. "That's all I got."

Bobby, Manny, and Gonzalez looked at each other, then at Sicari, unconvinced that he had told the truth. Bobby stared again at the mirror. By now, he had shed any pretense of calm, considered restraint. The time had come to find Jeffrey as quickly as possible—and by whatever means necessary.

"Salvi, listen," Bobby said with a short sigh, the menace in his streetwise voice as clear as the anger in his eyes. "You're gonna take us to Charles Jaynes, or we're gonna beat the fucking shit out of you, motherfucker, until you wish you were dead."

"Look, no problem," Sicari said. "All I want is to find Jeff. But all I got is a pager number."

Bobby maneuvered the Camry through heavy afternoon traffic toward the Cambridge courthouse, where he knew of a sidewalk pay phone that accepted incoming calls. Sicari was told to page Jaynes and wait for a reply. He was also given strict instructions not to mention Jeffrey during the conversation.

Bobby parked the car beside the phone, where Gonzalez stood close to Sicari as he dialed Jaynes three times.

"Something's not right with this fucking kid," Bobby said to Manny, shaking his head. The wait continued for several minutes.

Finally, the phone rang. It was Jaynes.

"Hello, who's this?" Jaynes asked.

Sicari, in a nervous staccato, blurted out a warning. "They think we had something to do with Jeff," he said, his rushed words cascading into each other. "I don't know what's going on."

Gonzalez lunged, but Sicari slammed down the phone before he could grab the receiver. Gonzalez, livid, slapped Sicari hard across an ear. "Salvi, what the fuck are you doing?" he screamed. "What is going on? We told you not to say nothing about Jeff."

Gonzalez pushed Sicari back into the car.

"What was that?" Bobby yelled at Sicari. "Some kind of code for him to get his shit together?"

Sicari stammered again that he only wanted to help, but Bobby and the others had turned a corner. They were now convinced that Sicari knew something about Jeffrey's disappearance.

"Listen, motherfucker, you better bring us to this kid Jaynes right now, or you're gonna be one dead piece of meat," Bobby muttered. "I want to know where he's at."

"Sure, sure," Sicari said, shaking. "We can find him at this car dealership in Newton."

In Bobby's mind, Jeffrey was not dead. He pictured Jeffrey sitting alone in a locked apartment, possibly sexually molested, passing time in captivity with a PlayStation computer game. During the twenty-minute drive to Newton, he planned his next move. Jaynes would be forced to lead them to Jeffrey. But Jaynes and Sicari would not outlive the day. For that purpose, concealed inside his leather jacket, Bobby had placed a loaded .38-caliber snub-nosed revolver.

Bobby reached Honda Village by 5:00 P.M., just in time for late-afternoon, rush-hour madness. Heavy traffic streamed in both directions as hundreds of bumper-to-bumper commuters merged on and off the nearby turnpike. With Sicari in tow, Bobby and his friends walked to the rear of the dealership, where a short, steep ramp descended into the gloomy basement and Kojak's reconditioning business.

"Okay, Salvi, where's this fucking kid?" Bobby asked, squinting as he scanned from wall to concrete wall.

Sicari pointed to Jaynes, who was busy cleaning a car. "That's him, right there."

Bobby moved toward Jaynes, who looked up just as Bobby locked his right arm around Jaynes's shoulders. "Come on, you're coming with me," Bobby said. "We're going for a walk."

"What's this about?" Jaynes sputtered.

"Don't worry about it," Bobby answered. "We're just gonna talk to you."

As they walked, Jaynes's confusion changed to fear. Bobby pressed the barrel of the gun into Jaynes's side, where a thick, limp roll of fat helped hide the weapon.

As Bobby half led, half pushed Jaynes up the ramp, Gonzalez thrust one of the fliers in Jaynes's startled face.

"You seen this little kid, motherfucker?" Bobby snarled quietly.

"I don't know. I haven't seen him. I don't know," Jaynes said.

"We're gonna find out about that," Bobby said, steering Jaynes around the back of the dealership and toward the Camry parked out front.

By now, Jaynes had begun crying loudly enough to attract attention from both the people inside Honda Village and the pedestrians on the street. An employee, watching the commotion, placed a 911 call to Newton police.

Sicari started to speak, but Gonzalez quickly cut him off.

"Salvi, shut the fuck up!" he snapped. "You don't say nothing! You're done! Just shut your mouth and let's go."

When they reached the car, Gonzalez opened the rear passenger door. "Get in!" he barked to Jaynes.

Jaynes bellowed for help, pushing back as Bobby and Gonzalez struggled to force him into the Camry.

"They've got a gun!" Jaynes wailed. "They're going to kill me!"

By now, the crowd had grown to forty people, who stood dumbstruck and frozen as they witnessed an attempted kidnapping in broad daylight on a busy street.

"This fucking kid had something to do with my brother not being around," Bobby shouted. "Anybody that comes near me, I'm gonna hurt you. Stay away!"

No one dared help Jaynes.

Gonzalez and Bobby pushed and pulled, screaming at their quarry and tugging furiously on his arms. Just then, a Newton police cruiser, speeding the wrong way and blaring its siren, braked to a squealing stop. Officer John Geary, a twenty-year veteran of the force, had been on routine patrol when he was dispatched to Honda Village. As Geary stepped out of his cruiser, he found himself outnumbered by a cluster of angry, violent, determined men.

"Freeze! Stay where you are!" ordered Geary, who immediately called for backup.

"Help me! Help me!" Jaynes pleaded. "They're trying to grab me! I didn't do anything! I haven't seen him for weeks!"

Geary had no idea what Jaynes meant.

"He did it!" someone yelled. "He kidnapped the Curley kid!"

Geary had not heard of Jeffrey's disappearance, but he saw that Jaynes was in trouble and pulled him away from his attackers. As he did, Bobby and the others pressed menacingly toward Geary, reaching for Jaynes and forcing the officer to back up toward a wall.

"We're gonna get you, you son of a bitch!" one of them thundered at Jaynes.

"We want him!" another yelled. "We're gonna get him! We're gonna take him!"

Within minutes, four more Newton cruisers arrived, and Geary had the reinforcements he needed. But during the confusion, before the police could restore order, Gonzalez hid Bobby's gun in the Camry and reparked the car down the street.

Geary isolated Jaynes, who told the officer he had no idea why he had been targeted. Minutes later, when Geary spoke to Bobby, he learned that they suspected Jaynes of kidnapping Jeffrey. Geary called Cambridge detectives, who asked that Jaynes be held for questioning. Geary ran a criminal check, saw the outstanding warrants, and handcuffed Jaynes on the spot. Bobby, his friends, and Sicari were told to follow police to headquarters, where investigators would begin to sort out the mess. "If you don't cooperate," Geary told Bobby, "we could possibly take out charges and arrest you for attempted kidnapping."

On the two-mile ride to the station, Jaynes continued to plead ignorance. "I don't know what they're talking about," he told Geary, shaking with anxiety. "I haven't seen that kid in weeks." At headquarters, Newton police placed Jaynes in a holding cell and waited for Cambridge detectives to arrive for a joint interview. Meanwhile, in the second-floor detectives' office, Sicari began to edge away from Bobby and the others.

"You know, you should be happy," Geary said to Sicari. "We've got this guy Jaynes. You guys—"

"I'm not with them!" Sicari shot back, referring to the Curley group. "They forced me to come over here and look for Jaynes. I'm Jaynes's friend."

Geary was surprised but didn't betray his confusion. "Well, you should feel lucky you're not Mr. Jaynes then," he said. "It looks like there's some serious charges. Good thing you're not involved in that."

Sicari turned white. "What do you think's gonna happen?" he asked.

"There's a missing person," Geary replied. "If there's evidence to hold Jaynes on kidnapping, we'll do an investigation. We'll get a statement from him, if possible, and see if he implicates anyone else."

"What's gonna happen if he says something?" Sicari added.

"If the evidence proves it, they'll be arrested," Geary said.

Sicari abruptly stopped talking.

Jaynes, in the meantime, sat alone in a cell, where he awaited a visit from Cambridge detectives John Fulkerson and Brian Branley and State Trooper Alan Hunte. Fulkerson, who lived two blocks from the Curleys, had just begun his night shift when he was briefed about Jeffrey's disappearance. He had suspected something was afoot when he awoke early that afternoon and saw helicopters circling the neighborhood. Still, when he arrived in Newton, Fulkerson's only information about Jaynes was that he had allegedly taken Jeffrey for rides in his Cadillac. "What happened, who did it, we weren't even close at the time, and we didn't have any ideas," recalled Fulkerson, thirty-four, a seven-year veteran of the force. "We figured he might know something, but we didn't know what he knew."

Jaynes was removed from the cell and brought to a conference room, where Fulkerson read him his Miranda rights and, wasting no time, asked whether he knew Jeffrey Curley. Jaynes said he had met Jeffrey in July in front of Sicari's apartment and that he had last seen the boy on Monday, three days before, about 2:30 P.M. outside the Harrington School. "I picked him up and gave him a short ride to near his house," Jaynes elaborated. "I saw Sal, so Jeffrey got out, and Sicari got into my car. That's the last time I saw Jeffrey." When asked about his relationship with Jeffrey, Jaynes told police, "Just friends."

His story began to unravel when Fulkerson asked for an outline of the previous day. Jaynes said he had stopped at Sicari's apartment in the early afternoon, driven to the Boston Public Library to visit Laurie Pistorino, and then taken Sicari to Honda Village, where they worked for a few hours.

So far, his story matched Sicari's.

After leaving Honda Village at 8:30 P.M., Jaynes continued, he and Sicari drove to New Hampshire and stopped at the first rest area across the border from Massachusetts. There, they parked in a dark, rear corner of the lot, near a Dumpster and far away from the "Welcome to New Hampshire" sign. Jaynes said they drank a few beers, moved to the backseat, "cuddled," and had sex before falling asleep until 7:30 A.M. At that time, Jaynes added, he took Sicari back to Cambridge.

Fulkerson was convinced that Jaynes was lying. At one point, Fulkerson noted, Jaynes denied renting an apartment in New Hampshire. The detective now began asking questions about Jeffrey, whom Jaynes dismissed as "a tagalong little kid" who "loved to run around the lot" at Honda Village. Jaynes admitted that Jeffrey visited the dealership often and that he had treated the boy to dinner at Vinny Testa's, bought him a bike, and even given him $10.

"How can you afford to be so generous to a 'tagalong little kid'?" Jaynes was asked.

"I don't know. I just can," he replied.

Jaynes stressed that he always brought Jeffrey home before 9:00 P.M. "so there wouldn't be any problem with Jeffrey's mother." Barbara did not know of their friendship, Jaynes said, and he had "never thought of asking permission."

"Even though Jeffrey was only ten years old?" the detectives asked.

"No," Jaynes replied tersely.

Ninety minutes after the interview began, Jaynes stopped answering questions. "I think I should now have my attorney here," he said.

The detectives gathered their notes and materials. As Jaynes rose to return to the holding cell, he left police with a startling and mysterious statement: "I want to tell you something about Sal, but I want my attorney present. I could help you guys find Jeffrey." That cryptic comment would be the last communication between the police and Jaynes, whose attorney arrived shortly to introduce himself to a polite but depressed client.

"I don't think he grasped the significance of what was going on around him," said Robert Jubinville, his lawyer and a dapper former State Police detective. "I think it's the first time he had ever been in a jail cell." Jubinville huddled with Jaynes, who asked simple questions about the process and what to expect next. At this point, Jaynes had only been charged with warrant violations.

By now, John McEvoy, the district attorney's first deputy, had traveled to Newton for an update on the high-profile, fast-moving investigation. If any deal were to be made in exchange for information, McEvoy was in position to make that happen. After conferring with his client, Jubinville approached McEvoy with a proposition: "John, give him a second. He'll tell you that Sicari did it, and he'll show you where the body is." Suddenly, authorities had crossed a grim threshold. What began as a routine search for a missing boy had now vaulted into a murder investigation. But whether Jaynes could be trusted, and whether Sicari had played a role in Jeffrey's disappearance, remained gaping, unanswered questions.

McEvoy, a tough, career prosecutor, began to consider Jubinville's offer, the defense attorney recalled. However, McEvoy had no need to be hasty. Jaynes was behind bars for the night, and Sicari was undergoing yet another round of questioning in Cambridge. Sicari had been whisked back to the Grainger

Room about 7:00 P.M., after Cambridge police, concerned for his safety and eager for another interview, dispatched a cruiser to Newton to retrieve their prize witness.

Sicari, who also wished to distance himself from Bobby Curley, agreed to reacquaint himself with Detective Sergeant Nagle. A former boxer and East Cambridge native, Nagle was nothing if not direct. And during this session with Sicari, his third of the day, he intended to determine conclusively if Sicari had been lying. Nagle read him his Miranda rights with another Cambridge officer and an FBI agent present, then opened with a series of simple questions: What's your name? Your date of birth? Your home address? How far did you go in school?

The sergeant then asked Sicari, again, to begin at the beginning: When did you last see Jeffrey? What happened next? What did you and Jaynes do in New Hampshire? When did you come back? This time, Nagle also asked Sicari to work backward from his visit to Manchester. At another point, he asked Sicari to talk about the middle of the evening. "If you're lying, you're going to be off," Nagle said later.

Nagle had never met Sicari before this day, but the detective felt he knew him. Nagle also had grown up and been battle-tested in the neighborhood. Although East Cambridge was within easy reach of the city's "lace-curtain" Irish, the cultural separation sometimes seemed enormous. "You fought every day going to school. You fought every day coming home," Nagle said. "So, you sort of know people. And I thought Sicari was a liar."

Despite that judgment, Nagle interviewed Sicari calmly. After all, Sicari was the best witness he had, and there was no sense in antagonizing him at this stage of the investigation. Indeed, Sicari was free to leave at any time, although it is unclear if he realized his options.

After a long round of questioning, Nagle ordered sodas for everyone in the room, and Sicari asked permission to phone his mother.

"I'm helping the police," Sicari told her at 8:50 P.M. "I'm fine, Ma. I'll be home in a while. I don't need you to come down."

Afterward, Sicari was asked if he would submit to a polygraph test by FBI Special Agent Thomas Donlan III.

"It's up to you, Sal," Nagle said. "It's your call."

"Oh, yeah, I'll do it. I'll do it," Sicari answered nonchalantly.

His willingness hurt him. When Sicari denied causing Jeff's disappearance or knowing where Jeffrey was located at that moment, the polygraph indicated he was lying. Sicari was unaware of the results.

Immediately after the exam, he told Donlan that Jaynes was a pedophile and had wanted to give Jeffrey $50 in exchange for sex. On the previous day, Sicari continued, Jaynes had disappeared several times into an upstairs area at Honda Village. Sicari did not see Jeffrey, he said ominously, but he knew something had happened to him.

By this time, Nagle had received critical, new evidence against Sicari. During a search of Jaynes's car at Newton police headquarters, officers discovered a receipt for concrete and lime, complete with time of purchase, from The Home Depot in Somerville. They also found a second timed receipt, from Bradlees in Watertown, for a Rubbermaid container. Nagle ordered detectives to view the corresponding store-surveillance tapes, which showed Sicari and Jaynes together at the registers. Now, conclusively, Nagle knew that Sicari had lied to him.

The time had come to confront Sicari. But when Nagle reentered the room, he saw Sicari standing, crying uncontrollably, and gasping for air. Donlan asked Sicari to tell Nagle what he had just said.

"I feel something may have happened to Jeffrey," repeated Sicari, who was hyperventilating.

"Whoa, what's the matter, Sal?" Nagle said. "What do you mean something happened to Jeff?"

"Charles Jaynes kept leaving when we were cleaning cars and going upstairs," Sicari said. "Charlie must have done something."

Nagle cut through the smokescreen.

"Sal, have I been with you three or four times during the course of the day?"

"Yeah."

"Have I treated you right?"

"Yeah."

Nagle walked toward Sicari. Pausing for effect, he raised his voice for the first time.

"Then why," he yelled, "are you jerking me around!"

"I'm not! I'm not!" Sicari answered.

"Yes, you are! Tell me about the bag of lime that you bought at Home Depot in Somerville at 10:21 P.M.!"

Immediately, Sicari stopped crying. An emotional wreck only seconds before, Sicari suddenly turned cold and controlled.

"Fuck it!" he said. "Lock me up!"

Nagle, too, reversed roles. "Sal," he asked solicitously, "what would I be locking you up for?"

Sicari did not answer. Instead, he retreated to one of the windows. Nagle, likewise, remained quiet as Sicari thought through his options: Do I save myself? Do I give up Jaynes? Do I have my lies together? What do I do? "The worst thing I could have done was get up and put the cuffs on him," Nagle recalled. "I knew there was more to this investigation."

After fifteen minutes of silence, Nagle emerged from the Grainger Room to find Fulkerson, who had just arrived from Newton. Following a quick briefing, Fulkerson asked permission to question Sicari with State Trooper Hunte.

"Yeah, go ahead," Nagle said.

Fulkerson walked into the room at 12:45 A.M. to find Sicari staring toward Central Square from one of the windows, his body obscured by a set of old, vertical window blinds draped over his back. Fulkerson, relaxed and empathetic, put a hand on Sicari's shoulder.

"Sal, my name's John Fulkerson. I'm a detective here in Cambridge. Would you mind sitting down and talking?"

Sicari wheeled toward Fulkerson.

"Just lock me up! I'm guilty," Sicari snapped. "Get my room ready. I'm guilty."

Then, just as quickly, Sicari reverted to silence.

"I'd just like to ask you a couple of questions," Fulkerson said quietly.

Several minutes later, Sicari walked slowly to the table and sat to Fulkerson's right. He pushed back, slouched in his chair, folded his hands, and buried his head in the hood of his sweatshirt. Fulkerson waited patiently for Sicari to speak, and he was prepared to wait all night. He knew the investigation had turned toward murder, and he sensed that Sicari was the weaker, more vulnerable link.

"I know what's going on. You could help us out with this," the detective told Sicari. "Just relax. Tell us what happened. Let's get this off your chest."

Fulkerson put his arm around Sicari, a gesture from someone who felt instinctively that Sicari wanted to talk. "That hard-guy stuff you see on TV—the good-cop, bad-cop stuff—that really doesn't work," Fulkerson said later. "I tried to be as compassionate as possible. The longer that he thinks he's your friend, and the longer that you can relate to him, the more information you're going to get. I knew it was too late for Jeffrey Curley, but now I was focused on getting these guys to justice."

Fulkerson told Sicari he had just come from Newton and had spoken with Jaynes. He did not disclose what Jaynes had said, but Fulkerson had caught Sicari's attention. "He knew it was bad for him," Fulkerson said. Finally, Fulkerson's strategy paid dividends. After twenty minutes of silence, after the detective's muted questions and gentle persuasion, Sicari began to cry. He lifted his chin, sat bolt upright, and looked Fulkerson directly in the eye.

"Okay, I'll tell you," he said. "I'm guilty, but I didn't kill Jeff Curley. Charlie did."

"Okay, start at the beginning, Sal," Fulkerson said.

Sicari outlined the previous thirty-six hours in microscopic detail. He walked police through the stop at Jeffrey's grandmother's house, the struggle in the car, the Rubbermaid purchase, the sickening scenes of molestation in Manchester, and the disposal of Jeffrey's body. As Sicari spoke, Fulkerson asked very few questions. He interrupted, gently, only when he or Trooper Hunte were confused or needed further explanation. Otherwise, the officers listened with a cool, professional detachment that masked an inner horror. "He just went on and on," Fulkerson said.

Sicari told the detectives what they could find in the Manchester apartment. The Boston College jersey would be next to the couch, he said. The Coors bottle would be in the kitchen, along with the waist button and the clothing label that Jaynes had kept as trophies. *Lion King* toys and paraphernalia would be everywhere.

This time, Fulkerson believed Sicari. "There was some discussion among us afterward whether he was more involved in the murder or not," Fulkerson recalled. "But it was just the way he was telling us. He was looking me in the eye; there was no hesitation. I believed him all the way."

The time was 3:00 A.M., and Fulkerson asked Sicari if he would ride with him to New Hampshire and Maine, where police would begin their search immediately.

"Are you willing to show us where you dumped him into the water?" Fulkerson asked.

"I'll go with you guys," Sicari replied. "But I won't go with anybody else."

With that, Fulkerson placed Sicari in handcuffs, charged him with the murder of Jeffrey Curley, and escorted him downstairs to the booking room, a small rectangular space tucked behind the first-floor reception area. As Sicari was channeled through a routine checklist of fingerprints, photographs, and standard questions, he seemed only marginally aware of his situation.

"How much time do you get for a murder charge?" Sicari asked George Sabbey, the booking officer.

"I don't know," Sabbey replied matter-of-factly, his eyes focused on the arrest report.

"I should get a few years knocked off for telling you guys I know where the body's at," Sicari said.

No response.

Standing before the Plexiglas divider that separated him from Sabbey, Sicari appeared completely at ease. He grinned, he joked, he answered questions quietly and politely, and he watched Sabbey work with almost childlike interest. He also handed over an earring, belt, pager, set of keys, and seventy-one cents in cash.

After Lieutenant Garfield Morrison, the overnight supervisor, read Sicari his rights, the suspect posed a stunning question. Would the charge, he asked, mean he no longer would be required to attend meetings for alcohol and abuse therapy? Sicari looked quizzically at Morrison, who kept his gaze trained downward. "Sal," Morrison said slowly, "I don't think you have to worry about that. I don't think you have to worry about that at all."

Fulkerson entered the room at 4:15 A.M. and let Sicari make one final call to his mother. Incredibly, he included a joke in the message. His booking number, he told her with a smile—his "lucky number"—was 37735.

"Come on, Sal. Let's go," Fulkerson said.

As Sicari hurtled north in an unmarked State Police car, Nagle drove home on deserted city streets. He had been up for nearly twenty-four hours, during which he had watched a missing-child report turn into the biggest murder investigation the city had ever conducted. Nagle's father also had been a homicide detective, one whose resume included the infamous Boston Strangler case. So, for Nagle, the gruesome particulars of such a job had long been familiar. Even as a kid, he recalled, police talk would dominate discussion around the Thanksgiving table. But something about the Curley case had touched him more than others. When he arrived home, his wife could sense something was wrong as she prepared to leave for work.

Nagle went straight to bed. When he awoke a few hours later, he noticed the strangest thing. One of his Rottweilers, a 150-pounder named Nitro, was curled near him on the bed. The sight confused Nagle because his dogs were banned from the bedroom. But then, lying alone in the morning, Nagle recalled the events of the previous day. And the dog's presence, a protective one, suddenly made sense. "I must have been crying," he said.

———

4

The Long
Journey Home

WHILE DETECTIVES interviewed Sicari, much of the Curley family searched for Jeffrey deep into the night. Barbara clung desperately to a fading belief that her son was alive. Most of the siblings, in-laws, and friends who ventured in and out of the tense, edgy condo that evening shared her stubborn faith.

When he returned home from Newton, Bobby updated his father that Jaynes had been arrested, but they both continued to believe that Sicari was complicit. Little information had come from Cambridge police headquarters during the lengthy and complicated interrogation. Until authorities knew exactly where they stood, they were reluctant to share any news that might raise or dash the family's hopes.

Part of the family fanned out toward the Museum of Science in Cambridge, near the Charles River, where they used flashlights to peer into abandoned buildings and patrol a confusing maze of new, nearby construction. Francine joined that group, despite a sore ankle. Overhead, the whir of police helicopters equipped with high-intensity lights and infrared heat sensors heightened the sense of emergency.

Bob, his brother John, and Bobby Jr. headed in another direction, toward Union Square in Somerville, to explore a ramshackle building filled with old radiators, where teenagers and young men from the neighborhood were known to drink and take drugs. Bob sat in John's truck while his brother and son scoured the lot. The scattershot nature of the search, particularly here in Somerville, seemed to Bob nothing more than the futile, desperate act of a family holding out for a million-to-one strike. We're just fucking wasting our time, he said to himself, staring at an endless stream of taillights in Union Square. We're just shoveling shit against the tide. Elsewhere, Shaun busily canvassed Broadway and other major streets in East Cambridge, tacking fliers on the few poles without them and distributing others to late-night pedestrians, the sober and the not-so-sober.

By midnight, most of the family had returned to the condo, where they tried to buoy each other's spirits before leaving for their separate homes until morning. Bob remained at the house with a few others. Barbara, as always, kept vigil at the driveway window. "I just couldn't leave," Barbara recalled. "I was just kind of frozen there for the longest time, until Bob couldn't take it anymore."

Bob pleaded with Barbara to sleep, concerned that she might collapse, physically and mentally, if she did not rest for a few hours. "Barbara, you haven't slept in a couple of days," he said. "You have to go upstairs and try to lay down. When Jeff comes home, you're not going to want him to see you like this." Barbara agreed and pulled herself slowly upstairs, where she lay down for the first time since Jeffrey had disappeared, in the same bed where Jeffrey had slept beside her.

Bob did not believe his words of hope, and he did not sleep, although a deep stillness had descended over the house. His thoughts, undistracted in the dead of night, revolved endlessly around the what-ifs and the might-have-beens for a father confronted with the unimaginable. Fear and self-reproach had been clamoring for Bob's attention when the phone rang at 3:00 A.M. On the other end was a Cambridge police officer. There was bad news, he said, and he wanted to send a priest. The details would wait.

When the knock came fifteen minutes later, four sets of hands reached to open the door from inside. Then, in a soft, somber tone, the devastating words were spoken: Jeffrey had been murdered. Bedlam erupted. Shouts mingled with sobs, rage with grief, anger with loss. Shaun screeched in agony, and Bobby ran screaming from the house to Sicari's apartment building, where he howled in anguish on the sidewalk below.

Bob lowered his head and cried, his instincts confirmed and his little son gone. But while pain racked Bob and all those around him, he realized he still had work to do. Barbara lay sleeping upstairs, and Bob knew he must be the one to deliver the news. He walked quietly into the darkened room, sat gently on the edge of the bed, and held the woman who had been his wife for nineteen years. Barbara stirred, her brief slumber broken by the embrace.

"Barbara, Barbara," Bob said in a whisper. "Salvi's confessed. They murdered our baby."

The words cut through the fog of Barbara's drowsiness. Her eyes widened in shock, then horror, and she flailed at Bob with her fists.

"You're lying!" she cried. "You're lying!"

"No, Barbara, I'm not. I'm not," Bob answered, cradling her in his arms. "Our baby's dead."

Barbara sobbed uncontrollably, her soul ravaged by the searing realization that her child had been snatched away, never to return, in an act that was at once unbelievable and irreversible. Her face, transformed and terrified, became a mirror of the depths of human suffering.

Bob let her cry, uninterrupted, until the spasms began to subside.

"What can I do?" he asked quietly. "What can I do?"

Through her grief, Barbara suddenly feared that her sons might hurt others or themselves, tragically compounding the murder's nightmare.

"Make sure that Bobby and Shaun are okay, that they don't go crazy. Right now, I can't deal with anybody," Barbara said. "And, Bob, please, whatever you do, don't let anybody ever forget who Jeffrey John Curley was."

Bob nodded and returned to the living room, where more of the family had gathered and where the sounds of mourning would last long past the dawn.

Francine was among the new arrivals, still recovering from the shock of a 3:30 A.M. phone call in which a woman's unrecognizable voice had screamed that Jeffrey was dead. Through the crying, she eventually identified the caller as her sister Margaret, who had relayed the terrible news while attached to a dialysis machine. Francine drove Margaret's husband, Charlie Francis, to Barbara's condo. His household had been hit particularly hard by the news. Charlie was Barbara's brother, and his wife was Bob and Francine's sister.

As the Curleys gathered to grieve, Sicari sat beside Fulkerson in the rear of a moving State Police car, his hands cuffed and attached to waist chains. The search had now officially shifted to the many, meandering waterways of southern New Hampshire and Maine, and its object from a missing child to a ten-year-old's body. Sicari appeared eager to cooperate and chatted nearly nonstop with Fulkerson. "Sal was talking with me just like a normal conversation, or as normal a conversation as it could be with someone who was just involved in killing a little boy," Fulkerson recalled.

The objective was to retrace the route that Jaynes and Sicari had taken from Manchester to the river where Jeffrey's body was dumped. The police realized the task was daunting, if not impossible: Sicari had little geographic knowledge of New Hampshire and Maine, and his journey with Jaynes had been done at night on unfamiliar roads.

Fulkerson played on the reservoir of trust he had developed during questioning. The pair talked easily all the way to Manchester, touching on family history and likes and dislikes; they even shared jokes. When they stopped at a Dunkin' Donuts at 5:00 A.M., Sicari kidded about how cops treat the place like a second home. Fulkerson returned the banter. When Sicari told him he never graduated from high school because he had failed gym class, Fulkerson broke into a laugh, asking, "How can that happen?"

"We talked about sports, football, and the fact that he liked dogs," Fulkerson said. "It seemed like he had been an abused kid, that he just wanted to be normal and do normal kid things, and that he didn't have the means to do it." Sicari spoke of his brother, who had been arrested for raping a ten-year-old and of the physical and emotional pain he had suffered at the hands of his mother and her boyfriends. "He made it seem, too, that Jaynes was the real bad guy," Fulkerson said. The detective kept his judgments to himself. "As much as I wanted to hate the guy, my goal was to get Jeffrey Curley's body back to his family. I knew it would torture the family if we didn't."

The police passed through Manchester and continued to Concord. Sicari was unsure where he and Jaynes had left the interstate to head toward Portsmouth, but he had an idea. "I remember four and sixteen," he said. "There was a state seal on a sign that looks like a badge." The police exited when they spotted a highway sign for Route 4. By 6:00 A.M., they had arrived in Epping, New Hampshire, about forty miles away, where Sicari was escorted to a bathroom at another Dunkin' Donuts. Then, on to Dover, twenty miles to the north. Back again to Epping. And, finally, on to Portsmouth.

All along the circuitous route, Sicari tried in vain to remember the bridge and the road where he and Jaynes had stopped. They scouted more than a dozen locations. "We drove along the water, along rivers, and notified different police departments up there," Fulkerson said. "We just kept riding around, and he kept describing the site to us: a white house on the right-hand side of the river, a bridge, a certain type of railing that they rested the Rubbermaid container on, and a light going on at the house." In Portsmouth, Sicari finally recognized his surroundings and directed police to the Dumpsters where Jeffrey's clothing had been discarded. Before leaving the city, they inspected more bridges, but Sicari was unable to identify any of them.

At 11:15 A.M., seven hours after they left Cambridge, Sicari returned to Massachusetts. He led police to the gas station where Jaynes had doused the rag, to the bicycle shop, and to the shops where Jeffrey had been forced into the Cadillac. "Charley killed him in the backseat," Sicari, exhausted, told the officers. "It took a long time for him to die." Police quickly examined the scene, took notes, and drove Sicari to Newton police headquarters, where he would be held until arraignment later in the day.

By now, the news of Jeffrey's killing dominated Boston's newspapers, television, and radio, and his Little League picture became an iconic image of the unimaginable. Reporters from around the country and Canada began making their way to Hampshire Street, where an impromptu shrine of flowers, candles, prayers, and stuffed animals grew to shoulder height and stretched for nearly a city block.

Inside the condo, Bob struggled with emotions that tugged him in jarringly different directions. As a man, he needed to grieve. But for his shattered family, he felt compelled to be a rock of stability. "Bobby and Shaun were hurt, Barbara was hurt, everybody was hurt," Bob said. "I wasn't really concerned with myself. I was worried about everyone else. But what could I do? Jeff was gone, and he wasn't coming back." Despite the pain, Bob began to look ahead. Okay, we'll deal with this, he told himself. What are we going to do next? What's the next step? We've got to bring Jeff home.

But bringing Jeffrey home was becoming extraordinarily difficult—far more so than Bob had imagined. When he heard from police that Jeffrey's body had been ditched in New Hampshire or Maine, he assumed the container had been left somewhere off I-93. The startling truth came via a television news report, in which Bob saw police divers searching the churning tidal rivers near Portsmouth. The revelation hit Bob like a body blow. "This is fucking going from bad to worse," he said. "This can't be happening."

From exhaustion, despair, and a sudden, strangling fear, Bob's legs buckled, and he slumped unconscious to the floor. Nothing that preceded that moment had terrified him as much as the thought of never seeing Jeffrey again. And nothing would hurt him as much afterward.

Bob revived several seconds later, his siblings gathered around him, and struggled unsteadily to his feet. But when he sat down, his head in his hands, he did so as a broken, beaten, empty man. He figured the odds of retrieving Jeffrey's body were very long, if not impossible. By then, however, police from three states—Massachusetts, Maine, and New Hampshire—had already begun to mobilize and analyze the scraps of information provided by Sicari.

While the search intensified, Arthur Kelly, a Massachusetts attorney, received a phone call at his home forty miles north of Boston. An abduction and murder had occurred in Newton, he was told, and an arraignment would be held that afternoon. The son of a former Newton police officer, Kelly knew nothing about the case, but he was one of a few dozen lawyers statewide on the so-called murder list, from which he could be appointed to supplement work from his private practice. For representing Sicari, he would be paid about $54 an hour. "I don't even believe I paid attention to any news about a missing child," said Kelly, a stocky forty-two-year-old father of two small boys, five and three. "But when I drove up to the courthouse, and I saw a number of TV trucks, I knew this was something more significant than a typical murder case."

Kelly proceeded to a holding cell, where he introduced himself to a murder suspect who appeared calm, polite, and cooperative. Sicari felt that he had done the right thing by assisting police and trying to locate Jeffrey's body. "I think he was made to feel, from the officers involved, that he was a hero, that the family would be at rest, that they would know what happened to Jeffrey, and that, more importantly, he had nothing to do with the death of the child," Kelly said.

Sicari's new attorney delivered the news that, no, he was not considered a hero. Instead, the state's charge of first-degree murder showed he was considered nothing but a cold-blooded killer. "I think, to some extent, he felt betrayed," Kelly said.

But if Sicari felt duped by police, a small army of them now assembled in Newton to protect him. An angry, vocal, and dangerous crowd, including the Curley brothers, had gathered behind the courthouse to await Sicari's short walk from the police station. Jeffrey's family had yet to hear the full depravity of the crime. And although Bob tried to prepare his boys for the worst, he feared they might disrupt the courtroom or try to attack Sicari. "I don't want any outbursts, or any crying, or any wailing, or anything like that," Bob lectured his sons.

When Sicari emerged from the police station, a bullet-proof vest cinched tightly around his chest, the crowd surged toward him. Fearing a confrontation, a half dozen wide-eyed police surrounded, pushed, and hustled Sicari across the parking lot that separated the station from the court. "Why are you protecting him?" someone shouted. "Let us do our own punishment!"

Sicari avoided vigilante justice, but he was unable to es-cape a cluster of reporters who frantically elbowed their way through the crowd to confront him. "Why did you do it? Why?" one television reporter yelled, her microphone thrust toward the suspect. Sicari looked straight ahead and shuffled into the courthouse, where Assistant District Attorney David Yannetti waited to summarize the grisly evidence against him for the first time in public.

Yannetti had been summoned to the Cambridge police station the previous night by John McEvoy while Sicari was be-ing questioned. When he received the call, Yannetti was only slightly familiar with the case.

"Have you heard about the little boy?" McEvoy asked.

"Yeah, I remember seeing something about that on the news," said Yannetti, who lived in a tiny, third-floor apartment in Boston's North End. "What's up?"

"Why don't you come down to the Cambridge police station," McEvoy continued. "We've got two guys we're interested in, and one of them is on his way to Cambridge now."

The news had been merely "background noise" on television, Yannetti said, and he took notice only because the report concerned a possible crime in his jurisdiction. As he drove to Cambridge, Yannetti was not even sure he would be assigned the case.

Yannetti recognized many familiar faces when he walked into the detectives' bureau. He had worked with these officers before and chatted easily with them as they briefed him. Soon, Sicari had made his statement, and Yannetti began mental preparations for the arraignment.

After heading home for a few short hours of sleep, he put on a suit and traveled to Newton, where he saw a scene unlike any he had ever encountered. The buzzing, hostile crowd at Newton District Court stunned Yannetti—as did the throng of reporters. Only then did he grasp the magnitude of the case. "It was at that time I realized that this is going to be major news, and it's not going to be the type of case where the press shows up for the arraignment just because they have to," he recalled. "This was really over the top." For the only time in his career, Yannetti was escorted into the building by a protective ring of burly state troopers.

Inside, the small court was packed with the Curleys, their friends, and reporters jostling for the best seats. Sicari, handcuffed and expressionless, exuded an air of tough, untouchable composure as he faced the judge. Yannetti had never prosecuted a case in a courtroom atmosphere as intense as this one. Spectators dabbed tears from their eyes. Mothers held their children. And Yannetti, knowing what was to come, studied his notes and rehearsed his arguments as he prepared to sketch the full, undisclosed horror of the crime.

As the proceedings began, the spectators sat hushed and morbidly expectant. But within minutes, gasps and sickened moans greeted Yannetti's description of sexual abuse, murder by suffocation, and necrophilia. "I wanted to kill him," Bob said of Sicari. "But I didn't want to give him the satisfaction that we were hurt as bad as we were."

Two hours later, Jaynes was arraigned separately on seventy-five outstanding warrants from eighteen courts. Charging him with murder was not yet feasible. Prosecutors did not have Jeffrey's body, they did not have a statement from Jaynes, and they did not wish to offer Sicari a deal to testify against his friend. "Things were very much up in the air with regards to Jaynes at that point," Yannetti recalled.

Jaynes's bail was set at $100,000 cash, and reporters peppered Yannetti with questions as he left the courthouse. "Why haven't you charged him with murder?" one asked. "What if he gets out?" another shouted. Yannetti realized that charging Jaynes based on Sicari's statement and convicting him were two different animals. The district attorney's office, he knew, needed a breather to weigh the evidence and build its case carefully. "I think that with one hundred thousand dollars cash bail," Yannetti told reporters, "he's going to have a difficult time coming up with that type of money right away. We're satisfied that he'll be held."

The Curleys were not as confident, and their anxiety about Jaynes's possible release only compounded the depression that filled the house. Barbara began to take heavy doses of medication, but she could not shake the nagging, haunting questions she asked herself, again and again, about Jeffrey's dying minutes. Her great, unanswered concern was that Jeffrey had been tortured, that he had called for her as he died, and that she had been unable to respond.

Barbara did not attend the arraignments, but she later agreed to accompany Bob to the front of the house, where the family made its first public statement about the murder. "If you people only knew," Bob said, scanning a crowd that stood eight to ten deep in a semicircle before him. "Sal was in my house, and he was telling me how sorry he felt. If you only knew how close he came to walking out of the Cambridge police station, you would be on your knees. You'd be throwing up."

The scene was carried on the evening news, and Bob's anguish immediately struck a chord. To many people who saw him on television, he represented the bedrock face of average, overlooked Massachusetts. Here was a simple man, scarred by tragedy, who spoke to the fears and frustrations of everyday families from struggling neighborhoods far removed from Harvard, MIT, and the polished lobbies of Boston's Financial District. He spoke to places where both parents worked and where the daily grind to earn a living and keep children safe seemed ignored by the media, the politicians, and the power brokers.

Ripples from the murder even reached Washington, D.C., where Senator Edward Kennedy of Massachusetts composed a letter of condolence to the Curleys. "Your Jeffrey left this life defending the values you instilled in him as parents," Kennedy wrote. "He was a young man whose inordinate courage brings inspiration into all of our lives. Mrs. Kennedy and I share your grief."

As the Curley household crumpled with tragedy, the neighborhood seemed to die a little, too. The old, comforting beliefs in family and community had been fractured, and East Cambridge no longer carried a gut-level conviction that its streets were somehow any safer or better protected than anywhere else.

State Representative Tim Toomey, a friend of the family who lived near the neighborhood, had never seen anything like the impact of Jeffrey's murder. "It was devastating. It was surreal. It was something that people just couldn't fathom," Toomey said. "We just didn't know how to grasp it, or even understand how something like that could happen to a young kid like him. It really shook the community to its core."

At the Harrington School, fewer pupils lined up after school for the bus. Instead, anxious mothers waited in idling cars to drive them home. Grief-counseling sessions were scheduled for students who previously had thought murder was fantastical, make-believe fare for television—if they thought about it at all. Now, they were asking questions.

Parents demanded answers, too, but answers were not easy to find. A meeting at the Harrington School, packed with five hundred outraged residents, turned ugly with anger. "It's beyond our comprehension, and we're up against it as a group," said Timothy Dugan, a child psychiatrist at Cambridge Hospital, who moderated the tense and fractious gathering. Drucilla Whiting, a seventeen-year-old, spoke for many when she admitted to an unfamiliar fear of random danger and a suspicion of neighbors who had lived among them for years. "I think what kills us the most was that Salvi was one of us," she said.

A virulently antigay streak also infected the mood. Many news reports had described Jaynes and Sicari as homosexual lovers, and a long-simmering, blue-collar resentment toward Cambridge's sizable gay population stoked some of the rage over Jeffrey's death. Bob, however, tried to tamp down those flames from the beginning. In public comments and private conversations, he urged the community not to channel its grief into a homophobic witch hunt.

He had no such qualms, however, about the death penalty. Before Jeffrey's murder, Bob had rarely thought about the morality or application of capital punishment. But in an off-the-cuff statement on Hampshire Street, while mingling with friends and neighbors, he set in motion a roiling tornado that would soon race across Massachusetts from Beacon Hill to the Berkshires.

When details of the crime circulated after Sicari's arraignment, public reaction was quick, loud, and vengeful. Almost immediately, calls to restore capital punishment bubbled to the surface from state politicians, talk show hosts, and the man in the street. If ever a case demanded the ultimate penalty, even in the country's most liberal state, the Curley murder was exhibit A for many citizens.

Nowhere was that sentiment more prevalent than among the throng outside Barbara's home. There, neighbors began to clamor for the death penalty in interviews with reporters who, searching for new angles to the ongoing drama, were eager to listen. One reporter asked Bob whether he wanted Jeffrey's killers executed. Bob's reply was typically direct: "For anybody who's opposed to the death penalty, you should have been sitting in our house, feeling what we're feeling."

Bob had not realized he was speaking to a journalist. But he meant what he said, and the effect was electric. Bob's call for the death penalty became an instantly irresistible story, highlighted in print, repeated on radio, and trumpeted on the television news. "Once I said that, it was off and running," Bob recalled. "I just blurted it out. I hadn't spoken with the family beforehand, and I wasn't really thinking too much about anything before I said it." For Bob, careful deliberation was not yet possible. As fear subsided, anger took its place. And Bob had found his target. "Being in the spot that I was in, I just couldn't see how anybody could be opposed to the death penalty," Bob said.

No one had been put to death in Massachusetts since 1947, and the state's highest court had ruled a death-penalty statute unconstitutional as recently as 1984. Despite Bob's feelings about the death penalty or how much support he generated, Jaynes and Sicari would not be executed in Massachusetts. No such law existed. But Bob began to look ahead, transitioning from grief to anger to activism against predators. Soon, like a river that gathers speed before a waterfall, the effort became an all-consuming crusade.

One of the first people to encourage Bob was Marilyn Abramofsky, a firebrand who fought relentlessly for tougher prosecution of juveniles after Kenny Claudio, a five-year-old boy who lived with her, had been raped and murdered by a fourteen-year-old neighbor in 1983. Certain elements of the case foreshadowed Jeffrey Curley's murder. Matthew Rosenberg abducted Claudio, a kindergarten pupil, as he played outside Abramofsky's home in the Roslindale section of Boston. Rosenberg beat and molested Claudio, drowned the child, and stored his body in a plastic trash bag in his closet.

Rosenberg, by statute, was tried as a juvenile and remanded to the custody of the state's Department of Youth Services, which was scheduled to release him at age eighteen.

The prospect horrified Abramofsky, who took her outrage to the State House, *The Oprah Winfrey Show*, *Geraldo*, and scores of other venues, in an effort to overhaul the Massachusetts juvenile judicial system. Along the way, Abramofsky founded a group called Parents of Murdered Children. But she also alienated many potential supporters with a brash, confrontational style that included threats of vigilante violence if Rosenberg were freed. "There will be a smile on this face when they lead me off to prison after he's dead," Abramofsky said.

Each time Rosenberg was scheduled for release, Abramofsky unleashed a new offensive to keep him in custody. The case resonated with court-affiliated psychiatrists, who repeatedly judged Rosenberg a danger to society. He was not freed until age twenty-three. In 1996, Abramofsky finally won what she had long sought when state lawmakers mandated that murder defendants fourteen and older must stand trial as adults.

One year later, when Jeffrey Curley was killed, Abramofsky remained an influential voice for the families of Massachusetts murder victims. She knew her way around the corridors of power in the State House, as well as where individual legislators stood on issues of crime and punishment, and she still burned with a passion that bordered on fury. So, when she heard the news about Jeffrey, she headed directly to the Curley home to offer condolences, lend support, and dispense advice.

Bob had never met Abramofsky before, but he knew her case. And when she hugged him at the door, Bob returned the embrace and listened. "I know how you're feeling," Abramofsky said. "But there's a lot harder to come. It really hasn't hit you yet that he's gone. Wait till a week from now, when you see people, and they're shopping, they're buying clothes, they're laughing. And you're thinking to yourself, My kid is dead. Why is everything just going on like nothing ever happened?" She encouraged Bob to be vocal and to ignore advice from the police to avoid the news media. "Murder is not a private thing," she told him. "Murder is public." She pledged that she would return to the house every day until Jeffrey's body was recovered.

Meanwhile, the drumbeat for capital punishment intensified, and Bob Curley became its undisputed champion. In interview after interview, he pressed his case to an audience that soon needed no introduction to this enraged Everyman. "I feel that it's God's way of ridding society of vermin like this that roam our streets," Bob told reporters.

To Bob, capital punishment was one more layer of protection for struggling blue-collar communities, where the need for two incomes inevitably and unfortunately produced latchkey children. "Families have to have two working parents now to survive the way society is," he said in a television interview. "And it's a breeding ground for these people to come in here and prey on the working-class people. They're just sitting back, licking their chops, waiting to get in here and abuse your child. Let's go get them and put the hurt on them. Until people are willing to make a stand, it's just gonna keep going on and on. They hurt me now. They hurt me as much as they can hurt me. And the next person who's gonna be hurt is God knows who."

On Sunday, two days after Sicari's arraignment, Bob and a half dozen members of the family met with District Attorney Thomas Reilly, First Assistant John McEvoy, Prosecutor David Yannetti, and a few State Police detectives to discuss the case. The meeting, in a second-floor conference room at the district attorney's office in East Cambridge, had not lasted long before Bob cut to the point that most concerned him. What chance was there to execute Sicari and Jaynes?

The anger from the Curley side of the conference table was palpable. They knew the death penalty was impossible in a state trial, so they asked Reilly if the case could be transferred to federal court, where capital punishment remained an option. "The main message from them was they didn't want us to stand in the way," Yannetti said. "He came in there wanting the death penalty and made that very clear to us. That was more important of a focus to him than the actual nuts and bolts of the evidence that we had at the time."

Reilly told the Curleys he would explore such a transfer but cautioned that the murder might not meet federal criteria because Jeffrey had allegedly been killed before he was taken out of Massachusetts. "Our function was to reassure them that we would do everything possible to get the harshest possible penalty on these two," Yannetti said.

Bob realized that the odds, even at the federal level, did not favor a death-penalty trial. As a fallback, he turned his eyes toward the State House. Former governor William Weld and Paul Cellucci, his lieutenant governor, had filed a death-penalty bill in each legislative session since 1991. And during each session, the bill would wither or fail.

After Weld resigned in July 1997 to stand unsuccessfully for confirmation as U.S. ambassador to Mexico, Cellucci assumed the title of acting governor. Less than three months later, the Curley murder occurred, and Cellucci was outraged like everyone else. Bob's calls for capital punishment struck a chord with this new, tough-on-crime governor.

Abramofsky, a well-known figure at the State House, arranged a meeting between the pair only days after Jeffrey's disappearance.

"Governor Cellucci, I'm with Jeffrey Curley's father," Abramofsky said by phone from the Curley home. "I was wondering if you could sit down and talk to him. He's devastated."

"Marilyn, when do you want it?" Cellucci quickly answered.

"Now," she replied.

"Now?" Cellucci asked incredulously. "Where are you?"

"Listen, I'll be right over," Abramofsky said in her trademark, rapid-fire delivery.

Bob took a seat in Abramofsky's car, accompanied by his brother Jim and two mothers from Parents of Murdered Children. Within fifteen minutes, they had negotiated the three congested miles to the State House, where Bob was escorted past the state trooper standing guard and into a private meeting with the governor. It was Bob's first visit to the historic State House, where the golden dome of Charles Bulfinch's architectural masterpiece had dominated the heights over Boston Common for two hundred years.

Inside the governor's third-floor suite, Bob suddenly found himself talking father to father with Cellucci about his loss. The discussion did not focus on the death penalty. Instead, Cellucci offered words of comfort interspersed with a parent's anger. "He really was caring," Bob recalled. "But he was also pissed off, and he wanted to do something about it."

For Cellucci, a small-town governor with two daughters, the case hit close to home. "Like everyone else in the state, I was just horrified by this crime," Cellucci recalled. "The security of living in a neighborhood was shattered for the Curley family and for a lot of people in Massachusetts. People were worried that you couldn't even go outside in the streets around your house."

Cellucci had voted against the death penalty as a young state representative from the semirural town of Hudson, forty miles west of Boston, where apple orchards and a cozy 1950s sensibility helped define a community where not much ever happened and where the residents liked it that way. His father owned a car dealership there, and Cellucci, a horse-racing fan and Robert De Niro look-alike, had risen through the ranks of local politics before his election to the state legislature in 1976. Like many Massachusetts Republicans in those early post-Watergate years, he did not ascribe to a rigid right-wing ideology.

Cellucci's thinking on the death penalty changed in 1988, when he managed George H. W. Bush's presidential campaign in Massachusetts and worked closely with the Boston patrolmen and the state trooper unions, who had endorsed the Republican. The police believed a death penalty would protect them if criminals knew they would be executed for murdering a law-enforcement officer. As a result, Cellucci said, "I wanted to say to the men and women who we ask to protect us that we're going to do everything under our power to protect you."

When Curley and the governor emerged from their meeting, reporters were waiting as the death penalty and Jeffrey's murder became linked at the highest level of state government.

"We want to deter this from happening again," Cellucci said grimly. "No one is saying the death penalty is a panacea, but I believe the two individuals in this case should not see the light again." Bob challenged state lawmakers to take a stand against "lowlifes" and predators. And Abramofsky, who had arranged the meeting, issued the same kind of unapologetic warning she had used in her long campaign to change the sentencing laws. "If they don't do something about this murder," she warned under the Bulfinch dome, "this house is going to be torn down."

For nearly a week, Bob Curley's private grief had morphed into a very public drama played out every day to a rapt audience of millions throughout New England. In the process, he had become the most recognizable "average" citizen in the state. He also had become increasingly comfortable with a limelight he had never sought but now would not avoid.

The world, however, looked much different to Mimi, who had entered an anonymous, private purgatory since the murder.

Since Bob awoke to the news of Jeffrey's disappearance, Mimi had seen him only five to ten minutes a day. He would stop by the house, brief her on the day's events, pick up a fresh set of clothes, and hurriedly return to Cambridge. Most of her news came from the television, where Mimi would watch her lover expose a pain that she could neither share nor ease. Mimi would watch Bob place his arm around Barbara or watch Barbara cry, embrace her husband, and lean on his shoulder for physical and emotional support. "I was part of it, but not really part of it," Mimi recalled. "I was seeing at a distance what was going on. He was married to Barbara at the time, it was his son, and I was just in the house on my own."

Mimi could not escape the case. She worked as a staff psychologist at a Cambridge Hospital clinic only two blocks from Barbara's home. On her commute to the office, Mimi would pass the TV trucks, the memorial shrine, and the throngs of mourning neighbors. "I was trying to be there for him, trying to be there for my patients, trying to be there for me, and I'd be losing my sanity," Mimi said. "I didn't have anyone to turn to. It was really tough."

At the clinic, terrified patients would talk about Jeffrey's killing. And as they talked, Mimi listened in torturous silence, unable and unwilling to speak of her relationship with Bob. One patient who lost a child to murder was retraumatized by Jeffrey's death. The daughter of another patient had been a classmate of Jeffrey's. And the son of yet another was hospitalized after he tried to commit suicide.

Mimi was reminded of her distant, yet intimate, relationship to the murder nearly everywhere she went. Even while shopping, Mimi saw a flier with Jeffrey's photograph. "It hit me then," Mimi said. "For the next week, I couldn't go to work. I was just glued to the television, waiting to hear if they had found the body. I just wanted to know, and I didn't have anyone to call."

That wait, for Mimi and the Curleys, seemed interminable. Divers from three states had converged on the Portsmouth police headquarters only hours after Sicari was whisked back to Massachusetts. "We are looking at this as a long-haul thing," said Massachusetts State Police Sergeant Greg Foley, who supervised the recovery effort. "If it takes me to Butte, Montana, that's where I'll go."

Massachusetts dispatched twenty divers from the eastern half of the state. Maine committed its entire dive team. And New Hampshire sent a full contingent from the state Fish and Game Division. In addition, State Police aircraft from all three states scanned the many rivers, coves, bays, and tidal shores near Portsmouth. As they did, police pilots soon found themselves jockeying for airspace with a swarm of news helicopters. "It was a circus atmosphere," said Sergeant Bill Freeman, who headed the Massachusetts dive team.

The search first focused on the dangerous, swift-moving Piscataqua River, which divides Portsmouth from Kittery, a seacoast community in Maine. "A lot of times we had to wait for slack tide, when the tide had stopped running," Freeman said. "That means we only had a twenty-minute window to actually do the dive and search around the bridges."

The effort expanded to Maine and the nearby York River, where police tried to simulate the movement of the Rubbermaid container that held Jeffrey's body. When police dropped a similar container off a bridge, the box sank almost immediately after the lid separated on impact. As a result, police targeted areas near or directly underneath the dozens of bridges they had selected. Later, they would discover that the container used in the crime, its lid sealed tight through impact, had drifted downstream.

John Fulkerson traveled to southern Maine the day after his ride with Sicari. In his travels, he crossed a two-lane bridge over the Great Works River in South Berwick. Everything about the location matched Sicari's description. "I'll never forget it," Fulkerson recalled. "I said, This is it. There's the house. There's the railing. There's the light. And there's a car like the one they saw when they turned around. Jeffrey Curley's right here someplace." Using the impact test as a guide, divers searched only the base of the bridge and found nothing. The search moved elsewhere, but Fulkerson, still drawn to the site, pressed for another dive at a later date.

Exhaustion and frustration, meanwhile, had begun to take a toll on the divers. The work was intense, the stakes were high, and each unsuccessful day brought increasing concern that Jeffrey's body had been carried out to sea. The strain was painfully evident in Cambridge, where a State Police forensic team arrived at the Hampshire Street condo on October 6, the fourth day of the search, to ask for DNA swabs from Barbara, Bob, and Bobby Jr. The request, which could help identify Jeffrey, sent Bob into a frenzy. "What the fuck is this?" he yelled at police. "You already got a confession. What the fuck are you doing here? Why are you wasting our time? Go fucking do some work!"

The next day, a glorious, sunny, autumn spectacular, proved worth the wait. Yannetti and McEvoy had decided after a days-long discussion to charge Jaynes with murder and kidnapping. Even though Jeffrey's body had not been discovered, prosecutors decided to press ahead with their circumstantial evidence. They could not compel Sicari to testify against Jaynes or even use his confession as evidence against a code-fendant. But they had the store surveillance tapes, testimony of repeated contact between Jaynes and Jeffrey, and articles of Jeffrey's clothing from Manchester. "We'd been working on it night and day for five days," Yannetti said. "On that fifth day, we said, What do we do? We have to charge him. When we did, we thought we'd have a very different case than what we ultimately wound up with." What they wound up with was a "miracle," Yannetti said. Fulkerson's hunch had paid off.

The miracle happened seventy-five miles to the north, at a sharp bend in the Great Works River, where a Maine State Police diver discovered the container holding Jeffrey Curley's body at nearly the same time that Jaynes was arraigned for murder. Working four abreast, a Maine dive team searched downstream from the bridge for fifteen minutes before they made the find in six feet of water. The sealed container was sitting upright on the river bottom, having traveled fifty yards before lodging in the trunk of a fallen tree. The code word for success, "lobster," was relayed to all police involved in the search.

Soon, the area around the bridge became jammed with police, reporters, onlookers, and several of Jeffrey's aunts, uncles, and cousins. After taking photographs to document the crime scene, police inserted the box into a body bag for overland transport to the state capital of Augusta. As they did, one Massachusetts State Police diver, Arthur Huntley, was struck by the scent of roses. "I had never smelled anything like that in my fifteen years of diving," Huntley said. "I was flabbergasted. Why would you have that smell, like perfume, like roses, you know?"

In Augusta, the state's chief medical examiner, Dr. Henry Ryan, cut the duct tape with a scalpel and slowly removed the lid. There, enshrouded in a plastic tarp, lay the body of Jeffrey Curley, entombed in a container filled almost to the brim with cool, cloudy water. Only a small portion of his face and feet were visible.

Jeffrey's body was removed from the box. A crooked front tooth was matched against a photograph of the boy. Fingerprints were taken. But there was no doubt who had been placed naked on the examining table. A detailed autopsy would wait for the next day, when a Massachusetts pathologist could arrive to observe. In the interim, Jeffrey's corpse was placed in cold storage overnight.

Word of the discovery was phoned instantly to the Cambridge command post outside Barbara's condo, where Detective Sergeant Lester Sullivan had continued to work during the long search. Now, he and District Attorney Tom Reilly faced the grim task of informing the family. Stepping just inside the door, Sullivan asked Bob and Barbara to speak with him privately in a semisecluded staircase. "I have some very bad news for you," Sullivan said. "They've located the body."

Bob and Barbara broke down. The sergeant relayed what specifics he knew, and Bob's mood pivoted instantly to anger bordering on violence. "I'll kill them!" he yelled. "I'll kill them!" Sullivan pleaded quietly, but insistently, for calm. The boys and other relatives remained in the living room, and Sullivan was aware of the powder keg of emotion that lay waiting there. "I know it's very painful, but I need you and Barbara to be the strength of this family and present the bad news," Sullivan said. "I will be with you, or I can present it for you, but I need you to maintain control for the rest of the family." And so they did, Sullivan said, despite as wrenching a display of grief as he had ever witnessed. Screams and sobs mixed yet again with cries for vengeance in the shattered household.

The autopsy was completed the next day. Yannetti, who flew to Maine in a State Police helicopter, steeled himself for the scene as he passed over beautiful countryside under clear, sunny skies. He had witnessed adult autopsies before—never one for someone as young as Jeffrey. As Ryan examined the body, Yannetti reached deep to summon all the professional cool he could muster. "It's something that will stay with me forever," he said. "There's something so unnatural about a ten-year-old boy on an autopsy table, being killed before he had a chance to live his life."

That evening, Jeffrey was returned to Cambridge, where a police escort led the grim procession to the Long Funeral Home. Bob also returned home, to Somerville, where he reunited with Mimi for the first time in a week. Psychically spent and physically exhausted, hollowed by the killing and unsure what the future held, each of them realized that nothing could ever be the same. "I had this sense that I had no right to feel anything because he was not my son, that this tragedy was Bob's," Mimi recalled.

Bob wanted to visit the funeral home with Mimi, before the rest of the family, to see Jeffrey for the first time since his murder. Reluctantly, Mimi agreed to go in the morning. What she witnessed has remained an indelibly harrowing memory. "They had the place locked up, but I knew he was in there," Bob recalled. "I don't think they knew I was coming, but it really wouldn't have mattered what they said, because I was going to go see him." There, in a small, open coffin, Jeffrey lay in a blue suit, white shirt, and blue tie. Rosary beads had been placed between his hands, and a single pink rose lay across his body.

Bob reacted with a visceral rage that alarmed Mimi, even though she had prepared herself for such an outburst. "I'm going to kill those motherfuckers!" Bob shouted, moving suddenly toward the coffin. "Look what they did!" Several of the staff rushed toward Bob, held him, and tried to calm him down. "It's okay, it's okay," they said. The dam burst, and Bob's rage dissolved in tears. Slumped and shuddering with pain, he gathered himself and approached the coffin. Bob placed a hand on Jeffrey's body, studied his placid face, and shared a final, lingering moment between an innocent child and his heartbroken father.

Several hours later, the doors opened to the public, and Cambridge firefighters monitored a steady stream of thousands who came to pay their respects over two days. Their number included the elderly and children, professionals and blue-collar workers, politicians and parents. And on Saturday, ten days after his disappearance, twelve hundred mourners filled Sacred Heart Church, spilling onto the sidewalk in a funeral that seemed suited more for a dignitary than a precocious ten-year-old. Bagpipes played the familiar strains of "Amazing Grace," 150 uniformed Cambridge firefighters formed an honor guard, police watched from horseback, and Bob and his sons helped carry Jeffrey's silver coffin on a striking, cloudless day. The Reverend Kevin Toomey, the brother of the neighborhood's state legislator, officiated at a Mass attended by Governor Cellucci and District Attorney Reilly.

In the rear of the church, far from the seats where Bob, Barbara, and the boys embraced throughout the service, Mimi sat quietly amid a shell of protective supporters, her hands held tightly by two close friends. "I tried to stay out of the way. I felt like a stranger," recalled Mimi, who had taken a sedative before the funeral. "Many times I would think, Would this have happened if he hadn't been with me?"

Mimi had not wanted to attend, but Bob insisted her presence was important. That presence, however, remained a silent, anonymous, and anxious one. "There was this moment when he was carrying the coffin with the boys," Mimi said. "He looked at me, and I looked at him, but I didn't talk to him that day. After the Mass, I just left."

———

Storm at the State House

BY THE TIME Jeffrey's body was buried in a simple plot at Cambridge Cemetery, outrage over his murder had become incendiary, stoked by a frightening series of gruesome killings that incensed the public and battered the facade of public safety throughout Greater Boston. Echoing the pleas of Bob and his family, a growing chorus of voices, whipped into a frenzy by talk show hosts and opinion shapers, clamored for the reinstatement of capital punishment.

Don Feder, a columnist for the *Boston Herald*, spoke for many when he wrote, "When the brutal killers of ten-year-olds are allowed to live, what does that say about our concern for innocent human life?" He derided Massachusetts as "the last bastion of delirious liberalism" and scoffed at the idea that life in prison without parole was adequate punishment. "Given their sexual proclivities, confining Jaynes and Sicari with men is like locking a chocoholic in a Godiva factory," Feder wrote two days after Jeffrey's funeral. "And if, in a decade or two, some sentimental governor comes along who decides that the duo has suffered enough—'model prisoners,' 'inspirations to others,' 'found Jesus'—these diseased animals could again feel the warmth of the sun on their backs and the grass beneath their feet."

Polling in Massachusetts had long shown deep support for the death penalty. And now, galvanized by Jeffrey's murder, proponents and sympathetic politicians sprang into action in the volatile weeks that followed. Public support might never be greater, they realized, and a better opportunity might never arise.

That support was fueled by anger over a two-year spate of murders, all highly publicized and all remarkable for their brutality, that had horrified Massachusetts since the 1995 slaying of Janet Downing by Eddie O'Brien, her fifteen-year-old neighbor in Somerville. In June 1996, the region was stunned again by the murder of Kristen Crowley, a twenty-seven-year-old woman from Peabody who had been abducted by two men outside a late-night convenience store and hauled into the brush. There the men, who had just left a nearby strip club, used a forty-five-pound rock to crush her skull. Three months later, a six-year-old boy was abducted in Lynn after a man reportedly offered him a bicycle. A massive search ensued, but Jesus de la Cruz was never found.

In September 1997, the public reeled once more when Catherine Rice and two small sons, ages four years and two months, were strangled in their Lowell home by Rice's former boyfriend, Peter Contos, a respected Air National Guard sergeant who was the boys' father. Contos disposed of the bodies, still clothed in pajamas, in his locker at the Air National Guard base on Cape Cod. Police discovered them there, blood-stained towels wrapped around their necks, stuffed in plastic bags and a backpack.

Two days later, Jeffrey Curley disappeared, and Eddie O'Brien was convicted on live television of the Downing murder. By then, the drumbeat of unconscionable violence had reached a crescendo, only to be reamplified two weeks later when Elaine Donahue of Reading, an obstetrics nurse and mother of four, was discovered battered and dead in a rented storage space. Donahue, who had been missing for nearly a month, was bludgeoned while she slept. The murderer was her husband, an impulsive gambler and self-employed accountant who had become angered by his wife's control of the family finances.

When his wife first failed to report for work, Edward Donahue expressed bewilderment to her coworkers and friends. He scoured the area with neighbors and joined mass vigils in which three hundred people prayed for Elaine's discovery. All the while, her body lay stashed in the basement of their home, where Edward continued to care for his three sons and one daughter. He was arrested after police, during a search of his home, discovered a receipt for a storage locker in nearby Lynnfield, where her body had been moved.

On October 21, four days after Donahue's stunning arrest, tragedy struck again. Annie Glenn was shot dead by an estranged boyfriend as she waited with her three children at a school bus stop in Lowell. Richard Kenney shot Glenn once, then leaned over her prone body to fire twice more as she struggled to protect herself. Kenney, the father of two of the children, was identified by one of them, a four-year-old boy. "Daddy shot Mommy," the boy told police who had rushed to the scene.

The surge of violence, exhausting and relentless, reinforced Governor Cellucci's determination to push through a death-penalty bill. The issue also gave Cellucci a striking opportunity to escape the outsized shadow of his predecessor, William Weld, and put a forceful, can-do stamp on his new administration. Cellucci and other Republicans in Massachusetts, vastly outnumbered in state politics, saw capital punishment as a platinum wedge issue, one that could attract the support of Democrats and independents who had tired of the barrage of violent crime. The Curley murder and others, Cellucci and his aides knew, could help push the death penalty through.

The Republicans also knew the polling numbers, which showed that the public supported capital punishment by a far greater percentage than did their elected representatives on Beacon Hill. In 1994, a Northeastern University survey found that 74 percent of Massachusetts residents favored the death penalty for first-degree murder. In 1995, a follow-up study showed only 45 percent support for the death penalty among

Massachusetts legislators. Nationally, public backing for the death penalty appeared similarly strong. In 1995, a Gallup survey found 77 percent in favor.

The Massachusetts numbers, in a state renowned for left-of-center politics, might have startled outsiders. In 1997, no one had been executed in Massachusetts for fifty years, a legacy perhaps of Puritan founders who had drastically pruned the number of capital offenses when they settled the colony. In seventeenth-century England, one could still be put to death for one hundred crimes, even for upending a drying rack for cloth. But in the Massachusetts Bay Colony, its ten capital offenses were limited to murder and a laundry list of religious affronts such as blasphemy, idolatry, and witchcraft. In 1692, Salem proved how deadly serious those transgressions were considered. The Puritan founders also insisted on the right of capital defendants to an attorney, the first right of its kind in North America and one not granted in England until the mid-nineteenth century.

Reluctance to impose the death penalty in Massachusetts waned in the early twentieth century, when violent crime spiked during a time of dramatic social change. Rapid immigration, spreading industrialization, and the economic troubles of the Great Depression had combined to alter the landscape of American life. Many Americans felt threatened by the upheaval. The notorious case of Nicola Sacco and Bartolomeo Vanzetti, widely considered to have been wrongly executed in Boston in 1927, is a prime example of the public's sense that capital punishment was appropriate in a society that seemed to be whirling out of control.

After 1947, when Massachusetts conducted its last execution, governors from both parties refused to sign death warrants for twenty-five years. That informal moratorium was reinforced by the tireless efforts of Sara Ehrmann, a longtime activist and organizer from Brookline. Ehrmann, whose husband had been a lawyer for Sacco and Vanzetti, helped persuade the legislature in 1951 to give juries the option of ordering life in prison instead of death for first-degree murder. By the dawn of the 1960s, amid postwar prosperity and relatively low crime, enthusiasm for the death penalty had declined across the country. The Gallup poll showed only 42 percent support in 1966, the lowest mark since the organization began asking a death-penalty question in 1936.

In the late 1960s, however, an alarming rise in crime sparked a steady, nationwide rise in support for capital punishment. The Gallup poll showed 66 percent support in 1976, then 75 percent in 1985, before the numbers crested at 80 percent in 1994. That surge met resistance from the U.S. Supreme Court, which ruled against the death penalty in 1972 in *Furman v. Georgia.* By a 5–4 decision, the majority objected to what justices called an arbitrary system with no clear guidelines for jurors. Justice Thurgood Marshall described the death penalty as "excessive, unnecessary, and offensive to contemporary values."

In 1976, however, the Supreme Court revisited the issue after Georgia and several states revised their laws. This time, the High Court upheld the death-penalty statutes, whose changes included greater discretion for judges and separate juries for trials and sentencing. In short order, dozens of states reinstituted the death penalty. By 1995, when New York joined the list, a total of thirty-eight states allowed capital punishment.

Massachusetts did not join the rush, although the legislature tried. The Massachusetts high court rebuffed two attempts by lawmakers to reinstate capital punishment in 1980 and 1984. The fight was not renewed until 1991. Over the next seven years, like legislative clockwork, Governor William Weld and Lieutenant Governor Paul Cellucci filed bills in every session to give Massachusetts a death penalty that would pass constitutional muster. The measures did not reach the House floor until 1994, when the chamber voted on the death penalty for the first time in nearly a decade. Speaker Charles Flaherty of Cambridge, who worked hard to defeat the bill, saw his lobbying efforts pay dividends in an 86–70 vote against the measure.

The debate resurfaced in the following year after the roadside slaying of a state trooper. The death of Mark Charbonnier, gunned down by a paroled killer during a routine traffic stop, infused death-penalty proponents with new urgency. With Charbonnier's murder fresh in the public mind, the state senate approved capital punishment for the murder of a police officer. The matter moved to the House once again, where the bill lost, 83–73, despite a small gain in support.

One notable opponent was Donna Fournier Cuomo, a Republican state representative from North Andover, who had won her first race for political office in 1993 as a tireless advocate for tough sentencing laws and the rights of crime victims. Cuomo was well known as the sister of Joey Fournier, a seventeen-year-old high school student who was murdered in 1974 in a gas-station robbery north of Boston. The killer was the infamous Willie Horton, whose later prison furlough became the subject of a controversial 1988 presidential campaign ad that portrayed Massachusetts governor Michael Dukakis as dangerously soft on crime and helped propel George H. W. Bush to the White House.

Fournier, a part-time attendant at the station, was stabbed nineteen times after emptying the cash register and handing the money to Horton and two accomplices. His body was stuffed in a trash can, where he bled to death. At the time of the killing, Horton was on parole after serving only three years of a nine-year sentence for attempted murder. He was captured after Fournier's death and sentenced to life in prison. This time, the sentence carried no parole. But in Massachusetts, life without parole did not exclude Horton from a program of unescorted weekend furloughs, even for inmates convicted of first-degree murder.

In June 1986, Horton left prison on his tenth such furlough and never returned. Nine months later, he terrorized a couple in their Maryland home, where over twelve hours he raped the woman twice, stabbed and pistol-whipped her fiancé, and then fled in the man's car. Horton was arrested after a police chase and ordered to serve two consecutive life terms plus eighty-five years. The sentencing judge, cuffing the Massachusetts correction system, declared, "I'm not prepared to take the chance that Mr. Horton might again be furloughed or otherwise released." Incensed by Horton's escape, Cuomo launched a crusade to end furloughs for first-degree murderers, holding rallies on the State House steps and organizing an ambitious petition drive that garnered seventy thousand signatures. Under angry, growing pressure, the legislature voted to abolish the program.

Despite her brother's death and his killer's weekend privileges, Cuomo did not vote for the death penalty in 1995. She had been a longtime opponent of capital punishment, and not even murder had influenced her to change that view. Two years later, in August 1997, Cuomo voted against the death penalty again when the Joint Criminal Justice Committee issued an unfavorable report on the latest Weld-Cellucci bill.

Although Cuomo opposed capital punishment, she remained adamant that violent criminals should face tough, sure punishment. At the beginning of the 1997 session, she filed a bill to extend the sentences for second-degree murderers. Under her proposal, such inmates would not be eligible for parole for twenty-five years instead of fifteen. Nor would the prisoners be eligible for "furlough, temporary release, or education, training or employment programs established outside a correctional facility" until they had served at least twenty-two years behind bars.

The bill was recommended by the Criminal Justice Committee, which sent the proposal to the Senate, where approval was all but certain before the bill was shipped to the House for enactment. Once in the Senate, however, the bill gained a certain political appeal. Here, in a noncontroversial measure about second-degree murder, death-penalty proponents believed they might have a vehicle for their long-elusive victory. So, with an eye toward winning bipartisan support in the House, Republican Minority Leader Brian Lees and Democratic Senator James Jajuga filed a narrow amendment to execute the killers of law-enforcement officers. Jajuga had been a State Police officer for twenty-one years and was the first recipient of the Hanna Medal of Honor, an award for bravery in the line of duty. The medal was named for another state trooper, George Hanna, who had been fatally shot during a traffic stop in 1983. The amended bill passed easily, 23–14, in a preliminary vote on September 17. Final approval in the Senate was expected the following month.

The bill received little attention outside the Senate, which had voted for capital punishment in 1994 and 1995. The House, where death-penalty bills routinely went to their legislative grave, would be another animal altogether. The murder of Jeffrey Curley, however, upended and changed that calculus. Legislators who had consistently rejected capital punishment suddenly were inundated with telephone calls from angry constituents demanding that they reverse their position.

One of those calls came from John Curley, Bob's older brother, who awoke early on October 5, four days after Jeffrey's murder, to read a brief newspaper article about Jajuga's death-penalty amendment. Jesus, I hate to see a police officer die, Curley said to himself. I agree with him on that—or any judicial officer, actually—but in my opinion a kid is just as important. A former military air-traffic controller in Vietnam, Curley was accustomed to decisive action. He picked up the phone at 8:00 A.M. and dialed Jajuga at home.

The senator's wife answered, and Curley began to explain why he believed that murders involving children should be added to the death-penalty bill. "Hang on a second," she said. "Jim, get over here and talk to this guy." Jajuga listened politely to Curley and invited him to meet at his State House office. At first, the senator was reluctant to expand the bill, convinced that a limited focus was best and wishing to avoid any perception of exploiting Jeffrey's death. By the end of the phone call, however, he had been persuaded. And on Tuesday, the senator and Lees filed a death-penalty amendment for the rape and murder of a child under fourteen. "They said it was important for them to do something meaningful," Jajuga said of the Curleys. "They said, 'Use us.'"

The Senate wasn't scheduled to consider the amendments for two weeks, a brief window during which activists on both sides mobilized for a short, intense fight. Lawmakers had never seen such outcry on any single issue, and many of them struggled with a wrenching decision that pitted the dictates of conscience against the realities of politics. For one legislator in particular, the question was excruciatingly personal.

State Representative Tim Toomey, whose district included Jeffrey's home, had voted against the death penalty twice before. Those decisions had been reflexive for Toomey, a product of a religious, Irish-Catholic upbringing that taught no one has the power to determine who lives or dies. But now, Toomey was torn. He knew Jeffrey from the neighborhood and had last seen him handing out water during a road race that passed Toomey's campaign headquarters. "When Jeffrey left the race," Toomey said, "he even took a couple of bumper stickers to give to people." Three days later, Jeffrey was dead.

The lawmaker was also a longtime friend of Jeffrey's uncle, Barbara's brother Arthur, who had worked in all of Toomey's campaigns from School Committee to City Council to state representative. The son of a Cambridge police lieutenant and the brother of a priest, Toomey had been one of the first people whom Arthur Francis called when Jeffrey disappeared. Toomey visited the Curley home during the maddening search, kept in close contact with police, and struggled to comprehend what had happened to his tight-knit community.

Soon, he would be struggling with a very different dilemma. Arthur Francis, the bosom friend who had campaigned tirelessly for him, made a request. He asked Toomey to change his vote on the death penalty. "I really, really wrestled with that," Toomey said. "I probably wouldn't be as successful in politics if I didn't have Arthur helping me all those years. He had never asked me for anything, but he asked me to consider doing that."

Something else helped Toomey rethink his position. The faces of the neighborhood children, he said, convinced him that some crimes are so heinous that society must respond with the ultimate penalty. "A lot of the young kids came up to me. They were very, very fearful," Toomey said. "They felt that having the death penalty was going to protect them."

Wrestling with his conscience, Toomey spoke at length with his brother, the Reverend Kevin Toomey, who officiated at Jeffrey's funeral. The priest, in keeping with church teachings, said he opposed any decision to support the death penalty. "He was somewhat disappointed," Tim Toomey recalled. "He would prefer that I not vote for it, but he knew what I was going through."

A war of opposing emotions raged back and forth in Toomey's mind. "There were the pros and cons, justice or revenge, the whole range of issues," Toomey said. "I mean, it was a massive conflict. But there was also the fact that I was angry, and that I thought these people just shouldn't live, to prevent them from ever getting out and doing something else to someone."

In the end, one week after Jeffrey's murder, Toomey became the first legislator to announce publicly that he would change his stance and back capital punishment. "This whole thing has completely stunned me, and the city is devastated," Toomey told reporters. "This crime is so horrific, I think we have to step back and say something is really wrong. These people aren't even human."

After Toomey's switch, speculation ran rampant at the State House as to who would follow and whether public pressure and private anger could erase the ten-vote margin that had squelched the death penalty two years before. Massachusetts had been jarred by all of the recent murders, but the Curley killing seemed to stand alone as a grim, new standard of depravity. And Cellucci, more attuned than Weld to street-level sentiment, did not need his advisers to tell him that the case, almost single-handedly, could alter the political landscape. To the governor, the case packed a visceral punch that would reach every lawmaker on Beacon Hill. "Any parent has got to feel that," Cellucci said of Jeffrey's death. "They've got to feel it in their heart."

For the Curley family, Jajuga's office soon became a State House headquarters where phone calls were made to legislators, strategy was mapped, and a sense of mission gained momentum by the day. Bob, at times, felt overwhelmed by the workings of a place so different from the firehouse. "There was so much activity. I really didn't know what the hell was going on," he said. "Here I am, Joe Schmo, working down in Inman Square fixing fire engines, and then two weeks later I'm involved in all this stuff."

Bob, John, and their brother Jim quickly became familiar with the corridors and crannies of the State House, where they would walk into legislators' offices for some old-fashioned, East Cambridge, one-on-one lobbying. Bob's approach, though respectful, was blunt. He would explain his stance and ask for support. If the lawmaker still opposed the bill, Bob would follow up: "How would you feel if you were in my shoes? How could you be against the death penalty then?"

John, the de facto family leader, had a more pugnacious style. "I used to walk into people's offices all day long," he said. "I aggravated the hell out of people." Often roaming the building alone, he prowled the State House with a list of state representatives and a notebook in hand, knocking on doors with no appointment and no advance warning. "They had no clue I was coming," said John, the lone Republican in the family. "I'd go in, tell them who I was, and ask whether they were voting for or against the death penalty. When they said they were against it, I'd want to know why."

Unlike Bob, John would grow heated if he did not hear the answer he wanted.

"Can you guarantee me these people will never kill another child?" John asked one legislator.

"Well, they'll be put away for life," the lawmaker answered.

"Oh, yeah? Well, what happens when we get another Mike Dukakis in office?" John shot back, referring to the infamous furlough program.

"Well, yes, you're right, there are no guarantees," the representative replied.

"Well, I can give you a guarantee," John said, his voice rising. "You put them to death, and they'll never hurt anybody again!"

If he offended some people with his brusque style, John knew that Fran Marini, a Republican who served as House minority whip, would welcome him. According to John, the pair became fast allies on the day he introduced himself with a stack of petitions collected by the family outside Jeffrey's home. Sitting in Marini's office, cradling the petitions in his lap, John made his pitch.

"I need someone to show everybody how many people are actually interested in the death penalty," John said.

"Well, how many petitions do you have?" Marini asked.

John lifted the stack, piled six inches high with thousands of names, and dropped the pile on Marini's desk with an authoritative thump. Marini stared at the stack for a few seconds, then stared at John, and finally looked back at the gift of political gold before him.

"Goddammit!" Marini said. "I'll bring up the son-of-a-bitch myself!"

As Marini went to work, he expected fierce resistance from House Speaker Tom Finneran, a fast-talking, iron-fisted politician from the Mattapan neighborhood of Boston, who knew almost immediately after the news of Jeffrey's killing that a hurricane was headed straight for the State House. Finneran, a Democrat who opposed the death penalty, favored postponing the vote for a year to give passions a chance to subside. Critics howled that Finneran, afraid he might lose, was simply stalling for time. "In my mind, I was thinking that the cumulative political effect of these murders would create a stampede in the legislature and that the effect would be something, in the end, that you just couldn't stop," Finneran recalled. "The public was demanding reciprocal justice. And given the hideous nature of some of these crimes, reciprocal justice for many in the public was, Light up the electric chair! Light it up, baby! I thought, Mother of God, this is going to be brutal." The day after Finneran publicly suggested a postponement, the hurricane blew that plan to pieces. On October 21, in the space of one eventful day, Annie Glenn was gunned down in Lowell, the minority leader vowed to stop House business unless Finneran set a vote, and the Senate convened to give all-but-certain approval to the death penalty.

Sitting in the ornate Senate gallery, the Curley family wore yellow ribbons bearing Jeffrey's name as they watched the debate. Below, they saw Jajuga, lashing the air with his arms, arguing vehemently that the death penalty is justified for anyone who would rape and murder a child. "The children of the commonwealth are crying out for someone to protect them, to say this egregious and outrageous behavior will not be tolerated," Jajuga said. "When we have one of our children savaged and ravaged," he added, pausing between the verbs for frightening emphasis, "we can ask the appropriate level of justice."

The amendment, prompted by Jeffrey's murder, spurred opponents to question whether politics was driving the debate. "What about the killers of Janet Downing, Elaine Donahue, and the two young boys whose bodies were stuffed in an equipment locker at Otis Air Force Base?" asked Robert Antonioni, a Democrat from Leominster, who led the Senate fight against capital punishment. He argued in vain. The amendment passed easily, 22–14, and the Senate had only gotten started.

Steven Panagiotakos, a Lowell Democrat, immediately requested the death penalty for murder by torture or extreme cruelty. Eleven minutes after the Jajuga vote, the measure passed, 20–16. Then, in a breathtaking expansion of the bill, Senator Richard Moore, a small-town Democrat from central Massachusetts, asked that twelve types of murder be punished by death. The motion included the previous amendments and added other categories, such as bombings or contract killings, which Weld and Cellucci had requested in the past. Moore's amendment was approved, 20–17, and the bill was dispatched to the House. The transformation had been stunning for its breadth and speed. A simple proposal to toughen restrictions on second-degree murderers, in a startling, rumbling burst of momentum, instead became the vehicle to express the frustrated rage of millions in the state.

Senator Marian Walsh, a Democrat from the middle-class West Roxbury neighborhood of Boston, watched the debate unfold with the unhappy assurance that passage was inevitable. Walsh opposed the death penalty, even though her district strongly supported capital punishment. Before the vote, she had received two thousand calls from constituents who urged her to change her position. She held fast, however, despite the 1995 murder of a close friend, Assistant District Attorney Paul McLaughlin, who was gunned down at a commuter-rail stop by a gang leader he was about to prosecute. "He ran all my literature drops. We were very, very close friends," Walsh said of McLaughlin. "I can't say that revenge has not visited my heart, but I just didn't let it stay. The reason we created a judicial system was because we wanted justice, not revenge."

As the focus shifted to the House, where three more categories of murder were added to the list, the pundits automatically assumed that Finneran, a master manipulator, would use a toolbox full of artifice and fear to orchestrate the outcome. So, when Finneran declared that Democratic lawmakers should vote their "conscience" on the issue, the pronouncement was greeted with snickers and head-shaking skepticism. "To say Tom Finneran isn't marshaling votes against the death penalty," recalled Rob Gray, the governor's press secretary, "is to say Bill Belichick isn't involved with the Patriots game plan." As a result, Cellucci prepared for the vote as if Finneran would be pulling the strings on the opposite sideline. The governor opened his legislative directory, sat for hours at his desk, and placed dozens of calls to freshman representatives, old friends, and legislators rumored to be wavering.

One of his targets was Anthony Scibelli, a Democrat who had represented the city of Springfield for forty-seven years and voted against the death penalty in 1995. In his mideighties, Scibelli had a reputation for turning the Massachusetts Turnpike into a state-run racetrack for his ninety-mile commute to Beacon Hill. Cellucci tossed his pitch: "Lookit, Tony," the governor said with a mischievous smile, "if you vote for the death penalty, we'll raise the speed limit on the turnpike."

Unlike his predecessor, Cellucci had no qualms about tackling this tedious, time-consuming work. As a former state representative and senator, Cellucci was well schooled in Massachusetts politics, in shoe-leather ways that Weld had never used, and he was confident of his ability to read and communicate with people. After all, this governor still mowed his own lawn and shopped for the groceries. The son of a car salesman, Cellucci once sold a dozen burnt-orange Oldsmobiles that his father thought would never move. Twenty years later, Cellucci beamed whenever he saw one of those garish cars still driving the streets of Hudson. Cellucci knew people, and he knew that winning votes on the death penalty meant being polite, but being direct. "The people of Massachusetts are crying out for justice," Cellucci would say to wavering legislators. "The vast majority of people in Massachusetts and your district want a death penalty. And I do believe it is a deterrent."

As the governor worked the phones, his staff scurried behind the scenes to push an issue that had rocketed to the top of their agenda. "It was an all-hands-on-deck situation," Gray said. "We knew the public wanted the death penalty, and we made the public aware there was an opportunity to get it done." News conferences were held to trumpet support from crime victims and their families. Editorial boards were contacted. Op-ed pieces were submitted. Key government officials were made available for interviews. And district attorneys who backed the death penalty were urged to join the fray. "We in the governor's office," Gray said, "applied every tool we could to try to get the death penalty through, because the Curley murder gave it a chance to get over the top."

All the momentum had shifted to Cellucci, as reports circulated almost daily of another state representative who had decided to switch. At the beginning of the session, death-penalty foes had counted an eight-vote cushion in their favor. But the intense, relentless public pressure after Jeffrey's murder had shredded that safety net.

Finneran ceded day-to-day management of the fight to William Nagle, the House majority leader, who represented the liberal mecca of Northampton in western Massachusetts.

Nagle's opposition had its roots in the tainted 1806 murder convictions of two Irish immigrants, Dominic Daley and James Halligan, who were hanged in Northampton at a time of nasty prejudice against foreigners in general and Catholics in particular. Defense counsel was not appointed until two days before their trial, the charge was based on one boy's suspect testimony, and neither Daley nor Halligan was allowed by law to testify in his own behalf. "My father was a rabid, first-generation Irishman," Nagle said. "When we'd drive by Hospital Hill where they were executed, he'd say to me, 'Those guys were hung because they spoke Gaelic, they were Catholic, and they were foreigners.'" The hangings, in a town of twenty-five hundred people, attracted an overflow crowd of fifteen thousand from throughout the Connecticut River Valley and beyond.

The legacy of the case, fraught with bias and mistakes, made a lifelong impression on Nagle, who was determined never to allow Massachusetts the chance to execute an innocent person again. As a result, Nagle approached the death-penalty vote, scheduled for a week after the Senate decision, with a tenacious single-mindedness. His office became the opposition headquarters.

Nagle was allied with a coalition of advocacy groups led by the American Civil Liberties Union (ACLU), which admittedly had grown complacent during the Dukakis administration, when a death penalty seemed out of the question. Now, Nagle and his friends knew they had a desperate battle on their hands and little time to prepare. "It was like watching two trains coming down the track toward each other," Nagle said. "And every day that went by, it got worse." To survive the collision, Nagle met daily with his team to pore over lists of lawmakers to call, schedule meetings with activists across the state, and plead with constituents to lobby their legislators.

Norma Shapiro, legislative director of the Massachusetts branch of the ACLU, and Ann Lambert, a private attorney who sat on the chapter's board of directors, emerged as Nagle's key lieutenants. They approached the challenge with an enthusiastic, full-throttle commitment that matched his. "We had assignments every single day on this," Nagle said. "If I said to Ann or Norma, go talk to ten people in this district, they would do it. And the next day we would meet regardless if it was eight in the morning or eight at night. Sometimes, we met two or three times a day." To Shapiro and Lambert, the effort was equal parts energizing and nerve-racking. "We had legislators who were helping us count noses, making sure that people were still with us," Shapiro said. "And we'd get messages from their staffs, saying, 'You have a problem with x, y, or z.' We'd go running right out to try to stop the problem, and we were not always necessarily successful."

Besides the ACLU, other groups joined the fight, including Massachusetts Citizens Against the Death Penalty, Amnesty International, the state's public defenders, the American Friends Service Committee, the Boston and Massachusetts bar associations, religious groups, and college organizations. "It took seven years," since Weld's gubernatorial election in 1990, "for all of us to really focus on a single mission, in a single way, in a concerted effort," Shapiro said. As a result, lobbying became disciplined. Visiting a legislator in his office was fine; picketing his house and following the family to soccer games was not. Shapiro, however, knew her side could not win the day on efficiency alone. "The noise out there was against us, and legislators are very sensitive to the noise," she said. "When you have people in church saying we need the death penalty, you know you've got a problem on your hands."

Shapiro and Lambert also felt they were constantly battling a shortsighted news media, which repeated, over and over, that polls showed three-quarters of the state supported capital punishment. A better indicator, Shapiro stressed, would be the Northeastern University poll from 1994, which also found only 38 percent support for the death penalty when respondents were given an option of life without parole. "It was very hard to convince legislators what the real polling looked like," Shapiro said. "The press was particularly bad for us."

As the climactic vote neared, the outcome remained too close to call, even for a head counter like Nagle, who prided himself on up-to-the-minute numbers. "It was a jump ball," he said. With each passing day, the pressure intensified from Boston talk show hosts who urged listeners to flood the State House switchboard with a deluge of outrage. According to Nagle, the strategy was chillingly effective. "Some of these people who called had never voted, and never would vote," he said. "But if you get a call from Johnny Jones down the street, and he tells you to vote a certain way, you say, 'Oh my God, what's that mean?'"

Finneran continued to insist that he would not pressure any lawmakers, but he did meet with several representatives. Some he invited to his office for a conversation. Others were conflicted and wanted to know why Finneran, who once supported the death penalty, had changed his position. One of those members was Nancy Flavin, a Democrat from the western Massachusetts city of Easthampton, who had voted against capital punishment in 1995 but now was torn and undecided.

Finneran explained to Flavin, as he explained to others, that his epiphany came through Bobby Joe Leaster, a twenty-one-year-old black man wrongly convicted of the 1971 murder of a variety store owner in the Dorchester neighborhood of Boston. Leaster served fifteen years in prison while Robert and Christopher Muse, father-and-son attorneys from Boston, championed his case with appeal after appeal. Finally, Leaster was freed after a schoolteacher, jarred by a *Boston Globe* story on the case, told authorities that Leaster had not been one of the two men he saw fleeing the store.

"What struck me about Bobby Joe Leaster were the parallels in our lives on some very basic things," said Finneran, who had met with Leaster. "We're roughly the same age. When he got into his situation, I was coming out of college, going to law school, falling in love, starting my family. And he's put away for fifteen years for a crime he didn't commit. I'm thinking to myself, God, if we had a death penalty, he would have been gone. So, while I'm marching the fifteen years from here to there, building a law practice and getting elected, he's sitting in a cell for something he didn't do. But there was no anger, no bitterness, no 'You motherfuckers ruined my life!' There was none of that stuff."

Flavin listened, Finneran recalled, but she remained in a quandary. On the morning of the debate, a day Cellucci proclaimed "Jeffrey Curley and Victims of Murder Memorial Day," the governor believed he was three or four votes short of victory. In the other camp, an anxious Democratic leadership was certain only that the decision would be razor-thin for either side.

For Bob and Barbara Curley, the day held the promise of delayed but righteous justice—if not for Jeffrey, then for future children preyed upon by predators. Barbara shivered in the morning chill as she joined more than a dozen relatives and supporters at an entry arch to the State House. She brightened when a television reporter asked for her thoughts. "My son would want me to do this for other children, so it doesn't ever happen to any other victims," Barbara said, her eyes bright and a smile crossing her face.

Bob did not share Barbara's enthusiasm. Pensive and edgy, he approached the day troubled by turbulent, barely contained emotions, which burst from their floodgates when he saw an elderly man, standing alone, protesting the death penalty with a handheld sign. His rage boiling and building, Bob eyed the man for several minutes. Finally, having seen enough, Bob stalked toward the man and began screaming uncontrollably. "You fucking left-wing burnout!" Bob yelled, his eyes bulging. "You've got nothing better to do than to come up here and take sides with Jaynes and Sicari? I should stick that sign up your fucking ass!"

Francine tried to pry Bob away. He turned, glaring at a sister he considered a saint. Today, none of that mattered. "Mind your own business!" Bob screamed at Francine before flinging a few, final words of abuse at the protester. Francine apologized to the man, who was flustered but forgiving. "I understand," he said calmly. Then, he quickly left.

The family regrouped inside the State House, where Donna Cuomo spotted them and offered her condolences. Asked how she intended to vote, Cuomo demurred and said she did not want to tip her hand. Francine, however, thought she saw an indication that the family would be pleased.

Bob seemed anything but pleased, however, as the long day progressed. And his mood grew even darker when Jim Braude, a liberal activist and media pundit, spotted Bob outside the House gallery and walked over to introduce himself. Bob, bracing for a conversation he didn't want, knew Braude by sight and reputation. "You took one look at him, you knew he was a leftie," Bob said. The firefighters at Engine 5 often saw Braude in the morning, crossing Inman Square on his way to the tidy, trendy confines of the 1369 Coffee House. Bob usually would be sitting on the second-floor couch, reading the sports pages, when an old-time firefighter from the neighborhood announced Braude's appearance with muttering disdain.

"There he is," the firefighter would say slowly, inflicting a wound with every word. "There's that fuckin', left-wing, liberal, fuckin' Braude."

Braude, a former public defender in the South Bronx who opposed the death penalty, had traveled to the State House as an interested observer. He approached Bob to say hello but received a double-barreled blast of vitriol instead. Bob lashed out at Braude with an expletive-laden rant that targeted his two small daughters. The underlying message, Braude said, was unmistakably clear: "If something were to happen to your kids, Mr. Liberal Asshole, let's see what your position would be."

Around the corner, at the small State House coffee shop, Marilyn Abramofsky awaited the vote. Scot Lehigh, a *Boston Globe* reporter, spotted her discussing strategy and asked why she supported capital punishment. "They had no problem killing our children. Why should the state have any problem killing them?" Abramofsky scoffed. "I want stoning, hanging, blowing their brains out."

Lobbying by both sides continued through twelve intense hours of debate. Cellucci invited a parade of twenty lawmakers to his office. Clergy buttonholed legislators in the hallways. And Nagle, scanning the chamber, occasionally left the podium to sit with individual members for a casual, collegial dose of deadly serious persuasion.

Above them, the large Curley entourage huddled in the gallery, holding photographs of Jeffrey as organized confusion unfolded below. Members wandered in and out. Chatter competed with oratory. And clerks and aides scurried to and from the podium where President-elect John F. Kennedy delivered his final speech before his 1961 inauguration.

For Bob, who had never been in the House of Representatives before, the scene seemed clipped from an old movie. "Are these people for real, making these big speeches and all this?" Bob asked the person beside him. "I really didn't think they did this stuff." What Bob saw, in a mixture of bemusement and awe, was a history-steeped room where dark wood and plush blue carpeting lay underneath five heroic paintings of important scenes from Massachusetts history. One of the paintings, titled *Dawn of Tolerance in Massachusetts*, depicted Judge Samuel Sewall's public repentance in 1697 for his role in the Salem witchcraft trials. The irony of the image, overlooking a debate on state executions precisely three centuries later, appeared to pass unnoticed.

As promised, Fran Marini, the minority whip, carried John Curley's stack of death-penalty petitions to the lectern, where he held them aloft with his right hand and passionately urged his colleagues to do the voters' bidding. "Jeff died on October 1," Marini barked in a loud, clipped voice. "This hasn't taken a year to collect. This hasn't taken a month to collect. This is simply a few weeks of our citizens asking us to vote for this bill." Mary Jane Simmons, a Democrat from Leominster, appealed more to the gut. "Don't let these people go on the street," she pleaded, "and do what they did to that beautiful child with the baseball cap."

Other lawmakers delivered equally charged speeches of resistance. One opponent, William McManus, a Democrat from Worcester, railed against the political threats he had received from constituents and others. "Shame on you people!" he said angrily. "This isn't the type of vote that is for sale. . . . I think it's disgusting, and I am not going to cower to it. And if it costs me an election, God bless it. I couldn't care less."

The depth of emotion and public pressure startled many freshman representatives, including Eugene O'Flaherty, a former public defender from Boston's tough Charlestown neighborhood. O'Flaherty, who received hundreds of calls from his district, had generally opposed the death penalty in his campaign but said he would consider capital punishment for the murders of police officers and acts of terrorism. Shortly before the debate, however, O'Flaherty's stance turned to complete opposition when he met Paul Hill, a native of Northern Ireland, who had been wrongfully convicted in 1975 of an Irish Republican Army pub bombing in England. Hill served fifteen years of a life sentence before being exonerated. "By that point," O'Flaherty said, "I was feeling personally comfortable, still politically worried, but personally comfortable with the decision I was making."

A few, such as Flavin, were tormented until the second they cast their votes. Questions of justice, morality, life, death, and unspeakable crime swirled in the heads of the undecided. Flavin, in tears, reluctant but resolved, finally pressed the yea button. "I saw that child's face," she later told Norma Shapiro of the ACLU. "I just kept thinking of that little boy."

After a seemingly interminable wait, the green lights for yea votes and red ones for nays flashed on a board in the front of the chamber. Spectators, reporters, and hushed politicians, eyes darting over the roster, strained to find the answer in the lights. "Holy Jesus," Finneran said, stunned, to a Republican on the rostrum. "You know you guys won?" The unthinkable had happened. By the slimmest of margins, 81–79, the motion had passed.

Joyous bedlam erupted in the gallery. As clergy and other opponents looked on in disbelief, John Curley bellowed, "Thank you for saving our children! We appreciate it!" He was summarily ejected.

To Bob, the scene mirrored a hockey game at the Gore Street rink. "Arms up, high fives, the whole bit," Bob said.

"Just like somebody had scored a game-winning goal." Demonstrations also broke out on the floor, where several members greeted their victory with cheering and hand slaps.

Nagle, devastated by the decision, was disgusted. "That was the mood, you know?" he said. "That was the lynch mob." The displays also saddened Tom McGee, a two-term representative from Lynn, who had made his maiden House speech against the death penalty. "It was a moment I'll never forget," McGee said. "In the pit of my stomach, I had this feeling when you know something isn't right."

After the vote, many legislators adjourned to a Beacon Hill watering hole called The 21st Amendment, named for the act that repealed Prohibition. Some crossed the street to celebrate; others, like McGee, came to commiserate. "It was one of the lowest times I've ever had in the legislature," McGee said. "It hit home that the death penalty was going to return to Massachusetts." Cellucci, who had just scored a major political coup, was ecstatic. "This is a victory for justice and for the people of Massachusetts," he told reporters. Finneran, by contrast, was pessimistically philosophical. "We live in a time in society when our culture is coarse, it is violent, and it has unacceptable, unspeakable levels of conduct that are not always condemned and almost condoned," he said. "In that type of situation, when society becomes unhinged from its traditional mooring, virtually anything goes. People react." Cuomo, who cried as she voted, joined seven other representatives who had changed their positions from 1995 to tip the balance. "I really did not want to disappoint the Curleys," she said, "and I believe the public believes the death penalty is going to make a difference."

Bob, leaving the gallery, was mentally exhausted. "I guess it's a step in the right direction," he said wearily to reporters. "But we have a lot of hard work ahead of us." The Curleys headed back to the Hampshire Street condo, upbeat and energized by what they believed was the climactic conclusion of their monthlong crusade. The family had no idea that the House bill, which differed from the Senate version, was

headed to a conference committee for negotiations before a
final vote. In their mind, the death penalty already was a locked-
down reality. And for the first time since Jeffrey disappeared,
the Curleys enjoyed a few hours of restrained celebration in
the very rooms where they had kept an agonizing vigil. "Everybody was pretty pleased at what had happened, yet there was
kind of a letdown for me," Bob recalled. "All the stuff leading
up to that point had been a distraction. And now, that night,
being a little happy on one hand, I was also asking myself,
How do we move on here?"

The next day, at the State House, Nagle was asking himself the same question. Once again, time was not a friend. The
bill would return shortly from conference committee, and the
House would be asked to enact the legislation. To reporters
who covered the initial vote and to nearly every other political
observer on Beacon Hill, that bit of business seemed a formal-
ity. "There seems little doubt that capital punishment will be
legalized," Doris Sue Wong and Adrian Walker wrote in the
Boston Globe.

Undeterred but under no illusions, Nagle went to work
to alter the outcome. His primary targets would be the eight
legislators who had switched their 1995 votes, figuring that
they now might regret the real-life effects of their change. The
results, however, were not encouraging. "I spoke to a lot of
people," Nagle said, "trying to convince them that this was a
historic moment, not only in Massachusetts but in the nation." His pleas, heartfelt and urgent, were not successful.

Instead, Nagle shifted his attention. In poring over the
legislative roster, he spotted one possibility, an obscure second-
term representative from the blue-collar city of Peabody, a
gritty enclave of fading tanneries and crowded, conservative
neighborhoods. John Slattery, a thirty-nine-year-old lawyer,
had already shown an independent streak by bucking Finneran
on several issues. He also seemed ambitious, was well spoken,
and had an innate scrappiness molded perhaps by several
childhood years spent in a tough Lynn housing project.

Slattery had backed the death penalty in 1995 and again in the first 1997 House vote. But Nagle and others, particularly Majority Whip Sal DiMasi of Boston, thought Slattery would listen, at least, to their arguments about the fatal potential of human error. Because Slattery had performed criminal defense work, DiMasi said, he "understood that potential more than any other person who had voted for the death penalty." Nagle and DiMasi liked their chances for an intellectual connection with Slattery. They also liked his fearlessness. "We wanted to switch somebody, but it couldn't be like throwing a Christian into the lion's den," Nagle said. "We needed someone who was articulate, who could debate, and who could stand his ground as the tank was coming at him. John Slattery was that kid."

Earlier in the year, Slattery had sat on the Joint Criminal Justice Committee during its preliminary deliberations on the death penalty. He had heard testimony about wrongful convictions, about doubts regarding deterrence, and about the high costs of capital punishment. Although he voted in favor at that time, Senator Marian Walsh, who cochaired the panel, said Slattery showed an earnest curiosity.

In the following months, Slattery continued to explore the subject with Walsh and close friends in the House, particularly McGee and Paul Demakis, both of whom opposed capital punishment. Again, he listened. But again, despite emerging questions, he joined the majority in the full House's 81–79 vote. "I was torn, but I thought my constituents generally favored the death penalty," Slattery said. "That first vote was a matter of saying, 'You know what? I'll just be consistent.' And that's what I did."

As the days between votes dwindled from nine to a few, Slattery spoke to lawyers he respected. Over and over, Slattery heard that juries make mistakes, that innocent people are executed, and that minorities are far more likely to be sent to death row. He was still processing this information late on November 5, the day before the final vote, when he received a visitor in his fourth-floor office. DiMasi had walked down the hall to speak with Slattery, a colleague with whom he often chatted during workouts at a nearby health club.

"John, I know this is a political decision," DiMasi said. "But, as a professional and as a human being, you know that mistakes are made in trials, and that mistakes that are made when there's a death penalty involved can be irreparable."

Slattery said that a switch might spell political suicide in his conservative district. But mostly, he sat silently, listening while DiMasi prodded him to consider the broader implications.

"Five or ten years from now, when you're not here, will you look back and say you made the right decision?" DiMasi asked. "That's the test you have to decide in what you're going to do, because I think you're going to have to live with that decision."

Slattery did not commit either way. But in his eyes, DiMasi recalled, Slattery appeared to be struggling.

Later that night, moved by the weight of argument, Slattery resolved to act. "If we can't be sure we're executing the right person, we shouldn't be executing anybody," Slattery said. "I just felt, at that point, that this was something I didn't want in Massachusetts."

Slattery at first confided his decision only to his wife, a nonpracticing lawyer who helped him weigh the repercussions.

"Are you prepared to leave the political arena?" she asked. "Because I'm not sure what will happen after you change your vote."

"Yeah, I'm prepared," Slattery said. "I think it's the right thing to do."

The following day reenergized the State House with a buzz of fresh anticipation. For proponents of the death penalty, this would be the day, finally, when Massachusetts became the thirty-ninth state to reinstate capital punishment. That afternoon, the Senate stayed true to form by approving the death-penalty bill reported out of conference committee, one that added the three new categories of murder endorsed by the House. The decision by the House, however, was not expected for several hours, which gave lobbyists on both sides time to work the hallways and offices of the crowded Capitol in a last, feverish attempt to upend or uphold the status quo.

Bob Curley, who thought victory had already been won, learned only that day that the bill would resurface. He alerted friends and relatives and hustled to the State House, where he saw Sister Helen Prejean, the author of *Dead Man Walking* and a fervent death-penalty opponent, plying her brand of gentle Louisiana persuasion. A friend stopped to introduce Bob, but the encounter quickly turned nasty.

"Bob, this is Sister Helen."

"I understand you are in great pain," Sister Helen said, her voice calm and empathetic. "Your son has been taken from you."

Bob responded angrily. Instead of kindness and condolences, he saw an enemy meddling in a stranger's tragic business.

"You don't know me. You don't know Jeff. Why the fuck are you doing this?" Bob snapped, his voice rising. "Who the hell are you to be against the death penalty, when nothing like this has ever happened to any of your loved ones?"

Bob stalked away, unmoved by her compassion.

The confrontation would not be the last for the Curleys. Bob's brother Jim spotted Eugene O'Flaherty and approached the legislator with an aggressiveness that bordered on intimidation.

"Stand up there and say, 'You know what? I believe in this. We have to take a stand. We have to save our children. We have to put an end to this whole thing right here!'" Jim Curley said. "I'm begging you, please do the right thing."

O'Flaherty, facing a press of TV cameras and reporters who had rushed to the altercation, would not agree. Curley, incensed, flew into a rage.

"So Jeff died for no reason!" he shouted.

"I'm not saying that," O'Flaherty answered calmly. "I believe this bill is not constitutionally sound."

With tensions rising dangerously, two fellow freshmen gently pulled O'Flaherty away from a velvet rope that separated him from Curley and the media.

Cellucci, who predicted that the winning vote would hold, delayed a trip to Canada with a Massachusetts trade mission. Instead, he stayed in Boston to monitor developments from the spacious confines of his corner office. With Finneran as speaker, Cellucci knew the unexpected was not only possible, but probable. Unknown to the governor, the machinery of the unexpected had already begun to move. When Slattery arrived at the State House, his mind made up, he called DiMasi and asked him to stop by his office. There, he delivered the thunderbolt.

"I'm going to change my vote, and I want to make a speech," Slattery said. "I may never get elected again in my district, but I'm going to do it because I think it's the right thing to do."

"I don't think you'll ever regret it," DiMasi said.

Slattery also informed Nagle, who warned him of an "acid bath of publicity" to follow. "You can expect to be vilified," he said. "Just be prepared for it." Nagle was elated, knowing he now had the votes to kill the death penalty with an 80–80 tie.

Before long, rumors of Slattery's defection had spread like wildfire throughout the building. Paul Haley, who pushed for the bill as chairman of the Ways and Means Committee, invited Slattery to his office for what became a frustrating, unpersuasive conversation. "It was obvious that there was going to be no reasoning with him," Haley said. Still, Haley delivered an impassioned speech on the House floor, defending capital punishment as a justifiable, necessary message from law-abiding society. "We are not choosing death here today," he said. "Those that have perpetrated the most heinous acts have decided that life should hang in the balance. We are stating unequivocally that, you rob someone else's life for your own twisted end, you put your own life in jeopardy."

Cellucci also summoned Slattery, who remained unmoved by the governor's arguments. Shortly afterward, sensing defeat, Cellucci held a news conference in which he divulged

Slattery's intentions. That announcement opened the floodgates of recrimination, and Slattery's office was immediately
swamped with outraged calls. Radio hosts had begun airing his
telephone number and whipping listeners into a frenzy with
allegations that Slattery had struck a backdoor deal to boost
his political fortunes.

Later, when Slattery took his seat in the House chamber,
three rows from the rear, his friend Paul Demakis saw someone who was extremely agitated. "I think the message to all of
us was, leave him alone," said Demakis, who had just been
given a glimpse of John Slattery's new life. "I went outside the
chamber before the vote, and this guy, with just a crazed look
on his face, says to me, 'Are you John Slattery?' Thank God I
wasn't, because he would have assaulted me."

As Slattery rose to address the chamber, now hushed for
the day's key speech, he ripped into the rumors that he had
sold his vote for Finneran's favor. "Let me start off by grabbing
by the lapels the argument that I had any connection to the
speaker of the House in arriving at a decision here tonight.
First of all, I take responsibility for my own acts," he said angrily, glaring at individual members throughout the room. "And
I don't need any one of you to tell me who's responsible for
my acts."

Slattery repeated his belief, stated the week before, that
some criminals deserve the death penalty. But since that first
vote, Slattery told the House, his discussions with lawyers and
constituents had "left me with an abiding conviction that we
can't be certain in the criminal-justice system that we always
get the right guy. And if I can't be certain that I'm getting the
right guy, then I have a very big problem with the death
penalty," Slattery said. "I don't want to be lying in my bed, at
12:01 A.M., fifteen years from now, knowing that somebody's
being put to death, that I helped to create the mechanism for
putting that person to death, and not being sure that that person being put to death deserves what he got." In conclusion,
Slattery said, "I need to be able to look myself in the mirror

the next day and like the person I see. And I can't do that if I feel that someone innocent might die because of me."

Soon, the bill awaited only the roll call that House members knew would doom the death penalty. Many in the gallery, however, did not know that the outcome had been determined. Finneran, subdued, addressed the chamber with the results. "Eighty having voted in the affirmative, eighty in the negative, the bill is not passed," he said.

The effect was either devastating or exhilarating. From the Curleys, a wave of cries and curses rolled toward the rostrum. Once again, John Curley was the loudest. "Are you out of your mind?" he screamed as Finneran pounded the gavel for order. At the opposite end of the gallery, lobbyists who had worked against the bill shed tears for their improbable victory. And on the floor, where drained members digested the outcome, two security officers told Slattery they would escort him from the chamber.

"You don't have to do that," Slattery said.

"No, we're walking you out," one of the officers answered firmly. "We don't want any issues in here. People are pretty upset, and we're going to get you out of the building. Do you have someone who can pick you up?"

"My brother," Slattery replied.

Upstairs, Bob left the gallery in a daze, unsure how the bill had failed but certain that the villain was Slattery. As he emerged, a pushing, jostling throng of reporters surrounded him, asking for his reaction. "It's disgusting, okay? They probably dug up some dirt on Slattery, and they threw it at him," Bob said. "It's up to the people out there to make a stand and get after these politicians. They just can't have their way and do what they want. It's an insult." Nearby, Finneran also spoke with the media. And as he did, the trembling brother of a murder victim shouted, "Coward!"

One floor below, Cellucci strode from his office, nearly red with rage, to rail at the bitter outcome. "We saw a phony vote, we saw a deal, we saw chicanery, and the will of the people was defeated tonight!" Cellucci said, seething. "Have you ever seen a phony vote like that?" Rob Gray, the governor's press secretary, went further. "He's a profile in cowardice," Gray said of Slattery. "The words 'spineless' and 'hypocrite' also come to mind."

The torrent of withering criticism had only begun for Slattery, who returned home to see a Peabody police cruiser parked outside for protection. Angry calls, some of them death threats, crackled over his telephone for days. "How would you like it if you were murdered?" one caller asked. "How would you like it if your kids were murdered?" another screamed. "Maybe they should put you and all the murderers on an island together," yet another suggested. "One guy threatened to come over to my house. I didn't know what he wanted to do, but I said, 'Hey, come on over,'" Slattery recalled. "He never did." For safety, Slattery moved his wife and three children, ages seven, five, and three, to his mother-in-law's home.

Despite the uproar, Slattery let much of the abuse pass without comment. "Once I've made a decision, I'm done. I felt I reached my decision based on the evidence and in an intellectually honest fashion," he said. "People can scream at me, and it's water off a duck's back. It doesn't faze me one way or another."

One attack, however, infuriated Slattery and his wife. The assault came from *Boston Herald* columnist Howie Carr, who wrote the day after the decision that "Judas Slattery" had sold his vote for "blood money." In Carr's view, Slattery had just endeared himself to a new bloc of friends, the murderers imprisoned throughout Massachusetts who certainly were rejoicing at the demise of capital punishment. "The only shocker," Carr wrote, "is that the Judas hails from the city of Peabody," where Kristen Crowley had been murdered by two men who "decided they wanted a 'piece of that'" before crushing her skull. Carr continued the offensive with a bit of Irish slang. "Rep. Judas Slattery has three children," Carr wrote. "One can only pray that none of his new-found friends ever decide they 'want a piece' of a Slattery spalpeen."

To Bill Nagle, however, Slattery's actions were nothing short of heroic. "No individual I served with compares to the courage he exhibited that day," Nagle said. "Over the years, I served with a lot of people, some very qualified people, and some very, very bright human beings. But for that particular day, he'll always be the one, my personal hero. He was willing to stand up, and it was amazing."

— 6 —

Uncharted
Ground

IN THE WEEKS following the State House dramatics, the ba-
nalities of everyday life slowly replaced the distractions that
had helped shield the Curleys from the horror of Jeffrey's murder. The television lights had been carted away, the memorial
shrine had long since been dismantled, and family members
had withdrawn to confront, finally, the magnitude of a tragedy
that had made their private loss a very public spectacle.

Bob, like Barbara and the boys, still warmed to the condolences of friends and strangers whenever he ventured outside. And at the condo, hundreds of letters from across the
country arrived in a steady, comforting stream. But despite
this support, Bob and his family found themselves ever more
isolated in their pain. "I can talk to people on the street, and
they tell me they know how I feel," Bob said at the time. "But
they don't. They can't know how I feel."

The tough-minded, almost defiant, stoicism that had been
a hallmark of both his neighborhood and culture became a defense mechanism that helped Bob get on with his life. But the
struggle, a constant and wearing one, was unlike anything he
had ever experienced. "I'm forty-two years old, and I try to
contain my emotions," Bob said then. "But you're just so hurt,
and you feel so violated, and you've got to try to have a disciplined attitude. If I start to fall apart, it won't serve anything."

One path in which Bob channeled his emotions was a dogged continuation of the death-penalty fight, which Governor Paul Cellucci pledged to wage in the next election against every legislator who voted against capital punishment. Indeed, Cellucci offered to campaign for any death-penalty supporter who would run against any of the eighty offending lawmakers. "This battle is not over," Cellucci said. "I intend to go to every part of this state, and I intend to let the people of Massachusetts know what happened, and I intend to support people for the House next year who are going to vote to bring the death penalty back."

Although those elections were a year away, the first test of the political appeal of capital punishment surfaced almost immediately in a special race to replace state Senator Paul White, a death-penalty advocate from Dorchester who had resigned midterm. Three of the four Democratic candidates, whose December 9 primary would essentially decide the race, opposed capital punishment. But the fourth hopeful, longtime Boston City Councilor Maura Hennigan, made its restoration an outsized, controversial cornerstone of her campaign.

Hennigan's staff enlisted Bob Curley's endorsement. The candidate held a news conference at the State House with members of the Curley family. She issued a flurry of press releases that trumpeted her support for capital punishment. And her campaign—without Hennigan's prior authorization, she said—even used the now-famous Little League photograph of Jeffrey Curley on its fliers.

The effect was electric. In a city with a storied history of bare-knuckled politics, even jaded, seen-it-all observers were horrified. One candidate, Eleanor LeCain, derisively commented that Hennigan seemed to be "running for state executioner instead of state senator." The Democratic campaign committee from Hennigan's own ward, in a stinging rebuke, declined to endorse a candidate. And State Representative Brian Joyce, the eventual winner, expressed disgust. "On such a personal matter of conscience, I understand and respect that reasonable people disagree," said Joyce, who had resisted enormous pressure during the State House debate to support the death penalty. "What I question is Maura's motive. By all accounts, it appears to be shameless political grandstanding." Hennigan made no apologies for her support of the issue, which she said resonated in the district's pivotal conservative suburbs. And besides, Hennigan added, she had been a long-time supporter of capital punishment.

At first, Bob backed Hennigan enthusiastically. He knocked on doors of homes and businesses. He stood in shopping centers. He shook hands in suburbs he had never visited before. And he recited his mantra that the death penalty could prevent the murder of another Jeffrey Curley. "It was all death-penalty stuff, just urging them to vote for her because she was for the death penalty and Joyce wasn't," Bob recalled.

Hennigan asked if Bob knew John Walsh, the anticrime activist and TV host of *America's Most Wanted*, whose son had been abducted and killed in Florida in 1981. Hennigan wanted Walsh to speak on her behalf, Bob said, but he never placed the call. "I was doing all this, but I had an uneasy feeling," he said. "I thought it was for the right reasons, but I just didn't know. Really, I didn't understand what the hell was going on. I was very naive in regard to politics."

Clarity came when Bob first saw the Hennigan flier with Jeffrey's picture. The message stunned him: Jeffrey had become a political poster boy for the death penalty. "Nobody asked me how I felt about it. It was just done," said Bob, who saw the flier by chance on the campaign trail. "What the fuck? They're gonna do this, and nobody's gonna ask me how I feel?" Without fanfare or an announcement, Bob walked away from the campaign. "I just said to myself, I'm out of here. That's it for me."

The issue failed to push Hennigan over the top. Instead of victory, she finished a distant third. Exit polls indicated that the rhetoric about capital punishment had motivated its opponents to vote. The same polling also indicated that voters, particularly the supporters of executions, were startlingly unaware of the state's penalty for murder. Only 11 percent of respondents knew that first-degree murder in Massachusetts carried a sentence of life without parole. Among capital-punishment supporters, nearly half believed that murderers usually served less than ten years in prison.

Angered by the flier, Bob wanted to shrink from the public eye. But he soon found himself pulled back into the full, harsh glare of the media spotlight.

Only eight days after the special election, Sicari and Jaynes's long-awaited superior court arraignment on murder and kidnapping charges was held in Cambridge. Unlike the separate arraignments two months earlier in Newton District Court, this proceeding brought the two defendants together before a judge for the first time. Courthouse security was bolstered in numbers and intensity, complete with bulletproof vests for the defendants and a ring of police escorts for Sicari and Jaynes, who were hustled past a hostile, jeering crowd less than a mile from the Curley home.

Inside, prosecutor David Yannetti once again detailed the grisly allegations against the pair, this time for Judge Judith Cowin. While he did, Sicari glanced toward the gallery packed with Curley family members. Bobby Curley was certain that Sicari pursed his lips and winked at him, a flippant gesture of nonchalant defiance toward a neighborhood tough guy he despised. "You fucking faggot!" Bobby yelled, lurching toward the railing that separated defendants from the public. "You're lucky you're behind there, or I'd kill you myself!" Cowin quickly ordered court officers to escort Bobby from the room. Later, after Sicari and Jaynes had been led away, most of the Curley family avoided a legion of reporters by leaving through a back entrance obscured from public view.

By this time, Bob had returned to the Fire Department, but his colleagues did not recognize the man who had left work on the afternoon of October 1. "When Bob came back, he was a basket case. He was frigging gone. I mean, he was like an empty skeleton walking around," recalled Bill McGovern, the longtime firefighter and neighborhood friend. "Bob was not a happy guy anymore. Now, he was sullen and very, very quiet. Everybody was afraid to talk to him because they figured he'd snap."

Despite appearances, Bob considered the firefighters a lifeline to sanity. One of them, whose brother had committed suicide, gave Bob a book on grieving. Others encouraged him to attend "Sparks" meetings on the Boston waterfront, where off-duty firefighters and fire buffs gathered, pagers on their belts, to chase the next blaze. During one meeting, Bob recalled, "Cambridge had a four-bagger—a four-alarm fire—and the place emptied out like somebody threw a hand grenade in the room."

To firefighter Fran Judd, an East Cambridge native raised in the housing projects near the Curley condo, Bob seemed burdened by questions about Jeffrey's supervision. In private conversations and public forums, Bob and Barbara heard murmurs and innuendos that their ten-year-old had been given too much freedom. "I think he probably felt there was a lot of negativity. You know, Why wasn't he there?" Judd recalled. "I never got into that. I thought he was a good father."

Others were not so sure. Some talk show hosts bluntly asked where Jeffrey's parents had been. The implication of gross neglect, delivered to a mass audience, was a stinging and embarrassing reprimand. Who the hell do they think they are to be telling me how to conduct myself? Bob thought at the time. They're not in my shoes. Who's supposed to be in jail? Me and Barbara, or Jaynes and Sicari?

The criticism also came through the mail. One letter, from a Brockton priest, warned Bob that he would go directly to hell, and never see Jeffrey, if he persisted in his campaign for the death penalty. For Bob, the landscape had shifted dramatically and unexpectedly. Once a tragic but empathetic figure, he now reminded many people of a horror they would rather forget.

But Bob could not escape his demons. The regular guy who would toss back a beer at the Druid, who would gab about sports after work, had all but disappeared. Fran Judd, for one, became concerned about Bob's mental health and would check on him almost surreptitiously at the firehouse. "When I'd leave, I'd go downstairs and shoot the crap with him, you know?" Judd said. "I suppose he wouldn't do anything foolish, but he didn't seem like the same guy. He was bitter, and you couldn't blame him." Certain topics of conversation became off-limits. "You didn't want to talk about your own kids. You kind of laid back from that," McGovern said. "We didn't shun him, but we said, Give him some space, let him heal, and when he's ready, we'll be there for him."

One conversation could not wait. McGovern became ill with stress when Jeffrey disappeared, and the condition worsened as the days passed without any sign of the boy's body. "I could not even go to the funeral, and it bothered me terrible," McGovern said. "My stomach just blew right out, and the more it went on, the sicker I got." Then, two months after Jeffrey's death, just as Bob returned to work, McGovern had a dream. "Jeffrey just came to me and said, 'Hey, Magoo, how're you doing? Everything's fine up here. Don't worry. I'm with God,'" McGovern recalled, his eyes welling with tears. "It was just his face, and he was smiling. I told Bob in the back room downstairs, and we had a good cry. I felt better after that."

While Bob struggled to adjust, Barbara and the boys endured a similar but less-visible version of hell. Barbara could not summon the strength to return to work, Shaun had dropped out of his senior year at high school, and Bobby, a tinderbox of volatility, refused to discuss his feelings during therapy sessions.

Barbara often was unable to dress herself. Instead, she relied on the help of Bobby and two sisters who had moved into the condo temporarily, one of whom even slept in the same bed with her. Jeffrey's grandmother, ill and frail, also came to live with her heavily medicated daughter. "I'd be curled up in a ball in the bathroom, crying my eyes out," Barbara recalled. "Everywhere I'd look, there would be Jeffrey. I'd hear his voice calling, 'Mommy, Mommy, Mommy.'"

Bobby now considered himself the man of the house, but one with frightening responsibilities. At nineteen years old, he often was the person to lift his mother off the bathroom floor, console her, and try to convince her of the improbability that better days lay ahead. "Every time she cried herself to sleep, I'd be the one there holding her," Bobby said. "I had to step up. I had to talk to her, because she wouldn't be all there. She was just crying, and she was not herself. She said things that really hurt me in the process, but I know she never meant it. I tried to let it go in one ear and out the other, but it's not easy, you know?"

Barbara had become a helpless, broken woman. But Bobby's life changed forever, too, the day Jeffrey disappeared. "Something in your heart's not there anymore," he said. "They could hang me by my feet for months on end, and it wouldn't bother me as much as that pain. They could take every penny I have, they could take everything from me, and it wouldn't bother me." Bobby withdrew from his social circle, distrustful and angry, winnowing his friends to only a select few and casting a wary eye on anyone who tried to draw close. "I didn't talk to nobody, not about what's bothering me. That stuff I keep to myself," he said. "Somehow, some way, I deal with it. It feels lonely sometimes, to tell you the truth, and I'm not really a lonely person."

Although Bobby tried to stay focused and positive, a mere sighting of the Sicaris could shatter his fragile self-discipline. Once, Bobby and Shaun threatened the Sicaris as the brothers passed the family's apartment building. "We seen them on the corner, giving us dirty looks like we did something fucking wrong to *them*!" Bobby recalled. In an instant, Bobby's rage found voice in a vile, threatening broadside that led to the brothers' arrest. Bobby spent a week in the Billerica House of Correction before the charges were dropped.

Shaun, however, was jailed for more than a month in Boston on a variety of charges. In one incident, he chased the Sicaris into their building with a hammer that he fully intended to use. "I came out of my driveway, and I see these people sitting outside in beach chairs, laughing and joking around like it's a celebration," Shaun said. "I pulled my truck over right in the middle of the street, got out, and chased them inside, pounding on the door. I was going to hurt them." Like his older brother, Shaun had been ripped apart emotionally. "Some days it made me angry, some days it made me sad, you know?" he said. "And being a teenager, you kind of don't want to be sad. You'd rather be angry and take it out on other people. And I took it out on Salvatore Sicari's family."

Shaun responded to therapy much better than his brother, but he also looked to friends and drugs to ease the pain. His mood-altering favorite was Ecstasy, which Shaun favored for the upbeat, "happy" high that provided an escape for several hours. "We'd head into Boston on Friday night," Shaun recalled, "and the clubs there would close at two in the morning. Everybody would still be riled up, you know? We'd be having a good time, so it's like, Why don't we go to New York?" Nearly a dozen times in the first months after Jeffrey's death, Shaun sought release in the New York rave scene, where clubs would open on Friday night and not close until Sunday morning and where patrons could gorge themselves on a mind-numbing orgy of music, sound, and nonstop dancing. "It was, like, take a hit of Ecstasy, go to the rave, dance with a bunch of girls, and, you know, kind of keep everything else outside the club and have a good time," he said. "I didn't get addicted to Ecstasy or nothing like that, but those were, like, really the only good times that I got to really have. It's sad to say that."

As Christmas drew near, the family thought not of the holiday but only of surviving yet another interminable day. There would be no Christmas tree in the condo and none of the presents that Jeffrey had wanted since the summer. No battery-powered car, no new skates, no bicycle. If anything, Barbara felt worse as the holidays approached than she had in those first horrific days after the murder. Disbelief had morphed into reality, and shock had taken new shape as painful, palpable grief.

Jeffrey's room had not been touched since his death, and Barbara could not bring herself to cross its threshold. Still, every so often, she caught herself expecting to hear Jeffrey's laugh or to see him running down the driveway. "Sometimes," she said, "I thought I'd wake up, and it'd all be a nightmare."

Jeffrey's younger relatives and friends continued to reel from the loss as well. Mary Downey, Francine's ten-year-old daughter, wrote touchingly of her heartache. "At least I have a memory to hold on to 'cause I had to let you go," Mary wrote in large block letters. "Sometimes when I'm in the dark, I feel scared, but you're the light at the end of the dark tunnel that I follow, and you lead me out of the dark and into the light. As tightly as I held, you broke away, and now you're gone. But I have your memory, and that won't get away."

Across the city from Jeffrey's home, in crowded Cambridge Cemetery, a small decorated pine tree and hundreds of flowers brightened a snow-covered plot on the fringes of the graveyard, where a stone bore Jeffrey's Little League image and a chiseled inscription to "Our Little Man." By Christmas, Barbara had traveled to the site only once, Bob twice. Nearly three months after the murder, Jeffrey's grave held no peace for the Curleys, no closure, no comfort. Instead, the family saw only a cold, black marker and a perpetual, engraved smile that reminded them of all they had lost.

After the holidays, the new year introduced the Curleys to the methodical pace of the state's judicial bureaucracy. The tornado of action that had defined the search for Jeffrey had been slowed and channeled into a flurry of motions and hearings preceding the trials. Lawyers questioned whether Sicari had been denied his right to remain silent, whether to hold two trials instead of one, and whether to empanel a jury far from the Boston media market that had made Jeffrey Curley a household name.

Arthur Kelly and Robert Jubinville, the defense attorneys for Sicari and Jaynes, argued before Judge Cowin in a pretrial hearing that Sicari had thrown up his hands at Cambridge police headquarters and indicated he did not wish to answer any more questions. As a result, the attorneys said, his confession should be suppressed. Yannetti argued that Sicari, instead of invoking his constitutional right to silence, was scheming to evade arrest when he refused to answer investigators for more than thirty minutes during the six-hour session. The prosecutor also noted that Sicari, on two occasions, had signed forms stating that he understood his rights to an attorney and to remain silent. In the end, Cowin sided with the prosecution and allowed the confession to be admitted at trial. She agreed, however, to hold two trials instead of one after Kelly expressed concern that Jaynes would testify against Sicari if they were tried together. She rejected a defense request for a change of venue to western Massachusetts.

Media interest in the trial, scheduled to begin October 26, more than a year after the crime, was predictably intense, and the New England all-news cable channel planned gavel-to-gavel coverage. Cowin, a former prosecutor with a reputation as a smart, tough jurist, clearly realized the extent of public scrutiny about to descend on Courtroom 12B, even if she wrote in one ruling that "there is nothing unique to this case that requires a change in venue." To limit what Kelly called the media's potentially "chilling effect" on jury selection, Cowin allowed only a single reporter to witness the process. She also barred reporters from conducting interviews inside the courthouse and on the sidewalks surrounding the building. The Boston news media were outraged by the ban, which attorneys for three television stations challenged as "unprecedented and unconstitutional." A single justice of the state's highest court quickly overturned the order, which he said infringed on "news gathering in its quintessential form."

Interest in the trial also ran high on Beacon Hill, where Cellucci was involved in the final days of a hard-fought campaign to determine whether he, an acting governor, would be voted into office in his own right. Help came from Bob Curley, who endorsed Cellucci during a State House news conference to promote the first Jeffrey Curley road race, designed to raise money for child-safety programs. Before a cluster of television cameras, Cellucci reiterated his support for the death penalty on the first anniversary of Jeffrey's murder. "We need to do everything we can to make sure that law enforcement and our criminal justice system have the resources to prevent these horrible crimes," Cellucci said. The campaign staff of his Democratic rival, death-penalty opponent Scott Harshbarger, lambasted the governor. "I think it's clear that Paul Cellucci stands for his own political convenience," said Ed Cafasso, a Harshbarger spokesman. "And he'll use anyone or anything he needs to position himself politically to further his own political interests."

Politics were not on David Yannetti's mind as he prepared for the biggest trial of his career. Much, but not all, of the tedious grunt work of lining up witnesses, conducting depositions, poring over evidence, and plotting strategy was now behind him as he went to battle backed by the formidable human and financial resources of the largest district attorney's office in Massachusetts. Although the public expected a conviction and the evidence seemed overwhelming, Yannetti faced enormous pressure to bring home the first-degree murder verdict that Middlesex District Attorney Tom Reilly, who was running for state attorney general, so desperately wanted.

Yannetti relished the fight. Reilly had hand-picked him, a bright, jockish star in the Middlesex office, as one of his premier homicide attorneys. And by the time McEvoy assigned him to the Curley case, Yannetti had already tried ten murders. A former long-distance runner at Bowdoin College in Maine, he loved both the law and the all-consuming intensity of high-profile cases. Quiet and self-effacing outside the courtroom, Yannetti seemed transformed before a jury, where he would pound home a point with impromptu theatrics, rhetorical flourishes, and long, dramatic pauses.

For six years, Yannetti had been living alone in a barely furnished apartment on a narrow street in Boston's heavily Italian North End. There, in the seven hundred square feet he called home for a sweetheart deal of $400 a month, he buried himself in the minutiae of the Curley case when he wasn't ensconced in the second-floor offices of the district attorney's homicide team. "You're getting up before dawn. You're cramming work into every nook and cranny of the day that you can, and still trying to get enough sleep so you're not bleary-eyed the next day," Yannetti recalled of his long, grueling hours on the case. "Maybe you'd go out to get something to eat on a Saturday night, but you're basically in the office," he said. "It's almost a twenty-four/seven deal."

Yannetti's strategy would be to portray Sicari as a full-fledged coconspirator in Jeffrey's death, which, if proved, would be enough to win the case. Under the legal theory of joint venture, which Yannetti pursued, Sicari would be as culpable as the actual killer if he shared the murderer's intent and was prepared to help during or after the crime.

Kelly, on the other hand, would seek to deflect blame from Sicari by putting Jaynes on trial in the minds of the jury. In his opening statement, Kelly conceded that his client, appallingly, did nothing to prevent Jeffrey's death. But, he argued, Sicari's actions did not rise to first-degree murder. Instead, Kelly said, the evidence pointed overwhelmingly to Jaynes, an admitted pedophile, as the mastermind of Jeffrey's seduction and the boy's remorseless executioner.

The Curley family filled the first row of the public gallery for all nine days of testimony, some of it mundane, much of it excruciating. Autopsy photos were displayed on a screen for the jury to examine, the Maine state medical examiner described Jeffrey's painful death in exacting detail, and acquaintances of Jaynes testified again and again about his unnatural attraction to young boys. Yannetti called fifty-five witnesses, including forensic experts from the Washington office of the FBI, in a meticulously prepared case that underscored the depth and breadth of the state's commitment to the trial. The defense called five.

Kelly delivered his closing arguments first, pacing like a boxer and jabbing the air. "Charles Jaynes, he killed that young boy. He seduced him and he killed him," Kelly said, his voice alternating between a whisper and a shout. "Salvatore Sicari did nothing to stop it. As reprehensible, despicable, and disgusting as that is, he did nothing. But he did not commit murder in the first degree."

Kelly led the jury through the testimony of witnesses who had connected Jaynes to his perversions and the crime. "Did we see any evidence whatsoever of Sal Sicari with such desires, intentions, or motives?" he asked. "We did not. It was Jaynes, and Jaynes alone, who had the motive, desire, and intent."

Kelly pleaded with the jury to put aside its revulsion and consider the evidence dispassionately. "You stood up and raised your right hand," he said, raising his own for emphasis, and swore "that you would look at this evidence with your mind and not your heart. I'm asking you to do that now. Because if you do that, you will find that the commonwealth has not proven this case beyond a reasonable doubt."

Yannetti immediately went on the offensive. "Mr. Kelly calls Salvatore Sicari's actions on October 1 and 2 unconscionable, despicable, reprehensible, wrong. I suggest to you that there's a more appropriate name for Salvatore Sicari's actions on October 1. That name is murder in the first degree," Yannetti said, his voice rising steadily. "When you boil it all down, this is a very simple case. Jeffrey Curley left Cambridge with two men, the two men who'd been spending time with him, the two men who'd been seducing him, and Jeffrey Curley never came home."

Yannetti became more animated as he continued. He beseeched the jury, he pointed directly at Sicari, and he grimaced at the horror of the crime. Jeffrey, he said, "was a ten-year-old boy who was made to feel like he was a big man. Me and Charlie and Sal. The three of us. The three musketeers. That respect turned to horror and disgust and terror when he realized why they were really treating him like they treated him." Yannetti mimicked Jeffrey's desperate attempts to ward off the gasoline-soaked rag and Jaynes's suffocating weight, flailing his arms in a wild-eyed reenactment of what Jeffrey experienced. "He struggled, he scratched, he clawed, with every ounce of might that his ten-year-old body could muster. You saw the autopsy photos. You saw all the red marks on Jeffrey Curley's face. You saw it on his chest, and his arm, and his eye." As he finished, Yannetti walked slowly before the jurors and showed them Sicari's booking photo. "I ask you, ladies and gentlemen, to find Salvatore Sicari guilty of murder in the first degree. And nothing less."

The jury deliberated for twenty-two hours over four agonizing days before they finally convicted Sicari of first-degree murder. As the verdict was delivered, Sicari stared ahead blankly, without emotion, just as he had for the entire trial and just as he did when Cowin ordered a mandatory sentence of life without parole.

The Curley family, however, erupted in an outburst of shouts, relief, and rapturous embraces before being muffled by a sharp order for silence. Then, Barbara and Bob Curley—one, tearful, the other defiant—delivered powerful victim-impact statements from the witness stand as Sicari, handcuffed and flanked by two court officers, watched impassively from the back of the jury box. "No justice can ever be served, because nothing can ever bring Jeff back," Barbara said, biting her lip and fighting back tears as she read from a piece of crumpled paper. "Part of each one of us is in the grave with Jeff forever."

If Barbara represented heartbreak, Bob embodied unquenchable anger. Seconds after he began to speak, Cowin admonished him not to look at Sicari. "What we've witnessed here the last two weeks, the people that come through here, is just a small glimpse of the dark side of society that's out there," Bob said, shaking his head and snarling in disgust. "We have to make a statement as a society that we won't allow crime like this. Crimes like this will go punished with the worst punishment we as a society can impose."

Bob did not mention the death penalty specifically. But Cellucci, who won election during the trial, wasted no time invoking what he pledged to make a priority of his first full term. "I have said for a long time that the two individuals involved in the Jeff Curley case are walking advertisements for the death penalty," he stated. "I am glad justice was done today." Capital punishment might not prevent all such crimes, Cellucci said, but the death penalty would give society the means to "express its outrage about some of this horrific violence."

Following the verdict, at a crowded news conference, Bob deflected questions about the death penalty. Such matters, he said, belonged to "the heavyweights" at the State House. He bristled when asked whether the conviction had brought closure to the family. "I hear this word 'closure' all the time, and I don't think I know quite what closure means," he said. "It'll be closure when you guys go home. But when the cameras go off, and six months from now when everybody forgets it, we're gonna have to live with it for the rest of our lives. I don't know if there can ever be closure for us."

Indeed, closure would be impossible for the near future. In less than three weeks, the Jaynes trial was scheduled to begin. One reporter asked Bob, as he moved toward the door, how the Curleys would prepare themselves for testimony that might surpass the gruesome ugliness that they had just heard. "We'll just try to get some rest today," Bob said wearily, "and worry about that tomorrow."

Inside, Bob realized he could not escape the trauma of Jeffrey's death. The tragedy had made him perhaps the most recognizable private citizen in the state, and his son's name had been indelibly attached to one of the most heinous crimes in Massachusetts history. Reminders of the murder could appear anytime, anywhere, and in the most innocuous of circumstances. Acquaintances and strangers often seemed uncomfortable around him, searching for words to express their sorrow or offer support. Ultimately, many of them were unable to say anything.

One such encounter occurred in a supermarket in Chelsea, a rough, working-class city across the harbor from downtown Boston. There, a woman bagging Bob's groceries began crying as she recognized the man who had come to embody every parent's worst nightmare. Bob returned her fixed, sorrowful gaze for an instant, but he could not utter a word. Nothing he could say, Bob felt, would make either of them feel better. Bob picked up his groceries, averted his eyes, and quickly left the store.

At home, Mimi noticed a dramatic change. The fun-loving, carefree Bob she met three years earlier had been replaced by an angry, driven man who immersed himself in causes that had never interested him before. He advocated for a tough sex-offender registry in the state, railed against NAMBLA, raised money for child-safety programs, received stacks of letters, and spoke with death-penalty supporters from across the country. David Brudnoy, a radio personality in Boston who backed the death penalty, invited Bob onto his talk show. And George Hanna, the father of a slain Massachusetts state trooper, called Bob often to share like-minded thoughts on the need for capital punishment. "I had a full plate. There was no time to sit around and feel sorry for myself," Bob said. "There was a lot of stuff to do, and I wasn't gonna let Jeff go for nothing."

Although she opposed the death penalty, Mimi understood Bob's motivation. She also knew that the work would help channel his anger. "It was a way to make meaning out of the meaningless," she said. "He found that it was important, because he could speak for other people who had similar things happen." But as Bob's media exposure increased, Mimi became worried that he would be manipulated and exploited by death-penalty advocates, many of whom struck her as fanatical and obsessive. "It just seemed like a circus that was getting out of hand. People were coming out of the woodwork," she said. "You know, this man was grieving. This man was a mess. He had no business being a champion of the death penalty."

Mimi did not try to dissuade Bob from his crusade, but its highly publicized intensity added another strain to a relationship whose rhythms and routines already had been twisted and rearranged. For Mimi, the murder resurrected a pernicious personal connection with child sexual abuse, whose victims she had counseled for years. That work had proved unbearable and eventually compelled Mimi to move to other forms of trauma therapy. Now, suddenly, Mimi found herself surrounded by the aftereffects of a similar horror. "Bob was finding out the realities of child sexual abuse and how pervasive it was," she said. "He was a new convert to the cause. But, for me, I had been there and done that. And now it was brought into my home."

Bob was right; closure was not possible. And neither would it be for Mimi, who soon found herself ensnared in a maelstrom of capricious, psychological demons that were holding her partner hostage. The emotional peace that Mimi had long sought and believed she had found began to crumble. And in the process, the crumbling of this rare relationship, one that had blossomed by chance and by courage, accelerated into a devastating implosion.

———

─── 7 ───

Collateral
Damage

The beginnings of that romance had the flavor of teenage flirtation, although the fire mechanic and the psychologist had seen plenty of life and shed their rose-colored glasses long before Bob began noticing Mimi walking to work at Cambridge Hospital. Mimi had moved into a modest, first-floor apartment on Inman Street, directly across from the firehouse, after her second marriage ended in divorce. The apartment happened to be visible from a small window in Bob's firehouse workshop, and the movements of this attractive newcomer immediately caught his attention.

Mimi, however, did not notice Bob. A small private practice plus two part-time counseling jobs at Cambridge Hospital and Wellesley College monopolized her time and thoughts, filling up her days and leaving her drained at night. Despite the demands and distractions of her work, a plaguing loneliness prompted Mimi, living alone, to consider returning to Colombia.

That thinking began to change in May 1995 as another semester was winding down at Wellesley College. Mimi had pulled up to the apartment with a car full of plants from her office when she saw Bob jogging through the square. *Oh my God, who is that guy?* she thought. But just as quickly, Mimi upbraided herself for giving him more than a passing glance. *Why do you even bother? You may never see him again.*

A few minutes later, Mimi heard a booming, friendly voice behind her. "Oooh, plants? I have a bunch of plants in the firehouse if you want some," Bob said with a grin. Mimi turned and saw the jogger. Startled for a moment, she quickly regained her composure, murmured a few words, and scurried into the apartment with her greenery. "Stay away from him," she muttered to herself. "This guy's a wolf. He probably talks to all the women around here."

Staying away proved to be no easy matter. On the three mornings a week she worked at Cambridge Hospital, Mimi invariably would fumble for her keys, leave the apartment late, and rush toward her office only a few blocks away. And just as invariably, Bob would be standing outside the firehouse as she passed.

"Where do you work?" he asked the first time.

Mimi did not break stride. Keep walking, she told herself.

The next time, Bob asked the question again.

"Oh, I work in the hospital," she answered.

About a week later, Bob tossed a follow-up.

"Are you a nurse?" he asked.

"No, I'm not," Mimi answered, smiling. "I'm a psychologist, and I know what you're thinking."

After that exchange, Mimi did not see Bob for several months, and she gradually relegated him to memory as she coped with a more pressing concern. A former student of hers, someone who had harassed and stalked her, had moved into an apartment across Inman Street. Mimi filed a restraining order, but the potential for unpleasant confrontations, even violence, frightened her as autumn turned to winter in late 1995.

Once, after a heavy snowstorm, she trudged to her car while nervously eyeing her surroundings. A man with a mustache stopped his truck.

"Hey, you don't say hello anymore?" he asked.

Mimi glanced warily at the man and recognized, to her relief, that this stranger was her unnamed admirer, who had been clean-shaven the last time she saw him. "Something lit up in my heart," Mimi recalled. "I thought I'd never see him again."

For the first time, Mimi spoke at length with Bob and told him of her worries about the neighbor. And when she did, she saw a dramatic shift in his demeanor, a change from light-hearted flirtation to genuine concern. "Keep an eye out for me, would you?" Mimi asked.

Afterward, they began talking more frequently, and Bob always asked if she felt safe. His interest and sincerity resonated with Mimi, who, in a moment of impulse, scribbled a note on a Christmas card that she placed on the windshield of his mechanic's truck. "I don't even know your name," she wrote, "but maybe some day we should have a cup of coffee!" As soon as she returned to her apartment, panic replaced giddiness. Oh no, what did I do? Mimi asked herself. She rushed outside, ridden with second-guessing, only to see Bob holding the card.

"Don't read it! Don't read it!" Mimi pleaded.

Bob smiled and said he thought the invitation was a good idea. Instead of coffee, he suggested they talk over drinks at the nearby Druid, where Irish accents and dark corners cloaked the place with a casual, Bohemian intimacy.

By this time, Bob had moved out of his house and begun to bunk at the fire station. His relationship with Barbara had broken down, but Mimi knew none of this. So, when he knocked on her door just before Christmas, Mimi was pleasantly surprised. She invited Bob into the apartment for cookies and sherry and almost immediately presented him with a question.

"Are you married?" asked Mimi, who had once seen a child's beach toy in his car.

"No, I'm divorced. I'm living with my mother on Gore Street with my two sons," Bob replied.

"Well, because if you're married," Mimi continued, "I don't want anything to do with you."

"No, no, I'm divorced," Bob said.

Mimi chose to believe him, this fire mechanic with a soothing, caring something that she found attractive. She had a doctorate, and Bob had struggled to finish high school. But there seemed to be a chemistry, and Mimi allowed the flame to flicker.

Soon afterward, Mimi invited Bob to a New Year's party that she energized with the Latin music and salsa dancing she craved. At one point, as Mimi danced intensely and alone to the rhythms of Colombia, Bob sat by himself on the couch, lost and transfixed, an outsider in an exotic culture he had never experienced. A friend of Mimi's noted Bob's predicament. "You're quite the bitch," she chided Mimi. "Look what you're doing to the poor man."

The relationship continued and deepened, but any hopes that Mimi entertained of a normal, grounded romance were jolted into another reality when her phone rang in late January. Bob was on the line, calling from Cambridge Hospital, where he had been admitted for an emergency colostomy. Mimi checked her schedule, saw that she had a cancellation, and made plans to visit him that night.

Again, Mimi knew only a fraction of the story. When Bob began feeling excruciating pain in his abdomen, he turned first to Barbara, not Mimi, and returned to his former home for advice and assistance. "I hadn't known Mimi very long, and I didn't know what the hell was going on with me," he said. "I didn't want to be a burden on her, and I didn't want to go to her house all sick, and in pain, and in agony." Instead, he found a ride to Hampshire Street, where Shaun was stunned to see his father, doubled over on the sidewalk, struggling in a snow-storm to find his footing. "Shaun, I think I'm dying," Bob said.

The boy had never seen his father helpless like this, pants hanging below his hips, hands clutching his stomach, his moaning constant and uncontrollable. Shaun helped carry him upstairs, where Bob asked Barbara to find a primary-care physician. Thinking the pain might be from kidney stones, Bob drank quart after quart of water and cranberry juice to flush away the hurt. When that failed to work, he took a taxi to the hospital's emergency room but was sent home when the medical staff could not pinpoint the problem.

The next morning, still in agony, Bob returned to Cam-bridge Hospital, where he was rushed into surgery. The last thing he heard before losing consciousness was an emergency room nurse who shouted, "We've got one going gray." A commotion followed, then Bob woke to find himself being placed in a hospital bed with a colostomy bag attached to his stomach. His colon had burst. "They told me what was going on and that I had almost died," Bob said. "I'm just looking at the bag, saying, What the hell is this?"

Bob phoned Mimi soon afterward. When she rushed into his hospital room, she was surprised to see a woman standing by the bed. Mimi looked at Bob, who rolled his eyes, and the woman turned to greet Mimi.

"Hi, I'm Bobby's wife," Barbara Curley said cheerily.

Inwardly, Mimi was furious and devastated. Outwardly, she was controlled and left quickly. Barbara assumed that Mimi was a hospital employee, and Bob reinforced that assumption.

"She's just some psychiatrist," he told Barbara. "She's crazy, and I told her I don't want to talk to her."

Mimi returned to her office in a blind, seething rage. At the end of her workday, she visited Bob again. This time, Barbara was not present, only a patient from India on the other side of a flimsy curtain.

"How dare you!" she demanded. "How dare you lie to me!"

Mimi snatched a pocket knife that lay near the bed and pointed the blade at Bob.

"I'm going to rip you where they cut you," Mimi said, spitting the words at Bob, prone and wide-eyed on the bed. "I'm going to kill you!"

With that, the Indian patient began wheezing in fright, stunned that a murder might be imminent in the adjacent bed. Mimi lowered her voice.

"You're lucky," she said to Bob. "Give thanks to your roommate that I'm not going to kill you. I don't want you ever to call me again—ever!"

Bob, however, did call Mimi a week later. About to be released from the hospital, Bob needed somewhere to recuperate.

"What do you want?" Mimi barked when she heard Bob's voice on the telephone.

"I'm being discharged, and I'm on my way there," he answered.

Mimi was flabbergasted. A man she hardly knew, someone who had deceived her, had just announced he would be at her doorstep in a few minutes in need of a bed and attached to a colostomy bag.

"Why don't you go to your house?" Mimi asked.

"Because, I told you, I don't live there anymore," Bob replied. Despite her help, Bob had told Barbara he would continue to live at the firehouse. The situation at Hampshire Street was too stressful, he said.

Mimi took pity on Bob, despite the mountain of negatives that had suddenly accumulated. Mimi knew he would have surgery in a few months to reverse the colostomy and that his survival was not guaranteed. In gauging the situation, she stretched the bounds of rationalization. Maybe this means something, she thought. Maybe God is putting him here so I can take care of him for three months, and that's the end of the story. So, let him recover.

Mimi had no expectations for the relationship beyond the second surgery. She spent full days at work, nurses tended to Bob's needs at the apartment, and, as a bonus, Mimi's longtime pet, Picasso, had a new companion. "The cat seemed to get along with him, so to me that was a sign that maybe he was okay," Mimi said, chuckling. "The surgery came, he didn't die, and then I went, Damn, now I'm stuck with this man."

As 1996 progressed, Mimi began to warm to the concept of a long-term commitment. "He was vulnerable, and I said, Well, he's not really married," Mimi recalled. "There had been the Bob before, the one who looked at me on the street. And then there was the guy who was very warm, and giving, and a great friend, someone who seemed innocent in some ways. I knew he wasn't completely innocent, but in his soul he was. There was something about him that seemed kind of soothing, caring, and concerned."

Bob eventually told Barbara that he had moved in with another woman, but he did not elaborate. He did not make the connection for Barbara between the woman she had met in the hospital and the new woman in his life. As a result, Barbara did not know Mimi's name or where they lived, even though their apartment was only a few blocks away. What Barbara did know was that her life had changed for the worse.

For Bob, life had taken the opposite tack. He had a vivacious companion, an outlet into a new, wider world, and a future of exciting possibilities. In 1997, Bob and Mimi began hunting for a house when their landlord, displeased by this unattached male occupant, decided to raise the rent. After a few months of frustrated searching, Bob and Mimi found their prize: a two-family home in East Somerville owned by an elderly Italian widow. "They had an open house, and we come in, and there's an old lady sitting in the corner, Mrs. Roselli," Bob recalled. "It looked like a funeral parlor with early-nineteen-sixties decor." When Bob pulled up a corner of the rug, he saw a beautiful hardwood floor. "It wasn't a cheery place, but we could see it had potential." Smitten, Bob and Mimi made an on-the-spot offer of $190,000. The bid was accepted, they moved in June, quickly rented out the first-floor apartment, and set about renovating the second floor and attic for themselves.

For Bob, the location was a wondrous revelation: large, roomy spaces and views of the Boston skyline. And less than two miles from Inman Square. Working on the house—stripping the walls, refinishing the floor, decorating the interior in a colorful, artsy, Latin style—helped bring Mimi and Bob closer. For this seemingly mismatched couple, the tumultuous childhoods they had both endured helped to deepen and strengthen their bond. "I think we gave to each other the missing part we always had," Mimi said. "I felt at home, with him, for the first time in my life, and he said he did, too."

Mimi was also struck by what she called Bob's "emotional language," an instinctive ability to recognize fear and sadness in others and react with understanding and comfort. For Mimi, she had never experienced such empathy in an intimate relationship. And its resonance proved thrilling. "On the surface, we had these huge differences, we had nothing in common," she said. "But under the surface, there was something very similar and very profound where we connected."

To Mimi's thinking, they both had been "orphaned" as children. In Bob's case, the dysfunctional marriage of his parents had isolated him emotionally. For Mimi, whose father never married her mother and maintained a separate family, she felt shamed and abandoned during her formative years. That fear of abandonment resurfaced when Jeffrey died. "It stirred up all the stuff with my father," she said. "Here's a man who's married with kids; my father was married with kids. I just became so scared."

But in the midst of his own pain, Mimi found reassurance from Bob. "I would say, 'Just take your things. You're just here because it's comfortable. You're along for the ride,'" Mimi recalled. "But he had a way of containing me. He was very, very loving and very patient." That assurance, often wordless, seemed to spring from a deep and hidden place of understanding how sadness felt. That warmth engendered trust, Mimi said, and trust engendered love.

Bob's trauma, however, would batter that love. The initial shock of the killing had strained their relationship, but the trials would prove devastating. The grisly public testimony, the intense media interest, and the actual presence of the killers in court propelled Bob up to, and often over, the border between rage and derangement.

The public rarely saw this side of Bob, who sat grim faced but stoic in the courtroom—first in Cambridge for Sicari, and then in the central Massachusetts village of East Brookfield, where Jaynes had been granted a belated change of venue. In their home in East Somerville, however, away from the public, Mimi saw a man transformed, mentally and physically, by his reacquaintance with the murder. Although Mimi avoided nearly all of the trials, she was forced to live them through the searing wounds they reopened in Bob. "After my day at work, I would come home to find a different person," Mimi said. "I didn't know

Jeffrey Curley in his Cambridge Little League uniform. This photo, published in newspapers and carried on television, became the indelible image of the murder victim. *Curley family photo*

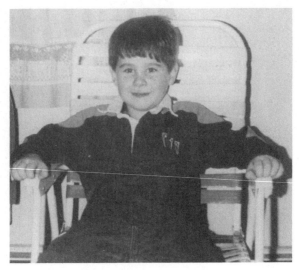

Jeffrey Curley, fearless and precocious, was a constant, energetic presence in his East Cambridge neighborhood. *Curley family photo*

The home of Muriel Francis, Jeffrey Curley's grandmother. The boy left through this door to accept his fateful ride with Charles Jaynes and Salvatore Sicari. *Police photo courtesy of Lawrence Frisoli*

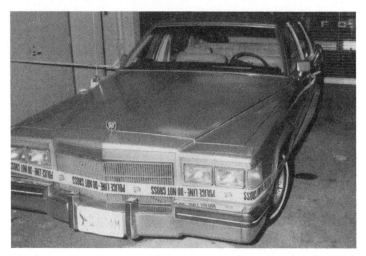

Charles Jaynes used this Cadillac, shown in police custody, to ferry Jeffrey Curley around Greater Boston. He later killed the boy in the car's backseat. *Police photo courtesy of Lawrence Frisoli*

Charles Jaynes used an alias to obtain this New Hampshire driver's license. *Police photo courtesy of Lawrence Frisoli*

The Manchester, New Hampshire, apartment where Charles Jaynes lived, shown in the condition the killer left it the morning after the murder. *Police photo courtesy of Lawrence Frisoli*

Jeffrey Curley's football jersey, folded carefully by Charles Jaynes and left on an end table in his apartment. The No. 8 was used by detectives to mark evidence. *Police photo courtesy of Lawrence Frisoli*

The clothing label and waist button, removed with a razor by Charles Jaynes, from the shorts worn by Jeffrey Curley on the day of his murder. *Police photo courtesy of Lawrence Frisoli*

Posters of child star Jonathan Taylor Thomas that Charles Jaynes placed on the walls of his apartment. *Police photo courtesy of Lawrence Frisoli*

While neighbors strain to hear, Bob Curley addresses a throng of news media near Barbara's condo on October 3, 1997. The search for Jeffrey's body has just begun in Maine and New Hampshire. *Boston Globe Photo/ George Rizer*

John Walsh, 12, joins a candlelight vigil in Cambridge for his slain friend Jeffrey. *Boston Globe Photo/Evan Richman*

A police diver searches murky waters in Portsmouth, New Hampshire, on October 3, 1997. *Boston Globe Photo/Thomas Hurst*

While divers continue to hunt for Jeffrey's body, friends and family members console each other on a Hampshire Street sidewalk. *Boston Globe Photo/Evan Richman*

Salvatore Sicari, still wearing the hooded sweatshirt in which he confessed, is rushed into court the following day by police. *Boston Globe Photo/Barry Chin*

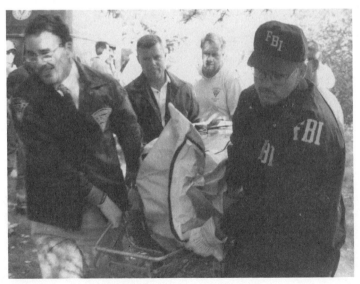

Authorities carry a protective bag holding the Rubbermaid container with Jeffrey Curley's body, shortly after its discovery in the Great Works River. *Police photo courtesy of Lawrence Frisoli*

An impromptu memorial tops a bridge railing in South Berwick, Maine, where the container holding Jeffrey Curley's body was dropped into the Great Works River. *Boston Globe Photo/Bill Greene*

Charles Jaynes, trailed by defense attorney Robert Jubinville at left, is led to his arraignment at Newton District Court on October 10, 1997. Jaynes's face had been scalded while in custody. *Boston Globe Photo/ David Ryan*

Jeffrey's wake at the Long Funeral Home in Cambridge attracted thousands of mourners over two days. *Boston Globe Photo/David Ryan*

Jeffrey's casket is carried from Sacred Heart Church in Cambridge. *Boston Globe Photo/Wendy Maeda*

The Curley family departs Sacred Heart Church following Jeffrey's funeral on October 11, 1997. From left, Bobby Jr., Barbara, Bob, and Shaun exit the services. *Boston Globe Photo/Wendy Maeda*

Bob Curley, holding Jeffrey's skates, sits on his son's bed on October 16, 1997, in only his second visit to the room since the murder. *Boston Globe Photo/Thomas Hurst*

Bob and Barbara Curley, at the Massachusetts State House, present petitions with thousands of signatures in support of the death penalty. *AP Photo/Gretchen Ertl*

Bob Curley, flanked by Barbara and Bobby Jr., react to the House of Representatives vote on October 28, 1997, to reinstate capital punishment. *Boston Globe Photo/Jim Davis*

Salvatore Sicari, in a typically unflustered expression, listens to testimony on November 3, 1998, in Middlesex Superior Court in Cambridge. *AP Photo/Patricia McDonnell*

Charlene Letourneau, a former girlfriend of Salvatore Sicari's who also knew Charles Jaynes, testifies at Sicari's trial. *Boston Globe Photo/John Blanding*

Prosecutor David Yannetti, during his arguments in Salvatore Sicari's murder trial, carries the Rubbermaid container used to dispose of Jeffrey Curley's body. *Boston Globe Photo/John Blanding*

Barbara Curley breaks down after the guilty verdict is announced against Salvatore Sicari on November 12, 1998. With her, from left, are Shaun, Bobby Jr., and Bob Curley. *Boston Globe Photo/Barry Chin*

The race begins in September 2000. The third annual Jeffrey's Run, held near the murder victim's home, raised money for child-safety programs.
Boston Globe Photo/Tom Herde

Bob Curley, right, attends Missing Children's Day at the Massachusetts State House on May 28, 2003. Also in attendance, from right to left, are Magi Bish, who lost her daughter Molly to murder; John Bish, her husband; Heather Bish, Molly's sister; and Matt Guertin, Heather's fiance.
Boston Globe Photo/David Ryan

Bob, Mimi, and Picasso the cat, shortly after the couple had met in the Inman Square neighborhood. *Bob Curley photo*

Five years after Jeffrey's death and a long journey down a tortuous road, Bob and Mimi were married in their home on February 22, 2003. *Bob Curley photo*

Bob and Mimi dance to the sounds of a Venezuelan trio at their wedding reception. *Bob Curley photo*

Jeffrey Curley's grave in Cambridge Cemetery is softened by snow in December 1997. *Boston Globe Photo/Bill Brett*

if he was psychotic. I didn't know if he was homicidal. I didn't know if he was suicidal because he would just go off about what he was going to do to them."

Bob's outbursts were horrifying, and they occurred often. The seams had begun to burst, and even Bob realized he had become unhinged. "I was going crazy," he said. Bob's face would become disfigured, his eyes would bulge, and he would scheme aloud about how to kill the murderers. Mimi would be cooking as Bob concocted his latest recipe for revenge. One monstrous rant involved hiding a knife inside his shoe, leaping over the courtroom railing, cutting Jaynes's throat, slicing open his chest, and throwing Jaynes's liver at his mother's feet. "If I'd been given the opportunity, I would have," Bob said later. "If I thought I could have gotten away with it, I probably would have done it."

Mimi could listen to only so much of the venom. "After a while, I'd say, 'Enough! Shut up! We have to eat!'" Mimi recalled. "And then, he would snap out of it, and we would eat. Later, I would ask him, 'Are you really going to do that?' And he would say, 'No, no, no, no.'" But even Mimi, a trained psychologist, did not know if Bob was being truthful. "I would think, maybe this guy needs to be hospitalized. Maybe the people in court need to be warned that something is happening. Maybe he's just venting," Mimi said. "But I never knew."

As a result, the quality of Mimi's life deteriorated as she engaged in a debilitating, daily struggle to maintain a professional focus at work and gauge whether Bob would harm himself or others. "It was a very fine line," Mimi said. "There were times when he would be in such despair that he would say, 'You know, I just want to hang myself.'" That possibility became one more wrenching piece of the harrowing obstacle course that Mimi was forced to negotiate each day. At work or while commuting, she often stiffened with fear at what the evening might bring. "I had these images," Mimi recalled. "I would say, What if I get home and find him dead?"

Mimi had expected Bob to crash emotionally after the first, consuming blitz of media coverage had dissipated. But when he did plummet, the foresight did not make the experience any easier. "He was here, but he was not here," Mimi said. "He was sad and sullen and absent. He was just broken. Totally." Normal conversations between them became impossible. And the tensions that pervaded every corner of their home exploded into fits of frustrated anger. "I would fight with him. I would punch him. I would scream at him. I would listen to him. I would cry," Mimi said. "I didn't know what I was doing, but I was losing the man I knew."

Mimi encouraged Bob to go to therapy, but he scoffed at the idea that anyone could understand the journey he had taken or somehow find a way to make his life easier. "You're my therapist," he told Mimi. But Mimi could not reach the caring friend and tender lover she had known before. "It was like we were in an ocean, and I was trying to throw him a life preserver," she said. "I just couldn't reach him, and that was very, very hard for me."

Now, in addition to counseling trauma victims, the Wellesley students, and her private patients, Mimi faced a monumental challenge in her domestic life. The resulting emotional overload, an incessant and uninterrupted burden that affected each and every day, nearly became too much to bear. "I was living it at home, I was living it at work, I was living it everywhere," Mimi recalled. For months, while she commuted to Wellesley College, Mimi would burst into tears, inexplicably, while traveling through Newton on the Massachusetts Turnpike. Only later did she realize that she had cried as she passed Honda Village, the place where Jaynes and Sicari had taken Jeffrey's body almost immediately after the murder.

Eventually, Bob relented and visited a Cambridge psychologist who ran a program for victims of violence. The sessions were excruciating for Bob, who regarded therapy as an admission of weakness by people not tough enough to figure out and endure their problems. Often, he sat fidgeting for almost the entire fifty-five minutes, waiting for questions that never got asked and unwilling to yield any insight into the demons prowling through his psyche.

"How are you doing today?" the therapist typically asked.

"Well, how do I look today?" he answered.

"You look good."

"Well, you look good yourself," Bob offered. "You look like Carly Simon. I'm not shittin' you."

Bob lasted only a few sessions. "I ain't got time for this. I ain't got a lot to say," he told Mimi. "I don't know what the hell to talk to her about. The Red Sox? The weather? What are these people going to say to me? What are they going to do to help me?" Mimi realized further persuasion was futile. In the end, she did not share her concerns with anyone about Bob's potential for violence. Instead, the perpetual turmoil that had become her life was relegated to a private hell endured by two tormented people trying to find their way through the darkness.

Mimi gained a reprieve when the Jaynes trial began in December, sixty-five miles west of Boston in a tiny, small-town courtroom. Judge Cowin granted the change of venue after the Sicari trial had produced incalculably adverse publicity about Jaynes's role in the murder. Bob did not wish to commute, so he stayed in a small motel in East Brookfield, where not much had happened since the 1862 birth of Cornelius McGillicuddy, the famous Connie Mack of misty baseball lore. There, among the rolling hills and sleepy roads, Bob found an outlet for his rage in the long, draining runs he took every morning. And at night, after the day's testimony, Bob made his way to a barstool at a local tavern, where he enjoyed a beer, a hamburger, and Boston sports on the television.

The locals soon recognized him as Jeffrey Curley's father from the TV coverage. "We'd be talking about sports or whatever, but not about the trial," Bob said. "They were just regular, working guys stopping off on the way home for a beer, just trying to be decent people." The interaction helped Bob escape, for a moment, the painful particulars of Jeffrey's story. Occasionally, he even managed a laugh, most memorably when he asked the regulars about the peculiar animals he had seen on his runs.

"What kind of horses are those?" Bob asked one night. "You know, the ones with the long necks?" The locals looked at each other, amazed, and burst into uncontrollable laughter. "Those aren't horses!" one man snorted. "Those are llamas!" Bob lowered his head and grinned. "Hey, what do you want from me? I'm from Somerville." For the rest of the trial, Bob smiled every morning when he jogged past the llamas in East Brookfield.

Although Mimi remained in Somerville, Bob often was joined by several members of his family. The trial lacked the wall-to-wall publicity that had surrounded Sicari's case, but the proceedings were no less intense for the Curleys.

And for Yannetti, the task had become even more difficult. Sicari had not agreed to testify against Jaynes, so his admissions to police could not be introduced as evidence. "We knew what Sicari alleged Jaynes did, but we couldn't use any of it, and a jury wouldn't be able to hear any of it," Yannetti said. "So, somebody could sign a statement, but you might as well have taken that paper and just thrown it away." Instead, Yannetti was left with circumstantial indicators—the store surveillance tapes, items of Jeffrey's clothing, and witnesses who placed the pair near the Great Works River—to convince the jury that Jaynes had killed the boy. "It became a mental exercise," Yannetti said, "because you have to subtract Sicari's statement and then make sense of them going to a Home Depot and getting a Rubbermaid container and concrete." The district attorney's office, however, never considered offering Sicari a deal to testify.

Robert Jubinville, who had defended dozens of alleged murderers, was unsure whether Jaynes grasped the case's life-altering potential. "He knew it was a trial, and he knew it was serious, I suppose, because I kept telling him that," Jubinville said. "He's grasping what's going on, but because of his immaturity, he's like, 'It's okay.'" Jaynes had lost more than fifty pounds in the fourteen months since his arrest. He now looked less like a sex-addicted monster and more like a chubby, baby-faced pushover.

Bob continued to fantasize about ways to kill Jaynes, but he and the boys, for the most part, managed to control themselves. Outside the courtroom, however, decorum sometimes broke down. Virginia Jaynes, the defendant's mother, was harassed. Sitting alone in the hallway, a friend of the Curley brothers approached to tell her he had just left state prison and that her son would be raped there and killed. Another time, at the diner where she ate, the owners were warned that the place would burn to the ground if they continued to serve her. Police were informed, and the threat was never carried out.

As the trial progressed, Charles Jaynes maintained a calm, unobtrusive, almost invisible demeanor—at least until Yannetti reprised the dramatic, theatrical closing argument he had used so effectively against Sicari. Vividly describing how the gas burned Jeffrey's lungs, pointing with an outstretched arm, Yannetti directed all eyes in the courtroom toward the defendant. Jaynes, broken by the attention, interrupted Yannetti with a loud, piercing whine.

"I didn't hurt him!" Jaynes cried. "I didn't hurt J.C.!"

Bob bolted from his seat. "You fat motherfucker!" he screamed. "I'll fucking carve you up like a turkey, you fat piece of shit. You're dead! Dead!"

Cowin pounded her gavel, demanding silence, and Jaynes was quickly led away.

After the outburst, Jubinville used his closing argument to place all blame on Sicari. It was Sicari, he argued, who murdered Jeffrey while using Jaynes's car, hid him in the trunk, and then talked Jaynes into paying by credit card for the lime, the concrete, and the Rubbermaid container. Jaynes was unaware of Jeffrey's murder, Jubinville said, until he and Sicari had reached the Great Works River. Only then, the lawyer added, did Sicari reveal that the boy had been killed and that his body lay in the trunk of the Cadillac.

The jurors, who deliberated nearly ten hours over two days, stunned the courtroom when they returned with a verdict of second-degree murder, which showed some uncertainty about Jaynes's intent. Bob shook his head in amazement, but

the family remained composed despite the decision. In the
end, one juror said later, the panel did not have enough evidence that Jaynes had planned and committed a first-degree
murder. Cowin sentenced Jaynes to the maximum term of life
in prison, but the conviction carried a possibility of parole after more than two decades behind bars.

Tom Reilly, the district attorney, approached Bob to express his disappointment. Bob listened politely as Reilly said
the prosecution had done its best and that law enforcement
would vigorously pursue the fight against organizations like
NAMBLA. But no words could erase Bob's feeling that justice
had short-changed him. The unsatisfying verdict, against a man
Bob considered the epitome of evil, had been a crushing coda
to more than a year of ever-present grief.

Bob rushed from the courtroom, grabbed the wheel of a
borrowed car, and sped out of the small parking lot with tires
squealing. As he headed toward the Massachusetts Turnpike
for the solitary journey home, he turned on the radio. An an-
nouncer teased listeners about an upcoming news report with
the words, "Drama in an East Brookfield courthouse." Bob
knew the outcome of that drama, but he was unprepared for
the script. When he heard Jaynes protest, yet again, that he
did not harm Jeffrey, Bob jabbed violently at the radio. "I don't
have to hear no more!" Bob wailed. Frantic and alone, Bob finally punched the button that silenced Jeffrey's killer.

8

Questions and Beginnings

W ITH THE END of the trials, Bob retreated from the spotlight once again, drained and disappointed. Although
David Yannetti had presented a painstaking case in the first
murder trials that Bob ever witnessed, Charles Jaynes still
managed to escape a first-degree murder conviction. For Bob,
the option of capital punishment now seemed even more
necessary.

But the battle had exhausted him, and the rage that had
upended his home life with nightly tirades had all but consumed itself. The fire could not burn without new fuel, and
Bob was spent. The killers had been convicted, the death-
penalty debate had been put on hold, and Bob had filed a civil
suit against NAMBLA. The time had come to heal, and Bob
realized he could not survive mentally, and perhaps physically,
if he continued in the role of embittered, howling Everyman
that he had played for more than a year.

Bob received some helpful advice in those early days after stepping down from the media stage—a stage he believed
he had left behind permanently. "I don't know who said it, and
I don't know where I heard it, but someone told me, 'They
killed Jeff. That's bad enough. Don't let it destroy you, and
don't let it destroy anyone else,'" Bob recalled. "That's the best
advice I ever heard: Jeff's dead, and let it end there."

Bob found a beginning in the garden that he and Mimi had created around their house. Mimi had never planted much before, and Bob had been a city kid who grew up thinking that a junkyard was a playground. Their yard in Somerville had limited physical options. A few feet were available on the south side, facing the Boston skyline, where a jungle of untended growth had filled the narrow space between the home and a chain-link fence. In the front, a tangle of weeds, bushes, and brush formed a similar dense patch on a short, slippery slope from the foundation to the sidewalk. The north side had barely enough room for a steep, narrow driveway, and the western edge of the lot, behind the home, had been given over to a parking area. Any evidence of horticulture, if it ever existed, had long since been obliterated. "The only thing I knew about gardening was how to ruin my grandfather's tomato plants," Bob said. "He had a big, beautiful garden—all the fruit, a big grapevine, and he even made wine in the cellar. Until I came along anyway, and that was the end of that."

Mimi studied gardening books, and Bob was relegated to much of the heavy weekend labor: hacking at brush, pulling up stumps, digging out rocks, and laying new stones for a border. The couple spent hours on their creation. Perennials were planted, as well as hydrangeas, rhododendron, roses, and lilies. Kitschy artwork also found a home in the form of small ceramic rabbits, frogs, elephants, and turtles nestled among the flowers. "I kept him busy. It was, Do a hole here, let's get this trunk out, clear that over there," Mimi said. "For rookies, we did pretty good." The work became cathartic in its productive tedium, a purifying freshener for two souls polluted by sadness and a chance to build something new, simple, and honest in a private, outdoor sanctuary.

The same could be said for changes under way inside the house. The second floor and attic sprang into new, colorful life with a lush patina of South American and global influences. The effect was both soothing and eclectic. Mimi added centuries-old Colombian pottery in rooms decorated with dark, intricately carved wood, exotic plants in suspended pots, and African and pre-Columbian ceremonial masks. The walls were stripped and glazed with swirling patterns of orange and red in one area, grass green in another. Hand-painted tiles adorned a winding, wooden staircase to a small bedroom that they fashioned from the once-forgotten attic. Tables and chairs in rich, muted shades of brown and couches covered in vibrant throws infused the home with a hint of Spanish colonial gentility. The sensation was one of walking in a foreign land, a soulful, breathing paean to Colombia's domestic rhythms and Mimi's worldly tastes.

Little of the place bore a hint of Bob's past, style, or preferences. It seemed almost as if Bob had arrived as a blank slate, a man without a history, someone whose social exposure had been so limited that his tastes were still unknown. Bob did bring an ability to learn and to suspend prejudgment. His openness had impressed Mimi since the beginning, and his willingness, even eagerness, to accept and absorb new ideas increased. The result deepened their friendship as well as their love. "I had been very lonely all my life, even when I was married, but he became my best friend ever," Mimi said. "We became complicit in lots of things. 'Oh, Bob, let's paint this wall,' I'd say. 'Let's work on the garden. Let's buy some paint.' And he'd say, 'Oh, sure. Okay.' We found things that we enjoyed doing together, cooking, little things. And that was our salvation, that we had this place to come back to. This house saved us. For a while."

While Bob recovered in the shadows, the drumbeat to reinstate the death penalty began to reverberate once again at the State House. Twenty-one new legislators had been elected in 1998 to serve in the House of Representatives, and Governor Paul Cellucci was determined to apply pressure, swiftly and firmly, while the memory of Jeffrey Curley's death remained fresh in voters' minds. He unveiled his new bill in February 1999 amid a friendly sea of police officers at a union hall in Dorchester. As the parents of three murder victims stood in support, the governor denounced those "monsters who do not deserve hope" and liberal legislators whom he ridiculed as being out of step with their constituents. Massachusetts residents, he urged, should "turn the heat up" on a legislature that had yet to warm, as most of the nation had, to the common-sense justice of eye-for-an-eye capital punishment. "I am more determined than ever to wage this fight for justice," Cellucci said, kick-starting another political donnybrook that was expected to match the intensity of the tumultuous debate of only sixteen months before.

Neither the Democratic leadership inside the House nor the death-penalty foes outside the building could predict the outcome. None of the supporters of capital punishment who remained in the House had changed their position. Indeed, several tallies suggested that only one vote separated the two sides. And Cellucci, undaunted by his previous defeat, broadened the bill to cover sixteen categories of murder that could be punished by death. "It will be right down to the wire," warned Bill Nagle, the House majority leader, who foresaw a reprise of the draining 1997 battle.

Unlike 1997, however, Nagle and his allies had been preparing for this war. Caught flat-footed by the dramatic swing in momentum after Jeffrey's murder, opponents of the death penalty began reorganizing immediately after the climactic tie vote that year. This time there would be no surprises, they vowed. And once again, Nagle was backed by a highly motivated coalition of interest groups and lobbyists, who looked to him for direction. They targeted new legislators who had never voted on capital punishment, as well as incumbent lawmakers who had reversed their positions in 1997 and opted to support the death penalty. Their arsenal included reams of statistical data, moral argument, and even some old-fashioned political calculation.

The activists saw two signs that the landscape had begun to shift. John Slattery, whose reversal in 1997 blocked the reinstatement of capital punishment, easily won reelection in 1998 despite an opponent who hammered Slattery about the vote in a district dominated by lunch pail conservatives. Even

Cellucci, who traveled to Peabody to campaign against Slattery, could not sway the election.

The second sign came from North Andover, where Donna Cuomo, a key supporter of capital punishment in 1997, lost her bid for a third term in a year when no incumbent opponents of the death penalty were defeated. "It helped legislators recognize that they could stand up and say, 'I have a moral objection,'" said Norma Shapiro of the ACLU. "People in the State House took notice of that."

People also noticed when Cardinal Bernard Law, the most influential Catholic in a predominantly Catholic state, declared in a 1999 news conference that support for the death penalty would be a sin. "The teachings of the church are very clear," Law said after Cellucci, a Catholic, reintroduced the death-penalty bill. "For a well-informed Catholic to support capital punishment, it would be morally wrong. And if one knowingly rejects the teachings of the church, it is wrong, morally evil, and a sin," he continued. "It's very difficult for me to understand how Catholics can come to that position." The implications were obvious for Cellucci, who attended Catholic high school and had earned two degrees at Boston College, a Jesuit institution. But the governor, undeterred, dismissed the cardinal's grave declaration as merely a difference of opinion.

Cellucci and Law would soon have an opportunity to pit the secular against the sacred. A marathon hearing on the bill was scheduled for March 21 in an ornate, old auditorium at the State House, where the governor and the cardinal would join dozens of others in arguing for or against the legislation. Cellucci planned to buttress his argument with testimony from the relatives of murder victims, who would sit beside him at the witness table, lock eyes with House members, and plead for the ultimate penalty. In the public's mind, one name belonged at the top of such a roster. So, three months after Bob Curley raced angrily from the East Brookfield courthouse, the governor's staff asked Jeffrey's father to take the microphone again, face the television lights, and demand that Massachusetts execute its killers.

Bob acquiesced, but only reluctantly. Since the Jaynes trial, he had begun to wrestle with nagging questions about a judicial system he had now come to know a little better. The discrepancies in the verdicts did not make sense to him. Sicari, the accomplice, would never walk free. But Jaynes, who was convicted of second-degree murder, could cling to the hope of parole. Bob also began to question why Jaynes, and not Sicari, had received a change of venue. "As bad as Sicari is, we would never have found Jeff if it had been up to Jaynes. He would have never talked," Bob said. "Charles Jaynes is as bad as they come, and Sicari was just an idiot tagging along." In Bob's view, justice seemed to have been skewed unfairly in favor of the worse defendant. "Let's face it, any time you're involved in the court system on any level, it doesn't take long to figure out there's a big difference between what's right, what's wrong, the law, justice, who can afford the best lawyer, and who can't," he said.

So, despite a creeping disillusionment with the system and his concerns about new media exposure, Bob agreed to appear at the hearing. "Yeah, I'll do it," Bob said halfheartedly. Cellucci had been a high-profile friend when Bob needed one in 1997. And now, Bob felt obligated to return the favor, particularly when the request came from the governor.

As Bob resigned himself to testify, the foes of capital punishment mobilized with a zealot's motivation. Families of murder victims who opposed the death penalty were invited. Like-minded congressmen and prosecutors joined the list. And Cardinal Law prepared to bring the full influence of the church to Gardner Auditorium.

To build momentum, Murder Victims' Families for Reconciliation (MVFR), an activist group that rejected capital punishment, organized a speaking tour. One stop included historic Faneuil Hall, the Cradle of Liberty in Revolutionary Boston, where an overflow audience listened to the soft Western twang of Bud Welch, a gas station owner from Oklahoma City, whose daughter had been killed in the truck-bomb explosion outside the Murrah Federal Building on April 19, 1995. That bombing, the worst act of domestic terrorism in United States history, took 168 lives. The victims included Julie Welch, a twenty-three-year-old translator for the Social Security Administration, who died instantly at 9:02 A.M., seconds after she met two clients in the building's front lobby. In an instant, in an explosion that shook his house eight miles away, Welch lost an only daughter whom he also considered his best friend. Julie's body was not recovered for three days, and Welch's initial shock and sorrow changed into blind and raging hate.

Like Bob, Welch wanted the killers put to death—without trials and without regrets. "Just fry the bastards," he said of Timothy McVeigh and his accomplice, Terry Nichols. So, when President Bill Clinton and Attorney General Janet Reno announced the day after the bombing that they would seek the death penalty, Welch embraced the news despite his previous lifelong opposition to capital punishment. Now, Welch longed for what he called a "quick fix" to deliver final, merciless justice.

In the months after Julie's death, Welch traveled daily to the smoldering ruins of the Murrah Federal Building. There, he mourned his daughter and railed against McVeigh and Nichols, antigovernment militants whose attack was payback for the deadly blaze two years earlier at the Branch Davidian religious compound in Waco, Texas. On that day, seventy-six church members, including twenty-one children, died in the bloody culmination of a fifty-one-day siege by federal agents. Fires killed many of the victims after tear gas had been released into the compound. Autopsies showed that some of the dead, including sect leader David Koresh, had died of gunshot wounds, possibly the result of murder-suicides.

Following Julie's death, Welch blamed himself for encouraging her to study foreign languages. And he blamed Julie, too, for not accepting an offer from Marquette University, where she had received a degree ten months earlier, to return for graduate studies. If different paths had been chosen, Welch told himself, Julie would not have been in the Murrah building when McVeigh drove up with a rental truck packed with five thousand pounds of fertilizer and race-car fuel.

For Julie, a woman who loved languages and sought to help others, the lure of home had been too strong. But there was more. For seven months before the blast, Julie had been dating an air force lieutenant whom she met through a young Catholics group at nearby Tinker Air Force Base. The couple were nearly ready to announce their engagement.

On the day she died, Welch had planned to meet Julie for lunch in a cherished weekly ritual at a Greek restaurant beside her office. He awoke just before 9:00 A.M. and had not yet left his bedroom when he felt the rumble that unhinged his life. Welch's son Chris stood in the kitchen, talking on a cell phone when the explosion occurred.

"Dad, what was that?" Chris asked.

"I don't have any idea," Welch said.

Within fifteen minutes, the television carried the stunning answer. And when Welch saw the rubble of the Murrah building, he knew his Julie was gone.

Welch's life soon careered into a self-destructive, alcoholic dead end. For ten months, each night after he closed his Texaco station, Welch would head home to pour himself a tall glass of rum. "The first thing I'd do when I'd come in that door would be to make a drink," said Welch, an earnest, avuncular man who looks people in the eye. "And if I drank enough by the time I went to bed, I could go to sleep. It was only the next day that I would pay for it." The hangovers first lasted a few hours in the morning, then past noon, and finally throughout the day. The drinking became worse, and Welch also started smoking more, ratcheting up his intake to four distracting packs a day.

Customers noticed the steady deterioration in their friend, who everybody knew had lost his daughter in the bombing. Some patrons even stopped using the gas station, unsure how to behave around a man who had suffered the insufferable.

"They could see clearly what was going on," Welch recalled. "They'd say, 'Bud, you're killing yourself.' And you know what? I'd say, 'I don't give a damn.' My thought was that the sooner I died, the sooner I would see Julie again."

The downward spiral continued through Christmas and into January. Each day, Welch would drive to the bomb site, and each night he would drink himself into a pain-numbing haze. The pattern continued until one cold afternoon when, his head throbbing and muscles aching from alcohol abuse, Welch stood beside the crater that had been the Murrah building and pondered what he needed to move forward. Obviously, the route he had chosen was not working. So, Welch asked himself three questions: Did he need the start of the trials, which were not scheduled for two years, to finally find peace? Did he need convictions? Did he need executions?

The answers did not arrive immediately. But after three weeks of anguished soul-searching, Welch found a path out of the maze of his misery. "I came to the conclusion that, when they take them from their cage to kill them, it simply wouldn't be part of my healing process," Welch said. "I wasn't going to gain anything from an act of hate and revenge. And hate and revenge, I realized, were the very reasons that Julie and 167 others were dead. I finally was able to clearly see what the Oklahoma City bombing was all about: It was about retribution."

Welch reached that conclusion privately, but the repercussions of the choice became national. A reporter, interviewing Welch on the first anniversary of the bombing, continued chatting with him after turning off his tape recorder.

"I bet you'll be glad when this is all over and McVeigh is executed," the reporter said.

Welch paused. "Actually, I'm kind of opposed to the death penalty," he said matter-of-factly.

Later, the reporter called Welch from the newsroom and asked if he could print the comment. Welch agreed, and his change of heart became public. The result was electric. Welch, a third-generation Okie who had been raised on a dairy farm, began traveling the globe to tell his story, and Julie's, to American university audiences, foreign lawmakers, and anyone else who would listen.

Welch's opposition to the death penalty had been foreshadowed by his Irish immigrant ancestors, who joined the Oklahoma land rush in the nineteenth century after trying their hands as Pennsylvania miners. In their eyes, the frontier punishment they observed was too arbitrary, and too prey to human biases, to qualify as justice. Welch inherited that point of view, almost as one inherits a religion, but he never thought deeply about the issue. After Julie's murder, however, he thought often about her conviction that the death penalty teaches hate and that hate begets hate. Finally, on that cold January day, he began to leave hate behind.

Three years later, Welch made what he considered his most important journey. During a speaking tour near Buffalo, Welch made time to visit Timothy McVeigh's father and sister, Bill and Jennifer, in a meeting arranged by a local Catholic nun. Welch felt compelled to make the trip after watching, by chance, a snippet of a television interview with Bill McVeigh. In three seconds, during which McVeigh stopped gardening to answer a reporter's question, Welch recognized the incredible pain that tormented this grieving father.

Welch sat with the McVeighs at their kitchen table in Lockport, New York, for ninety minutes, talking about their lives but never directly mentioning the crime that had shattered them all. Instead, Welch tried only to connect with two fellow human beings who also had suffered a horrific loss through the same terrible act. At one point, Welch nodded toward a photograph of Timothy McVeigh that hung near the table.

"What a good-looking kid," Welch said.

"That's Tim's high school graduation picture," Bill McVeigh said. Seconds later, a large, single tear rolled down the man's cheek.

Welch wanted the McVeighs to understand that he did not blame them for Julie's death and that he cared deeply about their anguish. That simple gesture of extraordinary compassion was

Welch's gift to Bill McVeigh and Jennifer, a twenty-four-year-old who, like Julie, had been attracted to teaching. In the process, Welch gave himself a life-altering gift as well. As he left, Welch shook hands with Timothy's father, sobbed with Jennifer, and then left them with this thought. "The three of us are in this for the rest of our lives. We can make the most of it we choose," Welch said, cradling Jennifer's face in his hands. "I don't want your brother to die, and I will do everything in my power to prevent it."

When Welch returned to Buffalo, he began crying without shame in his hotel room. The tears continued, uncontrolled, until the long day had reached an emotional, cathartic conclusion. When the sobbing ended, something else began. "All of a sudden, I had never felt closer to God than I did at that moment. After all the crying, this load was taken completely off my shoulders," Welch said. "I wish I could explain it to you." Re-energized and unburdened, Welch continued his evangelism for the abolition of the death penalty. By 1999, he had forged a reputation as one of the issue's busiest and best-known advocates.

That reputation brought him to the attention of Renny Cushing, the executive director of Murder Victims' Families for Reconciliation, who placed Welch high on a list of fourteen speakers he had compiled in advance of the State House hearing. Welch accepted Cushing's invitation to speak at Faneuil Hall and nineteen other venues and also agreed to appear on *Talk of New England*, a public-affairs television show. The program on New England Cable News, scheduled for the week before the hearing, would consider the death penalty from the starkly opposed perspectives of two men who had lost children to murder. Margery Eagan, cohost of the Emmy-winning show and columnist for the *Boston Herald*, invited Welch. Her partner, Jim Braude, placed a call to Bob Curley, his expletive-spewing antagonist during the State House debate in 1997.

Bob balked at the invitation. He had never met Bud Welch, but he assumed that Welch had been plucked from the ranks of "left-wing burnouts" whom Bob had long despised.

Bob was also concerned that Welch, a practiced speaker, would trap him, twist his words, and ridicule Bob's position as something straight from the talking points of a right-wing fanatic. After seventeen months of hell, Bob was tired of the controversy. Besides, Bob told Braude, he did not have a way to reach the station. When Braude offered to send a limousine, Bob said he would not ride in the same car as Welch. He answered every inducement with an obstacle and seemed beyond persuasion.

Disappointed, Eagan phoned Welch with the message that Bob did not wish to participate.

"He doesn't want to be at the same table with you," Eagan said. "He's afraid you're good at debating the death penalty."

"Margery, I would never attempt to back Bob Curley in a corner in any way or fashion," Welch said. "I don't do that. That's not my style. You call him back and tell him I'd be delighted to appear with him on or off television because I want to meet him."

After yet another phone conversation, Bob relented. He would appear on the program, he told the station, but he still insisted on a separate car.

Although the men sat less than a foot apart on the television set, the gulf between them seemed cavernous. Bob avoided eye contact with Welch for the first fifteen minutes of the half-hour segment, in part by twisting himself toward Braude and Eagan in an awkward body dynamic that kept Welch behind his left shoulder and out of sight. Both men sat with their hands clasped before them. Bob leaned back in a stiff gray jacket and tie, his narrow eyes rimmed by dark circles and his forehead creased by long, deep lines. Welch, more casual in a tweed jacket and white turtleneck, hunched forward toward the hosts, his demeanor as humble and homespun as Bob's seemed uncomfortable and defiant.

Welch had never been to Boston before the trip, but he quickly learned of Jeffrey Curley. In every speaking engagement, Welch faced questions about whether Jeffrey's murderers deserved the death penalty. As Welch had done hundreds of times before, he told his questioners the story of his rage, depression, recovery, and journey from revenge. On television, he did the same.

Bob listened intently, but he refused to look at Welch. Instead, when his turn arrived, Bob spoke of how the death penalty had been a therapeutic outlet, how he had refused to cower silently inside his house, and how he had chosen instead to fight against the monsters who had killed his son and would kill others. His path, Bob said, had been an instinctive reaction to an unspeakable loss, a road to sanity hacked out of a frightening wilderness of unimaginable sorrow. "They don't give you a handbook on how to grieve the loss of a loved one," Bob said.

Welch nodded, recalling the hopelessness that he also had experienced. But his road out of the dark days had taken a different direction, Welch said, toward a sense that hate and revenge would not help him heal. Welch validated Bob's pain, but he could not validate Bob's demands for eye-for-an-eye justice. Although Welch empathized with Bob's suffering, he would not soften his arguments for *Talk of New England*. The brutal, clinical consequences of capital punishment, he said, should not be confined to a few, silent witnesses, corralled out of public view in a small, secure room at 12:01 A.M.

When the camera turned to Bob, his cadence turned forceful and animated. Hate and anger *are* self-destructive, Bob agreed. But society has an obligation, he continued, to use the ultimate punishment against the most heinous criminals. "Some people view it as letting go and forgiveness. But then again, you have to draw the line somewhere," Bob said, his jaw tightening. "God's job is to forgive them. Our job is to keep people safe."

When Braude asked Bob if he could accept an iron-clad guarantee of life without parole, the harshest sentence allowed under Massachusetts law, Bob answered, "My position on the death penalty hasn't changed." Eagan then asked, "How would you feel if Jaynes and Sicari were killed by lethal injection?"

Before Bob could answer, Welch interrupted. The questions were unfair, he said. Jeffrey's death was still fresh, the pain too near, to consider any option other than revenge. Bob would never get over Jeffrey, Welch continued, and he would miss him every day. But with time, Welch suggested, maybe "he'll learn each day how to live that day a little bit better."

Bob glanced quickly in Welch's direction, again avoiding direct eye contact. But his demeanor had softened. To Bob's surprise, his supposed sparring partner had not come to castigate or diminish him. Instead, this folksy, gray-haired man had accepted his grief and understood his rage. The exchange touched Bob, who also connected with Welch when the Oklahoman spoke of his swift, unsettling transition from anonymous citizen to high-profile spokesman for a controversial cause.

"All I can say is pull me off the front page," Welch told Braude and Eagan. "Send me home to Oklahoma City right now and I'll pump gasoline. Just give my Julie Marie back."

Bob nodded knowingly. "I'm with you," he said.

The program ended with a summary of Welch's rationale for ending capital punishment. "I cannot see how in the world we can cage up a human being, and kill him, and teach our children that it's wrong to kill by killing," Welch said. Bob did not offer a rebuttal or even a last word. Instead, in an almost imperceptibly low voice, he thanked Braude and Eagan for the opportunity to appear on the program. For Braude, the program had been the most intense and moving he had experienced on a television set. That sense also resonated with the public, Braude said, which reacted with phone calls and on-the-street feedback that dwarfed any previous response that *Talk of New England* had received.

After the television camera had been turned off, Bob and Welch moved quietly toward the front of the studio, where two limousines were scheduled to return them separately to Somerville and Cambridge. When only one car arrived, Bob unexpectedly found himself in the awkward position of sharing a ride with Welch and Renny Cushing, who were bound for Harvard University and a speaking engagement at the John F. Kennedy School of Government. During the twenty-five-minute drive to Harvard Square—with Bob in front and Cushing and Welch in the rear—the three men spoke about their backgrounds, their families, and their tragedies.

Cushing, a former state legislator in New Hampshire, lost his father in 1988 when a neighbor knocked on Robert Cushing's door and greeted him with two fatal shotgun blasts. A retired elementary school teacher, the elder Cushing died on the living room floor in front of his wife, who had been watching a Boston Celtics playoff game on television.

Renny Cushing had always opposed the death penalty, and the murder of his father did not change his stance. But the killing did change his life. "For relatives of the murdered, part of you takes some responsibility for it. You failed your loved one because you couldn't protect them, and you'd do anything you could to change the history," Cushing said. "Part of what is hard about being a survivor is coming to grips with the fact that, try as you want to, you can't change the past. The best you can do is try to control the future."

To do that, Cushing channeled his energies into working against the death penalty and bringing together the relatives of murder victims who shared that goal. "There's this belief that all families of murder victims want the death penalty for closure," Cushing said. "And that, as a consequence, our political leaders are under this moral obligation to provide the execution solution for the victims' pain. We tried to shift that paradigm a little."

During the ride to Cambridge, Cushing spoke about his father. Welch spoke about his daughter, Marquette University, and her love of the Spanish language. And Bob, who mentioned the death penalty only briefly, spoke about the details of Jeffrey's death, as well as his ongoing efforts to bolster child-safety programs. But for most of the ride, the three men shared their stories, forged through pain and perseverance, about the task of coping with extraordinary evil.

Bob had never participated in such a discussion. In previous encounters, the relatives of murder victims had always supported the death penalty. This was new, unexpected, and confounding. Welch and Cushing both seemed like regular

guys, men who spoke straight from the heart and who both
knew firsthand the horrible pain of murder. How can they be
against the death penalty? Bob asked himself.

Welch had struggled with this question himself and seen
the struggle in others. He noted that Bob did not dwell on the
death penalty, either on the television set or in the limousine.
And Bob's repeated references to the work of child safety
showed Welch something else: that Bob had begun to bury his
hate in a constructive way.

In Harvard Square, they parted company as new friends.
As Welch and Cushing walked away from the limousine, Welch
gestured over his shoulder. "He's gonna turn around on this
thing," Welch said. "This is really a decent person, someone
who has suffered an unbelievable loss, but he's gonna change."

Ten minutes later, the limousine driver pulled up to Bob's
house, looked in the rearview mirror, and smiled at his passenger. Before he overheard the conversation in the car, the
chauffeur said, he had planned to ask Bob for an autograph.

"I thought you were doing the sports show," the driver
said. "I thought you were a baseball player."

"If I was a baseball player," Bob said with a chuckle, "I
wouldn't be living here in East Somerville, you knucklehead."

Unsettled by the encounter with Welch and Cushing,
Bob grabbed his bicycle and headed toward the Charles River,
where a loop from Cambridge to Boston and back again would
combine a workout with some serious thinking. As he pedaled,
Bob was consumed by jarring questions: How could Welch
and Cushing oppose the execution of murderers who had
shattered their families and lives? How could they reach that
point? What did this say about him? Was it unmanly even to
think this way? These questions were more than a mental exercise. The State House hearing, a full-blown media spectacle
where Bob once again would be asked to trumpet his support
for capital punishment, would be held in less than a week.

Suddenly, Bob was plagued by second thoughts. The reflexive justification he had used since Jeffrey's death now

seemed less certain. In Bud Welch and Renny Cushing, he had seen that opposition to the death penalty did not always signal weakness. "I always kind of viewed myself in a certain way," Bob said later. "You know what I mean? A certain class, a certain attitude, a certain edge, coming from where I came from. I always thought that if you were against the death penalty, you were a wimp." He had never met anyone like Welch and Cushing. Down-to-earth and unpretentious, these men were a different breed from the placard-carrying protesters he had encountered during the 1997 debate. And Bob had witnessed firsthand that punishment did not always fit the crime. Maybe, Bob thought, opposition to the death penalty was not necessarily abnormal.

Head down and legs churning, Bob tried to make sense of his hesitancy. But the questions were too big and the answers too obscure for him to reach any conclusions during a sixty-minute bike ride. He was, however, certain of one thing: He had made a commitment to Governor Cellucci to testify. And because of that agreement, he would not back out. "I was worried about how I'd be perceived if I didn't go and how I'd be portrayed in the media," Bob recalled. "I didn't want to look like a fucking dope, like a nutcase or something." Bob genuinely liked Cellucci, but he also feared the governor's clout. Nurtured in a neighborhood where broken loyalties brought repercussions, Bob worried that reneging on his commitment might invite payback. "That's a high level of politics, and I didn't know if there would be any kind of retribution," Bob recalled. "I was a little concerned, to be honest with you."

On the morning of the hearing, Bob reported to work as usual, dressed in his blue uniform and thinking ahead to his return to the spotlight. A packed auditorium, the cameras, a bank of reporters, and the rapt attention of a dais full of legislators awaited the words of the man who had come to symbolize the public's righteous vengeance. That man did not arrive in a limousine, as he had the previous week at New England Cable News. Instead, Bob rode his bicycle to the State

House, dressed in a suit he had quickly donned to replace the standard-issue clothing of the Cambridge Fire Department. A member of the governor's staff saw Bob pushing his bicycle through Doric Hall, a gilded remnant of the original building, and was startled by his appearance. Bob looked devastated, his pain raw and visible as he made his way to the governor's legal office. "It was a sad thing to see," the aide said.

Bob's voice would join a chorus of supporters of capital punishment, advocates who included high-ranking police officials, district attorneys, and other parents wounded for life by murder. The other side had also amassed a formidable array of speakers. Welch would be among them, as would Cardinal Law, Cushing, and a dozen other relatives of murder victims. The group included Andrew Pryor, the father of a slain nine-year-old girl from suburban Wayland, who once supported capital punishment but later changed his stance.

The hearing was convened by the Criminal Justice Committee, a seventeen-member joint panel from the House and Senate that was believed to be tilted toward the death penalty by a 9–8 margin. Cellucci knew that the committee's recommendation to the full legislature could push the issue either way, in what might be his last, best chance to enact the measure.

Outside the building, the event had taken on all the trappings and buzz of Opening Day at Fenway Park. Satellite trucks from every Boston television station squeezed into the cramped real estate beneath the golden dome. Inside, reporters staked claim to prize vantage points.

As the hearing neared, Maureen Hogan, a legal aide to the governor, escorted Bob to an elevator and the short walk to Gardner Auditorium. Bob was in turmoil. After speaking with Bud Welch and Renny Cushing, the prospect of ranting again for capital punishment gnawed at his conscience. His mind racing and palms sweating, Bob glanced nervously at Hogan. "I really don't want to get into this. You know, stepping into the spotlight again with this death-penalty stuff," Bob said in the elevator. "I don't feel comfortable doing it." With that, the door opened. Bob abruptly thanked Hogan, retrieved his bicycle, and left the State House. There had been no further explanations, no pleas for understanding from one of Cellucci's top legal assistants. He simply walked away.

As he coasted down Beacon Hill, the chill of March in his face, Bob did not yet know that a new ride had just begun. He smiled, pedaled briskly over the Longfellow Bridge into Cambridge, and returned to work a happy man from whom a tremendous burden had been lifted. Although he did not yet fully grasp what he had done, Bob knew this: He would no longer be Cellucci's angry front man. "I thought there was going to be a death penalty, at least it looked that way to me," Bob said. "And I didn't want Jeff to be remembered for the death penalty every time somebody was going to be up for an execution, or put on trial where capital punishment was involved. I just knew that Jeff's name would be dragged into it."

Inside the building, as Bob sped away, Cellucci pounded the drum again. "I believe we will save many lives," the grim-faced governor told the committee. "But if we can save even one life, it is worth it." Cellucci entered the chamber hoping to sway a legislator or two with his tough talk. Instead, he found himself on the receiving end of some unexpectedly pointed questions from a supposedly friendly committee member. Harold Naughton Jr., a Democratic state representative from Clinton who voted twice for the death penalty in 1997, prodded the governor for estimates about the imposing legal costs associated with capital murder cases. Cellucci could not provide an answer to the former prosecutor.

John Slattery, the governor's nemesis in 1997, asked Cellucci for any credible evidence that the death penalty is a deterrent. Again, Cellucci could not offer any statistics.

"I feel, with the death penalty, that you will execute an innocent person," Slattery said, staring down at the governor who had campaigned hard to unseat him.

"You're trying to protect a very narrow group of people," Cellucci shot back. "I'm trying to protect the six million people of Massachusetts."

To Martina Jackson, executive director of Massachusetts Citizens Against the Death Penalty, the governor's refusal or inability to provide any firm data to the committee had transformed him into an unwitting ally of the opposition. Jackson, whose grandmother was killed at Auschwitz the summer she was born, took pride in the fact that her grandmother's four daughters, including her mother, had opposed the death penalty.

Cardinal Law, who had reached out personally to lobby Cellucci on the issue, reiterated the Catholic Church's unequivocal stance on the death penalty. "The dignity of human life must never be taken away, even in the case of someone who has done great evil," Law said before an audience that included dozens of nuns and priests. "We do not help those whose lives have been shattered by the murder of a loved one. . . . We must not be motivated by vengeance."

Although the governor's supporters were outnumbered, their voices were no less anguished than they had been two years earlier. Susan Gove, the mother of Kristen Crowley, who had been bludgeoned to death in Peabody in 1996, testified for the bill and chided the cardinal for injecting himself into state politics. "What the cardinal must understand is that the cardinal has only one vote in this state," Gove told legislators. After the hearing, she rushed after Law and upbraided him in a crowded hallway before a cluster of reporters and television cameras.

"My daughter had a life, sir!" Gove said. "Don't you feel that the people who destroyed my daughter should deserve a punishment equal to the crime?"

"I believe that the crime against your daughter, the crime against her life, is not going to be taken care of by the killing of another person," Law replied. "It's the killing that has to stop."

Following the exchange, the pair embraced in a gesture of respect if not agreement. The same could not be said of lawmakers on opposite sides of the issue. Frustrated by the governor's resistance to his questions, Naughton told reporters as he left the auditorium that he would rethink his support for the death penalty, a stance cemented at a meeting the following morning when Cellucci still could not provide the requested figures. Later that day, Naughton cast the critical vote when the committee decided, 9–8, to send a negative recommendation to the House. After the vote, Naughton said that he continued to support the death penalty but that the state must first identify the funding to pay for legal fees and other expenses that could reach $7 million a case. Naughton said he also had been influenced by the recent exoneration of Anthony Porter, a death row inmate in Illinois who had come within two days of execution. Porter's double-homicide conviction had been dismissed two weeks before the Massachusetts hearing, aided by Northwestern University journalism students who found evidence that helped prove his innocence. Including Porter's release, thirteen inmates on the Illinois death row had been exonerated and twelve had been executed since the state reinstated capital punishment in 1977. To opponents of the death penalty, those life-and-death statistics delivered a jolting message about the fallibility of the justice system.

Naughton's decision all but ensured that the bill would not survive a vote in the full House. And Cellucci, painfully aware of the numbers, appeared to concede defeat. "Everyone I've talked to so far seems to have made up their mind," the governor said. In a reprise of 1997, Cellucci found a villain once again in House Speaker Tom Finneran, whom he lambasted for scheduling the vote before six vacancies could be filled in special elections. The empty House seats, Cellucci argued, meant two hundred thousand residents would be disenfranchised. "Why don't we just dismiss all of the legislators and let the speaker make the decision?" Cellucci said. "That apparently is what he wants."

Finneran defended his scheduling but did agree with the governor that the legislature seemed out of step with the state. In 1999, polls continued to indicate that most Massachusetts residents supported the death penalty. "This is one instance where representative form of government has given us a result that differs from a pure, undistilled democracy," Finneran said.

In the week between the hearing and the House vote, Bob began to question longtime friends about their feelings on the death penalty. "I started bumping into more and more people who I viewed the same way that I viewed myself—same place, same attitude, guys from Somerville, guys from South Boston, guys from East Cambridge," Bob said. And to his surprise, more of them opposed the death penalty than he had expected. The deck was stacked against the little guy, some said. Others rejected capital punishment for moral reasons. And some believed that fatal mistakes were inevitable.

Like most of his friends, Bob had never given much thought to the death penalty before Jeffrey's death. After any heinous murder, the notion of summary execution seemed reasonable to Bob and his peers. But when someone, particularly a middling mobster or ordinary workingman, was found to have been wrongfully convicted, Bob and his circle paid attention. In one high-profile case, Pete Limone and Joe Salvati, two fall guys from the Massachusetts underworld, were released from prison in the mid-1990s after serving more than thirty years for a murder they did not commit. That news, together with the long-suspected revelation that the pair had been framed by the FBI, provided reams of front-page fodder guaranteed to jump-start conversation in the firehouse. The news also planted seeds of doubt. "You hear about a terrible case and you think, Yeah, this guy deserves to die. You know, in a perfect world for me, Jaynes and Sicari should be executed every day from now till the end of time," Bob said. "But then, you start looking at the justice system, and there's always room for error."

The realization that mistakes are made—not only in evidence but in human judgment—struck Bob like a hammer the weekend after the hearing. Leaning back in a stiff, metal chair at the firehouse, savoring the slow progression of a quiet Sunday morning, the questions that had been circulating in Bob's mind suddenly began to crystallize into a startling conclusion.

A once-struggling student who had to be prodded, even threatened, by his sister to finish high school, Bob regularly scoured the two Boston papers, the *Globe* and the *Herald*, for tidbits about city crime and politics and whatever Boston sports team happened to be in season. On this March morning, the *Herald*'s front page devoted itself to the eye-catching story of a Massachusetts man, a two-tour marine veteran of Vietnam, who was nearing an execution date at San Quentin prison in California. Bob was drawn to the story instantly. Although he had not served in Vietnam, he knew many men from the neighborhood who had, and he knew that the domestic damage from Vietnam, more often than not, was felt in low-ceiling, blue-collar places like Inman Square.

"With every midnight hour, Manuel 'Manny' Babbitt's last days peel away and the Wareham native, who has spent nearly two decades on California's death row, moves closer to the mouth of the animal he calls the 'gray wolf,'" began the story by Ed Hayward. "On May 4, the day after his 50th birthday, Babbitt is slated to be strapped to a gurney; an intravenous brew will put him to sleep and then paralyze his heart and lungs. This is the punishment a jury meted out for the 1980 murder of Leah Schendel."

Schendel, a petite, seventy-eight-year-old grandmother, died of a heart attack after Babbitt savagely beat her during a botched robbery in a Sacramento housing complex for the elderly. Curley grasped the tabloid tighter and leaned forward to read more.

Babbitt, a black man raised in a cold-water shack on the overlooked fringes of Cape Cod, came from a large Cape Verdean family in which sixteen relatives had required psychiatric treatment or committed suicide. At the age of twelve, he survived a serious automobile accident but suffered a head injury that appeared to leave severe psychological and cognitive scars. Afterward, Babbitt trudged through school, aimless and impaired, repeating grades until he dropped out of junior high school at the age of seventeen.

Unable to read or write but inspired by a brother's military service, Babbitt walked into a marine recruiting station in Providence, Rhode Island, and asked to enlist during the height of the Vietnam War. With the help of the recruiter, he filled out an application his family does not believe he could understand. Within six months, Babbitt found himself at the bloody outpost of Khe Sanh, where isolated marines held out for seventy-seven days against overwhelming enemy numbers near the North Vietnam border. Although Babbitt survived the battlefield, he found himself besieged anew by posttraumatic stress disorder.

Troubled and unruly, Babbitt was discharged in 1970 and soon descended into a life of homelessness and crime. Convicted of robbery in Massachusetts, Babbitt was diagnosed in 1973 as suicidal and schizophrenic while in custody at the Bridgewater State Hospital for the Criminally Insane. He left the institution after three years, but his bizarre behavior did not end. He returned to his family in Wareham but often slept in the woods in a lonely search for solace. Family members finally encouraged him to live with his brother Bill in Sacramento. There, they hoped, Manny would benefit from the love and guidance of a married, responsible, older sibling.

Within months of Manny's arrival in California, Schendel was murdered. And only a few days after her highly publicized killing, while rummaging through a closet at his home, Bill Babbitt discovered a cigarette lighter that had been monogrammed with the initials "L.S." He also found hundreds of nickels stuffed into a piggy bank.

Puzzled about the nickels, Bill Babbitt recalled reading that Leah Schendel had recently returned from a trip to Las Vegas, where she amused herself at the casinos by pumping fistfuls of coins into the cheapest one-arm bandits. The stunning connection brought Bill Babbitt to his knees. Heartbroken but determined to do right, Bill discussed his options with his wife. Should he help his brother escape? Should he put him on a bus bound far from Sacramento? Could he live with himself if Manny killed again? In the end, disconsolate but determined, Bill approached the Sacramento police. "It was a difficult situation to turn your brother in, but I had to do the right thing because I love this country," Bill said later. "That could have been my mother who died."

The police assured Bill that his brother would not be subject to the death penalty because of his apparent mental illness. Instead, they said, Manny would be confined in a locked psychiatric facility, presumably for the rest of his life, where he would receive the help he so desperately needed. Satisfied, Bill told police he would lead them to Manny, who had been staying temporarily at their sister's house. Bill entered alone, greeted his brother matter-of-factly, and enticed Manny to join him for an afternoon of pool. Instead of a pool hall, however, Bill Babbitt led his brother to a waiting police cruiser. And as the police handcuffed Manny, Bill pleaded with his brother for understanding.

"Please forgive me," Bill said. "They're going to take care of you, Brother. You're going to be okay. Please forgive me."

Manny looked up, his hands shackled, about to begin another journey in dangerous, uncharted country.

"Brother Billy," he said, "I've already forgiven you."

Manny's journey, however, would not lead to a no-parole lifetime of incarceration and therapy. Instead, Babbitt's journey led straight to the "gray wolf" at San Quentin. The story horrified Bob, who felt he had much in common with Manny Babbitt's disadvantaged, bare-bones upbringing. Both men had been poor and marginally educated, and both had enlisted in the marines in an effort to escape troubled home lives.

Bob contrasted Manny Babbitt's fate with that of Ted Kaczynski, the infamous Unabomber, who had killed three people and injured twenty-three with mailbombs and other explosives over seventeen years. Kaczynski was arrested in 1996 after his brother, David, approached the FBI with suspicions that the Unabomber's antitechnology manifesto resembled his brother's writings. Although Attorney General Janet Reno sought the death penalty, prosecutors eventually offered Kaczynski a plea agreement that resulted in life without parole. Death for the poor black man, Bob thought. Life in prison for the Harvard-educated white man.

Suddenly, the thinking that Bob had done in the past week, as well as the doubts that had gained traction since the trials, began to fall into place like the tumblers in a combination lock. Now, the death penalty seemed less defensible. Once considered a hammer of justice, the punishment now seemed to Bob an emblem of inequity. A switch had been pulled in his mind, and its impact was immediate and profound. "It made me realize—being a poor guy, not educated, and from my background—that I'm closer to the guy who's going to be executed," Bob said.

Bob was unaware that Manny Babbitt's case had long been a cause célèbre for many Vietnam veterans and opponents of capital punishment. Both factions had argued passionately for years that Babbitt, irreparably scarred by mental illness, should be imprisoned for life instead of executed. That fight attracted Bud Welch, who lobbied Governor Gray Davis in California to spare Babbitt's life. And it attracted David Kaczynski, too. "Ted escaped by the skin of his teeth. And it was luck, it wasn't merits, it wasn't justice," said Kaczynski, who felt betrayed when Reno announced that prosecutors would seek the death penalty against his brother.

Later, after the plea agreement took execution off the table, Kaczynski received a phone call from Bill Babbitt in mid-1998. "This guy whose name I had never heard, from Sacramento, says, 'David, you don't know me, but I know you. I've read about you, and I think you might be the only person in the world who can understand what I'm going through right now,'" Kaczynski recalled. Because both men had turned in their brothers, and because both men knew the anguish of having exposed them to the death penalty, Kaczynski realized that Babbitt might be right. Who else could understand his emotional turmoil?

Bill Babbitt had become alienated from several of his siblings, who regarded him as a traitor. He endured cruel, racist comments about his brother by coworkers at the Sacramento transportation department, where Bill worked as a mechanic. And he despaired about the fate he unwittingly had sealed for Manny. "When Manny got arrested, I went back to my Bible,"

Bill recalled. "But besides my Bible, I had my marijuana, I had my booze, and I had my Derringer."

After outlining Manny's case for Kaczynski, Babbitt did not hear back immediately. Kaczynski was concerned that joining Bill's cause would reopen fresh wounds by resurrecting his family's story in the national news media. But after lengthy discussions with his wife, Linda, who first suspected the identity of the Unabomber, the Kaczynskis decided to help. When David Kaczynski finally called back in the spring of 1999, about the time that Bob Curley read the *Herald* story, Bill Babbitt was sitting on the edge of his bed, contemplating suicide.

"It's for you," Babbitt's wife said, handing him the phone.

Babbitt assumed the call was from a reporter, seeking yet another comment about the approaching execution. But instead of a reporter, Babbitt heard the calm, measured voice of a new, unexpected friend.

"Bill Babbitt, this is David Kaczynski," the caller said. "Bill, I'm coming to stand with you."

Instead of replying, Babbitt bolted from the bed. "Praise, Jesus! Praise, Jesus!" he shouted, while Kaczynski listened patiently. When Babbitt finally realized he had a phone conversation to finish, Kaczynski agreed to travel to Sacramento to attend Manny Babbitt's last-chance clemency hearing in April.

Three thousand miles to the east, Bob Curley also decided to become involved. He did not know how—he had no friends among the death-penalty opposition—but a doorway into the fight would open.

9

Resurrection

WHEN THE Massachusetts House of Representatives convened for six hours of debate, followed by a climactic
vote on capital punishment in 1999, the Curleys were nowhere
to be seen. No last-minute changes were expected this year,
no shouting in the hallways, no high fives on the chamber
floor. All the energy, so different from 1997, had shifted to the
better-organized opposition.

Still, the prospects for defeat did not deter Governor
Paul Cellucci from staging one, last, bitter rally on the broad
sidewalk in front of the State House. Flanked by the families
of murder victims and standing in front of a phalanx of police
officers, Cellucci pointed behind him, toward the Capitol's
gleaming golden dome, and railed against the lawmakers assembled there. "We have a House of Representatives that is
out of touch with the people they represent," Cellucci said,
his voice rising.

The governor was followed by a parade of somber supporters who, angry and embittered, recounted in graphic detail
the gruesome deaths of those they had lost. When the rally
ended, the governor conceded defeat in remarks to reporters.
He listed a variety of reasons: The economy is good. Momentum had waned. The other side is too formidable.

Inside the building, the process crept through a marathon session of theatrical debate to its predictable conclusion. In
desperation, Republicans offered a lengthy string of amendments

in a final, unsuccessful bid to make the bill palatable. Postpone the vote until the House vacancies are filled, they asked. Limit capital punishment to killers of law-enforcement officers. Target only those who murder again in prison. The list went on and on, to no avail.

John Slattery took the floor, and this time his fiery denunciations of the death penalty took no one by surprise. "Why is a cop's life more important than my mother's?" he bristled, surveying the chamber with defiance. At the end of the day, exhausted and resigned, the House voted, 80–73, to reject the bill.

On cue, Cellucci once again launched broadside after outraged broadside against Tom Finneran, the House speaker, whom he lampooned as a strong-armed con man bent on perverting the people's will. But, in defeat, even the governor and his supporters seemed to realize that a watershed moment had come and gone. The measure was dead, clinically and emotionally, and not even the resurrected memory of Jeffrey Curley's murder could revive its flagging chances. Opponents celebrated their hard work and brightening prospects for future success. Certainly, the activists believed, their efforts had made a difference in a legislature suddenly less enamored of state-sponsored lethal injection.

Another factor, too, might have played a role. Where was Bob Curley? He had neither testified at the hearing nor attended the debate. His voice also had been missing from the media run-up to the vote. Bob's absence throughout had been glaringly conspicuous. The activists could only speculate because Bob had not confided his concerns to anyone except Mimi. He had been content to sit out the latest skirmish and keep his new opinions to himself.

But Bob could not shake the image of Manny Babbitt, a mentally handicapped veteran, waiting in San Quentin for his date with death. Shortly after the vote, Bob was driving his mechanic's truck through Cambridge when he spotted Jarrett Barrios, a young, liberal state legislator, walking near Inman Square.

Bob stopped the truck, leaned out the window, and asked Barrios for a contact at Massachusetts Citizens Against the Death Penalty, a group that Bob had despised during the acrimonious debate in 1997. Barrios, who had noted Bob's absence at Gardner Auditorium, said he would put him in touch with someone. The conversation ended there, but Barrios's curiosity had been piqued.

He called Martina Jackson, the group's executive director, and relayed Bob's unexpected request. Jackson, as surprised as Barrios, eagerly agreed to phone Bob. When Jackson called, any trepidation she might have felt turned quickly to amazement. The person who answered was startlingly unlike the man who once cursed her during a death-penalty protest. This time, Bob was calm, solicitous, and anxious for a connection to the opposition. He hadn't made a decision, but he wanted to learn.

"There's a group that might be helpful to reach a conclusion," Jackson said. "It's called Murder Victims' Families for Reconciliation. Why don't you talk to Renny Cushing there?"

"Sounds like a plan," Bob replied.

That call led to a follow-up from Bob, which Cushing had been told would occur during a dinner meeting of his group. When he shared the news with other members, the gathering was stunned. Who? Bob Curley? *The* Bob Curley? It was true, Cushing assured them. Bob Curley wanted to contact California governor Gray Davis about the Manny Babbitt case.

Cushing was at the dining room table when Bob called. So was Andrew Pryor, the father of the murdered girl from Wayland. Also in attendance was Tom Lowenstein, political director for Massachusetts Citizens Against the Death Penalty, who was handed the phone shortly after Bob rang. Lowenstein had thrown himself into the Massachusetts death-penalty fray specifically because of Jeffrey Curley's murder. The son of former congressman Allard Lowenstein, a New York civil rights activist gunned down in 1980, Tom left behind a bartending job in

Northampton, Massachusetts, after reading a pro-death-penalty opinion piece by Jeff Jacoby, a conservative columnist at the *Boston Globe*. Jacoby had written with mock sarcasm about the potential reaction to Bob's push to prosecute Jaynes and Sicari in federal court, where a death sentence could be imposed. "Let's hope those Massachusetts authorities tell Curley where to get off," Jacoby said. "Let's hope they remind him in no uncertain terms that the death penalty is barbaric and medieval. . . . Let's hope they point out to him that the death penalty won't bring his butchered little boy back."

Lowenstein, seething, e-mailed every death-penalty opposition group he could find on the Internet to offer his services. "It was one of those rare moments where you get upset about something in the paper and get off your butt and do something about it," Lowenstein said. In short order, Lowenstein, an energetic idealist who favored black leather jackets and semiregular shaves, joined Cushing, Jackson, and other opponents who converged on the State House in the weeks preceding the 1997 vote.

While sitting in the State House coffee shop during that tumultuous period, Lowenstein saw Bob Curley for the first time. Escorted by a half dozen state troopers, Bob was rushing to yet another round of lobbying. Lowenstein was struck by the pain etched on Bob's face, a pain that he, himself, had felt after a mentally ill man shot his father in his Manhattan law office. Lowenstein was startled by the size of the State Police escort and by how the powers of the state had been mobilized for the governor's agonized new ally. "I'm sitting there with the antideath-penalty group, thinking, So, this is the way the government works this. I mean, who are they protecting him from? What's the worry up here?"

Lowenstein had never met Bob when he picked up the phone at that dinner gathering. As far as Lowenstein knew, Bob's concerns about Manny Babbitt might be a onetime exception for the no-compromise zealot he had seen marching through the State House. So, with a little anxiety but a little hope, Lowenstein put the receiver to his ear.

"Hello, this is Tom Lowenstein."

"Hi, this is Bob Curley," he heard. "Listen, there's this guy in California who's gonna be executed. He's a former marine, and this guy's got PTSD."

Lowenstein answered that he knew of Manny Babbitt.

"Look, I'd like to get in touch with Gray Davis. This guy shouldn't be executed," Bob continued. "I'd like some help in putting together a letter."

"Of course," Lowenstein said. "We'll help you write the letter. We'll do anything we can to help you."

Bob thanked Lowenstein but added an adamant, no-misunderstandings kicker. "I'm still for the death penalty," Bob said in a clipped, curt, businesslike tone. "I want to make that clear, okay? I still support the death penalty."

"Sure, I understand, Mr. Curley," Lowenstein said. "I understand exactly where you're coming from. I wouldn't try to convert you."

Lowenstein handed the phone to Cushing, who spoke briefly with Bob and encouraged him to call Davis. When the conversation ended, the ten people gathered at the table were teeming with questions. What did he say? How did he sound to you? What does this mean?

Bob's eagerness to join the fight for Manny Babbitt certainly was a cause for celebration. But perhaps more important, the group agreed, was Bob's need to underscore his continued support for the death penalty. That declaration was a telltale sign that a wall had been breached and that Bob was questioning his once-impervious beliefs. Anyone who opposed a single execution that strongly, the group believed, would eventually oppose them all. On this night and in this place, the leap was far from theoretical. Around the table, among friends bound by individual loss, others had also taken a similar, remarkable, and unexpected journey.

Bob followed up by writing to Gray Davis in Sacramento. He also placed a phone call to California in which he told a governor's aide about Jeffrey's story and why he opposed Babbitt's execution. If Davis was told of the call, Bob never heard.

Manny Babbitt's clemency hearing before the California Board of Prison Terms was held April 26, 1999. Bob did not attend, but Bud Welch was there, as were David Kaczynski, members of Babbitt's family, Vietnam veterans, and even Babbitt's fifth-grade teacher. The family of Leah Schendel also attended, as did prosecutors who scoffed at the notion that Babbitt's behavior could be linked to the siege of Khe Sanh, twelve years before the murder, or anything else he experienced in Vietnam. The facts and factors of the case were simple, the state said: A pathological criminal sought to rob an old woman, and then killed her when she became an obstacle.

Two days after the hearing, Bud Welch received a surprise phone call as he prepared to address a national convention of priests in San Antonio. The voice on the line belonged to Bob Curley, whom Welch had not seen since the Boston television show a month earlier.

"Bud, what are we going to do to save this guy out in California, this Vietnam vet?" Bob asked.

"You're talking about Manny Babbitt?" Welch said.

"Yes, him," Bob answered.

"Bob, I don't know what else we can do," Welch replied. "I just testified before the pardons board the day before yesterday."

The news startled Bob, who had been unaware of the hearing. He had no tool set for this situation, no options for fighting the machinery of a state determined to put a man to death. All his experience had been on the other side, and Bob, upset and deflated, felt helpless to alter a case that had changed his thinking so dramatically.

Davis ended any hope four days after that phone conversation, when he dismissed Babbitt's plea for mercy. "Countless people have suffered the ravages of war, persecution, starvation, natural disasters, personal calamities, and the like," the governor wrote. "But such experiences cannot justify or mitigate the savage beating and killing of defenseless, law-abiding citizens." The Schendel family praised Davis's "commitment to justice," but critics argued that the Democratic governor, eager to appear tough on crime, had approved the execution to further his national political ambitions.

On May 4, 1999, Babbitt became the seventh person executed in California since the state's reinstatement of capital punishment in 1992. Bill Babbitt stood on a riser as the lethal cocktail began its work, looking not at his brother but at the victim's family, whom Manny had asked him to forgive. The body was brought home to Wareham, Massachusetts, clothed in marine dress blues that fellow Vietnam veterans had purchased. There, in a cemetery plot donated by his former schoolteacher, Manny Babbitt was bid farewell in a flag-draped coffin as brother Bill struggled to hold up their grief-racked mother.

David Kaczynski watched from the fringes on a lush spring day, thinking how his brother had received a first-rate defense team, a plea bargain, and scrupulous attention from the national news media. Manny Babbitt, he knew, had benefited from none of those things. Kaczynski began to cry and could not stop, dissolving on the periphery of the burial in a rolling succession of heaving sobs. "Maybe I'd withheld a lot of tears because I felt I had to be strong, but the tragedy of the Babbitt family was just like a dam had burst," Kaczynski recalled. "I suppose I was crying for lots of folks. For Bill and his family, for my brother's victims, and for the grandmother's family, too."

Afterward, on the three-hour drive home to upstate New York, Kaczynski felt he had turned a corner. "I was coming to terms with the realization that the life I once had, the life I wanted back, was truly gone," Kaczynski said. "I now had seen things and experienced things that had changed me, and I wanted other people to know about them. I wanted somehow to put a face on the death penalty and let people see, in human terms, that it was cruel and unjust." Motivated by Manny Babbitt's execution, Kaczynski sought and was given the job of executive director of New Yorkers Against the Death Penalty.

The execution also impacted Bob Curley, who returned to a cocoon of routine, where he filled the empty spaces with the rhythms of the firehouse and the satisfactions of home improvements. He also watched the slow progression of his civil lawsuits against Jeffrey's killers and NAMBLA. One of them, a $200 million wrongful-death claim, was filed against Jaynes and Sicari in Middlesex Superior Court in a move that even Bob recognized as purely symbolic. "What am I going to get from these two stooges?" Bob asked at the time. "They're going to have a hard time coming up with that making license plates."

Once again, the Curleys became objects of public interest. They were asked in court to recount the lingering effect of Jeffrey's murder on their lives. Tears fell. The news media carried their familiar images. And the fifty-gallon Rubbermaid container, in which Jeffrey's body had been placed, was removed from storage and displayed again to grim-faced jurors.

Neither Jaynes nor Sicari appeared in court. Indeed, Jaynes instructed his lawyer not to present any meaningful evidence in his defense. Jaynes, his attorney said, wanted "to make it easier" on the Curleys. "I will trust in the jury to give a fair and reasonable award," Jaynes said through counsel.

That award was for a staggering $328 million, one of the largest ever granted in the United States for a child's murder. The family's attorney, Lawrence Frisoli, hailed the decision as a landmark deterrent. "This is a measuring stick by which to judge people who rape kids and get caught," Frisoli said. "We can't stop pedophiles from raping children, but we can make it harder on them."

Frisoli also hoped the huge award would help a second wrongful-death suit, against NAMBLA, in U.S. District Court in Boston. In that claim, the Curleys sought $200 million for what the family alleged were Web-based writings that incited Jaynes to murder Jeffrey. The family aimed, Frisoli said, to bankrupt the organization through unaffordable penalties and to send an unambiguous warning to any group that would use the Internet to promote pedophilia or other child abuse.

The lawsuit's connection with the Curley murder was guaranteed to generate publicity. But the case received an added jolt of controversy when the American Civil Liberties Union agreed to represent NAMBLA. "For us, it's a fundamental First Amendment case," said John Roberts, executive director of the ACLU's Massachusetts chapter. ACLU officials acknowledged the public's disgust with NAMBLA's goal of changing age-of-consent laws and allowing consensual sex between men and boys. But political advocacy, the ACLU said, is free speech regardless of the message, no matter how abhorrent. The ACLU compared NAMBLA with the Nazis who marched in Skokie, Illinois, in the late 1970s. "It is easy to defend freedom of speech when the message is something many people find at least reasonable," the ACLU said. "But the defense of freedom of speech is most critical when the message is one most people find repulsive. This was true when the Nazis marched in Skokie. It remains true today."

For all its initial controversy, however, the lawsuit figured to drag on for years with only minimal prospects for success. Outside state and federal court, Bob had other demons to confront. He lashed out at the city of Cambridge, faulting its efforts to protect children and lambasting a mandatory course in diversity training for all city employees. Bob derided the four-hour program, which one city official said would "develop an understanding of how we benefit from being part of a diverse workforce," as "feel-good crap." Derision led to disgust at the first session, where Bob exploded as the facilitator began extolling the advantages of cultural cross-pollination. "You fucking phony!" Bob yelled before storming out of the meeting. He refused to return.

In a twist of irony, Bob secured the services of Harvey Silverglate, a member of the ACLU board of directors and one of Boston's preeminent civil rights lawyers. Silverglate wrote to Cambridge officials, arguing that Bob was within his constitutional rights to refuse to attend. Afterward, the city allowed him to "opt out" of the program because of a "personal tragedy."

The waiver made Bob the only one of two thousand city employees who did not participate.

His distaste for diversity training did not necessarily mean Bob was any more conservative than the men he worked beside. Even if there were liberals in the firehouse, Bob was fond of saying, they wouldn't admit to it. As a result, Bob did not discuss the Manny Babbitt case with his coworkers. As far as Bob knew, everybody in the Fire Department was in favor of the death penalty. And among the public, Bob was regarded as the leader of the pack.

To Mimi, the only person in whom he confided his change of opinion, the shift was a sign of healing, an indicator that he had finally moved beyond the rage and grief that had consumed him for so long. "He told me what had happened with the man in California, and that he'd been thinking that the death penalty isn't only about race, it's also about class," Mimi recalled. "He would say, 'I'm a poor man, and this could have happened to me. This could have happened to people I know.'" Maybe, Mimi thought, Bob was connecting with the person he had always been.

Although Bob confined those feelings to the home, he immersed himself in a wide, public array of programs for child safety and the prevention of sexual abuse, and he soon became a well-traveled and hardworking spokesman for those issues. Through it all, Bob did not disavow the death penalty in conversations with other outreach workers, even though most of them were loud, liberal opponents of capital punishment. They had a natural empathy for Bob's ordeal, but they hadn't forgotten his merciless message from 1997. "At hearings or meetings," Bob said, "you could always feel the tension because of how they viewed me, as a big death-penalty supporter."

As best he could, Bob ignored the sideways glances and the unspoken questions. He'd chosen his path, he had important work to do, and his list of accomplishments grew quickly. Bob helped create the Jeffrey Curley Foundation, which raised money for programs to increase awareness about child safety.

He lobbied hard for a law, backed by Governor Cellucci, that made Massachusetts the last state in the nation to criminalize possession of child pornography. Previously, only producers and distributors of child pornography could be prosecuted in Massachusetts.

Bob and Barbara organized an annual road race, held near the date of Jeffrey's abduction, that provided scholarships for Cambridge students to pursue degrees in child psychology, social work, or similar fields to benefit children. Bob also touched the families of children who had been murdered or abducted. Parents such as Magi and John Bish, whose teenage daughter Molly vanished in 2000 from her lifeguard post, heard unexpectedly from Bob, a stranger, when he called to offer condolences and emotional support. Bob wrote letters to the opinion pages of New England newspapers, urged tougher registration laws for sexual offenders in the state, and worked with Jane Doe Inc., a non-profit organization that focused on the issue of domestic violence.

Bob's signature campaign led to the Jeffrey Curley Bill, enacted after a barnstorming effort to persuade the legislature to post a list of safety dos and don'ts at all public schools and on state-owned property. The "Eight Rules of Safety," developed by the National Center for Missing and Exploited Children, uses simple phrasing to deliver commonsense instructions, such as asking permission from a parent or supervisor before getting into a car with someone else or accepting gifts. They also are designed to empower children if they become victims of inappropriate contact. "I say 'no' if someone tries to touch me in ways that make me feel frightened, uncomfortable, or confused," one of the rules states. "Then I go and tell a grown-up I trust what happened."

Bob embarked on the crusade with a missionary's zeal, encouraged by Dan Moniz, a phone technician, who reached out to the Curleys in the first dark days after Jeffrey's disappearance. Moniz, who had been circulating the Eight Rules to town halls and police departments for several years before Jeffrey's murder, first saw coverage of the killing on a bank of televisions in an electronics store. Horrified by the news and thinking of his daughters, ages nine and ten, Moniz began crying as he watched.

Almost immediately, Moniz hatched an ambitious plan to recruit Bob and spread the Eight Rules statewide. First, he needed the courage to pick up the phone, call a grieving father he did not know, and make his pitch. After staring at the receiver for twenty minutes, Moniz finally placed the phone to his ear. On the other end, Moniz found an enthusiastic ally, and the two set right to work.

Bob and Moniz formed a persuasive and effective pair, addressing municipal officials in Cambridge, Somerville, Malden, Danvers, Lowell, and a dozen other communities. They appeared on any local cable outlet that would have them. The road show reaped big dividends in its three-year run. Cities and towns, touched by Bob's story and Dan's moral salesmanship, ordered thousands of posters with the Eight Rules of Safety. Each success gave the lawmakers on Beacon Hill one more reason to pass the Jeffrey Curley Bill. Finally, in February 2001, Governor Cellucci signed the bill into law at a bittersweet State House ceremony.

As the governor spoke, smiles creased many faces among the Curley family, their friends, and state officials gathered at the wide base of the Grand Staircase. But for Bob, the occasion resurrected reminders of why this moment had been necessary. Slouched in a gray suit, the corners of his mouth turned downward, Bob stepped forward to address the news media. Rubbing his chin and trembling with emotion, Bob spoke of his son. "I just hope that Jeff is looking down on this day now, just knowing how much I love him, and saying, 'Way to go, Dad. I knew you wouldn't let my fight be for nothing.'" Bob's words trailed off amid a swell of sustained, respectful applause that echoed off the marble floors and portrait-lined walls.

Despite the accolades, Bob remained as grim as the day he had stood on Hampshire Street and thundered for the death penalty. This time, however, Bob's turmoil was partly a product of the chasm between his public reputation on capital punishment and the private stance he refused to divulge. "I'd be sitting around the firehouse, and somebody would be reading the paper about some awful crime and say, 'Geez, if they only had a death penalty,'" Bob recalled. "And it always seemed to be when I was there. I'd say, 'Yeah, you're right.' Other than that, I'd basically keep my mouth shut, go about my business, and try to make an exit out the door." Outside work, as well, the death penalty managed to creep into conversation. "I wouldn't be introduced to somebody for ten seconds," Bob said, "and the first thing they'd say would be, 'That fuckin' Slattery,' or 'That fuckin' Finneran. They ought to put in an execution fast lane, the way Texas does it.'"

In Bob's mind, many people brought up the subject simply to make him feel better, to show some blue-collar solidarity with the icon of the state's death-penalty movement. Instead, the topic made him cringe. "After a while, it started to wear on me," Bob said. "I felt like a whore in church, like a fucking coward." But for someone from old-school Inman Square, the prospect of being labeled weak, or a "wimp," or an out-of-touch bleeding heart was simply not acceptable.

In the late spring of 2001, Bob decided he was done agonizing. Jeff's fourteenth birthday would be in a few days, on June 9, and Bob had been playing and replaying the surreal events of that horrible October nearly four years earlier. Finally, tormented enough, Bob resolved to remove the inner tensions that only he could feel. The time had come to make a public statement, lift the burden from his chest, and put the entire death-penalty issue in the rearview mirror.

Bob thumbed through his address book for the telephone number of a reporter for New England Cable News (NECN), a woman who called every several months to renew a standing invitation to talk on-air about the death penalty. Bob phoned to say he had changed his mind and that he wanted to talk publicly. The reporter, suddenly handed a good news story, drove to Bob's home and conducted an interview in the living room. Speaking calmly but earnestly, sitting in his favorite chair, Bob spoke of capital punishment as an attack on the working class, as the ultimate penalty inflicted unfairly on the poor. "You can't have it both ways," Bob said later. "You can't go back and forth and say this guy goes, and this guy doesn't because he has a better lawyer."

The interview was carried that night as part of NECN's twenty-four-hour cycle, but the news would take time to disseminate. The station's viewership at the time lagged behind that of the three network affiliates in Boston. But as far as Bob was concerned, a minimal amount of media attention would be fine. "For a long time, I'd struggled with what people would think," Bob said. "But when I made that call, I said to myself, Hey, I don't owe anybody anything. I said, I'm gonna tell it from my view. People can agree with me or they can disagree with me, but I do expect people to respect my view. If people don't like it, even if people from my own family don't like it, fuck 'em. After everything that had happened up to that point, I just felt I had an obligation to do this."

The next morning, relieved and refocused, Bob ambled downstairs to scan the morning newspapers. There, tucked inside the *Globe*, was a brief story about a conference at Boston College, scheduled to begin that day, for death-penalty opponents who had lost relatives to murder. Only a few miles away, only hours after he had announced his switch, hundreds of like-minded people would be sharing their tragic stories, offering mutual support, and validating a common conviction that no one should be killed in their name. "I couldn't believe it. I was stunned," Bob recalled. "I'm saying, there's some other, higher power operating here."

The conference, which had been planned for a year by Murder Victims' Families for Reconciliation, would be the first large gathering of survivors of murder victims in U.S. history. More than one hundred families converged on the college, as did dozens of academics, lawyers, activists, and clergy. The grandson of Mahatma Gandhi participated, as did Renny Cushing, Bud Welch, Sister Helen Prejean, and Cardinal Law.

As the conference opened that morning, word of Bob's change of heart had begun to ripple through Greater Boston. Newspapers carried stories of his switch. Puzzled neighbors asked each other if it were true. And Cardinal Law, welcoming home the prodigal son, left a long, sermonlike message on Bob's phone machine. "Robert, I'm very, very proud of you," he said.

The news also made its way to Boston College.

"I heard a rumor that Bob Curley was on TV yesterday and that he'd changed his mind about the death penalty," Cushing told Welch.

"You're kidding me. I had a feeling he was going to do that," Welch said. "I'm going to call him right now."

When no one answered, Welch began to leave a message: "Bobby, it's Bud Welch. I just wanted to give you a call. I'm in town—"

Before he could complete his thought, Welch heard a familiar, booming Boston accent.

"Hey, Bud, how you doing!" Bob said.

"Well, I'm with Renny Cushing, and we're sitting in the car on the campus of Boston College, and we've got this conference going on," Welch said. "Renny says you've changed your mind about the death penalty."

"Yeah, I have," Bob replied. "I've given a lot of thought to a lot of things you've said."

"Bob, I'm going to be addressing the full conference Saturday afternoon at one o'clock," Welch said. "I have an hour. Will you come and speak with me?"

Once again, as he had done before their joint television appearance, Bob said he didn't have a car. Then, he said his house would be difficult for a taxi to find. But this time, to squelch the exit strategy, Welch said he'd drive Bob himself. To avoid the maze of East Somerville, they agreed to meet at the firehouse.

On the ride to Boston College, Bob was unable to stifle his fears. He couldn't speak, he said. He didn't have a speech prepared. It wasn't possible.

"Bob, you don't want a speech written out," Welch said, falling back on the lessons he had learned. "You know Jeffrey. You know how Jeffrey was killed. You know the emotions you went through. You don't need that on paper."

As Welch drove to the college, the conference began to buzz with news of Bob's imminent arrival. A little while later,

Susannah Sheffer, a staff member for Murder Victims' Families for Reconciliation, spotted Bob in a hallway, huddling with Welch and Andy Pryor outside a panel discussion on the death penalty's potential to divide families already scarred by murder. Sheffer quietly left the classroom and introduced herself.

"Do you want to speak now," she asked Bob, "or would you like to wait?"

"Whatever you'd like me to do," Bob answered.

Sheffer slipped a note to Jennifer Bishop, chairwoman of the MVFR board, who was moderating the panel. "Bob Curley's here. He'd like to speak," the note read.

Bishop nodded as Bob sat in the front row to hear the horrific story of the murder of Bishop's pregnant sister and brother-in-law. In April 1990, the couple had returned from a family birthday party to find a sixteen-year-old stranger in their suburban Chicago home. The teenager shot Richard Langert, killing him instantly. He then fired at Nancy Langert's abdomen, which she shielded while pleading for mercy. Nancy bled to death, but not before crawling to her husband, dipping her fingers in his blood, and tracing a heart and a *U* on the wall.

Jennifer Bishop opposed the death penalty, even after the murders, and pledged to work against a political candidate who had sought to make sixteen-year-olds eligible for execution as a way to "honor" Nancy Langert. Bob listened intently to Bishop, who restated her opposition, and also to her father, who supported the death penalty. Soon, Bob knew, his own family would split starkly on the issue.

After the discussion, Welch strode to the podium and introduced Bob to the twenty-five people in the room. Bob needed no introduction. He thanked Welch, wrung his hands, and searched for the words to describe the events that had changed his life. "You got to bear with me, folks," Bob began, his face a wrenching reflection of his metamorphosis. "Prior to losing my Jeff, my only public speaking experience was with my baseball team in East Cambridge, so I'll do the best I can."

The audience laughed softly, and Bob managed a slight smile. Then, in simple language, Bob outlined the grisly details of Jeffrey's death, how Jaynes had been a member of NAMBLA, how Jeffrey had been "groomed" for abduction, and how Bob's rage had grown limitless and grotesque. Driven by hate, Bob said, "I led the fight in the state of Massachusetts to reinstate the death penalty."

Bob then told the group how he had changed and how Bud Welch, Bill Babbitt, and David Kaczynski had opened his eyes to another, more therapeutic possibility. The effect was immediate and transforming. The audience stood as one, crying and clapping, aware that this short speech had been an unscripted adventure into uncharted territory for a suddenly remade man. "It was one of those standing ovations where you feel like you're levitating," Sheffer said. "You don't even think you're standing. You're just standing because it's beyond words."

Bob was swarmed afterward, but he had other business directly ahead of him. Welch, who was scheduled to deliver the conference's keynote address, asked Bob to repeat his remarks for three hundred listeners. The speeches were nearly identical, as were Bob's pain, nervousness, and struggle to hold himself together. "You can imagine the anger, unbelievable anger," Bob told the larger audience of his reaction to Jeffrey's murder. "But time passes, and you get a chance to take a step back and look at things, and the way things are, and I started to take a look at the death penalty, and the way it's applied."

Bob paused, exhaling deeply as his shoulders began to relax. "It's been a long journey for me. It's something that I've kept inside of me from not long after I met with Bud two years ago," he said. "I don't know what effect it's gonna have on my relationships with people who look to me, or even my own family members," he added. "I don't think they know, but they know now." Soft, empathetic laughter pulsed through the auditorium. "It's ironic, because I'm gonna find out, because today is my Jeff's birthday. He would have been fourteen years old."

Gasps escaped from the audience, who knew the pain of birthdays for any family member who had outlived a child cut down by murder. And Bob, clearly, was in agony. He paused as the gasps subsided. But when he resumed, glancing at his watch, his tight control began to fray.

"I'm gonna be going to the cemetery at three o'clock, and we'll see what happens," Bob said, his voice breaking. "It's been a long, difficult journey for me, and I feel relieved that I'm here and am able to talk about it. I don't know what's gonna happen on the Fourth of July. Maybe I'll be rolling around the backyard, duking it out with my brothers or whoever, but that's all right. I choose my own path."

Bob, gaining confidence as he spoke, finished with an emphatic declaration of individual determination. "I want Jaynes and Sicari to stay in jail and to see me every day—to think of me, think of my Jeff, the strong, little boy that Jeff was," Bob said, his forehead knit in defiance. "I'm going to try to follow in Jeffrey's footsteps and be as strong as he was," Bob pledged, "and stand and be my own man."

Renny Cushing had tears in his eyes. "Everyone thought of their own pain and their own journey," he said later. "But they also recognized that this was Bob Curley. And for Bob to stand up and say, 'I've thought this over, and I don't support the death penalty anymore,' was incredibly powerful."

Bill Babbitt and David Kaczynski also wept. They had never met Bob, had not known Jeffrey's story, and were stunned and touched as Bob mentioned their profound impact on his decision. "From one human being to another human being who had lost a loved one, my heart went out to this man," Babbitt said. "They must have promised him a nice, cool drink out of this cup called closure. He probably entertained that and said, I know it's gonna taste good when I drink out of that cup. But then he saw David and I, saw how we were carrying on and not hating anybody, and asked, What are those guys having? I want what those guys got."

As Bob spoke, Babbitt noted the familiar "mask of pain"; Kaczynski heard the "conviction" in his speech. Both men recognized an irreversible conversion. "I could imagine the struggle, but I could see a sense of resolution," Kaczynski said. "It was amazing, because it was there. You knew this guy was not going back, no matter what happened from that point on."

After Bob's speech, Welch took the podium and looked down at the man he had met only once before, on the NECN set where Bob began his improbable journey. Welch clasped his hands together, his face riveted on Bob, the admiration evident in his gentle eyes and soft smile. "And I have to speak?" Welch said to the audience with a chuckle. "I'm not real sure I can do this."

Welch, however, talked for forty-five minutes about his relationship with his daughter Julie, his outreach to the McVeighs, his torturous battles with alcohol, and his unflagging commitment to fight the death penalty. Welch also told his listeners that, when he left Boston College, he would fly directly to Indiana to join a vigil protesting Timothy McVeigh's execution in two days. At 1:50 P.M., he ended his soft-spoken call to arms, mindful that he needed to help Bob make his appointment at Cambridge Cemetery, where the Curley family would be gathering for Jeffrey's birthday. Welch leaned down and whispered in Bob's ear, "Let's get out of Dodge."

The pair hustled out the door before they could be enveloped by embraces and congratulations. The Chevy Blazer that had brought Bob to Boston College was parked nearby, ready to ferry the men to East Somerville, where Bob would pick up Mimi's car and drive alone to the cemetery. But after they took their seats, Welch did not turn the ignition key. Instead, he began to cry, overcome by the events of the day and by the startling transformation of the plain, powerful man beside him.

Welch, who cries easily, was not surprised by his reaction. He did not expect, however, what happened next, when Bob Curley, relieved but exhausted, added tears of his own. The men sat for several minutes, sobbing on a college campus in the middle of the day, reflecting on their individual and mutual losses and on a journey that neither man had thought he could endure.

"It was very emotional for me inside that car," Welch recalled. "I'd had the privilege of introducing Bob, who had gone
through so much of a change. And to think I had influenced
that in some manner. I was having a good feeling about that
because I know what it is to live with retribution," Welch continued. "When you're living with revenge, you can't go through
the healing process. You just can't do it; it's impossible." Welch
saw a different man. In his mind, Bob had stopped blaming
himself for Jeffrey's death. This Bob Curley seemed more at
peace, had pushed revenge aside, and had reached the place
that Welch predicted he would find.

Welch wished Bob good luck as he dropped him off in Somerville. Bob, however, was worried and anxious as he drove the
four congested miles to Cambridge Cemetery, located near a
sharp, marshy bend in the Charles River. But he reminded
himself that his decision was his own and that his choice deserved respect, particularly from family members who had
wept and fought beside him in the death-penalty struggle. "I'd
finally gotten to a point where I wasn't going to be influenced
by anybody else's view on anything," Bob said. "I was going to
live and die with the consequences of what I thought."

Since the murder, the Curley family had gathered at Jeffrey's grave every year at 3:15 P.M. on his birthday, exactly the
time that Jeffrey had rushed from his grandmother's kitchen
and into the Cadillac. Barbara would be there, as would
Bobby, Shaun, Barbara's mother, Barbara's sisters, and Bob's
sisters Francine and Margaret. Francine would say a few
words of remembrance, prayers would be recited, and fourteen balloons would be released into the late-spring sky, one
for each year since Jeffrey had been born.

Bob had not spoken with any of his family since the television interview or newspaper reports about his change. But
they had all seen or heard the news, as Bob expected they
would. Barbara and the boys were furious, as were Barbara's
siblings, all of whom had no knowledge of Bob's long struggle

with the death-penalty issue and no warning that he would go public with his decision.

When Bob arrived at the cemetery, ten minutes late, the family had already assembled by the headstone. Their sorrow over Jeffrey's death, muted only slightly since the murder, now competed with the anger they felt at Bob's shocking reversal. As Bob walked the twenty-five yards from Mimi's car to the grave, all eyes turned toward him. Despite the silence, the tension was oppressive.

Finally, Barbara spoke for everyone. "How can you forgive the guys who killed the baby?" she asked, glaring, in stinging disbelief.

"It's got nothing to do with that," Bob replied.

"Yeah, what's up with this, Dad?" Shaun said, agitated. "You're being like a politician. You're flip-flopping. Come on. I mean, what's changed in the last four years?"

Bob tried to head off a confrontation, which could escalate rapidly among a family known for hot tempers and strong opinions. "Look, I just don't want Jeff to be known as a poster child for the death penalty," Bob said.

To Barbara, using Jeffrey to reinstate the death penalty would have been a tribute, a tangible sign that he had not died in vain, and a personal point of pride that his murder might prevent the deaths of other children. Bob's argument persuaded no one. And their body language, particularly among the boys, had become edgy, frustrated, and aggressive.

"Look, we're here for Jeff's birthday," Bob said calmly. "It's for Jeff, okay? I've got my view, and you've got your view."

Bobby, his eyes narrowed, looked at his father with bewildered disgust. "What the fuck is the matter with you?" he barked.

Before Bob could answer, Bobby thrust himself within inches of his father's face, a man he outweighed by thirty pounds, demanding an answer from someone he no longer understood. "I don't want to fucking find out what my father's thinking through the fucking media!" Bobby said.

"Hey, calm down, calm down," Bob answered. "Now's not the time or the place to be talking about this."

The anxious, agonized looks on the others showed that Bob was right. On an already difficult day, a shouting match or worse would be catastrophic for this crippled family. Bobby stepped back, Bob quieted down, and heads soon were bowed as murmured prayers and colorful balloons relieved some of the tension and replaced some of the ugliness.

Too much had been said, however, and reconciliation would have to wait. Bob left quickly when the memorial ended. Any solace it could give had been tainted by anger on top of anguish and by the sense that Jeffrey's legacy had been betrayed. "I just felt, That was my baby. How could you not want a death penalty?" Barbara recalled. "These guys planned this, you know what I mean? Bob was just so far away from what I thought his beliefs were that I couldn't even fathom it." As Bob walked away, an awkward, dejected guest at the grave of his murdered son, he tried not to blame Barbara or the family for their anger. "I fully understood the way they felt, because I felt the same way at the start," he said later.

But understanding did not make the confrontation easier to absorb. Although he had survived the first difficult test of his convictions, the repercussions would linger. Barbara and Bobby would not speak to him. "What my father did with his life at that point in time was his own fucking business," said Bobby, who was staggering under crushing burdens of his own. At twenty-three, he had been guardian of the home for nearly four years, caring for his mother when she cried herself to sleep, keeping Shaun away from drugs and out of trouble—a draining, demanding job that had been unwanted and unforgiving.

Now, after the graveside argument, the divide between Bob and his family had widened even further. On a day he renounced the death penalty, on the day he pledged to be his own man, Bob was mourning the loss of one beloved son and seemed to lose the other two.

—— 10 ——

The Road
Home

BOB HAD CHANGED, and so had the circumscribed world in which he lived. People who had known him as a relentless champion of the death penalty began to look at him differently. Invitations for television and radio appearances dried up. And even a few firefighters, stunned by his renunciation of capital punishment, joked with him in ways that sometimes hurt.

"You sucking up to Tom Finneran now, you fucking bum?" one firefighter asked after the news broke.

"What are you, fucking soft?" Bob said.

Bob realized most of his coworkers were teasing him with a firefighter's brand of merciless humor. But he didn't take all the remarks as a joke.

"How much did they pay you?" another firefighter asked.

"What the fuck are you talking about?" Bob shot back. "Who? Who's gonna pay me?"

Fran Judd, one of Bob's best friends at Engine 5, re-called that he was "horrified" by Bob's new views on the death penalty and that most of the men at the firehouse felt the same. "I believe in an eye for an eye, a tooth for a tooth, I really do," Judd said. "I mean, of all the people in the world who would have a reason to want the death penalty, you know?" For the most part, however, the firefighters left their friend alone to process his feelings in his own way. They might not agree with Bob on the merits of capital punishment, but his loss and courage demanded their respect, and they gave him that.

"This was a cause that I thought was the right thing to do," Bob said. "I could have gone and sat in a corner, and I think a lot of people would rather that I had done that, you know? If I've got a voice, I'm going to use it. But if you use your voice, the bottom line is that you're going to be criticized by people who oppose that cause. That's the way it is. People don't like it? Too bad."

Bob began lending his voice to groups that opposed the death penalty and to others that promoted child safety. He traveled to Washington, D.C., several times, even attending an October 2002 reception where he spoke with President George W. Bush during the White House Conference on Missing, Exploited, and Runaway Children. In December, Bob flew to Chicago, where Murder Victims' Families for Reconciliation had scheduled a public forum to persuade Governor George Ryan to commute all death sentences in Illinois. Ryan previously had declared a moratorium on executions in the state and was weighing whether to issue a blanket commutation before he left office in January 2003.

The principal speaker at the Chicago conference was Mamie Till Mobley, a black woman whose fourteen-year-old son, Emmett Till, had been kidnapped and murdered in Mississippi in 1955. Two white men accused in the gruesome killing, in which Till was brutally beaten before being shot in the head, were acquitted after only sixty-seven minutes of deliberation, although they later admitted their involvement. The murder drew global attention and helped spark the American civil rights movement.

Other speakers at the Chicago forum included Ross Byrd, whose father, James Byrd Jr., was murdered in 1988 when three white men beat him behind an East Texas convenience store, stripped him, chained his ankles to a pickup truck, and dragged him for three miles. James Byrd Jr., age forty-nine, was decapitated when his body struck a sewage drain.

Pieces of his remains were found at seventy-five places along the route. Despite his father's heinous murder, Ross Byrd opposed the death sentence imposed on two of the defendants.

Bud Welch, Jennifer Bishop, and Bob Curley joined Mobley and Byrd in what Renny Cushing hoped would be a compelling statement that not all victims' families supported the death penalty. Illinois prosecutors at the time had been mobilizing other families to oppose any commutation. "We are an integral part of the victims' rights movement, and we will not be silenced," Bishop said at the time. "Our voices deserve and need to be heard, too." Those voices were featured in *Deadline*, an acclaimed documentary about the reexamination of capital punishment in Illinois, which included part of Bob's speech in Chicago in opposition to the death penalty.

For Bob, the event was an eye-opening, ground-level introduction to important national opponents of capital punishment. Before the conference, he had never heard of Mamie Till Mobley, who made her last public appearance there before dying a month later. "I didn't know who the hell she was. I'd never heard of Emmett Till or anything," Bob recalled. "The Somerville public school system, you know?" He also became friendly with Ross Byrd, with whom he spent a memorable Saturday night on the town in Chicago, watching a college football game and hoisting a few beers.

The following month, Governor Ryan, a Republican who had decided not to seek reelection, made the controversial decision to commute the sentences of all 156 inmates on death row. Nearly all of the sentences were reduced to life without parole. Many prosecutors and victims' relatives were outraged, and Governor-elect Rod Blagojevich disagreed with Ryan. "I think a blanket anything is usually wrong," said Blagojevich, a Democrat. "We're talking about convicted murderers, and I think that is a mistake."

Ryan was adamant and unapologetic as he made the announcement at Northwestern University, where journalism students had uncovered evidence that exonerated death row inmate Anthony Porter nearly four years earlier. "Our capital system is haunted by the demon of error: error in determining guilt, and error in determining who among the guilty deserves to die. What effect was race having? What effect was poverty having?" Ryan asked. "Because of all these reasons, today I am commuting the sentences of all death row inmates."

Though energized by the decision, Bob was also happy to resume a predictable life bounded by the small triangle from East Somerville to Inman Square to his beloved cycling and running route along the Charles River. He was also ready to marry Mimi. And Mimi, who had watched Bob's mental and emotional health improve, thought the idea had merit, although she had no burning desire to marry for a third time. The decision, instead, was a leap of faith in a man who had shown he could be frighteningly erratic but who had touched her soul in a way that neither of her previous husbands had done. There was no simmering rage in Bob at this time, only small ups and downs, even little tantrums, but all of them manageable. Mimi and Bob had come through so much, endured so much pain, and better times seemed certain to lie ahead.

The wedding was set for February 22, 2003, one day after Mimi's forty-ninth birthday. Superior Court Justice Isaac Borenstein, a friend of Mimi's and one of the most liberal judges in the state, agreed to perform the civil ceremony in their home before a small group of guests. Bob dressed formally in a black tuxedo; Mimi wore a black dress draped with a shawl hand-painted with whirling symbols of life that she had bought at an artists' co-op in Harvard Square. As Borenstein presided, Mimi's family and friends, as well as many of Bob's siblings and in-laws, encircled the pair.

Even Bobby had decided to attend, incurring the ire of his mother, who felt betrayed that he would give even tacit approval to Bob's union with another woman. However, the two years since their confrontation at Jeffrey's grave had softened Bobby's attitude toward his father. Part of the shift was maturity; part of it a greater appreciation for what his father had suffered. And if old wounds hadn't completely healed, Bobby had chosen, at least, to try to move past them.

With his brother John behind his left shoulder and a lit candelabra above, Bob carefully repeated his simple vows. As Mimi listened for her cue, the golden ring between her right thumb and forefinger, she gently held Bob's hand and turned beaming toward the judge. Bob, his eyes closed, awaited the ring with a solemn, almost reverential expression. After Borenstein's declaration of marriage, the gathering erupted in a riot of Latin sounds, smells, and salsa. A Venezuelan trio, playing Colombian and classical Spanish music, provided a lush, soothing backdrop to the reception. Bob had learned some dance steps by then, and between fluted glasses of Champagne, he moved well enough to earn the compliments of Mimi's passionately expert relatives.

When the music slowed, guided by the sounds of the classical guitar, Bob held Mimi's hand, shifted gently from side to side, and looked deeply into the eyes of a woman who had remained his partner, improbably, through all the soul-testing darkness. Mimi returned the love with a soft, thankful gaze. For her, after all that had happened, the ceremony meant so much more than the formalities of mature, middle-age marriage. To Mimi, it represented a celebration of renewed and hopeful life.

The celebration continued in Cuba, where Mimi had engineered a honeymoon through a Cambridge travel agent who booked educational trips to the communist island. Neither Mimi nor Bob fit the typical categories of acceptable visitors to Cuba, such as journalists, athletes, or teachers. But the travel agent, accustomed to the ambiguities in the system, decreed that Mimi's reason for visiting would be to study mental-health issues and that Bob would analyze Cuban firefighting. Two days after their wedding, the couple left for Miami, where they boarded a flight to Cuba and a blissful vacation in Havana and its surrounding beaches and countryside.

Bob fell in love with the city, relaxing at harborside cafes with Mimi, walking along the white-sand beaches, and listening to street-corner musicians who played plaintively beneath the worn but haunting architecture of the old colonial capital.

The music would last for hours, some nights until dawn, as the sounds of the island danced from window to window to the open doors on their tiled terrace.

Bob also indulged his passions for cigars and baseball, chatting with old men who told wide-eyed tales of long-ago barnstorming visits by Babe Ruth and other American stars. One new friend, excited by Bob's deep knowledge of the game, invited him to his creaky Havana attic, where he let Bob gaze in awe at a collection of vintage baseball cards dating to the 1920s. There, the images of Lou Gehrig and other Yankees greats peered back from the depths of a worn and treasured shoebox. Bob found his way to Latin American Stadium, too, where he had been steered to watch the Cuban national baseball championship. A fat cigar in hand and a glass of beer at the ready, he passed a long, blissful afternoon in a raucous, dusty ballpark packed with rabid, roaring fans.

For Bob, the torment of the recent past seemed to have been consigned to memory. His partnership with Mimi had not only survived but been cemented. He had cleared his conscience on the death penalty. And his relationship with Bobby was improving. Perhaps most importantly, his thoughts of Jeffrey were not all painful ones. At last, life seemed good again. The man who had rarely ventured out of his neighborhood was flashing a wide, infectious smile at Latin American Stadium, blowing smoke rings in the air, and clapping with his new Havana friends for every stellar play. And, throughout the honeymoon, Bob never forgot the reason he had come to Cuba. "I'm pretty sure," he recalled with a grin, "I saw a fire engine go by on the second-to-last day."

After the vacation, back in Somerville, Bob and Mimi settled into a routine where work, home renovations, and a modest but satisfying social life had erected a tidy framework around them. In this world, normalcy equaled nirvana. But the extended honeymoon would soon be ended by the successive deaths, in April and December, of Bob's mother and his sister Francine. The losses hit Bob hard, especially that of Francine, who had been a surrogate mother to him when he was a rebellious teenager and who had held the family together during the dark, chaotic days after Jeffrey's disappearance. Throughout Bob's life, when trouble seemed everywhere, Francine had been the rock to whom he turned for moral and emotional support. And now, unexpectedly, she had died at the age of fifty-six. "I could never imagine Fran dying, you know?" Bob said later. "Here's someone who never drank, never smoked, and was as close to a saint in my eyes as you could get. She loved me, and I loved her."

For Bob, the deaths replaced a well of unfamiliar good feeling with one of foreboding. Always an intuitive man, Bob now saw signs of gloom in the everyday and the ordinary. He realized many of these fears were irrational, but he felt powerless to control them. "I used to say to Mimi that I feel there's this big, fucking wave that I'm running away from, a wave that's just waiting to overtake me, you know?" Bob recalled. "There was Jeffrey dying, and then my mother, and then Francine, and it was just a lot of stuff building, building, and building. I felt that the wave was just gonna wash over me, and take me out, and that was gonna be it." Bob became almost paralyzed with paranoia, worrying after he left the house that he had forgotten to turn off the oven. He agonized over his work at the firehouse, haunted that he had neglected some chore that would cause a mechanical breakdown and result in a preventable death. "It got to the point where it was crazy," Bob said later. "I used to think, what if I screw something up, and somebody's grandmother has a heart attack around the corner, and Engine 5 can't get there, and she dies because of that? I used to worry about one of my kids getting killed, or Mimi getting killed, and it used to really scare the shit out of me."

Bob's superiors in the Fire Department seemed to recognize that he had suffered a relapse. Although all three mechanics had been transferred on paper to headquarters near Harvard Square, Bob was allowed to spend much of his day at Inman Square. The duties there were nearly nonexistent; the responsibilities, negligible. "It kind of got to the point where they were like, you know, just go down to Inman Square and don't get in any trouble," Bob said. "They didn't want me doing anything on the fire engines. I'd basically go around to the firehouses and check the lights, change the oil, that kind of thing. They probably kept me on light work because they saw I wasn't doing too good," Bob said. "They probably knew it better than I did."

One day in August 2004, Bob was told to replace a tire on one of the big trucks at another station. It was a routine job, one that he had done hundreds of times—and one that would get him out of the cramped back shop at Inman Square. Bob rolled a tire across a wet, puddled floor, and put his shoulder to the tread as he walked up a wooden ramp to his mechanic's truck. Bob didn't notice that oil had spilled on the wood. And after a few steps, sliding on a slick mixture of oil and water, Bob lost control and tumbled off. Both man and tire bounced on the cement floor, where Bob lay crumpled in excruciating pain. He had wrenched his back and pinched a nerve, and the injury led to an indefinite disability leave.

Bob would recover at home, where Mimi was busy planning for a four-year course in psychoanalytic training that would start the next month. Combined with her private practice, whose income she now needed more than ever, Mimi expected to be out of the house at least twelve hours a day. Almost immediately, Bob began to withdraw, and Mimi did not need much analysis to figure out a reason. Once again, Bob had been disconnected from his lifeline at the firehouse. But unlike the months following Jeffrey's death, this time he did not have an all-consuming crusade to distract him. Bob spoke occasionally with acquaintances from the child-safety and abolitionist groups with whom he had worked, but even there, his links steadily weakened.

Soon, Bob began each day without a plan, with nowhere to go, and with no other friends who were out of work or had time on their hands. Instead, Bob found, he began to think about Jeffrey every day and in ways that he had not experienced since the murder. "I didn't try to avoid places that Jeffrey had been, but different things would pop up," Bob recalled. "I'd see kids, Jeffrey's friends, and they'd have to introduce themselves to me because they were seventeen years old, and I didn't even recognize them. You lose track of time. It doesn't really hit you until you see these kids, and Jeff's not there."

Mimi noticed that Bob became moodier when certain dates approached—holidays, birthdays, the day Jeffrey disappeared. "Bob, what's the matter?" Mimi would ask.

"I don't know."

"What happened last year around this time?"

"I really don't know," Bob would answer.

Then, Mimi would remind him that his mother, or Francine, or Jeffrey had died.

"You're right. I hadn't thought about it."

Mimi recognized in Bob the "unthought known," a condition in which a person experiences extreme sadness without knowing why, but the timing of which can often be linked to traumatic, tragic events from the past.

Mimi also believed that Bob might be suffering from guilt, although he never acknowledged having any regrets about their relationship and the changes it had caused in his parenting. "Do you feel guilty that you were with me?" Mimi asked. "Do you feel that if you hadn't been here, this wouldn't have happened?" Bob consistently and adamantly denied any such feelings, but Mimi could not push them out of her own head. "Well, I feel guilty," Mimi told him. "Maybe this is irrational, but sometimes in the back of my mind I think this wouldn't have happened if you had been there." Mimi realized that Jaynes and Sicari could have abducted Jeffrey, whom they had carefully targeted, whatever the domestic situation had been on Hampshire Street. Still, the haunting questions about any tangential role she might have played never disappeared.

Bob kept his innermost feelings to himself, or, more likely, never probed deeply enough to understand what he truly felt or why he was prone to such mood swings. And he rarely spoke about the murder. "He didn't talk about Jeff. He just didn't talk about it," Mimi said. "But I sensed it was always there. I don't think he ever put that behind him."

For a month after his injury, Bob could turn to Mimi to keep his own overwhelming thoughts at bay. But when Mimi began her analytic coursework in September, an already small world began to feel more claustrophobic. Everyone who had clamored for his attention was gone. The cameras had long ago moved on to other stories. And all the energy that Bob once directed outward began to reverse direction. Bob was a time bomb, and the fuse had been lit. "I couldn't run, my back was in pain, and I didn't have the structure of work," Bob said. "I started feeling like a useless piece of shit. I mean, how many times are you going to drive around Inman Square?"

During the interminable winter, Bob looked forward to the arrival of spring and a daily release at the beach, where he planned to listen to sports talk radio, read the newspapers, and kibitz with his sun-worshipping buddies at the L Street Bathhouse in South Boston. At a minimum, he believed, the beach would give him a destination and a place to while away the day. And at first, it did provide a taste of freedom, made more enjoyable by the case of beer that Bob would haul to the beach every day in an ice-filled cooler. To buy the beer, Bob would drive each morning to Rockingham, New Hampshire, just across the Massachusetts border, where he could pick up a case of "the good stuff," usually discounted Samuel Adams or Bass heavily. Besides, the round-trip up and down I-93 helped shorten each wide-open day by two hours of easy driving.

The weekday routine developed a clockwork precision: Out of the house by ten-thirty, at the beach by one o'clock, and home by six-thirty. Then, Bob would lay on the sofa, watch whatever he could find on television, and wait for Mimi to return by seven-thirty. Mimi did not know of Bob's excursions to New Hampshire, and he felt no obligation to tell her. "I needed an escape, and that's what I was trying to find in the drinking," Bob said. "I thought it was helping."

At the beginning, Bob worked out in the bathhouse gym, took a swim, and talked with the many characters who made L Street a quirky, near-legendary world unto itself. Before long, however, the routine turned disastrous as Bob began drinking heavily every day on a nearly empty beach. What once seemed an escape became an addiction, and Bob's sense of alienation only deepened. "The more I sat there, the more isolated I became, and it just kind of snowballed," Bob said. "I just got to that place where you shut it down."

Now, instead of mingling with the bathhouse crowd, Bob was sitting by himself in a fold-up beach chair, listening to sports chatter through his headphones, and drinking beer after beer until the cooler filled with stacked-up empties in a tepid pool of melted ice. Not even a change of scenery, even a summer at the beach, could help Bob avoid the inevitable confrontation with his sublimated emotions. "I was just getting more depressed. There was nothing to do, same old thing. And at the end of the day, you're fucking drunk on top of it," Bob said. "I didn't want to talk to anybody. I had no outlet, no escape, no nothing." The daily reminders of Jeffrey's death, the estrangement from some of his family, and his own relentless questions about whether he could have prevented the murder added ever more weight to the burden. "All this stuff catches up to you, but I tried to put it aside," Bob said. "I didn't really have any respect for the magnitude of what had happened to me, and I never dealt with it the way I should have. I was just dead inside."

The dead zone expanded to Bob's house, where Mimi would return from work to find a distant, disengaged husband with a TV remote in one hand and a glazed look in his eyes. Mimi tried to speak to Bob, but he wouldn't respond. Instead, he usually stared glumly at the television while Mimi sought other ways to reconnect with the man she had known and nurtured. After a while, saddened and exhausted, Mimi realized the effort was fruitless. "It was his body, his shell, but it was not him," she said.

The relationship also became complicated by a worsening financial strain. Much of Bob's disability income was needed to pay alimony, leaving little for him to contribute to maintaining the household and forcing Mimi to pay almost all of the couple's bills. "I was getting very, very resentful," she said. "I had to get up, run to work, come home at night, and this guy is sitting there after I don't know what he's been doing during the day."

Mimi suspected he was drinking, but Bob never admitted his habits or divulged his routine. Instead, Mimi found herself smelling him for telltale hints of alcohol or searching in hard-to-find places where he might be hiding a bottle. "I felt like a fool, because I think I'm pretty smart," Mimi said. "But I also drew the line that I was not going to be his babysitter." She tried confronting Bob. "What have you had?" Mimi asked many times. "Are you taking something? Are you smoking something? Are you drinking?"

Bob denied everything, but the undeniable result was that, only two years after their marriage, Mimi had been dragged into a corrosive partnership that began to destroy her. "I was just fed up dealing with this life," she said. "It was stalled, it was dead, and I had seen all this stuff." Ordinary, mundane tasks became difficult, draining obstacles. "I couldn't focus. I couldn't concentrate. I couldn't even read a magazine," she recalled. "I had secluded myself from my friends, and I was worried that I was getting very, very far away from the things that were important to me."

Mimi started to fight back with a rescue strategy of passive, gradual disengagement. "I could sustain being different from him in so many ways, but we always had that emotional connection," Mimi said. "Without that, though, there really was nothing. I thought, I have to regain my soul. I have to regain who I am. I have to remember where I come from. This is not my life." Even Bob's work against the death penalty, which Mimi had once considered a sign of healing, became an irritant. "I wasn't interested in hearing that stuff," she said. "I was fed up, burned out, and I didn't give a shit. I just felt that too much had been brought into my life that I didn't have control over. I didn't care."

As the gulf between them widened, Bob drifted even more to alcohol to escape the numbed, meaningless repetition that had become his life. The relationship reached an ugly nadir one summer night in August 2005. That evening, Bob agreed to cook steaks while Mimi relaxed in the living room. The time passed without conversation, another strained chapter in a badly damaged marriage, as Mimi read and Bob remained in the kitchen. After thirty minutes, with neither the smell of steak nor any sound from the cook, Mimi broke the silence.

"Bob, what's happening?" she asked sharply.

"It's coming, it's coming," Bob answered with annoyance. Ten minutes later, Mimi pressed again. "Bob, what is going on?" she asked, insistent and frustrated.

Bob took a few steps toward the living room and mumbled almost incoherently. "I just threw them out," he muttered.

"You threw them out?" Mimi asked incredulously.

"Yeah, they got burned."

"Bob, they didn't get burned!" Mimi answered. "I haven't smelled anything getting burned!"

Bob's face began to twist into the crazed, contorted shape that Mimi had not seen since the trials. His eyes bulged, his mouth tightened, and the rage that had been absent for seven years found renewed expression in him. This time, however, the fury was not directed against Jeffrey's killers. The object, instead, was Mimi. He lunged toward her, grabbed her by the wrist, and began to drag her down a long, wooden staircase to the trash barrels outside. "Nothing's burned?" Bob snarled. "Come with me! Come, and I'll show you!"

Mimi was terrified and screaming. Bob's grip had broken her wrist, but he continued to pull her maniacally toward the trash. At the bottom of the stairs, Mimi broke free and ran frantically upstairs to call the police. Bob stayed behind. "I don't get scared that easily, but in that moment I was horrified," Mimi recalled. "Those were the eyes I had seen when Bob talked about slashing Jaynes. He looked like a madman."

When the police arrived, Bob was sitting calmly in a lawn chair, oblivious or uninterested in Mimi's shaken state and his own legal predicament. "I don't know what she's talking about," he told the officers. Mimi declined to press charges and have Bob arrested. What he needed, she told police, was a hospital more than a jail cell. She did ask the officers to escort Bob into the house to retrieve some clothes. Later that night, she changed the locks while Bob headed to the Somerville home of Arthur Downey, Francine's widower, who had taken care of him so often during his unpredictable, unfocused teenage years.

For Mimi, the end had arrived. "That was it," she said. "I can't be with someone who is going to be violent with me. I said, I'm divorcing this guy. I don't want to be married to this man. Here's where I draw the line." Her attorney advised Mimi to obtain a restraining order. "If you were my daughter," the lawyer said, "that's what I would tell you to do." Mimi, however, was wary. Bob had never been violent before, and she did not expect him to return to the house. A friend of Mimi's asked her to consider the context of Bob's actions, inexcusable as they were, and the consequences of legal action. "He's dealing with his grief; he's dealing with his trauma," the friend said. "Keep him out. But if you file a restraining order, the media are going to be here. You don't want to do that to him, and you don't want to do that to yourself." Upon reflection, Mimi agreed. She had the power to shatter whatever remained of Bob's disintegrating world. Out of pity or exhaustion, she chose to spare him that blow, however deserved that option seemed.

For Bob, life had rewound nearly forty years. Once again, he was living with his brother-in-law Arthur, sleeping in the attic, with little money, in a world defined by turmoil. Arthur, a former marine drill instructor whom Bob idolized, never passed judgment on him. But Bob, ashamed and despondent, could sense the disappointment as he continued to drink away his days on a South Boston beach.

Bob had cut himself off from friends, although coworkers would call occasionally to ask if he'd recovered from his back injury, which he hadn't. In those conversations, Bob never talked about his drinking, where he was living, or what had happened between him and Mimi. In those calls, he sounded like the same guy from Inman Square: plugging away, trying to make the best of things, sharing a joke. But word had circulated on the street that Bob had hit the bottle. Even Barbara and his sons heard the rumors, which made sense to Bobby after his father began approaching him for money. "I knew he was doing something he shouldn't have been doing, that he was going through a tough time," Bobby said. "So I just told him, 'If you ever need anything . . .'"

What Bob needed became apparent on the first morning of September, a Thursday, when he biked to the beach at 6:30 A.M. to begin a day like many others in that lost and lonely summer. Bob leafed through a day-old copy of the *Boston Herald*, the crime-sports-and-politics tabloid, and stopped at a column by Joe Fitzgerald, an old-school reporter who wrote about ordinary guys, overlooked neighborhoods, and everyday heroes in the blue-collar corners of a gentrified city.

Bob read of Chris Mulligan, a thirty-three-year-old alcoholic and marine veteran, who was found dead shortly after the *Herald* printed a letter in which he had asked forgiveness from his mother and two sisters. The letter had caused a stir because of its street-level humanity, which spoke directly to struggling, disappointed men just like Bob. "The disease of addiction can be a slowly painful death that begins by seducing your soul, slowly tearing it out, and holding it hostage along with the souls of the ones you love most," Mulligan wrote. "I am an addict in recovery, and only another addict can fully understand this. Not a day goes by that I don't crave something that can stop the pain," said Mulligan, a product of the city's Charlestown neighborhood.

"I had been living at home as a typical prodigal son the day my mother dropped me off at a hotel with all my worldly possessions. She says it was the worst day of her life. Well, Mom, I share that feeling with you. [But] what you did for me that day saved my life," Mulligan continued. "I am getting better.

One of the main reasons is my family. I feel their love every day. They give me a strength that's so ingrained in my heart and soul that there is nothing I cannot beat."

Two days later, Mulligan was found dead on the deck of his apartment. According to the *Herald*, neighbors reported that he had been drinking heavily during a heat wave. Bob, sitting alone on the beach, shook his head and laughed when he read of Mulligan's death. "Another rummy bites the dust," he chuckled, dismissing the story as just another news blip about a blame-dodging loser. He'd known guys like that his entire life.

Or so he thought. The more he read, the more Bob realized he was reading about himself. By the time he finished the column, he began to cry. "What the fuck am I laughing at?" Bob said. "I'm sitting over here with my thumb up my ass, no nothing going on here, and I'm laughing at this kid?" Bob put the paper down, gazed at the morning stillness of Dorchester Bay, and made the pledge of a frightened man who had just seen the path to a lonely, early grave. "What the fuck kind of a life is this?" he said. "I've got to pull out of this and get back on track. This is not me."

Bob walked slowly from the beach, steadied his bike, and began pedaling to Somerville, lost in thought as streams of early commuters began clogging the highways into Boston. Back in his room, Bob dug out his cell phone and called Mimi, who heard the familiar voice but did not answer. "I'm going to change, Mimi," Bob said, his voice both subdued and sincere. "I'm going to take care of things. Either I'm going to get help, or I'm gonna die."

Bob told Mimi he planned to contact a doctor at McLean Hospital in suburban Belmont, where, in the past, he had forced himself to sit through a few frustrating counseling sessions at one of the country's top psychiatric facilities. Mimi called ahead to tell the psychiatrist to expect a call. "I know you can't talk to me because of confidentiality reasons, but you can hear my message," she said. "Bob is going to see you, but he is probably not going to convey what happened between us because I don't even know if he remembers." Mimi told the doctor about the incident, that police were summoned, and that she was extremely concerned about Bob's mental health and well-being.

Bob phoned the psychiatrist shortly afterward. "Hey, I need some help here," he said.

"Sure, come on over. We'll have a talk," the doctor answered.

The "talk" never materialized. When Bob walked into McLean, drawn and disheveled after months of steady drinking, the psychiatrist was startled.

"I gotta fuckin' straighten up here, brother," Bob said.

"Let's go," the doctor said sharply.

"Where we going? " Bob asked.

"You'll find out when we get there."

Bob was too tired to press for details. Instead, he followed dutifully as the psychiatrist escorted him to an in-patient facility at McLean, where Bob could sober up for three days while undergoing a battery of analysis and preliminary treatments.

The doctor pounded home how serious and damaging his problem had become. "You've got to stop this," he said.

"I am gonna stop," Bob answered.

"Stop drinking," the doctor repeated slowly.

"Okay." Bob nodded.

"Stop . . . drinking," the psychiatrist said again, pausing between the words for no-nonsense emphasis.

After three days at the hospital, Bob was released to a "sober house" of his choosing, where he could spend up to a month in a residential setting with supervision. Bob ran his finger down a list at McLean and selected a house in Quincy, just south of Boston and ten miles from Somerville. "Yeah, we have a place for you. Come on down," a staff member said.

The place Bob found was unlike anything he had ever experienced. Most of the residents were chronic alcoholics or drug addicts who had no intention, or will power, to change their ways. Some continued to shoot heroin at the "sober house," others popped Oxycontin, and more than a few residents placed calls on their cell phones for special drug deliveries to a supposed oasis of sobriety.

Without a home and nearly without hope, Bob wallowed in self-loathing and fearfully pondered the future from his new, small piece of hell. "It was awful," Bob said. "I was ashamed. I was embarrassed. How did my life get like this?" Bob fled, disgusted, after a week and returned to the attic in Arthur Downey's house. The experience had left him shaken but more determined to remain on the life-altering course he had promised himself.

Bob immediately enrolled in a three-week program that combined intense therapy for both substance abuse and trauma. He stayed clear of alcohol. He began attending Alcoholics Anonymous meetings. And he reached out to Mimi every so often to express his remorse. "I'm a different man," he'd say. "You'll see." Mimi was not convinced. "I was clear one hundred percent that it was over," she recalled. "I just didn't want to have anything to do with him. I couldn't trust him. And when the trust is broken, there's nothing left."

Over time, though, Mimi's resolve began to soften. She invited Bob to take some clothes from a batch her friend had just brought from Colombia. But when Bob arrived at the house, Mimi would not engage him, other than to point toward the coffeepot and silently indicate he could help himself. As he rummaged through the clothes, Mimi glanced quickly at his face. And there, in his eyes, she saw a genuine repentance that reminded her of the caring man who had touched her soul a decade before. "He looked so tormented by what he had done," she said. "And I didn't want to see him like that." Mimi's friend also noticed the sorrow. "You know, he really loves you," she said after Bob had left.

Through the autumn, Mimi kept her distance. But her friends would intercede for Bob, without his knowledge, and tell Mimi of his affection. Gradually, guided by their eyes, Mimi began to see a man who had suffered, endured, and now recognized all that he had lost. "Knowing Bob from before, I knew him to be a good man," Mimi said. "And I knew, as upset as I was, that he would not have wanted this to happen to him. God, life had been horrible to this man."

By Christmas, four months after being banished, Bob returned to the house, a changed and sober man—just as he had promised. "I realized that it's just not yourself that you're hurting," Bob said later. "You think you're not bothering anybody, you're not hurting anybody, that people just need to leave you alone, you know? But you look around, and you see all the people that care about you, and how they're hurting because of you."

In retrospect, Bob knew he might never have changed if Mimi had not forced him to confront his demons. "She did what she had to do to help me out," he said. Bob was also grateful to a stranger named Chris Mulligan, a troubled man who became much more than just another "rummy" in a newspaper. "I think," Bob said, "he saved my life."

Into
the Light

W HEN THE "Monsignor" speaks at Alcoholics Anonymous meetings at a nineteenth-century church in downtown Boston, mixed among upscale shops and trendy restaurants in one of Boston's premier neighborhoods, the group pays close attention. Some are thieves who have served time in prison. Others are young professionals only a few years removed from college. And some are Beacon Hill socialites who just left the jewelry counter at Lord & Taylor. Most of the two-dozen people who sit here in a wide circle on metal folding chairs do not know the Monsignor by name. To them, he is just another recovering alcoholic, like themselves, trying to do the right thing and seeking reinforcement from others who struggle with the gnawing desire for another drink. And then another. And yet another until the mind loses track of the glasses or the bottles.

But a few know the identity of the Monsignor, a term of endearment given by one of the circle to Bob Curley, who checks more baggage outside these gatherings than anyone else and never discloses the full, staggering story of his long, personal walk with the devil. Instead, he brings to the meetings an unfiltered message that gets straight to the point and comes straight from the heart. In life as well as recovery, Bob has little time to waste anymore.

At one session, Bob leads the group in readings from Step 12 of the famed recovery program, focusing this night on the effects of alcohol on marriage. It's a subject he knows well, and Bob keeps his head down as he bends far forward and reads in a low monotone.

As the readings progress, Bob listens intently. At times, he sits with his arms folded and chin buried in his chest. At others, he clasps his hands behind his head and leans back in his chair. Dressed in khaki shorts, a T-shirt, and sandals, Bob appears the most at ease of anyone in the group, whose members mostly sit motionless as tales of desperation, crime, and ruin follow one another in harrowing, confessional succession.

"I failed miserably with life," says one former executive in his late sixties.

"I have no clue how to stay sober without you guys," says a younger man, who once slept on park benches but now wears a suit to work.

"I've been sober for thirty days," another man says to applause.

When Bob's turn arrives, he challenges a previous suggestion that alcoholism usually affects the well-to-do. "I don't see that," he offers, shaking his head slightly. Then, eyes trained on the parquet floor, he is characteristically blunt. "Things are going well," he says. "I'm glad to be here, glad to be sober, and grateful for another beautiful day. That's about it."

After an hour, Bob rises, grasps the hands of the people to either side of him, and leads the group forward into a tight circle. Together, they recite a familiar prayer: "God, grant me the serenity to accept the things I cannot change; courage to change the things I can; and wisdom to know the difference." Following a few, brief good-byes, Bob walks out the door, passes a window display of luxury fashions, and slips into his car for the quick ride home to Somerville.

Since he bottomed out on the beach, the meeting in the Back Bay has been only one of several AA groups that Bob frequents. There is another in Charlestown, hard by the tough Bunker Hill housing projects, where the Chris Mulligans of the world can meet every day if they choose. There's also one in Somerville. "I got in touch with guys I know, regular jamokes like me, who just don't drink anymore," Bob says. "They'd tell me, 'You'll be all right. And even if it ain't all right, it's gonna be better than if you're drinking.' Now, someone can see a guy like me and everything that I've gone through and figure, If he can't drink for one day, maybe I can, too. You know what I mean?" Bob makes the AA rounds faithfully, not only because he likes the people but because he pledged he would never visit that South Boston beach again with even a single beer beside him. His marriage and his work for child safety are far too important.

Bob returned to the Fire Department in the summer of 2006, his back made healthy again through a tedious program at Spaulding Rehabilitation Hospital in suburban Woburn. "For once in my life, I paid attention to what I was supposed to be paying attention to, and I was kind of a little more receptive to being helped," Bob said. He even returned to South Boston as part of his recovery, walking at first and then running a little at the track at Columbus Park, only a short jog from the spot where he would mask his pain with daily drink. Eventually, as he became stronger, he entertained thoughts of one day entering the Boston Marathon.

During his dark period, Bob cut off communication with many of the organizations with which he had worked for better child protection and against the death penalty. But after he returned home, Bob reestablished himself as a passionate, articulate spokesman for those issues. To other advocates, Bob became a dependable friend who needed only to be asked to join a committee, speak to the public, or testify at the State House.

He also showed no hesitation when someone lost a child to a high-profile act of violence. Bob had reached out this way for years, both to comfort the parents of victims and to find solace for himself. Magi and John Bish, reeling from their daughter's disappearance, experienced that rare generosity of spirit soon after Molly was abducted from her lifeguard station in central Massachusetts in 2000. Bob telephoned them simply to offer his support and let them know they weren't alone.

Ever since, he has attended each annual vigil for Molly, whose body was discovered in 2003, and even organized a work party to build a ramp to the Bish home when John suffered a debilitating stroke in 2007. "Bob's help has been a gift," Magi Bish said. "He's showed us, from the earliest days, that you will survive and that the presence of evil, even in the worst of times, can bring out the best in people."

Bob has further contributed to the annual success of Missing Children's Day, an event promoted by the Bish family, in which family members and others gather at the Massachusetts State House every May to remember children who are missing and to comfort those who miss them. "Bob has always chosen to speak," Magi said. "He has such heart, but you can sense the sadness and the hurt. He's not afraid to show that, and I think that's good." She also knows Bob's work from a special task force formed by Governor Jane Swift in 2002, when the two of them joined the panel to help evaluate services available in Massachusetts to victims of sexual assault and abuse.

The task force included Richard Hoffman of Cambridge, an author and poet whose memoir about the sexual abuse he suffered as a ten-year-old led to the conviction of his former sports coach, a man who had assaulted more than four hundred children over four decades. Hoffman first met Bob as he moved through the receiving line at Jeffrey's wake. Hoffman disagreed with Bob's calls for the death penalty, but he had been impressed by Bob's efforts to calm the homophobic rage that erupted around the killing.

A year later, Hoffman formed an indelible impression of the man at a conference in Rhode Island for victims of sexual abuse. While Hoffman waited to deliver the keynote address, in which he planned to mention Jeffrey's murder, he noticed Bob walk into the room alone. Afterward, Hoffman introduced himself to Bob.

"I hope you didn't mind that," Hoffman said.

"No, no," Bob answered. "Not at all."

Hoffman, who had not met Bob since Jeffrey's wake, was stunned that he had attended the gathering. "Here's someone coming to a conference of adult survivors of sexual assault. Not as a speaker but just because he wanted to understand," Hoffman said. "This was not a sociologist going out to do a study. This was somebody who was out there with his heart still like a piece of raw meat. A lot of people would just close down, but he didn't. He wanted to learn what the hell the nature of this evil is all about. It just took tremendous courage."

Several years later, Bob reached out to Hoffman when the clergy sex-abuse crisis engulfed the Roman Catholic Archdiocese of Boston. Bob was furious about the unfolding allegations that priests had abused hundreds of youths in the archdiocese over decades, and that the church had failed to investigate or punish the predators adequately. "We've got to do something. We've got to shake this up," Bob told Hoffman. As a result, a hastily arranged news conference was held at the State House, where Bob and Hoffman, among others, demanded that an independent commission be convened to delve into the scandal. The Governor's Task Force on Sexual Assault and Abuse was formed a short time later.

Bob and Hoffman also lent their voices to the Enough Abuse Campaign, created in 2004 by the Massachusetts Child Sexual Abuse Prevention Partnership to increase awareness about the problem and develop innovative ways to combat what the American Medical Association had termed "a silent epidemic." The partnership, a statewide collaboration among twenty-three public and private entities, received seed money for its campaign from the U.S. Centers for Disease Control and Prevention, which ranked its proposal the best among applicants throughout the country. The campaign, according to its Web site, seeks to energize "those who believe that we have had enough secrets, enough shame, enough hurt, enough confusion and enough denial that child sexual abuse is a serious epidemic." In an audio link, Bob underscores why more information and communication are indispensable to the fight. "The only thing I ever taught Jeffrey about sexual abuse was all that I was ever taught, and that's, Don't talk to strangers."

Bob's willingness to spread the word also benefited Deborah Savoia, who worked hard to toughen the sex-offender registry in Massachusetts. "I don't know if there's one time that I've called him that he hasn't gone out. Bob has always stepped up to the plate, trying to make sure another parent doesn't go through what he's gone through," Savoia said. "You've got to remember that when he speaks in front of people, he's reliving everything that happened to him and his child. Yet, he does that, and he asks for nothing in return."

While Bob's work on child-safety issues expanded, the death penalty came to define him less and less in the public's eye. He attended the annual Sacco and Vanzetti memorial in Springfield, Massachusetts, on the anniversary of their notorious 1927 executions. He also testified several times at the State House against new attempts to reinstate the death penalty, an effort that faced longer and longer odds with each election cycle.

Although Bob Curley's work against the death penalty diminished gradually, his legacy on the issue endured for all those who worked against him in 1997 and later stood beside him following his watershed speech at Boston College. To Tom Lowenstein, whose father was murdered at the hands of a crazed gunman, Bob's role in the 1997 debate stands as a cautionary example of how victims' families can become movable pieces in the political chess game. "One of the important lessons about Bob is that the death penalty is not about the victim's family," Lowenstein argued. "If you're for the death penalty and they can trot you out, they'll do it. But if you turn around and say, 'I'm not sure how I feel about this,' they'll put you on ice as fast as they can." Bob said he experienced that dismissal firsthand when, after his public reversal on capital punishment, his telephone calls on child-safety issues no longer were welcome at the U.S. Department of Justice under Attorney General John Ashcroft, a staunch proponent of the death penalty.

To Renny Cushing, who for years had been supporting victims' families who opposed the death penalty, Bob stands as an empowering example of someone who, despite suffocating grief, came to that stance largely on his own. "For Bob to stand up and say, 'I've thought it over, and I've come to the conclusion that I don't support the death penalty anymore,' is incredibly powerful," Cushing said. "I find that people who spend so much time fixating on how their loved one died, end up forgetting how they lived. And that can consume your life, too. The murder claims more than one victim."

Bob understands that concept instinctively. Over the years, he has never lost the hatred in his eyes when he speaks of Jaynes and Sicari. But he has found a way to move beyond his rage and refocus on the potential of the positive. The man who has emerged can befriend people from opposite ends of the ideological spectrum, make his own decisions, and give an opinion that matters to those who take the time to listen.

The liberal pundit Jim Braude, who cohosted the television show that played a pivotal role in Bob's thinking, developed an abiding respect for a man who made, in Braude's view, a change of striking, singular courage. "It was a huge personal transformation at a huge political moment in Massachusetts," Braude said. "I'm an admirer of anybody who is big enough and honest enough to admit they were wrong, particularly when you know you're going to suffer some public ridicule."

The transformation was not limited to Bob's views on the death penalty. Margery Eagan, the other host of *Talk of New England*, was struck by the difference in Bob's appearance when she interviewed him some time later. "Before, he had looked very dark, just very gray," Eagan said. "And then you meet him again, sitting at his house, and everything is bright and colorful and cheerful. I remember thinking that day that he was just a very different guy."

To Mimi, Bob's impulse to help others was one more sign of healing. She credited Alcoholics Anonymous for much of the insight and support that helped Bob rechannel his energies. And the fellowship he found there, Mimi said, helped provide a feeling of family that Bob had often seemed to be seeking. "He has found a sense of meaning there and connectedness, and I think that saved him," Mimi said. "At the latter stages of health, you sublimate what happened to you and look instead to help someone else. That's what he wants to do." Jimmy Tingle, a nationally known comedian from Cambridge, also became one of Bob's most important lifelines to recovery, faithfully calling his old friend from the neighborhood every day to keep him focused.

Despite her leap of faith, Mimi did not set unreachably high expectations when she gave Bob a second chance. "It was more like, let's wait and see," she said. "He had been very good to me, even in the midst of all the craziness, and part of me understood, when I put on my psychologist's hat, what he was going through. I don't think I could have done what he did, you know?" Mimi's ability to step back and evaluate the relationship, despite the hurt, helped persuade her to open the door. Maybe, she thought, Bob's long depression and ugly climax were sadly inevitable—possibly even necessary to force him to confront his grief. Maybe he will get better, she thought. He's admitted that he has a problem, he's doing something about it, and he's working. Together, they bought a condo in Florida near Mimi's half sister, visited Colombia, sampled ethnic restaurants in and around Boston, and continued to improve the home and garden where so much of their recovery from Jeffrey's murder had occurred.

The Fire Department, as always, provided a shelter where Bob could find comfort in the work, the easy banter, and the unspoken camaraderie of his coworkers. That bond, Bob knew, extended well beyond the firehouse doors, even ten years after the tragedy. Several firefighters, for example, answered Bob's call for volunteers to build the wheelchair ramp for John Bish.

Although Jeffrey's murder had long since disappeared from daily conversation, many firefighters still could glimpse its lingering effect. Bill McGovern, who has known Bob as long as anyone in the department, said his friend had reclaimed some of his old, upbeat personality—but only to a point. "He's gotten better, but he's not the same Bob I knew ten years ago, twelve years ago, fourteen years ago," McGovern said a decade after the killing. "I don't think he ever will be, unfortunately." However, McGovern added, one important trait has remained. "If I ever got in trouble and asked Bob for a favor, without a doubt he'd be right there," McGovern said, nodding his head slowly in the firehouse. "He's just a great guy."

To Mimi, the friendship of firefighters like McGovern and a busy schedule have helped Bob avoid the psychological triggers that can spark angry, self-destructive behavior.

"He can't be without lots of empty spaces in his life. He has to be engaged," Mimi said. "But he created a structure, and he created enough support around him, and that is going to help." Bob, for his part, agreed to see a therapist. "He had lost everything and finally realized he needed it," Mimi said of the counseling. "It came to a point where he knew he had to have help, or he would just sink."

Bob readily admits he is radically changed, and he credits Mimi for the love she showed during Jeffrey's disappearance and its aftermath, for her patience during his manic bloodlust for revenge, and for her willingness to hope for a better day between them. "She was determined that she was going to straighten me out, she was going to help me, and she was going to stick with me through the whole thing," Bob said. "And she did."

Bob also credits Mimi's no-excuses approach and her decisive move to end the relationship in the wake of violence. If Mimi had not forced him from the house, Bob said, "maybe I would have hit that beach in South Boston and not bounced back." In retrospect, he said, "it might have been easy for other people to sympathize with me and just not have the courage to try to set me back on track. Somebody else, somebody not as strong as she is, probably wouldn't have taken that course. It was hard for her to change the locks, but you've got to do what you've got to do."

Besides tough love, Mimi brought home a professional toolbox that seemed ideally suited to deal with Bob's profound and complex troubles. First at Children's Hospital in Boston and then at the Cambridge Hospital clinic, Mimi's experience with victims of sexual and domestic trauma helped hone her skills and sensitivity to deal with Bob's personal crisis. "She always got me back to normal things as quick as she could, without me even realizing it," Bob said.

What he does realize is how lucky he is, despite the long litany of past and painful horrors. And for that good fortune, Bob is grateful. "She loves her cat, and she loves me, too," Bob said, smiling. "I scratch my head and wonder how I'm still here and how I'm not completely insane, you know?" he said. "I look around and see a lot of people I know who are sick, not doing good, they're struggling, and I count my blessings every day. It sounds corny, but it's true."

A few miles away in East Cambridge, life after Jeffrey held no such promise for Barbara Curley. Her world, instead, became a dark place of dire ailments and incessant heartache, where the memory of her child remained fresh and ever-present in the small home where they had lived. From the beginning, Barbara's family helped care for an inconsolable woman who had lost the will and hope to continue living. She often had trouble dressing herself. She continued to be heavily medicated. And she took a year off from work by necessity, before returning for a time to a part-time job as a secretary for the Cambridge schools. Barbara also was battered by a cruel succession of debilitating physical problems. Breast and ovarian cancer, treated by chemotherapy and radiation, ravaged her already frail body. She developed diabetes.

As a result, Barbara became a grieving recluse in her own home, which she rarely left and where she often imagined she heard Jeffrey. "Everywhere I look, Jeffrey is there. I hear his voice calling, 'Mommy, Mommy, Mommy,'" Barbara said a decade after the murder. "I think about what they did to him, and what he must have gone through, and that he must have been crying for me."

After that first year following Jeffrey's murder, Barbara moved in with her mother, who had become seriously ill and needed intensive dialysis. What helped give Barbara the strength to face each day, she said, was her concern for Bobby and Shaun, who she feared would spiral downward. "My whole world is my two boys," she said. "I did not want them to turn their feelings into hate and revenge. That's all that went through my head. That's the only thing that I could think about."

Together, the three participated in therapy, but only for a short time as a family. The sessions helped purge some of Shaun's anger, but Bobby never opened up in counseling and regarded the sessions as a waste of time. His roiling anger was a problem he would analyze and conquer alone, Bobby said, and not something that any therapist would medicate away, even temporarily. "When it all happened, the doctors wanted to put me on this, that, and the other fucking thing," said Bobby, who belongs to the pipe fitters union. "I truly believe the medication only makes you worse, and that's why I've never taken anything."

Instead, Bobby said, he has tried to stay strong for his mother's sake and to focus on the positive, as difficult as that seems. The manner of Jeffrey's death, together with the insidious trap laid by its architects, have infected his life with a profound mistrust that continues to color his relationships with all but his closest friends. "Now, when something bad happens, you sort of look at people a little more," Bobby said. "Let me put it like this: If someone goes missing, I don't think it's a complete stranger that had something to do with it." He said he will not read the state's sex-offender registry because if someone on the list lives nearby, he might not be able to control his rage.

The world he knew before Jeffrey's murder no longer exists, Bobby said. "It just fucks with your head, some things that words can't even describe," he explained while looking at the beach from his condo in Revere, just north of Boston. "Psychologically, it does things to you that you don't even realize.

That day changed me forever." Still, despite the shadows, Bobby believes he has a divine patron. "I just think that God's on my side, you know? He knows I make a lot of right decisions, and he helps me."

Like his brother, Shaun lives with dark, persistent suspicion. "I can't trust no one no more. It's just real sad," he said. "There's all this anger, and all these memories, and all these thoughts that weigh on my shoulders every day." A licensed carpenter, Shaun continued to live at the Hampshire Street condo with his mother, wife, and two small children. For him, the tragedy reinforced the importance of family and the need to protect the most vulnerable within that circle.

In many ways, his primary responsibility became Barbara, who moved back to the condo after her mother died in the summer of 2007. Without a job, with little money, and still in fragile health, Barbara spent days at a time in the condo basement, which Shaun painstakingly renovated into an apartment for her. "She comes up, and I cook her dinner," Shaun said. "But she still can't go upstairs to the second floor because of Jeffrey, the nightmares, the visuals. I don't think she'll ever work again. I think she's too shattered. I tell her, 'I'll pay everything. I'll feed you. I'll pay the water, the gas, lights, cable, everything.' I can't leave my mother, you know?"

In addition to her daunting physical problems, Barbara remains plagued by guilt and second-guessing. "In the end, the fact is that this was done by Charles Jaynes and Sal Sicari," Barbara said at her kitchen table. "But even today, you blame yourself, you know? You say, maybe there was something I could have done."

Not a day passes that she doesn't think of Jeffrey. Often, the thoughts are happy ones. "I talk to him every day in my mind," Barbara said. "I know he watches out for us." She thinks fondly of Jeffrey's bold declaration that he wanted to live in Disney World, where Barbara once dispatched him with an uncle, aunt, and cousin. "I had to work, and we had to pay for the house, so I came up with the money so my brother could take him," Barbara recalled. "I wanted to take him myself at some point." Instead, she was rewarded by the vicarious pleasure of Jeffrey's awestruck memories of a children's paradise, where a city kid from East Cambridge could lose himself in an all-day fantasy of castles, thrill rides, and candy, and where the goblins and pirates were all make-believe.

Barbara reflects on how close they had become, and the memory of that bond is both heartening and heartbreaking. "His world just shined when he saw me, and mine shined when I saw him," Barbara said, dissolving into tears. "He absolutely adored me, and I adored him."

Barbara takes comfort in knowing that she and Bob fulfilled the promises they made to each other in that awful moment when she heard Sicari had confessed. "We both did what we promised each other we would do," she said. Bobby and Shaun overcame much of their anger. Barbara exposed them to counseling. And Bob kept his word by raising awareness about the dangers facing children.

That awareness extended to NAMBLA, which most New Englanders did not know existed before the Curley murder seared its name into the region's consciousness. In April 2008, Bob and Barbara dropped their $200 million federal lawsuit against the organization after a judge declared that the key witness for the family was mentally incompetent to testify.

Nevertheless, Bob and Barbara insisted that the effort had been worthwhile, if only for illumination. "Maybe this is going to prevent some kid from being kidnapped. Maybe it's going to prevent some kid from being raped," Bob said. "Maybe reading the Eight Rules of Safety means that some eight- or nine-year-old boy or girl comes in contact with somebody, the kid does the right thing, and the guy goes on his way."

The frustrating part of this work, Bob said, is not knowing when or whether it makes a difference. But the effort is worth that frustration, he continued, because any effort is better than inaction. For Bob, that maxim also applies to capital punishment. "Maybe a guy like me, talking about the death penalty and being able to look at it the way I have, maybe that's going to prevent some innocent guy from being put to death," he said.

When Bob thinks back to his rants for capital punishment, he shakes his head in bemused disbelief. From unknown fire mechanic, to media magnet, to icon of a death-penalty crusade he never sought to lead, Bob sometimes must remind himself he has not lived a dream. "I look back and say, How did this happen? Why did this happen?" Bob said. "I still can't believe that all this happened to me. I still can't."

Bob is not an overtly spiritual man. But Jeffrey's murder, he senses, happened for a reason, and it happened to a family whose public sorrow would touch countless others. From the earliest days after the murder, Bob began to believe that Jeffrey's death greatly superseded its gruesome details and shock value. "It seemed to be something bigger than me and bigger than life," he recalled. The legacy of Jeffrey's killing might never be one, singular, towering accomplishment, Bob mused, but possibly "a lot of little, good things along the way." And if that's the case, he can live with the result.

Like Barbara, Bob thinks constantly of Jeffrey. He thinks of him when he sees Jeffrey's friends in the neighborhood, driving their cars and walking with girlfriends. He sees Jeffrey when he passes Donnelly Field, where the sound of Little League chatter fills a summer night, and the Gore Street ice rink, where he changed Jeffrey's diapers while Bobby and Shaun skated during hockey games. He sees Jeffrey when he runs along the Charles River on a beautiful day and recalls the priceless joys of a simple game of catch.

And when he sees his sons, Bob imagines how Jeffrey would have grown from boy to man. "Maybe he'd be playing hockey at Fitchburg State College or Salem State," Bob says. "Maybe he would have been in the navy. Maybe he would have been hammering nails with his brothers. Who knows?" Bob looks around his house, where so much of Mimi's influence is present, and envisions Jeffrey there on weekends, helping with small renovations or getting his hands dirty in the garden.

Bob still dreams about Jeffrey, but most of those dreams are pleasant. The nightmares return only occasionally, when he confronts Jaynes and Sicari in the same kind of violent, thrashing fantasies that tormented him during the trials. Now, when Bob sees Jeffrey in his dreams, his son is always in a safe place. He's laughing and joking, and in constant motion as the ten-year-old child he will always remain.

Bob sees Jeffrey riding his bike, doing wheelies, and flexing his muscles as he yells to his father, "Dad, I'm doing my push-ups and my pull-ups. I'm getting strong."

And in his dreams, just as he did in life, Bob will answer with a laugh, "You sure are. I can smell you over here!"

In East Cambridge, Jeffrey's legacy is preserved in neighbors' memories of a precocious kid with a perpetual smile and in a tragic reminder that community vigilance is a constant, unfortunate necessity. There, residents will always remember where they were, and what they thought, when the news of Jeffrey's murder spread like fire from house to house. Those neighbors, more than they know, helped Bob and his family endure, however imperfectly, an excruciating ordeal and its agonizing aftermath. The pain will never disappear for the Curleys, but neither will their gratitude. "There were a lot of good people out there who helped us, just by a kind word," Bob said. "That's the thing that really sticks out from those days, the simple kindness toward us."

In ways that constantly evolve, Bob has tried to return that goodness—to the friends who cried with him, to the strangers who reached out, and to the people who need a lift today. "A big focus has been just trying to do decent things, just trying to do the right things, just trying to help people the best I can," Bob said.

For many people, Bob will always be the kid from Inman Square, the kid from the corner who loved his friends, looked up to the veterans, laughed with the characters, and never felt compelled to explore beyond his crowded but colorful neighborhood. He's still an average guy, unremarkable to the casual observer, except for a wrenching journey that began in utter darkness and followed a twisting, torturous path to light.

And because of that experience, because of one horrible, transforming event, Bob Curley made a difference. Through a rejection of vengeance and through Mimi's heroic patience, he discovered within himself the emotional means to move on—without Jeffrey, but with the knowledge that, despite incredible suffering, he had triumphed over his darkest impulses. He has made a difference in the lives of recovering alcoholics and of families crippled by tragedy through the humble, understated example of his mere survival.

And on the death penalty, the signature cause that catapulted him from obscurity to unwanted fame, Bob's opposition will never be quantified, its effect never translated into numbers. But his voice, that of the man who pushed Massachusetts to the brink, remains profound, powerful, and resonant. More than a decade after the awful day that changed his life forever, Bob lives simply and by a simple maxim.

"I'm gonna do the best I can," he vows.

For Jeffrey's sake.

Epilogue

O N NOVEMBER 7, 2007, dozens of witnesses jockeyed for seats in a State House hearing room. The subject was the death penalty, and the Joint Judiciary Committee had convened to consider testimony on the latest effort to reinstate capital punishment in Massachusetts. Tellingly, the public hearing on what Governor Deval Patrick derided as an unfortunate "annual ritual" would no longer be held in the sumptuous, spacious confines of Gardner Auditorium. Instead, a large, boxy room served as an antiseptic setting to rehash the old arguments.

Bob Curley spoke first. Dressed in jeans and a blue shirt, his weathered face furrowed by deep lines, Bob addressed the panel without notes. "My name's Robert Curley. I'm from Somerville, and on October 1 of 1997, my ten-year-old son was kidnapped, and he was murdered," Bob said.

The committee members knew his story well, particularly Eugene O'Flaherty, who had risen since his tumultuous freshman year in 1997 to become House chairman of the panel. Bob reminded the lawmakers that he had led the charge for capital punishment after Jeffrey's death. But over time, he said, he met relatives of murder victims who saw the discussion differently and helped to change his mind.

Everyone in the room, legislators and the public, listened with rapt attention. "It took me a long time to get to the point where I did change my opinion on the death penalty," Bob continued. "It took me a long time, and it just didn't happen to me overnight. But that's just the way I see it and pretty much all I have to say."

Bob was followed to the witness table by other relatives of the slain, by academics, politicians, clergy, and activists. The committee heard from Carol Steiker, a Harvard law professor, who told the legislators that in 2006, for the first time in its history, the Gallup Poll showed more Americans in favor of life without parole than the death penalty. "The citizens of Massachusetts know there are better alternatives to the death penalty, and they are right," Steiker said. "The death penalty will not make us safer, and it can only brutalize all of us—not only the dangerous offenders but also those of us who believe, with the great jurist Benjamin Cardozo, that the death penalty is 'an anachronism too discordant to be suffered.' Looking all around us, we continue to see that the tide has turned on this issue."

After two rancor-free hours of testimony, Robert Creedon Jr. of Brockton, the Senate chairman of the panel, scanned the room and invited supporters of the death penalty to take the microphone.

No one stepped forward. Creedon waited several seconds, looked left, then right, and finally grasped the gavel. "There being no further business before this committee," he said, "this hearing is closed."

The bill was resoundingly defeated.

———

NOTES

The sourcing for this book came almost exclusively from personal interviews by the author, his coverage of the murder as a reporter for the *Boston Globe*, and his review of police and legal documents related to the murder of Jeffrey Curley. Archival newspaper stories of important events in the book, particularly concerning the Massachusetts legislature's debate on capital punishment in 1997, were also referenced. The following notes, for the most part, denote where the author used quotes obtained by other reporters and newspaper columnists. Subjective descriptions of characters in this book, their emotions, and their motivations were offered by sources close to the characters described. In nearly all cases and wherever possible, multiple sources corroborated these assessments.

4. THE LONG JOURNEY HOME

86 "Why are you protecting . . ." Judy Rakowsky, *Boston Globe*, October 4, 1997.

90 Timothy Dugan, Cambridge Hospital child psychiatrist. "It's beyond our comprehension . . ." Mac Daniel, *Boston Globe*, October 8, 1997.

90 Drucilla Whiting. "I think what kills us . . ." Mac Daniel, *Boston Globe*, October 8, 1997.

96 Marilyn Abramofsky. "If they don't do something . . ." Jon Keller, *Boston Globe*, opinion piece, October 9, 1997.

97 Massachusetts State Police Sergeant Greg Foley. "We are looking at this . . ." Caroline Louise Cole, *Boston Globe*, October 7, 1997.

5. Storm at the State House

103 "When the brutal killers . . ." Don Feder, *Boston Herald*, October 13, 1997.

105 "Daddy shot Mommy." Daniel Vasquez, *Boston Globe*, October 23, 1997.

112 State Representative Timothy Toomey. "This whole thing . . ." Adrian Walker and Frank Phillips, *Boston Globe*, October 9, 1997.

115 State Senator Robert Antonioni. "What about the killers . . ." Doris Sue Wong, *Boston Globe*, October 22, 1997.

122 Marilyn Abramofsky. "They had no problem . . ." Scot Lehigh, *Boston Globe*, October 29, 1997.

123 State Representative William McManus. "Shame on you people . . ." Doris Sue Wong and Adrian Walker, *Boston Globe*, October 29, 1997.

124 John Curley. "Thank you for saving . . ." Doris Sue Wong and Adrian Walker, *Boston Globe*, October 29, 1997.

125 Governor Paul Cellucci. "This is a victory for justice . . ." Doris Sue Wong and Adrian Walker, *Boston Globe*, October 29, 1997.

125 State Representative Donna Cuomo. "I really did not want to disappoint . . ." Doris Sue Wong and Adrian Walker, *Boston Globe*, October 29, 1997.

125 Speaker of the House Thomas Finneran. "We live in a time . . ." Doris Sue Wong and Adrian Walker, *Boston Globe*, October 29, 1997.

125 Robert Curley. "I guess it's a step . . ." Doris Sue Wong and Adrian Walker, *Boston Globe*, October 29, 1997.

132 Robert Curley. "It's up to the people . . ." Tina Cassidy, *Boston Globe*, November 7, 1997.

132 Paul Cellucci. "We saw a phony vote . . ." Scot Lehigh and Frank Phillips, *Boston Globe*, November 8, 1997.

133 Rob Gray. "He's a profile in cowardice . . ." Carolyn Ryan, *Boston Herald*, November 7, 1997.

6. Uncharted Ground

136 Cellucci. "This battle is not over . . ." Frank Phillips and Scot Lehigh, *Boston Globe*, November 8, 1997.

136 Eleanor LeCain. "Running for state executioner . . ." Patricia Smith, *Boston Globe*, December 5, 1997.

136 State Representative Brian Joyce. "On such a personal matter . . ." Adrian Walker, *Boston Globe*, December 4, 1997.

144   Cellucci. "We need to do everything we can . . ." Jill Zuckman,
      Boston Globe, October 2, 1998.
145   Ed Cafasso. "I think it's clear . . ." Jill Zuckman, *Boston Globe*,
      October 2, 1998.

8. QUESTIONS AND BEGINNINGS

169   Cellucci. "Monsters who do not deserve hope . . ." Scot Lehigh
      and Frank Phillips, *Boston Globe*, February 17, 1999.
171   Cardinal Bernard Law. "The teachings of the church . . ." Diego
      Ribadeneira, *Boston Globe*, March 20, 1999.

9. RESURRECTION

198   "Let's hope those Massachusetts authorities . . ." Jeff Jacoby,
      columnist, *Boston Globe*, October 7, 1997.
202   Robert Curley. "What am I going to get . . ." Matthew Falconer,
      Boston Globe, March 30, 1999.
202   Lawrence Frisoli, Curley family attorney. "This is a measuring
      stick . . ." Ralph Ranalli, *Boston Globe*, August 24, 2000.
202   Charles Jaynes. "I will trust in the jury . . ." Ralph Ranalli, *Boston
      Globe*, August 22, 2000.
203   John Roberts, executive director, Massachusetts chapter of
      ACLU. "For us, it's a fundamental . . . " Ralph Ranalli, *Boston
      Globe*, August 31, 2000.

10. THE ROAD HOME

219   "We are an integral part . . ." Jennifer Bishop, Murder Victims'
      Families for Reconciliation, newsletter, December 3, 2002.

ACKNOWLEDGMENTS

In a nonfiction work with so many moving parts, the list of people who contributed their time, insight, passion, and suggestions is a lengthy one. But any acknowledgment of these contributions must start with the Curley family and with Bob's wife, Mimi, whose courage to tell their story had a profound effect on me. I will be forever grateful to them for their patience, their recollections, and their simple willingness to sit across a kitchen table and express, as well as relive, the sorrow that they have experienced.

To Bob Curley and Mimi, Barbara Curley, Bobby Curley Jr., Shaun Curley, the late Francine Downey, John Curley, and the late Muriel Francis, my heartfelt thanks for the many hours in which you educated and enriched me.

My thanks, as well, to the many fine members of the Cambridge fire and police departments who, without exception, were generous with their time and thoughts. To Bill McGovern, Fran Judd, and the crew of Engine 5, I'll never forget the hospitality of "The Nickel." And to John Fulkerson, Pat Nagle, Lester Sullivan, and Frank Pasquarello, whose police work was critical after Jeffrey's disappearance, thank you for your painstaking reconstruction of the investigation.

Likewise, I am grateful to John Geary of the Newton police for his vivid recollection of the fracas involving Charles Jaynes at Honda Village, and to Bill Freeman and Arthur Huntley, who searched for Jeffrey's body with the Massachusetts State Police dive team.

My research benefited immeasurably from the cooperation of the attorneys in this case. Thank you to David Yannetti, the prosecutor, who first sat down with me several years ago when the outlines of this book had only begun to take shape. In follow-up interviews over the years, his help and advice continued to prove invaluable. My gratitude also extends to the defense attorneys, Arthur Kelly and Robert Jubinville, who never failed to respond to requests for an interview or an accuracy check. And I owe a debt to Corey Welford, the press liaison for the Middlesex District Attorney's Office, whom I bombarded with call after call for information and contacts.

The death-penalty debate in the legislature is a central part of this story, and I was fortunate to glean some of the background and context of those tumultuous times from many current and former Massachusetts politicians. I thank John Slattery, Bill Nagle, Paul Cellucci, Tim Toomey, Tom Finneran, Sal DiMasi, Marian Walsh, Paul Haley, Eugene O'Flaherty, Tom McGee, Maura Hennigan, Paul Demakis, and Bradley Jones for their interest and accessibility. Each of them was a pleasure to interview.

A debt is also owed to the passionate activists who joined that discussion. Norma Shapiro and Ann Lambert of the ACLU honored me with their time and buoyed me with their good humor. Renny Cushing, Tom Lowenstein, and Susannah Sheffer of Murder Victims' Families for Human Rights were inspirational in their dedication to the fight against capital punishment. And Martina Jackson, executive director of Massachusetts Citizens Against the Death Penalty, is the embodiment of commitment.

Magi Bish, who lost a daughter to murder, showed that the human spirit truly can be indomitable. Dan Moniz, who led the crusade to promulgate the "Eight Rules of Safety," was a marvel of energy. And Richard Hoffman, an author who suffered sexual abuse as a child, moved me with his admiration of his friend Bob Curley.

Marilyn Abramofsky showed me the power of plain speaking and the possibilities of believing in a cause. And Sister Helen Prejean showed me a down-to-earth godliness.

Giving voice to emotion played a critical role in understanding the depths of feeling of this book's main characters. Outside of the Curleys, no one did this better than Bud Welch, Bill Babbitt, and David Kaczynski. Welch welcomed me into his Oklahoma City home for two compelling interviews about the loss of his daughter Julie in the 1995 bombing of the federal building there. Babbitt and Kaczynski turned a long lunch in Schenectady, New York, into an unforgettable seminar on the impact of the death penalty and the factors that led to their wrenching decisions to turn over their brothers to the authorities.

The people who knew Charles Jaynes and Salvatore Sicari also provided invaluable insights. I particularly wish to thank Charlene Letourneau for helping me understand the relationship between the killers. I wish her peace. Her friend Michelle Ward also provided useful background and helped Charlene find the courage to speak about her troubled past. Input from Kris McGovern and Wayne Garber about Sicari and his family, their onetime neighbors, is appreciated. Rebecca Moffitt, who once taught Jaynes, provided a chilling example of his depravity.

My contacts in the news media were unfailingly helpful. A special thanks goes to Jim Braude, who painted a dramatic picture of Bob Curley's important appearance on *Talk of New England*. Likewise, to Margery Eagan, his cohost, and to Doreen Iudica Vigue, a former colleague at the *Boston Globe*, who is communications director for New England Cable News. Doreen's work in compiling video from the station's coverage of the murder investigation and the death-penalty debate provided me with an irreplaceable visual record.

No mention of the media, however, would be complete without mentioning *Globe* editor Martin Baron, who approved a leave of absence to write the book, granted an extension, and was supportive throughout.

Toby Leith and Joel Swanson of the *Globe* helped me find my way through a thicket of technical issues.

Thanks, too, to Karen Miranda, a psychologist and professor whose insights into human behavior were enlightening. Professor Alan Rogers of Boston College helped me navigate the history of the death penalty in Massachusetts. And the late Larry Frisoli, the Curley family lawyer, allowed me access to all his police and legal files on the case.

Writing this book became an all-consuming job of long, intense days in which a heinous crime was the harrowing and inescapable focus of my work. To Judy McClellan, who welcomed me into her beautiful home on the Fire Island Inlet as an oasis for writing and reflection, your bottomless generosity can never be repaid. Your integrity, heart, patience, and support became inspiring life lessons. A nod of the cap, too, to Chloe, a warm but feisty Chesapeake Bay retriever, whose undemanding companionship was a comfort and a revelation at the many times I needed that.

And to Steve Kurkjian, who allowed me the run of his house near a stunning perch on Cape Cod Bay, a special remembrance for Manomet.

Bringing this book from idea to reality would not have been possible without the encouragement and expert direction of Todd Shuster, my literary agent, and Rachel Sussman, who worked patiently with me on developing the proposal. A special thanks, as well, to my editor at Da Capo Press, Bob Pigeon, who saw the possibilities of a story in Bob Curley's saga and took a chance. And a well-done to Katy Brunault, who offered incisive critiques and cheerful commentary throughout the project.

Finally, I wish to thank my family—especially my mother, Rita; father, Jim; and sister, Lesley—for their unfailing belief that this was possible. And to my daughter, Fiona, the light of my life, who was born four months after Jeffrey Curley and remains for me a vibrant, loving reminder of why we must always cherish our children.

INDEX

Abramofsky, Marilyn, 91–92, 94, 96, 122
ACLU. *See* American Civil Liberties Union
Addiction, 231, 233
African Americans, 9
Alcoholics/Alcoholics Anonymous, 233, 234, 237–239, 243–244
Alfaro, Roque, 35
American Civil Liberties Union (ACLU), 118–119, 203
American Friends Service Committee, 119
American Medical Association, 241
America's Most Wanted (TV show), 137
Amnesty International, 119
Antonioni, Robert, 115
Ashcroft, John, 242
Astrology, 14
Avant, Jacquelyn, 35

Babbitt, Bill, 190–191, 192–193, 201, 211, 212
Babbitt, Manuel "Manny," 189–193, 195–201
clemency hearing for, 200

Barrios, Jarrett, 196–197
Baseball, 12, 222
Beer, 38, 226. *See also* Curley, Bob: drinking heavily
Bicycles, 19, 22–23, 31, 55, 57, 70, 104, 182, 183
Bish, Magi, John and Molly, 205, 239–240, 244
Bishop, Jennifer, 210, 219
Bisson, Dale, 35
Blagojevich, Rod, 219
Borenstein, Isaac (Superior Court Justice), 220, 221
Boston Alliance for Gay and Lesbian Youth, 15
Boston Bar Association, 119
Boston College, 208, 209–210
Boston Globe, 14, 120, 122, 126, 133, 188, 198, 208
Boston Herald, 103, 177, 188, 189, 231, 232
Boston Red Sox, 5–6
Boston Strangler, 77
Bradlees department store in Watertown, 39–40, 73
Branch Davidian compound (Waco, Texas), 173
Branley, Brian (detective), 69
Braude, Jim, 122, 177, 180, 243

Bridgewater State Hospital for
    the Criminally Insane, 190
Brockton, Massachusetts, 13, 15,
    43
Brudnoy, David, 150
Bush, George H. W., 108
Bush, George W., 218
Byrd, James Jr. and Ross, 218–219

Cambridge Cemetery, 143, 213,
    214–216
Cambridge Fire Department, 3,
    4, 5, 6, 102, 122, 138–139,
    153, 158, 204, 217, 223,
    239, 244
Cambridge gay population, 90
Cambridge Hospital clinic, 96,
    97, 153, 246
Cambridge Little League, 12
Capital punishment. See Death
    penalty
Cardozo, Benjamin, 254
Carr, Howie, 133
Carr, Tracy, 49
Catholic Church. See Roman
    Catholic Church
Cellucci, Paul, 94–96, 102, 121,
    122, 171, 172, 196, 205, 206
  clout of, 183
  and death-penalty, 105, 107,
    109, 112, 115, 116–117,
    125, 130, 132–133, 144–
    145, 148, 169–170, 185,
    187, 195
  and death-penalty supporters,
    136
Cement/concrete, 40, 41–42, 44,
    46, 47, 73, 164, 165
Charbonnier, Mark (state
    trooper), 107–108
Charles G. Harrington School.
    See Harrington School

Chelsea, Massachusetts, 149
Children's Hospital (Boston),
    246
Child-safety programs. See under
    Curley, Bob
Christmas holidays, 142
Civil rights movement, 218
Claudio, Kenny, 91
Clinton, Bill, 173
Closure, 149, 151, 181, 212
Concrete. See Cement/concrete
Contos, Peter, 104
Cowin, Judith (judge), 138, 143–
    144, 148, 163, 165, 166
Credit cards, 18, 35, 43, 165
Creedon, Robert, Jr., 254
Crime, rise in, 107
Crowley, Kristen, 104, 133, 186
Cruz, Rochelle, 23
Cuba, 221–222
Cuomo, Donna Fournier, 108,
    109, 121–122, 125, 171
Curley, Barbara (mother of
    Jeffrey Curley), 6, 7–9, 10–
    11, 19, 34, 37, 38–39, 49,
    62, 70, 79, 80, 88, 121,
    214, 215, 216, 231, 246–
    247, 248–249
  and confirmation of Jeffrey's
    murder, 81
  father of, 8, 29
  filing missing-person report,
    51
  grieving after murder, 140,
    142–143
  health problems, 246
  marriage of, 8, 9
  and Mimi, 157
  mother of, 11, 214, 247, 248
    (see also Francis, Muriel)
  See also Curley, Jeffrey:
    relationship with his mother

Curley, Bob (father of Jeffrey
    Curley), 1–2, 3–6, 7, 8, 12,
    34, 53, 62, 86, 87–88, 123,
    124–125, 126, 135, 138,
    143, 167–168
  accomplishments of, 204–205,
    250
  and activist Jim Braude, 122
  and Alcoholics Anonymous,
    234, 237–239
  back injury of, 224, 239
  and Bud Welch, 177–180,
    181–182, 209, 213
  at Cambridge Cemetery with
    family, 214–216
  and child-safety programs,
    144, 150, 181, 182, 204,
    205, 218, 239, 242, 249
  civil lawsuits against Jeffrey's
    killers and NAMBLA, 202–
    203
  and confirmation of Jeffrey's
    murder, 81
  and death penalty, 90–91, 93,
    113, 171–172, 206–207,
    207–208, 222, 242, 250 (see
    also Curley, Bob: opposing
    death penalty)
  and discovery of Jeffrey's body,
    100
  and diversity training for
    Cambridge city employees,
    203–204
  dreams of Jeffrey, 250–251
  drinking heavily, 226, 227,
    228, 229, 230, 231 (see also
    Curley, Bob: and Alcoholics
    Anonymous)
  and elderly protester at State
    House, 121
  emergency colostomy of, 156–
    157

  and hearings of 1999, 182,
    184–185
  informed of Jeffrey's
    disappearance, 52
  at Jaynes trial, 165, 166, 250–
    251
  and John Slattery, 132, 207
  at Long Funeral Home, 101
  and Manny Babbitt case, 191–
    192, 192–193, 196–197,
    198–200, 202
  and Marilyn Abramofsky, 92
  marriage of, 8, 9 (see also
    Mimi: marriage to Bob
    Curley)
  and Maura Hennigan
    campaign, 136, 137
  as most recognizable "average"
    citizen, 96, 149
  opposing death penalty, 207–
    216, 218, 219, 239,
    249–250, 252
  as paranoid, 223
  parents of, 160, 222
  questioning judicial system
    and death penalty, 171, 182,
    188, 191–192, 199
  realizing Jeffrey was dead, 58,
    59, 80
  and retrieval of Jeffrey's body,
    84–85
  return to Fire Department
    after murder, 138–139,
    139–140
    after Sicari conviction, 148–
    150
  and Sister Helen Prejean, 129
  statements to media, 88–89,
    207–208
  suspicious of Sicari, 59–60, 79
  on Talk of New England TV
    show, 178–180

Curley, Bob (*continued*)
  in therapy, 162–163, 234, 245
  being violent with Mimi, 229–
    230, 233, 245
  See also Mimi
Curley, Bobby Jr. (brother of
    Jeffrey Curley), 6, 8, 11–12,
    27–28, 37–38, 39, 49, 51,
    52, 80, 138, 140–141, 214,
    215, 216, 220, 222, 231,
    247–248, 249
  arrested for threatening
    Sicaris, 141
  and Charles Jaynes, 66–68
  and confirmation of Jeffrey's
    murder, 81
  revolver of, 66, 68
  searching for Jeffrey, 54–55
  suspicious of Sicari, 60, 64–
    65, 66, 79
Curley, Jeffrey, 1, 6–8, 9–10, 12,
    19–20, 110, 117, 185
  autopsy of, 100–101, 146, 147
  funeral of, 101–102
  grandmother of. *See* Francis,
    Muriel
  and home of his father and
    Mimi, 12
  legacy of, 252
  murder of, 32–33
  relationship with his mother,
    8, 10, 11, 12, 22–23, 25,
    28, 249
  relationship with Jaynes, 20–
    22, 23, 24
  search for body of, 84–85, 97–
    100
Curley, Jim (brother of Bob
    Curley), 94, 129
Curley, John (brother of Bob
    Curley), 79, 80, 110, 113–
    114, 123, 124, 132, 221

Curley, John (father of Bob
    Curley), 4, 5
Curley, Shaun (brother of Jeffrey
    Curley), 6, 7, 10, 11–12,
    26–27, 37, 38, 39, 49, 51,
    52–53, 59–60, 80, 140,
    156, 214, 215, 216, 247,
    248, 249
  and confirmation of Jeffrey's
    murder, 81
  jailed for incidents with
    Sicaris, 141–142
  questioned by police, 53–54
Cushing, Renny, 177, 180–182,
    183, 184, 197, 199, 208,
    209, 212, 243
Cushing, Robert, 181

Dahmer, Jeffrey, 48
Daley, Dominic, 118
Davis, Gray, 192, 197, 199–200
"Dawn of Tolerance in
    Massachusetts" (painting),
    123
Deadline (documentary), 219
Dead Man Walking (Prejean),
    129
Death penalty, 2, 90–91, 93, 113
  and class, 204
  commutation of sentences in
    Illinois, 218, 219
  death threats concerning, 133
  as deterrent, 185
  and exoneration of Illinois
    death row inmates, 187
  groups against, 119
  hangings in 1806, 118
  hearings of March 21, 1999,
    concerning, 171–172, 182,
    183–187
  legal costs, 185, 187
  life without parole as option

for, 119, 138, 219, 254 (*see also* Life without parole sentence)
and mental illness, 191
and murders of children, 110, 115
and murders of police officers, 108, 109, 124, 196
Northeastern University survey on, 105–106, 119
opponents of, 119, 170, 172, 183, 184, 186, 187, 188, 192, 195, 196, 198, 204, 210, 219, 243 (*see also* Nagle, William; Slattery, John; Welch, Bud)
petitions concerning, 114, 123
as protecting children, 111
and Puritan founders, 106
and sixteen-year-olds, 210
states allowing, 107
support for, 103–104, 105–107, 114, 117, 119, 125, 127, 136, 137, 150, 169, 170, 171, 184, 187, 195, 204, 210, 242, 253, 254
for terrorism, 124
for torture or extreme cruelty and other types of murder, 115
See also under Curley, Bob
De la Cruz, Jesus, 104
Demakis, Paul, 126, 131
Democrats, 6, 114, 115, 116, 120, 121, 123, 136, 145, 185, 219
Desir, Henock, 21
DiMasi, Sal, 127–128, 130
Divers, 84, 97, 98, 99
Diversity training, 203–204
DNA swabs, 98
Domestic violence, 205, 246

Donahue, Edward, 105
Donahue, Elaine, 104–105, 115
Donlan, Thomas III (FBI agent), 73
Donnelly Field, 9
Door-to-door canvass of neighborhood, 54
Dover Point Variety Store (New Hampshire), 49
Downey, Arthur (brother-in-law of Bob Curley), 230, 234
Downey, Francine (sister of Bob Curley), 9, 34, 52, 53, 56, 58, 79, 82, 121, 214
daughter of, 143
death of, 222–223
Downey, Mary, 143
Downing, Janet, 25, 104, 115
Drew, Jason, 36
Drinking alcohol, 174. *See also* Beer; Curley, Bob: drinking heavily
Drugs, 43, 142, 233–234
Duct tape, 35, 44, 46
Dugan, Timothy, 90
Dukakis, Michael, 108, 113, 118

Eagan, Margery, 177, 178, 179, 243
East Cambridge, Massachusetts, 1, 4, 20, 23, 89, 251
Ecstasy drug, 142
"Eight Rules of Safety" for children, 205, 206, 249
Ellis, Tashika, 23, 24, 28, 29
Enough Abuse Campaign, 241

Faneuil Hall (Boston), 172
FBI, 61, 73, 188, 191
Feder, Don, 103
Federal Bureau of Investigation. *See* FBI

Finneran, Tom (House Speaker),
114, 116, 117, 120–121,
124, 125, 130, 132, 187,
196, 207, 217
First Amendment, 203
Fitzgerald, Joe, 231
Flaherty, Charles, 107
Flavin, Nancy, 120, 121, 124
Fliers, 54, 56, 61, 66, 80, 97
of Hennigan campaign, 136,
137
Flutie, Doug, 46
Foley, Greg (state police
sergeant), 97
Fournier, Joey, 108
Francis, Arthur (uncle of Jeffrey
Curley), 29–30, 111
Francis, Charlie (brother of
Barbara Curley), 52, 82
Francis, Margaret (sister of
Francine Downey and Bob
Curley), 82, 214
Francis, Muriel (mother of
Barbara Curley), 11, 28, 29,
30, 34, 140, 214
Freeman, Bill (state police diver),
97–98
Frisoli, Lawrence, 202
Fulkerson, John (detective), 69–
70, 74–75, 77
and search for body of Jeffrey
Curley, 98, 99
Furman v. Georgia, 107

Gallup poll, 107, 254
Garber, Wayne, 60
Garvin, Greg, 49
Gavell, James, 36
Geary, John (police officer), 67–
69
Georgia, 107
Glenn, Annie, 105, 114

Gonzalez, Elvis, 55, 56, 60, 64,
65, 66–68
Gove, Susan, 186
Gray, Rob, 116, 117, 133
Great Depression, 106
Grief counseling, 89
Guilt, 225, 248

Haley, Paul, 130
Halligan, James, 118
Hanna, George (state trooper),
110
father of, 150
Hanna Medal of Honor, 109
Harrington School, 7, 89–90
Harshbarger, Scott, 145
Hate, 176, 179, 211, 212, 243,
247
Hayward, Ed, 189
Hennigan, Maura, 136–137
Hill, Paul, 124
Hispanics, 9
Hockey, 12, 124–125
Hoffman, Richard, 240–241
Hogan, Maureen, 184
Home Depot in Somerville, 40,
73, 74
Homophobia, 4, 90, 240
Honda Village (Newton,
Massachusetts), 21, 22, 35,
36, 66, 70, 73, 162
Horton, Willie, 108–109
Hunte, Alan (state trooper), 69,
74, 76
Huntley, Arthur (state police
diver), 99

Illinois death row inmates'
exoneration, 187. See also
Death penalty:
commutation of sentences
in Illinois

Inman Square, 3, 4, 5, 62, 122,
   189, 207, 223
International Bicycle Centers, 31
Internet, 202–203
Irish immigrants, 176

Jackson, Martina, 186, 197
Jacoby, Jeff, 198
Jajuga, James, 109, 110, 112,
   115
Jane Doe Inc., 205
Jaynes, Charles, 13–17, 29, 43,
   55, 60, 65, 66–67, 90, 198,
   211
   alias of (Anthony Scaccia), 13
   apartment of, 13, 14–15, 17,
      44–46, 76
   arraignments/bail for, 88, 138
   attorney of, 71
   Cadillac of, 20, 23, 31–33, 36,
      44, 46, 47, 48–49, 57, 165
   change of venue for, 163, 172
   charged with murder and
      kidnapping, 98
   described, 14
   and Detective Nagle, 61
   and disposal of Jeffrey's body,
      46, 47–48
   father of, 14. (see also Jaynes,
      Edward, Sr.; Kojak's
      Reconditioning)
   goal of being a famous killer,
      49
   mother of, 13, 36, 40, 43–44,
      165
   murder of Jeffrey Curley, 32–
      33 (see also Jaynes, Charles:
      and disposal of Jeffrey's
      body)
   as necrophiliac, 45–46
   outstanding arrest warrants for,
      13, 57, 68, 71, 88
   as sexually attracted to boys,
      15, 16, 20, 24, 41, 73, 146
   and souvenir trophies of
      murder, 45, 46, 76
   wrongful-death claim against,
      202
   See also Curley, Jeffrey:
      relationship with Jaynes;
      Trials of Sicari and Jaynes
Jaynes, Edward, Jr., 36
Jaynes, Edward, Sr. (Kojak)
   (father of Charles Jaynes),
   17, 21. See also Kojak's
   Reconditioning
Jaynes, Virginia (mother of
   Charles Jaynes), 40, 165.
   See also Jaynes, Charles:
   mother of
"Jeffrey Curley and Victims of
   Murder Memorial Day," 121
Jeffrey Curley Bill, 205, 206
Jeffrey Curley Foundation, 204
Joyce, Brian, 136–137
Jubinville, Robert, 71, 143, 164,
   165
Judd, Fran, 139–140, 217
Juries, 127, 144
Justice Department, 242
Justice system fallibility, 187. See
   also Curley, Bob:
   questioning judicial system
   and death penalty

Kaczynski, David, 191, 192–193,
   200, 201–202, 211, 212–
   213
Kaczynski, Linda, 193
Kaczynski, Ted, 191
Kelly, Arthur, 85–86, 143, 146–
   147
Kennedy, Edward, 89
Kennedy, John F., 123

Kenney, Richard, 105
Kojak's Reconditioning, 21, 66
Koresh, David, 173

Lambert, Ann, 118–119
Langert, Richard and Nancy, 210
Latchkey children, 93
Law, Bernard (Cardinal), 102,
    171, 172, 184, 186, 208,
    209
Leaster, Bobby Joe, 120–121
LeCain, Eleanor, 136
Lees, Brian, 109, 110
Lehigh, Scot, 122
Letourneau, Charlene, 17, 18,
    36, 40–43, 44
Liberals, 6, 103, 122, 170, 196,
    220
Life without parole sentence,
    119, 138, 148, 179, 219,
    254
Lime, 40, 44, 46, 47, 73, 74, 165
Limone, Pete, 188
Lion King, The (movie), 14, 46
Llamas, 164
Long Funeral Home, 101–102
Loving Boys, 16
Lowenstein, Allard, 197
Lowenstein, Tom, 197–199, 242
L Street Bathhouse (South
    Boston), 226, 227

McEvoy, John (deputy district
    attorney), 71, 86–87, 93,
    98, 145
McGee, Tom, 125, 127
McGillicuddy, Cornelius, 163
McGovern, Bill, 10, 138–139,
    140, 244–245
McGovern, Kris, 18, 19
McLaughlin, Paul, 115

McLean Hospital, 232, 233
McManus, William, 123–124
McVeigh, Bill and Jennifer, 176–
    177
McVeigh, Timothy, 173, 213
Maine, 48, 97, 98
Manchester, New Hampshire,
    13, 43, 47. See also Jaynes,
    Charles: apartment of
Manny, "the Portugee" (friend of
    Barbara Curley), 64, 65
Marijuana, 43
Marini, Fran, 114, 123
Marshall, Thurgood, 107
Massachusetts
    criminalization of child
        pornography in, 205
    Governor's Task Force on
        Sexual Assault and Abuse,
        241
    high court in, 91, 107, 144
    informal moratorium on death
        penalty in, 106–107
    Joint Criminal Justice
        Committee, 109
    Joint Judiciary Committee, 253
    juvenile judicial system in, 92
    penalty for first-degree murder
        in, 137–138
    Senate/House, 110, 115, 116,
        125–126, 128, 169, 184,
        196
    sex-offender registry in, 242,
        247
    State House, 94, 112, 113,
        121, 126, 169, 171, 183–
        184, 195, 206, 240, 241,
        242, 253
    State Police, 61, 93, 107–108
    support for death penalty in,
        103–104, 105–106, 107,

119, 187, 253 (*see also*
Death penalty: support for)
Massachusetts Bar Association,
119
Massachusetts Bay Colony, 106
Massachusetts Child Sexual
Abuse Prevention
Partnership, 241
Massachusetts Citizens Against
the Death Penalty, 119, 186,
197
Massachusetts Turnpike, 116
Media, 62, 84, 85, 92, 97, 150,
160, 177, 184, 201, 206,
207–208
first public statement by
Curley family, 88–89
implying gross neglect of
Curley family, 139
and John Slattery, 131
and trials of Sicari and Jaynes,
144
See also Press
Merrill, William, 48
Middlesex Superior Court, 26
Mimi (woman living with Bob
Curley), 6, 10, 12, 52, 96–
97, 101, 102, 149, 150–151,
204, 234–235, 252
beginning of relationship with
Bob Curley, 153–156, 157–
158
buying new house with Bob
Curley, 159
concerned about Bob Curley's
psychological condition,
160–162, 225, 226, 227,
228, 232–233
dissatisfied with marriage,
228–229, 230
garden and house of, 168–169,
244
and healing of Bob Curley,
243–244, 245–246
marriage to Bob Curley, 220,
221
and violence of Bob Curley,
229–230, 245
Minorities, 127
Miranda rights, 69, 72
Missing Children's Day, 240
Missing-persons cases, 51, 53
Mobley, Mamie Till, 218, 219
Moffitt, Rebecca, 14, 15
Moniz, Dan, 205–206
Moore, Richard, 115
Morrison, Garfield (police
lieutenant), 77
Mulligan, Chris, 231–232, 235
Murders, 91, 97, 104–105, 112,
114, 115, 116, 118, 120,
133, 145, 170, 181, 196,
210, 218–219, 239–240
families of murder victims,
205, 211, 219, 242, 243,
254 (*see also* Murder
Victims' Families for
Reconciliation)
murder of state trooper, 107–
108, 110
murder trial of Eddie O'Brien,
25–26, 27
penalty for first-degree murder,
137–138
sentences for second-degree
murderers, 109–110, 115,
166
and Willie Horton prison
furlough, 108
wrongful convictions, 188
See also Death penalty; Life
without parole sentence

Murder Victims' Families for
     Reconciliation (MVFR),
     172, 177, 197, 208, 210–
     212, 218
Murrah Federal Building
     bombing, 173, 175
Muse, Robert and Christopher,
     120
MVFR. *See* Murder Victims'
     Families for Reconciliation

Nagle, Patrick (detective), 77–
     78. *See also* Sicari,
     Salvatore: and Detective
     Nagle
Nagle, William (House majority
     leader), 117–119, 119–120,
     122–123, 125, 126, 127,
     130, 133, 170
NAMBLA. *See* North American
     Man/Boy Love Association
National Center for Missing and
     Exploited Children, 205
National Guard, 61
Naughton, Harold, Jr., 185, 186–
     187
Nazis, 203
NECN. *See* New England Cable
     News
Necrophilia, 46
Neil, Robyn, 20
New England Cable News
     (NECN), 177, 207
Newton, Massachusetts, 14, 67
     Newton District Court, 87
New York City, 15, 142
New Yorkers Against the Death
     Penalty, 202
New York State, 107
NHD Hardware, 35
Nichols, Terry, 173

North American Man/Boy Love
     Association (NAMBLA),
     15–16, 41, 150, 166, 167,
     211
     wrongful-death suit against,
     202–203, 249
North Andover, Massachusetts,
     171
Northeastern University survey
     on death penalty, 105–106,
     119
Northwestern University, 219

O'Brien, Eddie, 26, 27, 104
     verdict and sentencing of, 34
O'Connor, Thomas (deputy
     superintendent), 61
O'Flaherty, Eugene, 124, 129, 253
Oklahoma City bombing, 173,
     175

Panagiotakos, Steven, 115
Parents of Murdered Children,
     92, 94
Pasquarello, Frank (police
     officer), 53
Patrick, Deval, 253
Pedophilia, 16, 202, 203. *See also*
     Jaynes, Charles: as sexually
     attracted to boys
Pelligrini, William, 15, 24
Photographs, 20–21, 62, 84
     autopsy photos, 146, 147
     See also Fliers
Piscataqua River, 48, 97–98
Pistorino, Laurie, 13, 16–17, 21,
     36, 70
Politics, 6
Polygraph tests, 73
Pornography, 15, 20, 41
     child pornography, 205

Porter, Anthony, 187, 219
Portsmouth, New Hampshire,
    47, 48, 83
Posttraumatic stress disorder,
    190
Prejean, Sister Helen, 129, 208
Press, 87, 90, 117. *See also*
    Media
Pryor, Andrew, 184, 197, 210
Public defenders, 119
Puritan founders, 106

Radicals, 6
Rape, 19, 62, 83, 91, 108, 110,
    115, 202, 240
Reilly, Thomas (district attorney),
    26, 93–94, 100, 102, 145,
    166
Reno, Janet, 173, 191, 192
Republicans, 6, 105, 109, 113,
    114, 219
Revenge, 179, 214, 247, 252
Rice, Catherine, 104
Right to an attorney, 106, 144
Roberts, John, 203
Rockingham, New Hampshire,
    226
Roman Catholic Church, 8, 102,
    171, 186
  sex-abuse crisis of, 241
Rosenberg, Matthew, 91–92
Rubbermaid Rough Tote
    container, 40, 44, 46, 73,
    83, 98, 99, 164, 165, 202
Ryan, George, 218, 219–220
Ryan, Dr. Henry, 99

Sabbey, George (police officer),
    76
Sacco, Nicola, 106, 242
Sacred Heart Church, 102

Salem witchcraft trials, 123
Salvati, Joe, 188
Sarchioni's store, 26, 27
Savoia, Deborah, 242
Schendel, Leah, 189, 190, 200
Scibelli, Anthony, 116
Selvig, Fabio, 31
Sewall, Samuel, 123
Sexual abuse, 150, 204, 240,
    241, 246. *See also* Rape
Sexual-offenders laws, 205, 242
Shapiro, Norma, 118–119, 124,
    171
Sheffer, Susannah, 210, 211
Sicari, Robert (brother of
    Salvatore Sicari), 19, 83
Sicari, Salvatore, 17–19, 21, 28–
    29, 30–33, 43, 68–69, 70,
    71, 90, 165, 198
  arraignments of, 86–87, 138
  attorney of, 85–86
  and Bob Curley, 58–59
  and Charlene Letourneau, 17,
    41
  confession of, 75–76
  criminal record of, 19
  and Detective Fulkerson, 74–
    75, 82–83
  and Detective Nagle, 57–58,
    61, 63–64, 72, 73
  and disposal of Jeffrey's body,
    46, 47–48
  as homophobic, 4
  locking Jeffrey in trunk of
    Jaynes's car, 23
  mother of, 72–73, 77
  retracing route when Jeffrey's
    body was dumped, 82–83
  talking about Charles Jaynes
    after murder, 56–57, 59, 63,
    73, 75–76, 83, 164

Sicari, Salvatore (*continued*)
    as volunteer, 55–56, 61
    wrongful-death claim against,
        202
    See also Trials of Sicari and
        Jaynes
Silverglate, Harvey, 203
Simmons, Mary Jane, 123
Skokie, Illinois, 203
Slattery, John, 126–128, 130–
    131, 133, 134, 170–171,
    185, 196, 207
    addressing House after vote
        (1997), 131–132
Smith, William, 48–49
Snow, Sharon, 22
Somerville, Massachusetts, 3, 4,
    6, 25, 40, 52, 79–80, 104,
    219
Spaulding Rehabilitation
    Hospital, 239
Sports, 12
Steiker, Carol, 254
Suffolk Downs racetrack, 5
Suicide, 97, 161, 189, 193
Sullivan, Lester (detective), 53,
    54, 56–57, 100
Supreme Court, 107
Swift, Jane, 240

Talk of New England (TV show),
    177–180, 243
Talk shows, 139
Tarp used after Jeffrey's murder,
    35, 36, 44
Television, 62. *See also* Media
Therapy, 247. *See also under*
    Curley, Bob
Thomas, Jonathan Taylor, 15, 46
Till, Emmett, 218, 219
Tingle, Jimmy, 244

Toomey, Kevin (Reverend), 102,
    112
Toomey, Tim, 89, 111–112
Trials of Sicari and Jaynes,
    160
    Jaynes trial, 149, 160, 163,
        164, 165–166, 250–251
    pretrial hearing, 143–144
    Sicari trial, 146–148, 160,
        250–251
    victim impact statements,
        148–149
21st Amendment (bar), 125
Tyson (Curley family dog), 27,
    28, 29, 30, 37, 57–58

Unthought known, 225
U.S. Centers for Disease Control
    and Prevention, 241

Vanzetti, Bartolomeo, 106, 242
Vietnam War veterans, 189–190,
    192, 200, 201, 231
Vinny Testa's restaurant, 21, 70
Volunteers, 54, 55–56

Walker, Adrian, 126
Walsh, John, 137
Walsh, Marian, 115–116, 127
Ward, Michelle, 42–43
Watertown, Massachusetts, 39–
    40
Welch, Bud, 172–180, 182,
    183, 184, 192, 200, 208,
    209, 210, 211, 213–214,
    219
Welch, Julie, 173, 174, 180
Weld, William, 94, 105, 107,
    109, 112, 115, 117, 119
Wellesley College, 153
White, Paul, 136

White House Conference on
   Missing, Exploited, and
   Runaway Children,
   218
Whiting, Drucilla, 90
Windsor Tap, 38, 63
Wong, Doris Sue, 126

Yannetti, David (prosecutor), 86–
   87, 93, 94, 98–99, 100–101,
   138, 143, 147–148, 164, 167
closing arguments of, 165
preparing for Sicari trial, 145–
   146
York River, 98